Corruption Scandals and Their Global Impacts

Corruption scandals receive significant press coverage and scrutiny from practitioners of global governance and bilateral and multilateral donors. Across the globe, the annual publication of Transparency International's Corruption Perceptions Index (CPI) and the World Bank's Worldwide Governance Indicators elicits spirited denials and accusations of targeting, of neo-colonialism. Poor measures on corruption indices and the ensuing negative publicity can have serious consequences both externally, through a freeze or retraction of donor funding, and internally, through reducing availability of public funds and harming the credibility of serving governments and institutions.

Corruption Scandals and Their Global Impacts tracks several major corruption scandals across the world in a comparative analysis to assess the full impact of global corruption. Over the course of the book, the contributors deliberate the exposure and reporting of corruption scandals, demonstrate how corruption inhibits development on different levels and across different countries, the impact it has on the country in question, how citizens and authorities respond to corruption, and some local, regional and global policy and legislative measures to combat corruption.

The chapters examine the transnational manifestation of corruption scandals around the world, from developed countries and regions such as the United States and the European Union, to BRIC countries Brazil and Russia, to developing countries such as Belarus, Jamaica, Kenya and Nigeria. In each case, chapters highlight the scandal; its impact; the local, regional and global responses; and the subsequent global perceptions of the country. Concluding with a review of the global impacts of corruption scandals, this book provides an important comparative analysis which will be useful to students and scholars of international development and politics, as well as to development practitioners, donors, politicians and policy makers.

Omar E. Hawthorne is Lecturer of International Relations at University of the West Indies, Kingston, Jamaica.

Stephen Magu is Assistant Professor of Political Science at Hampton University, USA.

Routledge Corruption and Anti-Corruption Studies

The series features innovative and original research on the subject of corruption from scholars around the world. As well as documenting and analysing corruption, the series aims to discuss anti-corruption initiatives and endeavours, in an attempt to demonstrate ways forward for countries and institutions where the problem is widespread. The series particularly promotes comparative and interdisciplinary research targeted at a global readership.

In terms of theory and method, rather than basing itself on any one orthodoxy, the series draws broadly on the tool kit of the social sciences in general, emphasizing comparison, the analysis of the structure and processes, and the application of qualitative and quantitative methods.

Anti-Corruption in International Development
Ingrida Kerusauskaite

Corruption Scandals and their Global Impacts
Edited by Omar E. Hawthorne and Stephen Magu

For more information about this series, please visit: www.routledge.com/ Routledge-Corruption-and-Anti-Corruption-Studies/book-series/RCACS

Corruption Scandals and Their Global Impacts

Edited by Omar E. Hawthorne and Stephen Magu

LONDON AND NEW YORK

First published 2018
by Routledge
2 Park Square, Milton Park, Abingdon, Oxon OX14 4RN

and by Routledge
711 Third Avenue, New York, NY 10017

Routledge is an imprint of the Taylor & Francis Group, an informa business

© 2018 selection and editorial matter, Omar E. Hawthorne and Stephen Magu; individual chapters, the contributors

The right of Omar E. Hawthorne and Stephen Magu to be identified as the authors of the editorial material, and of the authors for their individual chapters, has been asserted in accordance with sections 77 and 78 of the Copyright, Designs and Patents Act 1988.

All rights reserved. No part of this book may be reprinted or reproduced or utilised in any form or by any electronic, mechanical, or other means, now known or hereafter invented, including photocopying and recording, or in any information storage or retrieval system, without permission in writing from the publishers.

Trademark notice: Product or corporate names may be trademarks or registered trademarks, and are used only for identification and explanation without intent to infringe.

British Library Cataloguing-in-Publication Data
A catalogue record for this book is available from the British Library

Library of Congress Cataloging-in-Publication Data
A catalog record for this book has been requested

ISBN: 978-1-138-30797-1 (hbk)
ISBN: 978-1-315-14272-2 (ebk)

Typeset in Times New Roman
by Apex CoVantage, LLC

Contents

List of figures	vii
List of tables	viii
List of contributors	ix

1 Introduction: corruption scandals and global governance   1
OMAR E. HAWTHORNE AND STEPHEN MAGU

**2 The management or mismanagement of corruption in
Trinidad and Tobago**   16
ANN MARIE BISSESSAR

**3 Examining the potential impact of whistleblowing on
corruption in the Caribbean's financial sector**   34
PHILMORE ALLEYNE AND MARISSA CHANDLER

**4 A fish rots from the head: corruption scandals in
post-Communist Russia**   57
LESLIE HOLMES

**5 Toa kitu kidogo: when "chai" is not tea – and Kenya's
corruption scandals**   77
STEPHEN MAGU

**6 Campaign donation and extradition of the connected
in Jamaica**   97
OMAR E. HAWTHORNE

**7 Big, bigger, biggest: grand corruption scandals in the
oil sector in Nigeria**   120
SOPE WILLIAMS-ELEGBE

vi *Contents*

8   **A spoonful of laws doesn't help the bribery go down: persistent contributing factors of corruption in the US pharmaceutical and medical device industry**   145
    MIKHAIL REIDER-GORDON

9   **The Foreign Corrupt Practices Act in the US and extra-territorial enforcement of an international anti-bribery regime**   171
    JEFFERY RAYMOND MISTICH

10 **The dynamics of corruption in Brazil: from trivial bribes to a corruption scandal**   189
    LIGIA MAURA COSTA

11 **"The theory of the world in-between": corporatism and mafia-ness in the new type of corruption in Italy**   204
    DAVIDE TORSELLO AND MARIA GIULIA PEZZI

12 **Belarus: do stones thrown into a marsh make rings?**   219
    PAVEL SASCHEKO

13 **Conclusion: lessons learned**   237
    OMAR E. HAWTHORNE

    Index   251

Figures

2.1	The determinants of parliamentary performance	27
6.1	PM Portia Simpson Miller mum on Trafigura scandal	101
6.2	Painting the Trafigura scandal	101
6.3	Protesters in support of Mr. Christopher 'Dudus' Coke	110
9.1	Number of ratifications/legislations implemented by year	175
9.2	The bribery game	179
9.3	Number of FCPA enforcements by year	184
12.1	Publications on corruption cases (1–545)	222
12.2	"Peak" publications	223

Tables

2.1	The responsibilities of the three Joint Select Committees	23
2.2	Size of Joint Committees in Trinidad and Tobago	29
3.1	2016 Corruption Perceptions Index scores for selected countries in the Caribbean	40
10.1	Brazilian cases of grand corruption or political corruption from 1987–2008	191
10.2	Brazil: Corruption Perceptions Index	195
10.3	Locations of the "Car Wash" investigation, first phase	197
10.4	Judicial work related to the Car Wash operation, January 5, 2017	199

Contributors

Philmore Alleyne is Senior Lecturer in Accounting in the Department of Management Studies at The University of the West Indies, Cave Hill Campus, Barbados, and is also a chartered accountant by profession. He conducts research in whistleblowing, accounting and auditing issues, corporate governance, business ethics and finance and lectures in accounting and auditing courses.

Ann Marie Bissessar is Professor of Public Management with the Department of Political Science at The University of the West Indies, St Augustine Campus, Trinidad and Tobago. She is currently the Dean of the Faculty of Social Sciences. She is the author/co-editor of 19 books and approximately 80 journal articles with peer-reviewed journals. She served as a member of the Integrity Commission 2010–2013 and sits as a member of the United Nations Office on Drugs and Crime (UNODC) Academic Initiative Against Corruption (ACAD).

Marissa Chandler is a Research Assistant in the Department of Management Studies at the University of the West Indies, Cave Hill Campus, Barbados, and is actively involved in the campus's strategic development initiatives. Ms. Chandler conducts research in whistleblowing, corporate governance and business ethics and has research interests in industrial, organizational and social psychology.

Ligia Maura Costa is Professor and head of the Department of Social and Legal Sciences at Escola de Administração de Empresas de São Paulo, Fundação Getulio Vargas (FGV-EAESP), member of the United Nations Office on Drugs and Crime (UNODC) Academic Initiative Against Corruption (ACAD), and a lawyer in São Paulo, Brazil.

Omar E. Hawthorne is Lecturer of International Relations at the University of the West Indies, Mona, Kingston, Jamaica. She is also a member of the United Nations Office on Drugs and Crime (UNODC) Academic Initiative Against Corruption (ACAD). Her research interests include corruption, good governance, global security and US foreign policy.

Leslie Holmes has been Professor of Political Science at the University of Melbourne since 1988. He also teaches every year in Warsaw and Beijing, and

x *Contributors*

occasionally at the International Anti-Corruption Academy in Vienna. He has authored or edited 16 books, and his work has been published in 16 languages. He specializes in post-communism, corruption and organized crime.

Stephen Magu is Assistant Professor of Political Science at Hampton University, teaching teaches courses in World Civilizations, International Relations, and Research Methods. His research interests include International Political Economy IPE, US foreign policy, foreign policy in Africa, and democracy and governance in Africa.

Jeffery Raymond Mistich is a Political Scientist at Florida State University. His research focuses on the international institutions that shape international political and economic interactions.

Maria Giulia Pezzi is a Post-Doctoral Research Fellow at Gran Sasso Science Institute (GSSI) as a member of the Social Sciences research unit, working on a research project on the development of peripheral (inner) areas in Italy. Her current research focuses on tourism policies and heritage-making strategies from a bottom-up perspective.

Mikhail Reider-Gordon is a Vice President in the International Services practice at an international policy and consulting firm. She focuses on regulatory, political and cultural challenges where the intersection of transnational financial crimes, corruption, money-laundering, IP theft and cybercrime collide with corporate and institutional ethics and compliance, risk and responsibility. She is currently, the Rule of Law Officer within the American Bar Association's Section of International Law.

Pavel Sascheko is Head of Division of the Scientific Center of the Prosecutor General's Office of the Republic of Belarus. He is also Associate Professor and Chair of Criminal Law and Criminology of Academy of Ministry of Internal Affairs of Belarus. He is the co-author of several books and the author of numerous articles on anti-corruption, criminal law and prosecutor's supervision which have been published in Belarus, Bulgaria, China, Russia and Slovenia.

Davide Torsello is Professor of Anthropology and Organizational Behavior. He has extensive experience of ethnographic field research in organizations and communities in Japan, Italy and Eastern Europe. He is the Director of the CEU Center for Integrity in Business and Government. He has published over 60 journal articles and 10 books.

Sope Williams-Elegbe is a Professor in the Department of Mercantile Law and the Deputy Director of the African Procurement Law Unit, Stellenbosch University, South Africa. She specializes in public procurement law, anti-corruption law, international economic law, development law and commercial law. She is the author of several publications in the areas of international trade, anti-corruption and public procurement.

1 Introduction

Corruption scandals and global governance

Omar E. Hawthorne and Stephen Magu

Corruption and its manifestation: an inherently human enterprise?

The expression "but I know it when I see it" was first used by Associate Justice of the US Supreme Court Hon. Potter Stewart in *Jacobellis v. Ohio* to explain his finding that the movie *The Lovers* (*Les Amants*) did not, in his view, contain obscenity; he implied that obscenity could perhaps not be well defined, but one would recognize it when one saw it. Sometimes the same is true of corruption: you know it when you see it – or when you hear about it; it ranges from brash notions of "eating the national cake" to a benign suggestion to "buy lunch", "tea" or "chicken", to "facilitate business", sometimes codified as "missing files" that magically reappear when money changes hands, and bundles of cash passed discreetly, or briefcases brought to offices by burly bodyguards. In other places and times, it manifests as exceedingly complex, shadowy, pay-to-play, influence peddling, and underhand, covert meetings in back rooms where only the elites have admittance; it is about contracts and passports and oil deals and weapons acquisitions and cover-ups.

Rose-Ackerman and Palifka, while arguing that their list is inclusive rather than exhaustive, highlight eight types of corruption: bribery, extortion, exchange of favors, nepotism, cronyism, judicial fraud, accounting fraud, public service fraud, embezzlement, kleptocracy, influence peddling and conflicts of interest (2016: 8–9). The authors and contributors to this volume highlight other types of corruption, including, for example, "tenderpreneurship" and "javelin-throwing", in addition to instances that fall within the Rose-Ackerman and Palifka framework, such as self-dealing, kickbacks and bribes. In other times and places and as the world becomes increasingly interconnected, corruption is (not-so/-well) well concealed behind bits and bytes, 0s and 1s, traveling at light speed through the ether of the internet, its nefarious purposes carried out by shadowy lawyers with postal boxes for addresses in exotic locations such as the Cayman Islands, Jersey Islands, Panama and a multitude of tax havens; in such cases, you really don't know it when you see it. Sometimes, it takes prosecution in a second jurisdiction for a country to catch on to the fact that graft occurred, as was the case with Smith & Ouzman in the UK in the early 2010s.

2   *Omar E. Hawthorne and Stephen Magu*

The genesis of the concept of corruption, *corrumpere*, intimates "mar", "bribe", "destroy". Corruption goes by other synonyms; dishonesty, fraud, graft, sleaze, bribery, unscrupulousness, criminality, moral depravity, decadence. The appearance of the term in written literature appears to have manifested itself especially profoundly in the early 19th century, decreased drastically in the early to mid-20th century and regained frequency later into the 20th century and the early decades of the 21st century. The magnitude of the funds moved through corruption has increased significantly even as its use decreases. Today, several major manifestations of the practice of "graft" or "corruption" are broadly considered. They range from simple bribery that might involve the exchange for money for a favor, pay-to-play, nepotism, cronyism, no-contract bidding, different forms of manipulation of the supply and procurement systems and chains, flouting international procurement (for example, of military equipment that may require no-bidding contracting), while other forms of corruption include "tenderpreneurship" and "javelin-throwing".

Corruption is not a new phenomenon. Kautilya's *Arthashastra*, written around 2,000 years ago, discussed corruption and corruption scandals. Even Shakespeare in his plays gave corruption a prominent role. *The Financial Times*, in its December 31, 1995, end-of-year editorial characterized 1995 as the year of corruption. That was also the year of the birth of watchdog group Transparency International. The degree of attention over the last two decades being paid to corruptions has led many to ask why and why so much attention now. For some political economists, the end of the Cold War also helped to stop the hypocrisy of developed industrial countries, which often ignored political corruption that existed in many developing and emerging market economies that were in their political camp.

The increase in the number of democratic governments, coupled with free press, helped to create an environment that facilitated discussion on the once-taboo topic of corruption. The increased role of non-governmental organizations such as Transparency International, amongst others, in publicizing the problems of corruption, has been successful in creating anti-corruption movements in many countries. Hawthorne (2015: 37) makes the case that it would appear that government corruption is more pervasive in countries where the structure of opportunities a/nd incentives are conducive to corrupt behavior. Sandholtz and Koetzle (2000: 31) assess another dimension that is related to the political sphere, that relating to "repertoires of cognitions, feelings, and schemes of evaluation that process experience into action". Furthermore, Sandholtz and Koetzle add that "the effectiveness of democratic institutions in curbing corruption, however, depends on the presence of a set of democratic norms" (2000:31). Hawthorne (2015: 37) adds that in some societies where the government seems to have its hand in economic creation and development there is a positive correlation between the degree of state control of the economy and corruption. Hence, the political culture of a society might also affect how that society and its people conceptualize what is corruption. And, only when a society start disaggregating corruption, demanding accountability, and in what seems to be a dominant feature in corruption scandals, once an insider or an

Introduction 3

active civil society individual makes public such corrupt activities which result in a scandal, it continues to be business as usual.

Defining corruption scandals

It is important to highlight the differences between *corruption* and *corruption scandals*, despite the terms being used interchangeably by several authors. Corruption, defined as the misuse of public office for private gain, by no means implies the publicity of the actions, but instead just their occurrence, whereas corruption scandals can be defined as the revelation of corruption that generates a strong public reaction. Corruption that does not become scandalous can be considered "successful" in the sense that it achieves secrecy, which is a key concern of those committing the acts (Balán 2011: 460). Corruption is also one of the most difficult crimes to detect, report on and measure the impact. A corruption scandal implies both public disclosure of corruption as well as the public upheaval that follows. Applying Theodore Lowi's (1988) views, in addition to John Thompson's (2000), corruption scandals have a certain temporal and sequential structure. Balán expounded on Lowi's and Thompson's position and argued that three stages can be distinguished: (1) the trigger stage, when information on the transgression is leaked; (2) the spread stage, when the information is made public; and (3) the response stage, when those involved in the scandal react (2011: 460).

The duration and intensity of each stage may vary from scandal to scandal, but the general structure allows for comparisons across corruption scandals that initially seem to be unique events. Bearing in mind the differences in the stages, the trigger stage is pivotal for a number of reasons – in that this stage involves the disclosure or leaking of detrimental information. One must become cognizant that not all corrupt acts are triggered to become scandals; that is, there is no automatic transformation from corruption to a scandal. Furthermore, more disclosure of information does not automatically imply more corruption in a society and vis-à-vis a country perceived to be highly corrupt does not imply a likelihood for more disclose of corrupt events. Subsequently, using Balán's (2011: 460) premise, the disclosure of information requires two main components. First, information must be previously concealed, which implies that someone is revealing previously unknown events. Second, information must come from reliable and credible sources, which is a function of the sources' proximity to actors involved in the transgressions. Hence the individuals that have access to the undisclosed information and the credibility and reliability of sources are fundamental.

The second stage – the spreading of the information to the wider society – is crucial, and the role of media in addition to civil society actors is key. In some instances, individual journalists and newspapers may have political agendas that sometimes push either for or against the publication of certain corruption scandals. And, as for Thompson (2000), the media is far from "innocent". But, with a competitive media market and at minimum a level of media independence, an individual willing to disclose information can find the means. Social media is a game changer. In that the rapid rate at which disclosed information can be shared and viewed via online portals, this added dimension in the spreading of information sometimes takes on a life of its own and in stark difference from the role of traditional media. The Panama Papers, although shared with a journalist once the information became available on social media, turned average citizens into investigative journalists trying to research on their fellow citizens.

The response stage to a scandal can become the trigger for new scandals, building chains of scandals. The knowledge of corrupt activities is often available to political actors due to their proximity to the acts. And thus members or associates of a political actor's party or staff can be expected to possess information about their misdeeds. Hence, leaking, be it selective or publicly denouncing, as Tumber and Waisbord (2004: 1034) point out, "everyone in politics . . . realizes if you examine more closely and for long enough, damaging information can be found on almost anyone." The role of whistleblowers or an "insider" is rather pivotal. As Waisbord argues, "had [insiders] not come forward with sensitive and compromising information, most reporters agree, it is doubtful that most exposes would have ever surfaced" (2000: 196).

Corruption scandals have become an important aspect of politics. The prevalence of the scandals that have occurred throughout the world and their impacts are relevant to today's society, as are the lessons learned from them and how they can or will transform societies going forward. Beyond economic conditions of a country, the extent to which scandals shape approval might ultimately depend on the type of scandal. A scandal related to the misuse of public funds might be perceived to be graver than a scandal related to claims about the personal character of a public official. The literature is somewhat ambiguous, and there is no broad consensus about the theoretical underpinnings of what attribute to one and not the other.

Corruption scandals continue to shake the political landscape of Brazil, but what is often lost in the debate on Brazil's corruption scandals is that several institutions and anti-corruption movements have ascended to the challenge. The Brazilian corruption scandals are pivotal for not only this generation, but also will be studied for decades to come. Noting that across Latin America vigorous investigations have not only implicated the elites of politics and business circles, but these previously deemed untouchables have been arrested, charged and in some instances convicted for acts of corruption. Brazil is replete with lessons for judicial institutions and cooperation for other countries to grapple with. Amidst the corruption scandals and investigations, the democratic institutions of Brazil are seemingly holding their mandate.

Quite often, some political corruption scandals emerge as a power struggle even within the same political party. An insider may selectively leak information on wrongdoings in an attempt "leapfrog" and strengthen their position in relation to a rival. Conversely, as David Apter (1962: 157) emphasizes, "when there is a [weak] opposition, factionalism and intraparty intrigue become the prevailing political style". Leapfrogging can generate chains of scandals, as both those who leak and those who are involved in the scandal remain in the government, allowing for new leaks in response to corruption scandals.

Corruption: "cost of doing business"?

Is corruption a blot on the inherently good nature of humanity, or merely the cost of doing business, opportunities that present themselves to accrue revenues that one might otherwise not have had the opportunity to? If it is so widely pervasive, should it be considered part of the business fabric, where it can be written off as part of business costs, as Jeffrey Mistich points out the practices in some European countries prior to the adoption of the extra-territoriality facet of the US Foreign Corrupt Practices Act (FCPA)? On average, most firms can expect to lose 5 percent through corruption costs, but it would cost far more for them to prevent and/or prosecute corruption. For instance, Iyer and Samociuk argue that the recovery of $10 million requires an extra $100 million, and thus perhaps unjustifiable in the eyes of the business. When costs of investigations are factored in, for example, $1 million to investigate a $10 million loss, with the costs climbing to between 30 percent and 100 percent of the amount lost, it seems that preventing, finding and prosecuting graft presents increasingly diminishing returns (Iyer and Samociuk 2006: 6).

Additionally, sometimes in doing business with the government there is the added "tax" of corruption. Before "Mani Pulite", more widely referred to as the "Tangentopoli scandal" in Italy, Nordio (1997) noted that Minister Martelli, an essential member of the Socialist Party, in a speech in Bari admitted that the Italian political parties had on their payrolls a small army of employees. The salaries of these employees had to come from somewhere. Mr. Martelli's speech enunciates a problem with political parties and campaign finance in that the need to generate funds for activities related to political parties gives the opening for bribery. Jamaica's Trafigura Beheer political campaign bribery scandal, among others, is a perfect example of how pressures build to generate funds. Rose-Ackerman perhaps captures the link between democratic political campaigns and corruption best when she notes, "Democracy gives citizens a role in determining their political leaders. Corrupt elected officials can be voted out of office. But democracy is not necessarily a cure for corruption." Politicians will campaign on anti-corruption platforms and the usual rhetoric of being tougher on corruption, but as the various corruption scandals explored in the text show, the web of corruption often entangles those who campaigned with some of the strongest anti-corruption rhetoric.

The views of some of economists in the 1980s and 1990s which seemingly advanced the view that corruption might promote growth have been largely dispelled and the broad consensus now holds that corruption is unequivocally bad. The idea that corruption "oils the mechanism" or "greases the process" of Leff (1964) and Huntington (1986), the bidding competitions and highest bribe model of Beck and Maher (1986) and Lien (1986) and the concept of bribes as supplements for low wages put forth by Tullock (1996) and Becker and Stigler (1974) have all been shown to not be conducive to growth and development. Corruption and rent-seeking as political glue or as a wage supplement may be helpful in the short run, but they may lead to major problems over the long run, as it has been shown for a number of the cases discussed throughout the course of this text.

6   Omar E. Hawthorne and Stephen Magu

Furthermore, corruption distorts markets and the allocation of resources. It reduces public revenues while increasing public spending, resulting in larger fiscal deficits that affect any government's fiscal policy.

Measuring corruption

If corruption could be measured in its entirety, it could probably be eliminated. It goes far beyond the payment of bribes; thus measuring total bribes paid does not fully capture corruption, as it inadvertently ignores corrupt acts, which are not accompanied by the payment of a bribe. Furthermore, if we were to measure acts of corruption instead of the bribes paid, it would be a near impossible task – dealing with unimportant actions and not being privy to all the information. Due to the nature of acts of corruption, the scale at which it occurs and because in order to measure it with accuracy would require individuals involved in illegal acts to self-declare, it is near impossible to measure with accuracy. We instead rely on assessments and survey indices that measure the perception of corruption. A growing range of indices are being developed that focus on measuring corruption and good governance; some of the more established indicators are Transparency International's (TI) Corruption Perceptions Index (CPI) and the World Bank's Worldwide Governance Indicator. Both are composite or aggregate indicators, in that they combine different measures of a similar thing into a single measure. For TI's CPI, on average, 14 sources are used, including the Asian Development Bank's Country Performance Assessment ratings, the Heritage Foundation, Freedom House's Nations in Transit, the World Economic Forum's Global Competitiveness Report, and Varieties of Democracy. The World Bank, on average, uses 25 sources for its Control of Corruption indicator. The items used to create the indices measure very different things, despite having similar-sounding titles. Often, the only commonality in the measurement tools is a combination of terms such as "accountability", "corruption", "democracy", or "transparency". Additional tools of assessment and measurement, such as the Global Integrity Index, the Global Corruption Barometer, the Global Competitiveness Report, the Political and Economic Risk Consultancy and Political Risk Services, have also added to the debate – these public opinion surveys have sought to capture snapshots of corruption worldwide. While these surveys measure the perceptions of corruption rather than corruption per se, they provide a good lens into how a country is perceived by others, as well as by the people within a country itself.

Corruption, in general, comprises acts that are illegal. The acts are normally secretive or hidden, and quite often without an act of scandal or an investigation they rarely come to light. It is difficult to determine absolute levels of corruption for countries based on empirical data. It might be the case that acts of bribery are not reported, and if and when they are reported, the resulting investigation might be lengthy and/or the timeline for prosecution and/or conviction might not necessarily transpire yearly (Hawthorne 2015: 33). TI's CPI is perhaps the best-known index. This composite index, which began in 1995, has been largely credited with putting the focus of corruption on the international agenda. TI's CPI, the most popular measure of corruption, is a flawed instrument (De Maria 2008; Hawthorne 2015). Many policymakers embrace the CPI, and politicians often use it to score points against a rival government if there is a change in the ranking. But quite often, leading figures, especially in the developing world, will place greater focus on the rank on the CPI and not necessarily the CPI score. However, change or stagnancy in the perceived score is actually more important than the rank, which policymakers highlight. At the same time, TI makes clear that the index cannot be compared year-to-year as the components used in the index vary. Furthermore, as De Maria (2008) argues, given the challenges in gathering empirical data on actual corruption, TI's CPI, which is based on capturing perceptions of corruption of those in a position to offer assessments of public-sector corruption, is the most reliable method of comparing relative corruption levels across countries.

Global measures of corruption

Composite indicators remain the most widely used measurement tools partially because of their near-global coverage. The debate about perception-versus experience-based indicators is not lost on the contributors to this volume. Perception-based indicators are the most frequently used measurement tools; they rely on the subjective opinions and perception levels of corruption in any given country among experts and citizens, in contrast with experience-based indicators that attempt to measure actual personal experiences with corruption. There are divergent opinions as to whether these indicators would need individuals to acknowledge knowingly breaking the law and giving or accepting a bribe. Oftentimes, the experience-based indicators show less corruption than the perception-based indicators due to several contributing factors. For example, individuals quite often will not implicate themselves in acts of corruption, but rather without actual evidence will deduce that corruption is taking place. Such sentiment is driven by perception of inefficiencies in the system or the perception that corruption is high due to different index rankings and public opinion polls and periodic anti-corruption campaigns.

Because corruption cannot be measured empirically, perception-based indicators seek to assess corruption through indirect measures by aggregating varying opinions or by measuring good governance and levels of public accountability mechanisms. Subsequently, the demand-and-supply debate with regards to corruption has largely been focused on public-sector corruption and not necessarily corruption in the private sector. Useful tools to evaluate private-sector corruption, such as the Bribe Payers Index, must be more actively engaged. As shown in some of the corruption scandals explored in this text, international entities sometimes pay bribes in foreign countries. Based on a demand-and-supply analysis of corruption, quite often the international entity involved in acts of corruption rarely suffers much of a price, given that the allegations often are wrapped up in court proceedings for years, if they even ever get to that level. In some countries, corporations have been fined for involvement in corruptions in other countries, but the "punishment" is often few and far between.

8 *Omar E. Hawthorne and Stephen Magu*

Regional activities and initiatives to combat corruption

The subsequent chapters in this book will detail selected individual countries' corruption scandals and actions, as well as joint, regional and global agencies' actions, resolutions, declarations and recommendations to combat corruption within, outside and affecting their borders, and with extra-territorial implications and jurisdiction, including agencies and legislation aimed at eliminating corruption. Efforts to combat corruption have ranged from regimes, such as UN General Assembly declarations and resolutions, non-binding EU instruments, technical assistance programmes, naming and shaming and annual reports issuing from TI and the World Bank.Globally, in October 2003, the UN General Assembly adopted through resolution 58/4 the United Nations Convention against Corruption (UNCAC) which to date has 140 signatories and 183 parties (United Nations 2017). Nationally, for example, the US has the SEC and the 1977 Foreign Corrupt Practice Act(s); the European Union has the OECD Convention on Combating Bribery of Foreign Public Officials in International Business Transactions and the Council of Europe's Criminal Law Convention on Corruption to address the vice (OECD 2008).

Further afield in Asia, the former Soviet Republics of Armenia, Azerbaijan, Georgia, Kazakhstan, Kyrgyzstan, Russia, Tajikistan and Ukraine endorsed the OECD Anti-Corruption Network for Eastern Europe and Central Asia (ACN), also known as the "Istanbul Plan", in 2003. In Africa, the African Union (AU) bloc has attempted to address issues of corruption through the 2003 African Union Convention on Preventing and Combating Corruption, which aimed to "promote and strengthen the development in Africa by each State Party, of mechanisms required to prevent, detect, punish and eradicate corruption and related offences in the public and private sectors" (AU n.d.: 6). Individual countries, including those that this book concerns itself with, have national frameworks, agencies and varying legislation intended to prevent and punish corruption; yet, as the TI's CPI shows, corruption remains a significant constraint to social and economic development.

Globalization of corruption

The increasing interconnectedness of the global economy has facilitated increased possibilities and occurrence of corruption. Although practices that range from bribes to payoffs of persons in positions of authority in exchange for access and/or resources is not new, their format has changed as the world has changed: independence, for example, changed the relationships between the Global South and the former colonial powers. In the Congo Free State, Union minière de Haut-Katanga, with the help of the Force Publique, had managed to entrench a system of forced labor, 20 cents-a-day wage, debt slavery, and punishments, including mutations, amputations and high taxes. During World War II, the headquarters of the company moved to New York; when the Congo Free State became independent, Union minière de Haut-Katanga continued to do business in the country, despite its egregious historical practices, until the country ran out of the critical minerals radium and uranium – although in the new economy Mobutu Sese Seko "took a cut from virtually every business in his country" (Bisariya 1982: 7).

The global cost of corruption is staggering. How widespread it is, how far it reaches into government and/or the private sector or the extent to which nationals of different countries are involved in or touched by corruption – no one has the exact numbers: Richardson points out as much, writing that "the clandestine nature of corruption makes estimation difficult" (2001: 76). Yet, even as this difficulty persists, there are some estimates in disparate contexts: Cater notes that the former director of the World Bank Institute programme on global governance Daniel Kaufman's estimate that "the total annual bribery of public officials by individuals and the private sector can be estimated at $1 trillion" (2013: 64) excludes private-sector fraud or embezzlement of public funds, and that some political leaders have been known to amass up to US$30 billion over their lifetimes. Specific country figures might shed more light on the pervasiveness of graft: the Center for Global Financial Integrity estimates that illicit outflows from China between 2000 and 2008 averaged US$240 billion, for a total of US$1.428 trillion (Cockcroft 2013: 73). It also manifests in such countries as Nigeria, which experienced a –0.5 per cent per capita GDP growth between 1975 and 2003, despite oil revenues in the region of US$600 billion (2013: 73). Corruption in the developed world was estimated by the World Bank at US$80 billion (Richardson 2001: 76), far exceeding the total amount of development aid disbursed to the countries.

Book outline

As a global phenomenon, it is useful to not only consider the definitions and types of corruption, the cost thereof, its reach and the impacts and implications; it is also useful to survey how corruption manifests itself around the world and how some organizations, countries and regions, as well as global efforts, attempt to deal with the phenomenon. The subsequent chapters examine disparate countries around the world and some of the corruption incidents, scandals and responses that have made the headlines. The chapters detail the corruption, scandals and legislative and policy responses, and in some areas assess the success of the same. Ann Marie Bissessar, in Chapter 2, examines the management or mismanagement of corruption. Bissessar dissects the theoretical framework of literature on corruption; for Bissessar there is no dearth of academic literature on the theme of corruption. Indeed, Heidenheimer and Johnson's (1989) edited volume *Political Corruption* and Anechiarico's (1998) *Pursuit of Absolute Integrity* stand out as classics in the field. Add to that Rose-Ackerman and Palifka's (2016) *Corruption and Government* and the much-publicized *The Panama Papers* (Obermayer and Obermaier 2016) and one would expect that much of the debate surrounding this theme has been exhausted. Yet, surprisingly, little has been done to explore the extent to which the mechanisms to curb corruption in small island states have attained success. This chapter interrogates parliamentary scrutiny, particularly of the Public Accounts Enterprise Committee in the twin-island republic of Trinidad and Tobago. It contends that in plural, developing societies such as Trinidad and

Tobago, parliament and parliamentary processes as a mechanism to minimize corruption within governmental agencies is often more a theoretical construct rather than a practical tool.

In Chapter 3, Philmore Alleyne and Marissa Chandler examine the potential impact of whistleblowing on corruption in the Caribbean financial sector. For Alleyne and Chandler, the various financial scandals that have occurred in the Caribbean over the past decade have made corruption a cause for concern in the region. As such, regulators are tasked with finding anti-corruption strategies unique to the Caribbean experience, but this has not been easy. Therefore, the chapter discusses a few of these major corruption scandals, such as the Allen Stanford, Colonial Life Insurance Company (CLICO) and the Hindu Credit Union (HCU) cases, and the current status of the Caribbean on the CPI. Findings reveal that there is severe political interference in the region, inadequate whistleblowing legislation and that whistleblowing is not fully embraced in the Caribbean. As a result, potential whistleblowers prefer to utilize anonymous channels, and that there are instances where observers of wrongdoing prefer to remain silent. The authors propose that whistleblowing can be an effective anti-corruption strategy that may aid in the elimination of corruption from the Caribbean's financial sector. Recommendations include enactment of whistleblowing legislation, acceptance of whistleblowing in organizations and societies, as well as improving the ethical organizational culture in the region.

Considering that hardly a day passes without news broadcasting a corruption scandal someplace in the world, recent scandals in China, Russia, Equatorial Guinea, Peru, South Africa, Egypt and elsewhere emphasize the extent of corruption globally, especially in the developing world. In the 21st century, combating and overcoming corruption is one of the most important challenges. Corruption is a global concern, and it represents a serious threat to the basic principles and values of government, undermining public confidence in democracy and threatening to erode the rule of law. It is most opportune that, in Chapter 4, Leslie Holmes illustrates that relative to its level of economic development, Russia is widely perceived to be the most corrupt country on earth. Yet ever since first coming to power in 2000 – at least until mid-2017 – Russia's leader, Vladimir Putin, has claimed that his government is committed to fighting corruption. Questions on the awarding of Russia's bid to host of the 2018 World Cup continue to challenge this claim. One reason for the gap between the rhetoric and actuality is that, allegedly, corruption can be found at the very highest levels of the system. This chapter focuses on four major corruption scandals, including one surrounding Russia's first post-Communist president and another relating to its current prime minister. It argues that Russia's best-known anti-corruption campaigner had by 2017 got so under Putin's skin that the president is now downplaying the significance of corruption in Russia – much to the annoyance of many Russian citizens.

In Chapter 5, Stephen Magu examines some of the major corruption scandals that have ravaged Kenya since its independence over half a century ago, the governmental responses, civil society and western donors' responses, national, regional and global legislative frameworks that address corruption in Kenya and the inexplicable reality that few, if any senior government and private-sector officials accused of corruption have ever been convicted. He especially discusses Kenya's most egregious, brazen scandal, the Goldenberg scandal, which was an export compensation scheme where Goldenberg International exported fictitious gold to earn Kenya foreign exchange, at a time when most western donors were withholding aid. The cost of the scandal to Kenya's economy was US$158 million, approximately 10 percent of Kenya's economy. Kenya would then reel from one scandal to another, most related to security equipment contracting: the 2013 general election ballot materials acquisition from Smith & Ouzman in the UK, the Euromarine scandal to purchase a navy ship, the Police Forensic Lab, the Anglo Leasing scandal and a US$6.91 million scandal from the National Youth Service. Despite successive presidents declaring that "there are no sacred cows", as the chapter highlights, all the appropriate legislative and judicial frameworks have not saved Kenya from the perennial corruption scandals: the lack of political will and commitment to purge the vice continues to bedevil successive governments, and Kenya's efforts to rid herself of corruption remain woefully wanting.

Omar Hawthorne, in Chapter 6, examines the frequency of corruption scandals in Jamaica. In Jamaica, numerous institution-building efforts have been undertaken with the aim of improving administrative propriety and reducing corruption. Corruption has persistently increased in spite of anti-corruption policies and institution-building. Jamaica's corruption scandals have in the recent past had more attention paid to them, with calls for more concerted actions towards prosecution and merging of anti-corruption entities as one, with the Integrity Commission. Corruption scandals have revealed billions of dollars lost with little or no repercussion and accountability. This chapter examines the frequent occurrence of corruption scandals in Jamaica but focuses primarily on two major corruption scandals: (1) the bribery scandal involving the international firm Trafigura Beheer in 2006 and the People's National Party and the legislative amendment that was passed as a result of this corruption scandal and (2) how the extradition request of an alleged international organized crime boss, Mr. Christopher Coke, by the US resulted in a political scandal for the sitting prime minister and turmoil once the security forces attempted to arrest Mr. Coke for extradition. The chapter concludes that political will, tenacity and a change in the political culture are key variables to complement the institutional response to curb corruption.

Sope Williams-Elegbe, in Chapter 7, examines Nigeria's reputation for systemic corruption, its consistently low CPI scores and a 2017 report by the National Bureau of Statistics and the UN Office on Drugs and Crime that notes the insidious nature of public-sector corruption. Although many countries have problems with petty or bureaucratic corruption, in Nigeria the pervasiveness of grand corruption in the last decade presents one of its largest problems, as law enforcement is often ill-equipped and powerless to address corruption committed by the extremely wealthy and powerful political elite. This chapter examines the most significant grand corruption scandals in Nigeria in the last decade. It will be seen that there has been a marked increase in the amounts of money that are implicated, and the impunity with which these acts of grand corruption have been committed.

Unfortunately, the systemic and collective nature of corruption in Nigeria makes it almost impossible for even the dreaded Buhari administration, which was elected on an anti-corruption platform in 2015, to appropriately deal with these cases of grand corruption. The chapter will further consider approaches and challenges to the fight against corruption and the successes recorded, to date, by the Buhari administration.

Mikhail Reider-Gordon, in Chapter 8, examines corruption scandals in the pharmaceutical industry, by examining the US medical–industrial complex, a multi-trillion-dollar sector of the economy providing jobs as well as many and varied products to the marketplace. While the US has led global anti-corruption efforts for decades, it has failed to tackle these same issues within this industry. The evidence of the influence and degree of bribery committed in the US health-care industry is well-documented. In health care, bribery occurs primarily between pharmaceutical and medical device companies and healthcare providers. Mechanisms of "inducements" considered bribery in foreign markets are categorized as "marketing" domestically and remain legal. What laws do exist domestically only apply to government-funded programs and not the private marketplace. Extensive research has demonstrated that marketing to healthcare providers can take many forms; even the smallest of gifts or meals have been shown to influence provider behaviors such as prescribing. By failing to acknowledge the underlying drivers of corruption, domestic laws have remained inadequate to curb these behaviors. The enforcement of domestic bribery has been slow and the definition of acceptable industry marketing behaviors allows for wide latitude of interpretation. This chapter focuses on where US domestic laws have failed to curb corruption in the US healthcare industry, examining current laws and guidelines and demonstrating their failure. Further, it is proposed that bribery can be curtailed only with the adoption of stand-alone laws, harsher penalties and the engagement of key stakeholders such as the insurance industry and consumers.

In Chapter 9, Jeffery Raymond Mistich explains the historical evolution of anti-bribery legislation in the US and subsequently throughout the entire OECD. Mistich undertakes an extensive discussion of the Lockheed scandals and how they led to the consideration of extending anti-bribery legislation to business deals abroad, highlighting the singular focus of US anti-corruption legislation on American companies and businesses, and the weaknesses of this approach. American companies could do business abroad and bribe officials and companies there, and if the country did not have anti-bribery legislations, then companies could get away with it. The revisions and adoption of legislation that strengthened the issues addressed in the Foreign Corrupt Practices Act is addressed in this chapter. Fixing these loopholes explains why the US has adopted the anti-bribery regimes that it has today and how compliance is achieved through the extraterritorial enforcement provisions written into the agreement. Special attention is given to the domestic politics in the US that led to the unprecedented creation of an anti-bribery law, and how that law spread to the international community. The chapter concludes with a discussion about the most recent enforcements of bribery law and the future of anti-bribery prosecutions under the OECD Anti-bribery Convention.

Introduction 13

Ligia Maura Costa, in Chapter 10, examines the dynamics of corruption in Brazil: from trivial bribes to a corruption scandal. In the 2000s, Brazil was on the fast track to become a developed country. However, recent slow economic growth has not only compromised this optimist vision, but it has also revealed just how widespread government corruption is throughout the country. The "Car Wash" investigation has splashed the reputation of the government, political parties, firms and Brazilian society as investigations have revealed kickbacks paid to politicians, businesspeople and bureaucrats; systematic bribes; distorted public decisions; money laundering; trading in influence and other related illicit activities. Based on legal and socio-economic theories, this chapter focuses on the dynamics of corruption as perceived in Brazil as result of the recent spiral of scandals related but not limited to the state-run oil and gas company Petrobras. This chapter responds to three traditional questions: What are the causes of corruption behind the "Car Wash" investigations? What are the consequences? And what are the available means for an efficient fight against this universal phenomenon? The purpose of this chapter is to answer these and other questions using an analytical narrative based on secondary data analysis based on information from sources such as reports from the police, prosecutors, court hearings, judicial decisions and the media. The results of this study explain the way that Brazil has been tackling corruption through an analysis of selected aspects on recent corruption investigations and the influence of the new anti-corruption legislation on the results of these criminal cases. This study might help companies in formulating entry strategies in this emerging and challenging market where corruption is still far from being abolished.

In Chapter 11, Davide Torsello and Maria Giulia Pezzi examine the theory of "the world in-between": corporatism and mafia-ness in the new type of corruption in Italy. Torsello and Pezzi make the case that over the last two decades, anthropology has chosen to deal more programmatically with corruption. It has done so by interrupting a silence that has distinguished this from other social sciences since the times of the discipline's sophisticated theorizations of clientelism. Furthermore, corruption has become a complex phenomenon to the study of which mainstream theoretical frameworks appear increasingly narrow. The main strength of anthropological analyses of the study of corruption has been the one that renders problematic some common assumptions that situate corruption in contexts of weak institutional development, porous state structures and difficult economic conditions. This chapter develops the argument that present-day corruption, in the case of Italy, is a complex social mechanism that includes various tasks, roles and personalities that allow the symbolic creation of what those implicated call "the world in-between" (*il mondo di mezzo*). By looking at the case of Mafia Capitale, a mafia-like organization that operates in Rome, this chapter argues that the new Italian form of corruption is based on a sophisticated mechanism of social interaction that allows different sets of actors to perceive a sense of sameness and of membership in a strong corporatistic structure.

In Chapter 12, Pavel Sascheko examines corruption scandals in Belarus. For Sascheko, The Republic of Belarus is a state, famous for its vast swamp and marsh

14   *Omar E. Hawthorne and Stephen Magu*

areas called the "lungs of Europe". Specific features of this former Soviet Republic include the commitment to tradition and maintaining the existing situation. Belarus also acts cautiously with respect to governance and amending domestic legislation, trying to find the best course of action and a balance between the interests of different groups of the population. In this regard, the central question in the examination of the linkage between corruption and governance in Belarus is whether corruption scandals constitute a "stone" which is capable of "making rings". To answer this question, corruption cases that occurred in Belarus from June 2014 to June 2016, as well as amendments to domestic legislation, are examined. This chapter identifies a set of key traits of corruption scandals that occurred in Belarus and their consequences with respect of governance. Sascheko also provides a detailed examination of some of the major scandals that have been the focal points of Belarusian media, including how well these scandals are articulated in the national press, indicating the levels of interest amongst the public.

In Chapter 13, Omar Hawthorne assesses the corruption scandals in the various countries included in the text and further analyzes their domestic and global impacts while noting that corruption is not limited to any one country and/or society. In the interdependent and global economy, the interconnectedness of states via trade, bilateral treaties and commerce undoubtedly requires that the issue of corruption be addressed. However, it should not be addressed in piecemeal isolation; rather, on matters where sharing of information and reforming legislation is needed, states should work together to address corruption. Politically, when leaders opt to abuse their power for personal gains the effects are devastating for countries and the impact seemingly has more lasting effect.

References and further reading

African Union. (N.D.) "African Union Convention on Preventing and Combatting Corruption." (Web). Accessed on 8/30/2017 from: www.eods.eu/library/AU_Convention%20 on%20Combating%20Corruption_2003_EN.pdf

Anechiarico, F. (1998) *The Pursuit of Absolute Integrity* Chicago: University of Chicago Press.

Apter, D. (1962) "Reflections on the Role of a Political Opposition in New Nations." *Comparative Studies in Society and History* Vol. 4: 157.

Balán, M. (2014) "Surviving Corruption in Brazil: Lula's and Dilma's Success Despite Corruption Allegations, and Its Consequences." *Journal of Politics in Latin America* Vol. 6, no. 3: 67–93.

Beck, P. & Maher, M. (1986) "A Comparison of Bribery and Bidding in Thin Markets." *Economic Letters* Vol. 20: 1–5.

Becker, G. & Stigler, G. (1974) "Law Enforcement, Malfeasance, and Compensation of Enforcers." *The Journal of Legal Studies* Vol. 3, no. 1: 1–18.

Bisariya, Chetan, Ed. (1982) *Uranium: The Element Which Changed the World.* Chetan Bisariya.

Cater, C. (2013) "Corruption and Global Governance." In Sophie Harman & David Williams, Eds. *Governing the World? Cases in Global Governance.* New York, NY: Routledge.

Cockcroft, L. (2013) *Global Corruption: Money, Power and Ethics in the Modern World.* New York, NY: I. B. Tauris & Co. Ltd.

de Maria, W. (2008) "Measurements and Markets: Deconstructing the Corruption Perception Index." *International Journal of Public Sector Management* Vol. 21, no. 7: 777–797.

Hawthorne, O. (2015) *Do International Corruption Metrics Matter? The Impact of Transparency International's Corruption Perception Index.* Lanham: Lexington Books.

Heidenheimer, A. & Johnson, M. (1989) *Political Corruption: A Handbook.* New Brunswick, NJ: Transaction Press.

Huntington, S. (1986) *Political Order in Changing Societies.* New Haven: Yale University Press.

Iyer, N. & Samociuk, M. (2006) *Fraud and Corruption: Prevention and Detection.* Aldershot, UK: Gower Publishing.

Leff, N. (1964) "Economic Development through Bureaucratic" *American Behavioural Scientist* Vol. 8, no. 3: 8–14.

Lien, D. (1986) "A Note on Competitive Bribery Games." *Economic Letters* Vol. 22: 337–341.

Lowi, T. (1988) "Foreword." In Andrei Markovitz & Mark Silverstein, Eds. *The Politics of Scandal.* New York: Holmes & Meier Publishers.

Nordio, C. (1997) *Giustizia.* Milan: Angeto Gorinie Associaii.

Obermayer, B. & Obermaier, F. (2016) *The Panama Papers: Breaking the Story of How the Rich and Powerful Hide Their Money.* London: Oneworld Publications.

OECD. (2008) *Corruption: A Glossary of International Standards in Criminal Law.* Paris: OECD.

Richardson, P. (2001) "Corruption." In Peter J. Simmons & Chantal de Jonge Oudraat, Eds. *Managing Global Issues: Lessons Learned.* Washington, DC: Carnegie Endowment for International Peace, pp. 75–106.

Rose-Ackerman, S. & Palifka, B. (2016) *Corruption and Government: Causes, Consequences, and Reform.* Cambridge, UK: Cambridge University Press.

Sandholtz, W. & Koetzle, W. (2000) "Accounting for Corruption: Economic Structure, Democracy, and Trade." *International Studies Quarterly* Vol. 44, no. 1: 31–50.

Thompson, J. (2000) *Political Scandal.* Cambridge: Polity Press.

Tullock, G. (1996) "Corruption Theory and Practice." *Contemporary Economic Policy* Vol, 14, no. 3: 6–13.

Tumber, H. & Waisbord, S. (2004) "Political Scandals and Media across Democracies." *American Behavioral Scientist* Vol. 47.

United Nations (2017) United Nations Treaty Collection, Chapter XVIII, Penal Matters, 14. United Nations Convention against Corruption. Accessed on 8/29/2017 from: https://treaties.un.org/Pages/ViewDetails.aspx?src=IND&mtdsg_no=XVIII-14&chapter=18&lang=en

Waisbord, S. (2000) *Watchdog Journalism in South America.* New York: Columbia University Press.

Williams-Elegbe, S. (2012) *Fighting Corruption in Public Procurement: A Comparative Analysis of Disqualification or Debarment Measures.* Oxford, UK: Hart Publishing Ltd.

2 The management or mismanagement of corruption in Trinidad and Tobago

Ann Marie Bissessar

Introduction

In much of the academic literature on mechanisms to curb or minimize corruption in countries worldwide the emphasis has been on legislation or institutions such as the Integrity Commission or anti-corruption agencies. The chapter first presents a descriptive overview of the mechanisms that have been established to curb and prevent corruption in Trinidad and Tobago. However, the primary purpose of this chapter is to interrogate one critical institution, the Parliament, and its primary role and responsibility to curb or minimize corruption in the twin-island republic of Trinidad and Tobago. The major argument of the chapter is that while the Parliament has established the necessary processes for oversight, the success so far in curbing corruption by governmental agencies within these countries has been poor. The chapter accordingly probes and tries to arrive at explanations for the limited success of the Parliament in fighting corruption in the twin-island state. It focuses specifically on one committee, namely the Public Accounts Enterprises Committee which has oversight for Ministries/State Enterprises and Service Commissions. Unfortunately, because of the limitations involved in writing a single chapter, the actual cases undertaken by the Public Accounts Enterprises Committee and more in-depth data cannot be presented but would be forthcoming in other chapters.

A historical overview

The twin-island Republic of Trinidad and Tobago is 11 km (6.8 mi) off the northeast coast of Venezuela and 130 km (81 mi) south of the Grenadines. The *transplanted* populations of the islands are the descendants of the East Indian indentured servants who make up 35.4% of the total population, the African-descended population which comprises 34.2% of the population, mixed/other 15.3%, mixed African/East Indian 7.7%, other 1.3% and unspecified 6.2% (2011 est.). The countries experienced a change of ownership during the 1800s, moving from the Spanish and then finally were acceded to the British. In 1962, the combined country of Trinidad and Tobago attained its independence from Britain. It should be recalled that before granting independence to its colonies, however, the British experimented with a number of governance models before finally introducing an adapted form of the Westminster model. For instance, one of the earliest models of administration was a system of Crown Colony administration. Later, the administrators attempted to establish a unified civil service, and finally a West Indian federal system was proposed. When the federal 'experiment' failed, the countries, starting with Jamaica, requested and attained independent status and introduced the governing system later referred to as the Westminster Whitehall model of government.

The Westminster Whitehall model of government was a two-tier system of government, comprising a central government arrangement and a local government arrangement. Each of the two spheres of government was made up of three parts:

- The elected members – who represented and approved policies and laws;
- The executive committees – who coordinated the making of policies and laws;
- The civil servants – who were responsible for implementation of governmental policies.

The foundations upon which this hybrid model of government was based included a written constitution. As in Britain, three arms of government – the Executive, the Legislative Branch (the Parliament) and the Judiciary – were established. The Parliament in ex-colonial societies such as Trinidad and Tobago had supreme authority and was only superseded by the written constitution. The functions of the Parliament resemble those in Britain, and they include:

1 Formulating laws, revising exisiting laws and repealing outdated laws;
2 Representing and articulating the views of the wider population;
3 Overseeing the activities of the executive branch of government to ensure accountability to the citizenry.

One can suggest, however, that when the Westminster Whitehall model was introduced in Trinidad and Tobago 1962, (entornointeligente, 2017) the original intension to ensure accountability may have been limited to oversight of the management of government's revenue and expenditure. By the latter half of the 1960s, however, with a number of allegations of corruption[1] emerging, it was obvious that new oversight mechanisms had to be introduced and existing mechanisms and processes strengthened. What was also obvious was that the determination to establish the various mechanisms required that the multi-dimensional nature of corruption had to be taken into account.

The multi-dimensional nature of corruption and the introduction of appropriate anti-corruption mechanisms

Without doubt, the typology defining the types of corruption has grown immensely. Whereas previously three broad types of corruption had been identified, namely grand, petty and administrative, this had now been extended to include systemic (endemic), sporadic, political, and legal and moral corruption (Byrne, 2012). Essentially these terms define the 'what' of corruption. Begovic (2005) argues, however, that irrespective of the scope of this phenomenon, economic theory has collapsed these typologies into two views, what may simply be alluded to as the 'where' of corruption. Simply put, corruption is either exogenous to the political process or endogenous. In other words, corruption can be located within the government or it can arise from outside the government, from external sources. It is reasonable to assume, then, that if the 'placement' or the 'where' of corruption is limited, then the remedies to curb this malady will not be expansive. But this is not the case. Rather countries around the world have introduced a variety of mechanisms, including legislation and institutions, many of which often duplicate, if not contradict, the functions of the others.

In the case of Trinidad and Tobago, for example, a framework of domestic leglislation, policy initiatives and special institutions, along with international conventions and multilateral and bilateral treaties, were introduced or endorsed. Some of the international conventions include:

1 The Inter-American Convention Against Corruption, ratified on 15 April 1998;
2 The United Nations Convention against Corruption (UNCAC), which was ratified by Trinidad and Tobago on 31 May 2006. Trinidad and Tobago agreed to be reviewed by selected peer members (Argentina and Palau) in 2013.

In addition, Trinidad and Tobago entered into a number of multilateral and bilateral treaties, including those regarding:

1 Mutual legal assistance
2 Extradition

Trinidad and Tobago has concluded both multilateral and bilateral treaties in relation to rendering and requesting mutual and legal assistance as well as in relation to extradition. Trinidad and Tobago has concluded these treaties with Commonwealth as well as non-Commonwealth countries, such as the United States and the Netherlands (see the Mutual Assistance in Criminal Matters Act, Chap. 11:24, and the Extradition [Commonwealth and Foreign Territories] Act, Chap. 12:04).[2]
Domestic legislation includes the following:[3]

- *The Mutual Assistance in Criminal Matters Act*, Chap. 11.24, facilitates mutual assistance in criminal matters within the Commonwealth or countries designated under the act. This facility to provide mutual assistance is generally rendered on the basis of a bilateral treaty or agreement or multilateral convention, and it provides a means for one state to obtain evidence from another state for use in a criminal investigation and/or prosecution.
- *The Central Authority of Trinidad and Tobago* was established under this act, and section 3 of the act provides that the Attorney General is the Central Authority. To give effect to the act, a unit has been established in the Ministry

of the Attorney General and is headed by a Director with the support of legal and administrative staff.

- *The Extradition (Commonwealth and Foreign Territories) Act*, Chap. 12:04, provides procedures for extradition between Commonwealth and non-Commonwealth jurisdictions. This act states the circumstances in which an offence may be extraditable, as well as the circumstances in which the extradition may be refused.
- *The Prevention of Corruption Act*, Chap 11:11, provides for certain offences and punishment of corruption in public office. The elements of the offence of *corruption in office* (section 3), *corrupt transactions with agents* (section 4), *corruptly using or communicating official documents* (section 5), and the *grounds for the presumption of corruption in certain cases* are set out in section 7.
- *The Proceeds of Crime Act*, Chap. 11.27, establishes the procedure for the confiscation of the proceeds of certain offences and for the criminalizing of money laundering. Bilateral agreements for the provision of mutual legal assistance exist between Trinidad and Tobago and the United States (4 March 1996), the UK (5 January 98) and Canada (27 January 2000). Section 3 of the act provides a mechanism for the determination of confiscation of the proceeds of specified offences.
- *The Integrity in Public Life Act*, Chap. 22:01, provides for the establishment of the Integrity Commission, making provisions for the prevention of corruption of persons in public life by providing for public disclosure; it regulates the conduct of persons exercising public functions and preserves and promotes the integrity of public officials and institutions. An exercise to review the act and the organizational structure of the commission is underway with the intent to enhance its ability to achieve its statutory mandate.
- *The Freedom of Information Act*, Chap. 22:02, gives members of the public a general right (with specified exceptions) of access to official documents of public authorities. The intention of the act was to address the public's concerns about corruption and to promote a system of open and good governance. In compliance with the act, designated officers have been appointed in each ministry and given the statutory authority to process the applications for information.
- *The Police Complaints Authority Act*, Chap. 15:05, provides for the establishment of the Police Complaints Authority (PCA) and establishes a mechanism for complaints against police officers in relation to, among other things, police misconduct and police corruption. The PCA is given the power to receive complaints from members of the public, to undertake investigations in relation to those complaints and, when a case is established against the officer, to refer the matter to the Commissioner of Police or the Director of Prosecutions for necessary action. The PCA is an independent body. Its purpose is to ensure that when a member of the public makes a complaint it is dealt with thoroughly and fairly.

20 *Ann Marie Bissessar*

Other special initiatives established by the state to prevent corruption include the following:

- *The Caribbean Financial Action Task Force (CFATF)*. This is an organization of states and territories of the Caribbean region that have agreed to implement common countermeasures against money laundering. The CFATF is also an associate member of the Financial Action Task Force (FATF), which is an intergovernmental body established in 1989 by the ministers of its member states.
- *The AML/CFT Standards*, also known as the *FATF Recommendation*. These standards are important for financial institutions to develop internal controls to protect themselves from exposure to money laundering and the financing of terrorism and to comply with regulations on anti-money laundering (AML) and combating the financing of terrorism (CFT). The FATF on money laundering has developed international standards on AML/CFT. Within this comprehensive general framework, individual countries are responsible for introducing local legislative and regulatory regimes.
- *The Financial Intelligence Unit (FIU)*. The FIU of Trinidad and Tobago, incorporated under the Financial Intelligence Act of 2009, has been established to implement the anti-money-laundering policies of the FATF, an intergovernmental organization set up by the Group of Seven industrialized countries. The main objective of the FATF is to develop and provide international policies to combat money laundering and terrorist financing.
- *The Anti-Corruption Investigations Bureau (ACIB)*. This is a group of police officers and civilian staff who are specially trained in investigating white-collar crime. The ACIB was established in January 2002 to deal in a holistic manner with the question of investigating corruption, particularly in the public sector. The bureau was provided with the resources required to carry out its mandate, including personnel with special expertise, legal advice, staff and accommodation. The bureau is required to keep the Attorney General informed of the findings of its investigations. It is to be noted that the question of prosecutions remains the responsibility of the Director of Public Prosecutions because of his clear and exclusive constitutional mandate.
- *The Egmont Group of Financial Intelligence*. Trinidad and Tobago's FIU is a member of the Egmont group – an informal group of FIUs formed to enhance international cooperation. The goal of the Egmont group is to provide a forum for FIUs around the world to improve cooperation in the fight against money laundering and financing of terrorism and to foster the implementation of domestic programs in the field.

With so many mechanisms in place, it would be expected that the number of incidents or allegations of corruption in the twin-island republic of Trinidad and

Tobago would be considerably reduced. Yet, this country is ranked the 101st least corrupt nation out of 175 countries, according to the 2016 Corruption Perceptions Index (CPI) reported by Transparency International.[4] No doubt it could be argued that this increase in the allegations of corruption may have emerged as a result of one or more of the following variables, namely:

*   Globalization and the removal of barriers to trade;
*   The porous borders of the country and its use as a transhipment point for drugs;
*   Weak regulatory controls;
*   The instability of governments with a limited five-year term;
*   High levels of crime;
*   High levels of patronage or cultural factors.[5]

While the number of variables that may give rise to corrupt practices may be expanded, essentially as Polterovich (1998) pointed out, these can be collapsed into three groups, namely: fundamental factors rooted in the imperfection of economic institutions and economic policy, organizational factors (weakness of government) and finally societal factors, which he suggests depend on the prehistory of the country and are connected with the mass culture and norms of bureaucratic behavior. In the case of Trinidad and Tobago,[6] the data clearly suggest that a large number of allegations of corruption are linked directly to state agencies and departments. These allegations allude to over-spending by government and state agencies, lack of proper processes for procurement, patronage and weaknesses in accounting procedures and policies. In other words, the major sources of corruption appear to occur 'within' the governmental ministries or state agencies. This is where the Parliament of the country, and more specifically the Committees of Parliament, play an important role because they are required to ensure that there is accountability as well as transparency in the expenditure of public funds.

Parliament and its processes

As noted previously, the Parliament of Trinidad and Tobago, like parliaments in many countries, exercises three major functions, namely, legislation, representation and oversight of the executive branch of government. In the case of the Parliament of Trinidad and Tobago, there are 11 units and approximately 330 members of staff. The Parliament is bicameral, comprising an elected House of Representatives (the Lower House) and an appointed Senate (Upper House). The Head of State, the President, is elected by members of both Houses for a five-year term. The Lower House comprises 41 members, while the President appoints 31 senators: 16 on the advice of the Prime Minister, 6 on the advice of the Leader of the Opposition and 9 at the discretion of the President.

22 *Ann Marie Bissessar*

Complex issues of Parliament are referred to small groups/committees for detailed study and recommendations. There are four broad types of committees which consider matters referred to them or which fall within their mandate and report their recommendations to the House. These are:

- Committees of the Whole;
- Sessional Select Committees;
- Special/Joint Select Committees (established on an ad hoc basis);
- Watchdog Committees.

Sessional Select Committees deal with the regulatory functions for the House and include the Standing Orders Committee, the House Committee, the Committee of Privileges and the Regulations Committee. The Special Select Committees are ad hoc committees which are set up to consider and report on specific matters referred to them. Such issues may be legislative, financial or investigatory. The Watchdog Committees, as the name implies, perhaps are the most critical committees. They include the Joint Select Committee established under the constitution (section 66a) and include members of both the Lower House and the Senate. These committees are empowered to inquire and report to both Houses of Parliament with regard to Government Ministries, Municipal Corporations, Statutory Authorities, State Enterprises and Service Commissions. The Watchdog Committees include the Public Accounts Committee (PAC), as well as the Public Accounts Enterprises Committee (PAEC), established under section 119 of the constitution. (See Table 2.1 for a list of the ministries/departments reviewed by these committees.)

As noted previously, the PAEC (within all parliamentary jurisdictions) is responsible for examining the audited accounts of all State Enterprises. These committees allow citizens to participate through written submissions and to appear before public hearings (by invitation) to canvass issues of concern. The committees report to the legislature on the use of public funds and other matters. These committees, if effective, can have a major influence on revealing inefficiency or misuse of funds and in recommending improvements to policy, legislation and administration.

During the course of its deliberations, the PAEC obtains evidence from the Accounting Officers of the ministries, who are the Permanent Secretaries, Heads of Departments and other responsible officers. It also regularly summons Accounting Executives of Public Finance, State Accounts and National Budget or their nominated representatives. It is the duty of the Permanent Secretaries to personally appear before the committee to explain and justify the financial activities of the departments under the purview of their ministries. The recommendations of the committee may contain directives to government departments and ministries, and such directives are deemed to be those of Parliament. Copies of committee reports are also distributed among Officers of the Ministries, Departments, and Local Authorities.

Table 2.1 The responsibilities of the three Joint Select Committees[7]

JSC appointed to inquire into and report on ministries with responsibility areas listed as (GROUP 1) and on the Statutory Authority and State Enterprises falling under those ministries	JSC appointed to inquire into and report on ministries with responsibility areas listed as (GROUP 2) and on the Statutory Authorities and State Enterprises falling under those ministries	JSC appointed to inquire into and report on Municipal Corporations and Service Commissions (with the exception of the Judicial and Legal Service Commission)
Ministry of Arts and Multiculturalism (9 Statutory Authorities/State Enterprises)	Local Government (3 Statutory Authority/State Enterprise)	Police Service Commission
Office of the Attorney General (10 Statutory Authorities/State Enterprises)	National Security (3 Statutory Authority/State Enterprise)	Public Service Commission
Community Development (3 Statutory Authority/State Enterprise)	Office of the Prime Minister (5 Statutory Authority/State Enterprise)	Statutory Authorities Service Commission
Education (4 Statutory Authority/State Enterprise)	People and Social Development (7 Statutory Authority/State Enterprise)	Teaching Service Commission
Energy and Energy Affairs (22 Statutory Authority/State Enterprise)	Planning, Economic and Social Restructuring and Gender Affairs (3 Statutory Authority/State Enterprise)	Arima Borough Corporation
Finance (23 Statutory Authority/State Enterprise)	Public Administration (4 Statutory Authority/State Enterprise)	Chaguanas Borough Corporation
Food Production and Land and Marine Resources (8 Statutory Authority/State Enterprise)	Public Utilities (7 Statutory Authority/State Enterprise)	Couva/Tabaquite/Talparo Regional Corporation
Foreign Affairs	Science, Technology and Tertiary Education (24 Statutory Authority/State Enterprise)	Mayaro/Rio Claro Regional Corporation
Health (8 Statutory Authority/State Enterprise)	Sport and Youth Affairs (5 Statutory Authority/State Enterprise)	Penal/Debe Regional Corporation
Housing and the Environment (5 Statutory Authority/State Enterprise)	Tobago Development (2 Statutory Authority/State Enterprise)	Point Fortin Borough Corporation
Justice (4 Statutory Authority/State Enterprise)	Tourism (2 Statutory Authority/State Enterprise)	Port-Of-Spain City Corporation
Labour and Small and Micro-Enterprises Development (8 Statutory Authority/State Enterprise)	Trade and Industry (18 Statutory Authority/State Enterprise)	Princes Town Regional Corporation

(*Continued*)

24   *Ann Marie Bissessar*

Table 2.1 (Continued)

Legal Affairs (1 Statutory Authority/State Enterprise)	Works and Transport (14 Statutory Authority/State Enterprise)	San Fernando City Corporation
		Sangre Grande Regional Corporation
		San Juan/Laventille Regional Corporation
		Siparia Regional Corporation
13 ministries	13 ministries	4 commissions
54 boards	43 boards	1 corporations
49 enterprises	40 enterprises	
Total: 117 entities	Total: 96 entities	Total: 18 entities

The PAEC, as well as the PAC, by law, must be chaired by a member of the Opposition.[8] In essence, the functions of this committee in the case of Trinidad and Tobago is similar to that of Sri Lanka and includes:

1   Probing whether the allocated funds have been used by the respective ministries, departments and local authorities with the maximum efficiency and whether the financial regulations have been duly complied with;
2   If any excess has taken place, to find out whether it was done with proper authority and whether it can be justified. If over-expenditure is justifiable, the committee can make suitable recommendations to parliament to allow the same;
3   If excess cannot be justified, to make recommendations regarding action to be taken to prevent such occurrences in the future;
4   The committee can also make recommendations relating to underutilization of funds as well as over-expenditure on extravagance (Yapa, 2014).

While the functions of these committees are outlined and the processes clearly established, it appears though that in many countries the effectiveness of these committees is currently under review (Yapa, 2014; Victoria, 2000; Wehner, 2003). In evaluating the effectiveness of PACs and PAECs, a number of broad recommendations have been proffered. These recommendations were effectively summarized in one report (2006)[9] which suggested that there were three imperatives to improve the effectiveness of these committees, namely:

1   The need to build capacity; that is, the provision of adequate resources to improve the ability of parliaments and their PACs to perform their functions;
2   To allow committees a measure of independence/freedom from political and legal constraints to carry out duties, and;
3   To set up channels to allow for information exchange, which was a commitment to keeping PACs up-to-date with best practices.

In keeping with these imperatives, therefore, included in the majority of reports (globally) were the proposals that:

- The relationship between the PAC and the auditor general in defining respective remits should be strengthened;
- The committees should establish a clear focus on accountability;
- The committees should develop technical capacity;
- The committees should issue formal and substantive reports to parliament at least annually and;
- The committees should establish a procedure with the government for following up on its work.

In other words, the various reports focused on improving the process and the relationship of these committees. In the case of Trinidad and Tobago, though, Staddon (2012) was more expansive. One of the gaps identified in his report was the legislation that established these committees. He noted for instance:

> There is a discrepancy between the Standing Orders of the Senate and the Standing Orders of the House of Representatives in relation to the JSCs. Standing Order 79b. (2) Of the House of Representatives states:
>
>> A JSC referred to in sub-paragraph (1), shall be empowered to study and report on all matters relating to the mandate, management and operations of the Ministry or body which is assigned to it by the House. In general the Committee shall be severally empowered to report on –
>>
>> (a) The statute law relating to the ministry/body assigned to it;
>> (b) The program and policy objectives of the ministry/body and its effectiveness in the implementation of same; Other matters relating to the management, organisation of the ministry/body, as the Committee deems fit.
>>
>> (Staddon, 2012: 22)

He went on to add:

> In most jurisdictions, select committees are only able to scrutinise a small amount of the policy and actions of government departments and agencies. However, this appears even more marked in Trinidad and Tobago with just two committees devoted to 26 ministries. It may be unrealistic to expect Trinidad and Tobago to have a committee system which parallels government departments and some form of grouping is inevitable given the size of the Parliament. But a question mark must remain as to whether the current system allows appropriate oversight of government departments and specialization among committee membership. Perhaps one way of ensuring this would be to establish subcommittees (which is permissible in the Standing Orders). This would allow members to specialize in certain areas and ensure a greater division of labour within the committee. It should be noted, however, that while

26 *Ann Marie Bissessar*

subcommittees play an important role in some larger parliaments, such as the United States Congress and German Bundestag, their role has been limited in most Jurisdictions.

(Staddon, 2012: 24)

Apart from the issue of the legislation, Staddon (2012) also raised concerns such as the size and quorum of the committee, the capacity of the committee, as well the limited output of the committee, which he illustrated by way of a table.[10] He assessed the committee based on the following factors (Staddon, 2012: 37):

- A clear mandate, clear roles and responsibilities of the committee (parallel government departments) with a degree of autonomy and the power to set its own agenda;
- The size of the committee – large committees are unwieldy and small numbers limit the quantity and quality of ideas needed for effective work;
- The quality of the chairperson;
- The quality of support staff and resources available to the committee (including the experience of the clerks and the existence of special advisers supporting the committee);
- Consensus-building and a nonpartisan approach;
- The general quality of membership;
- Powers to take evidence and conduct inquiries (and the amount of time taken on each inquiry);
- The degree of media interest;
- The readiness of departments to provide evidence and useful material and to respond to reports.

He accordingly noted, based on these criteria, major constraints in the operations of the various committees. While Staddon (2012) did allude to other factors, it was evident, however, that he afforded minimal attention to two critical factors that were previously raised by Polterovich (1998), namely organizational and societal factors. In other words, minimal attention was devoted to the governance structure which defined the environment in which the PAEC would operate. This structure is best defined by one report[11] entitled "Parliaments that work." An excerpt from this report suggested:

Among the key variables here are the relations between the state, the market and civil society, the extent of political space and support for active citizenship, and the impact of the global village. Secondly, performance is heavily influenced by parliamentary culture, the set of motivating and constraining beliefs and practices. What are the values and expectations associated with being a Member of Parliament? What is the relationship between leaders and followers? Thirdly, parliamentary performance is dependent on the organizational capacity of parliament, including the strengths and weaknesses of the political and administrative sides of parliament.

(p. 7)

This relationship has accordingly been illustrated in Figure 2.1.[12]

The Determinants of Parliamentary Performance

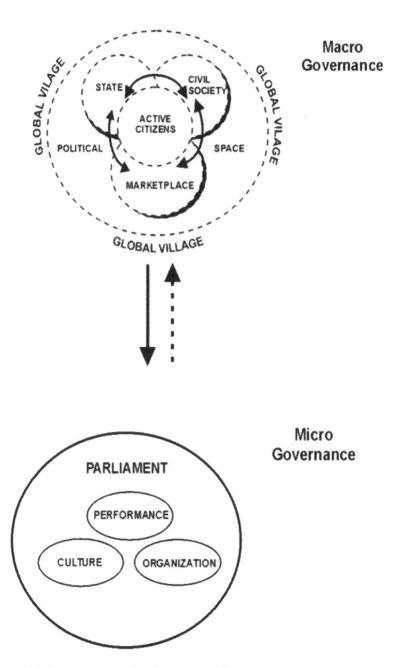

Figure 2.1 The determinants of parliamentary performance

28 *Ann Marie Bissessar*

Given this arrangement, then, the question emerges whether the effectiveness of the committees is limited as a result of weak processes or whether it is due to the ratio of the government and opposition members sitting on these committees.

Recommendations of the Public Accounts Enterprise Committee

The committee's recommendations followed the examination of the audited financial statements of the Sports Company of Trinidad and Tobago (SporTT), Community Improvement Services Limited (CISL), Community-Based Environmental Protection and Enhancement Programme (CEPEP), Point Lisas Industrial Port Development Corporation (PLIPDECO) and the Solid Waste Management Company Limited (SWMCOL). Four "trends" were identified: the limited capacity of the Investments Division of the Finance Ministry in overseeing and monitoring State Enterprises, the late submission of audited financial statements to Parliament, a lack of approved strategic plans for the current period and the absence of an internal audit unit at those State Enterprises.

The chairman noted that a recommendation has been made to the Investments Division that it be more proactive in its oversight responsibility by conducting regular site visits as well as monitoring and evaluating the quarterly reports of all State Enterprises. This recommendation can be very insightful towards inproving the structure and procedures of the Investment Division when monitoring State Enterprises. The committee also recommended that the division take a leading role in ensuring that State Enterprises comply with the existing performance monitoring manual, which sets out guidelines on accountability, transparency, value for money and performance.[13]

It was also recommended that each of these enterprises establish internal audit units and implement internal audit functions, with line ministries taking urgent steps to hire an internal auditor for these entities. Other recommendations include immediate steps by the Auditor General's Department to assist in implementing proper audit practices and adherence to international financial reporting standards. The chairman recommends that the State Enterprises' performance manual become a legal document because right now it is only a set of guidelines, and thus does not carry any legal sanction, and hence state enterprises are not restricted to following the manual. The committee ensures that these recommendations are properly implemented to improve the delivery of services and goods by these entities to the country.

Summarizing the Trinidad and Tobago experience

It is evident that in the case of Trinidad and Tobago the processes of Parliament are established and adhered to. However, clearly, this has not facilitated any meaningful improvements in reducing the alleged cases of corruption or over-spending by ministries and departments. As discussed, Staddon's report in 2013 attempted to identify existing weaknesses. What Staddon's report failed to do, however, was to

Corruption in Trinidad and Tobago   29

address the relationship between the governing party and the opposition party. He also failed to understand the dynamics of relationship within a ministry or state department where the minister held responsibility for that ministry (Tanzi, 1995). Nor did he address the issue of implementation of the recommendations at the administrative level. This chapter cannot attempt at this stage to address all these concerns but rather will focus on the ratio between government and opposition members sitting on the committees.

The relationship between the government and opposition members of parliament

Previously, it was felt that the governing and opposition members under a West-minister Whitehall model of government presented a seemless mechanism where the opposition served as a 'shadow government' or a 'government in waiting'.[14] This philosophy proposes that often there is consensus between government and opposition members of parliament. Yet, it has been suggested that conflict of interest as well as party loyalty may be the most common ethical dilemma faced by legislators. Scholars of parliamentary politics argue, for instance, that the relationship between government and opposition is based on, and derived from, a power relationship that depends of factors such as the structure of government, the strength of the government and constitutional arrangements. It is extremely important to also understand the power dynamics as they relate to the strength of members of the various groups sitting on the committees. In the case of Trinidad and Tobago, for example, it is evident that the composition of the governing group outweighs the opposition team.

Table 2.2, for example, clearly illustrates the numerical strength of the Government as opposed to the Opposition. Given this arrangement, then, it is evident that what may well happen behind the closed chambers of the Parliament is conflict rather than consensus between the two groups. In addition, it will not be surprising that the strength in numbers may well determine the outcomes of the decision taken by the committee. Perhaps this goes contrary to Satrori's (1978) argument.

Satrori (1987) suggested that committees can serve both as a potential for conflict as well as an arena for consensus. According to Satrori (1978) committees are the ideal forum for decision making since they are small, face-to-face groups. Furthermore, he argues that members interact on a basis of 'give and take' and that conflict

Table 2.2 Size of Joint Committees in Trinidad and Tobago

Committee Size	House	Senate	Government	Opposition	Independent
12 (current practice)	6	6	7 (58%)	3 (25%)	2 (17%)
11	6 (5)	5 (6)	7 (64%)	3 (27%)	1 (9%)
10 (suggested practice)	5	5	6 (60%)	3 (30%)	1 (10%)
9	5	4	5 (56%)	3 (33%)	1 (11%)

Source: Staddon (2012: 29).

30   *Ann Marie Bissessar*

resolution is often facilitated as these committees work behind closed doors. Contrary to Satrori's (1978) view, one study conducted in 17 western democracies produced another point of view. Data from this study revealed that in more than half of all the committee decisions documented, conflict and majority rule prevailed over consensus and unanimity. This may also be relevant in Trinidad and Tobago as well.

No doubt the counterargument will be that while there is an undecided numerical advantage of the government as opposed to opposition members on the committees, the chairman of these committees according to the constitution, must be a member of the opposition. Yet, that, too, becomes a moot point if the powers of the chairman are defined. Documents produced for committee members by the Committees Office of the Parliament describe the role of the chairman as follows:

- Collaborates with committee members in making strategic planning decisions;
- Ensures that all rules established by the committee are respected;
- Requests on behalf of the committee the appearance of witnesses or the production of papers;
- Conducts proceedings in an orderly and fair manner;
- Rules on the relevance of questions to witnesses;
- Ensures that the committee receives advice from the secretary in relation to matters of procedure and availability of resources.

In addition, it has been noted that the chairman

1   Does not have the power to decide questions of privilege (such decisions rest with the House after a report from the committee) and does not vote except in instances where there is equality of votes in which case he/she has a casting vote;
2   Does not have the authority to unilaterally summon any person before the committee without approval from the committee;
3   Can cancel a meeting that he has set, but not one set by the committee.

Given the above then, it can be suggested that the powers of the chairman are limited (Staddon, 2012)

In summary, then, apart from the numerous challenges highlighted by so many reports on the Parliamentary Committees which limits their ability to act as checks and balances on the executive, one other point is clearly the relationship between the Government and the Opposition members in committees. In the case of Trinidad and Tobago, one major flaw seems to be that the Government members far outweigh the Opposition members, and even the role of the chairman is extremely limited. The interactions between members as well as the governance arrangements between the Parliament and the civil society will of necessity be the subject of discourse of another chapter. In conclusion, however, it is evident that given the numerous challenges in providing oversight of the administration of the executive why Trinidad and Tobago now occupies the position of 101 out of 175 most corrupt countries globally.

Notes

1 In the 1960s and 1970s, Trinidad and Tobago was rocked by scandal after scandal – the DC-9 affair, the Caroni Racing Complex, the Radar scandal at Chaguaramas, the Gas Station racket, and the Tesoro affair.

2 Bilateral agreements for the provision of mutual legal assistance exist between Trinidad and Tobago and the United States (4 March 1996), UK (5 January 1998), and Canada 27 Janury 2000. Taken from Mechanism for Follow-Up on Implementation of the Interamerican Convention against Corruption. www.oas.org/juridico/PDFs/tto_legal_framework.pdf

3 The discussion on the various mechanisms was taken from: http://siteresources. worldbank.org/EXTAML/Resources/396511-1146581427871/AML_implications_ complete.pdf

4 https://tradingeconomics.com/trinidad-and-tobago/corruption-rank Trinidad and Tobago is the 101 least corrupt nation out of 175 countries, according to the 2016 Corruption Perceptions Index reported by Transparency International. Corruption Rank in Trinidad and Tobago averaged 69.44 from 2001 until 2016, reaching an all time high of 101 in 2016 and a record low of 31 in 2001.

5 For more on this see Teuta Vodo's 2012 paper, "Identifying the Most Crucial Factors Giving Rise to Corruption in the Albanian Courts." Faculty of Political and Social Science, Université Libre de Bruxelles, Brussels, Belgium. Paper presented in the World Congress of the International Political Science Association, Madrid, 2012. Vodo, however, looked at the judicial system.

6 "It is alleged that a senior Petrotrin official pushed through the deal and within weeks of the disputed 29 August 2012, Petrotrin payout; US$750,000 of the US$1.25 million upfront commission was paid into a Houston bank account in Texas, USA, in the name of Member source Credit Union, and was allegedly transferred to two private bank accounts at the Ellerslie Plaza branch of Scotiabank,".www.entornointeligente.com/articulo/70759/Petrotrin-investigating-lease-operators-06092017

7 Table taken from Anthony Staddon, pages 23–24. He notes that

the Table (3)shows the Ministries, Statutory Authorities, State Enterprises, Municipal Corporations and Service that fall under the purview of each Committee. Essentially, the ministries have been split equally between JSCs 1 and 2 along with their relevant statutory authorities and state enterprises. This division has been calculated on an alphabetical basis and no attempt has been to group similar ministries together or to consider the number of statutory authorities and state enterprises falling under those ministries. The third JSC is devoted to Municipal Corporations and Service Commissions (with the exception of the Judicial and Legal Service Commission).

8 Much of this has been summarized from the following: Anthony Staddon. 2012. "A Study on Parliamentary Scrutiny and Existing Parliamentary Practice." A consultancy paper. February. www.ttparliament.org/documents/2181.pdf

9 Report of the CPA Parliamentary Financial Scrutiny Workshop, held from 7 to 15 February 2006 in Canberra and Sydney, organized with the World Bank Institute and La Trobe University. http://dev.cpahq.org/uploadedFiles/Information_Services/Publications/CPA_ Electronic_Publications/Parliamentary%20Financial%20Scrutiny%20The%20Role%20 of%20Public%20Accounts%20Committees.pdf- PARLIAMENTARY FINANCIAL SCRUTINY: THE ROLE OF PUBLIC ACCOUNTS COMMITTEES (PACS)

10 See Staddon (2013: Table 8, page 24). http://www.ttparliament.org/documents/2181.pdf

11 "Parliaments That Work: A Conceptual Framework for Measuring Parliamentary Performance." https://view.officeapps.live.com/op/view.aspx?src=http%3A%2F%2Fwww1. worldbank.org%2Fpublicsector%2Fbnpp%2FMeasuringParliamentaryPerf.doc The Parliamentary Centre and the World Bank Institute have undertaken a project to develop a conceptual framework and indicators for measuring the performance of legislative institutions. The entitled the project "Parliaments that Work."

32 *Ann Marie Bissessar*

12 "Parliaments That Work: A Conceptual Framework for Measuring Parliamentary Performance." https://view.officeapps.live.com/op/view.aspx?src=http%3A%2F%2Fwww1.worldbank.org%2Fpublicsector%2Fbnpp%2FMeasuringParliamentaryPerf.doc
13 See http://trinidad-tobago.financialsweb.com/financial/paec-report-better-financial-reporting-required-from-state-enterprises – loop-trinidad-amp-tobago.html Author PAEC report: Better financial reporting required from State enterprises – Loop Trinidad & Tobago
14 This view is supported in: www.parliament.uk/about/how/role/parliament-government

References and Further Readings

Ackerman, S. and Palifka, B. (2016). *Corruption and Government: Causes, Consequences and Reform*. Cambridge: Cambridge University Press.

Anechiarico, F. and Jacobs, J. B. (1996). *The Pursuit of Absolute Integrity How Corruption Control Makes Government Ineffective*. Chicago: The University of Chicago Press Books.

Bank, W. (n.d.). *World Bank*. Retrieved August 10, 2017, from http://siteresources.worldbank.org/EXTAML/Resources/396511-1146581427871/AML_implications_complete.pdf

Begovic, B. (2005). *Corruption: Concepts, Types, Causes and Consequences*. Washington, DC: Center for International Private Enterprise.

Byrne, E. (2012). *Political Corruption in Ireland 1922–2010, a Crooked Harp?* Manchester: Manchester University Press.

CIPE. (2005). Retrieved July 19, 2017, from www.cipe.org/sites/default/files/publication-docs/032105.pdf

Corruption, M. F.-U. (2000). *Corruption*. Retrieved August 17, 2017, from www.oas.org/juridico/PDFs/tto_legal_framework.pdf

Corruption Rank. (2016). Retrieved August 10, 2017, from https://tradingeconomics.com/trinidad-and-tobago/corruption-rank

Cpahq.org. (2006). *Parliamentary Financial Scrutiny: The Role of Public Accounts Com*. Retrieved August 18, 2017, from http://dev.cpahq.org/uploadedFiles/Information_Services/Publications/CPA_Electronic_Publications/Parliamentary%20Financial%20Scrutiny%20The%20Role%20of%20Public%20Accounts%20Committees.pdf-

entornointeligente. (2017). Retrieved August 20, 2017, from www.entornointeligente.com/articulo/70759/Petrotrin-investigating-lease-operators-06092017

Heidenheimer, A. J. and Johnston, M. (1989). *Political Corruption*. New Brunswick, USA: Transaction Publishers.

Mattson, E. D. (2004). "Conflict and Consensus in Committees." In H. D. Hallerberg (Ed.), *Patterns of Parliamentary Behaviour*. Burlington, VT: Ashgate, Palgrave Macmillan.

Obermayer, B. and Obermaier, F. (2016). *The Panama Papers: Breaking the Story of How the World's Rich and Powerful Hide Their Money*. Panama: The International Consortium of Investigative Journalists.

officeapps. (2012). *Parliaments That Work: A Conceptual Framework for Measuring Parliamentary Performance*. Retrieved August 11, 2017, from https://view.officeapps.live.com/op/view.aspx?src=http%3A%2F%2Fwww1.worldbank.org%2Fpublicsector%2Fbnpp%2FMeasuringParliamentaryPerf.doc

Polterovich, V. M. (1998). Corruption Factors. *Matekon, 4* (summer), 3–15.

Satrori, G. (1987). *The Theory of Democracy Revisited*. Chatham, NJ: Chatham House Publications.

Staddon, A. (2012). *Activities on Strengthening Parliamentary Practices in Trinidad And Tobagoa Study on Parliamentary Scrutiny and Existing*. Port-of-Spain: Trinidad and Tobago Parliament.

Tanzi, V. (1995). "Corruption: Arm's-Length Relationships and Markets." In *The Economics of Organised Crime* (pp. 22–26). Cambridge: Cambridge University Press.

uk government, p.-g. (2016). *parliament.uk*. Retrieved August 22, 2017, from www.parliament.uk/about/how/role/parliament-government

Victoria, V. (2000). *Report of the Public Accounts and Estimates Committee on Commercial in Confidence*. Melbourne: Parliament of Victoria.

Vodo, T. (2012). *Identifying the Most Crucial Factors Giving Rise to Corruption in the Albanian Courts*. Brussels, Belgium: Université Libre de Bruxelles.

Wehner, J. (2003). Principles and Patterns of Financial Scrutiny: Public Accounts Committees in the Commonwealth. *Commonwealth and Comparative Politics, 41*, 21–36.

Yapa, P. (2014). The Oversight Committees in Developing Countries – Public Financial Control and the Expectations Gap – Some Empirical Evidence from Sri Lanka. *Asian Journal of Finance & Accounting*. Retrieved August 8, 2017, from www.macrothink.org/ajfa

3 Examining the potential impact of whistleblowing on corruption in the Caribbean's financial sector

Philmore Alleyne and Marissa Chandler

Introduction

Kreikebaum (2008, 82) posits, "corruption is recognized as an issue of serious political, economic and moral significance representing a cost for growth and development." It is an ageless, pervasive problem that has affected society from the beginning of time, though to varying degrees (Kreikebaum 2008; Everhart et al. 2009). Recognizing the pervasiveness of corruption and the negative impact it has had on the economic and social development of countries, the World Bank has provided support to more than 600 anti-corruption programs (Peyton and Belasen 2012).

Within the Caribbean, however, corruption continues to be very prevalent, as reflected by the region's relatively low rankings on Transparency International's Corruption Perceptions Index. Given the region's history, these rankings are unsurprising. The Caribbean, also referred to as the West Indies, is composed of a number of islands, including Barbados, Trinidad and Tobago, Jamaica and Guyana, which were colonized from the 17th through 19th centuries by the British, Dutch, French and Spanish powers. These European powers settled in the Caribbean islands to engage in farming, fishing and trade, but as time passed sugar cane became one of the major crops on the islands. As a result, black African slaves were imported and sold throughout the Caribbean to work on the sugar plantations (Mason et al. 1989), and therefore many in the Caribbean are of West African descent (Graham 2002). Today, the Caribbean population comprises a variety of ethnicities, religions (although Christianity is the most dominant) and languages, including Spanish, French, Dutch and English, the latter of which is the main language of the region. In addition, the Caribbean has a thriving financial sector, which comprises local and foreign commercial banks, credit unions and international business companies. With such a vast history, there is a need for anti-corruption mechanisms or strategies that are geared towards the unique Caribbean context. As such, the authors propose that whistleblowing should form the basis of any anti-corruption strategy that is developed for the region.

Whistleblowing, most commonly defined as a disclosure of unethical conduct, is a concept that has received more attention in academic discourse in recent years. Many authors have examined this concept and the various influences on a decision to whistle blow, particularly due to several international scandals involving whistleblowers. The most popular of these scandals was Enron, where Sherron Watkins, a CPA, wrote a memo to Kenneth Lay (the CEO) about the accounting irregularities she noticed; a memo which was later publicly disclosed in her testimony to Congress (Miceli et al. 2008). Watkins resigned from Enron, dissatisfied with how her disclosures were dealt with and the treatment she received (she was demoted). A few months later (late 2001), the company filed for bankruptcy and Watkins was hailed as a hero for her actions, especially in the face of organizational pressure (Lacayo and Ripley 2002; Lucas and Koerwer 2004). However, the consequences of the Enron scandal could have been reduced had her report been taken more seriously.

This chapter will therefore seek to discuss the potential impact whistleblowing can have on corruption in the Caribbean's financial sector. The following sections will review the relevant literature on corruption and whistleblowing before moving on to a discussion of corruption in the Caribbean. After this discussion, the authors will show how whistleblowing could be the key to addressing corruption in the Caribbean, before concluding the chapter.

Definitions and interpretations of corruption

Corruption is most commonly defined as "the abuse of public power for private benefit" (Everhart et al. 2009, 1579; Doig and Riley 1998; Peyton and Belasen 2012; Shabbir and Anwar 2007) and is further noted by Akinseye-George (2000) to be the "mother of all crimes". Furthermore, the Oxford Dictionary (according to Shabbir and Anwar, 2007) defines corruption from a moral and ethical standpoint, noting that it involves dishonest or illegal behaviour from persons in authority and involves making someone change their behaviour standards from moral to immoral acts. Gould (1991) supports this moral–ethical definition by noting corruption to be "an immoral and unethical phenomenon". Corruption can be either active or passive; "offering a pecuniary or other advantage to somebody for an improper action beyond his duties is called 'active' corruption. We speak of passive corruption when such an advantage is not combined with a legal offence" (Kreikebaum 2008, 82).

From an ethical and moral standpoint, corruption presents an interesting dichotomy. According to Schollhammer (1977), there is a clear conflict between conducting business in an ethical manner and maximizing profits, specifically as the latter may entail engaging in activities that may contravene the former. Thus, organizations can end up being both victims and culprits with reference to corrupt practices while pursuing these two potentially conflicting ideals. As Crane and Matten (2004, 320) note, "corporations might on one hand provide a context that to some extent encourages behaviour that is of dubious legality and, on the other, be expected to ensure that employees fulfil their legal obligations." In fact, financial profits may eventually win out for many businessmen, as striving for money "dominates their lifestyle and personal relationships" (Kreikebaum 2008, 85), and they may be tempted to use their company and employees for their own private purposes.

36 *Philmore Alleyne and Marissa Chandler*

Several types of corruption have been proposed in the literature, ranging from grand corruption (corruption deeply embedded at the higher levels of government organizations) to petty corruption (small-scale corruption that occurs at the lower echelons in society (between poor citizens and public officials)). Several causes of corruption have been identified, including government spending, regulation, and size and scope of the public sector, whereas economic freedom, political freedom, GDP per capita, increased levels of education and average income, and press freedom have been seen to be able to reduce corruption in developing economies (Doig and Riley 1998; Peyton and Belasen 2012; Shabbir and Anwar 2007). However, economic freedom is seen to play the largest role in combatting corruption (Peyton and Belasen 2012), and Shabbir and Anwar (2007) note that when democratic norms are adopted for longer periods, the level of corruption can be reduced. These authors also note that economic factors (such as economic freedom, education, income) contribute far more in reducing the level of corruption in developing countries than non-economic factors (such as press freedom and democracy).

Impact of corruption

According to the literature, even the mere presence of perceived corruption can significantly impact on a country's economic growth (Buscaglia 1999; Everhart et al. 2009; Seligson 2002; Shabbir and Anwar 2007). However, Everhart et al. (2009, 1590) also note that the impact of corruption on economic growth is not direct, but is rather an indirect effect on growth "via its interaction with public investment and governance quality". However, the consequences of corruption extend beyond stunting of economic growth and include reduction in investments and investment incentives, decreased private savings, increased transaction costs, lower tax revenues for government, a decline in the quality of the bureaucracy, hampering of political stability, misallocation of resources and impacts on both the public and private sector (Buscaglia 1999; Seligson 2002; Doig and Riley 1998; Everhart et al. 2009). Additionally, corruption usually reflects that the state is poorly functioning (Della Porta 2000; Doig and Riley 1998; Everhart et al. 2009).

At an organizational level, corruption decreases income growth for the poor, can cause businesses to fail and can increase income inequality (Seligson 2002). Additionally, corruption is a conduit by which fraud and organized criminal groups can develop, function and grow which then poses an additional threat to many countries with reference to international security (Buscaglia 1999; Doig and Riley 1998).

Corruption has detrimental effects on the efficiency of the social system. This point is emphasized by Kreikebaum (2008), who note that even when some firms avoid short-term gains by staying away from bribes and corruption and possibly lose business to those who engage in such activities, in the long term they avoid the negative consequences of corruption, which overall makes for a more successful organization.

Whistleblowing

Definitions and interpretations of whistleblowing

Near and Miceli (1985, 4) define whistleblowing as "the disclosure by organization members (former or current) of illegal, immoral or illegitimate practices under the control of their employers, to persons or organizations that may be able to effect action." It is also defined as "a disclosure of information by an employee or contractor who alleges wilful misconduct carried out by an individual or group of individuals within an organization" (Figg 2000, 30).

Whistleblowing can be done internally (reporting the information to a source within the organization) or externally (to the media or regulators). Although there are some who regard only the reporting of wrongdoing externally as whistleblowing, there is a strong preference for internal whistleblowing, as much of the research suggests that "nearly all whistle-blowers initially attempt to report wrongdoing via internal channels before or instead of external channels" (Mesmer-Magnus and Viswesvaran 2005, 282). This preference could be due to the employee's desire to address the wrongdoing internally before any public scrutiny or legal action befalls the organization and potentially causes irreparable damage to its reputation (Alleyne 2016; Alleyne and Pierce 2017).

Factors influencing whistleblowing

Contrary to the beliefs of those who oppose whistleblowing, whistleblowers are not motivated by self-interest, but rather make a positive and significant contribution to organizations and by extension the society. It has been argued that whistleblowers have helped to save billions of dollars and numerous lives through their disclosures of pertinent information with reference to fraud, corruption, mismanagement and wrongdoings committed by public and private organizations, government and their officials, thereby protecting citizens, employees and consumers.

However, it must be noted that the decision to blow the whistle is not an easy task (Elias 2008). The observer of the wrongdoing can either stay silent, report internally, report externally or leave the organization (Mesmer-Magnus and Viswesvaran 2005). Thus, many factors are considered before the individual decides to whistle blow. This decision, as noted by Alleyne et al. (2016), can be influenced by ethical sensitivity (awareness of the wrongdoing), ethical competence (strategy in dealing with ethical dilemmas) and perseverance (the ability to follow through on the ethical course of action). Research has also shown that individual characteristics such as age, gender, educational level, job position, locus of control, ethical reasoning, job performance, organizational commitment, professional commitment, work attitudes, value orientation, tenure and approval of whistleblowing also influence an individual's decision to whistleblow (Bowling and Lyons 2015; Cassematis and Wortley 2013; Hooks et al. 1994; Kaplan and Whitecotton 2001; Mesmer-Magnus and Viswesvaran 2005; Nayir and Herzig 2012; Near and Miceli 1996; Seifert 2006; Sims and Keenan 1998; Taylor and Curtis 2010). However,

38 Philmore Alleyne and Marissa Chandler

Graham's whistleblowing model also proposes that there are other factors that influence whistleblowing, which will be discussed next.

Graham's model of principled organizational dissent

Graham (1986) proposed the principled organizational dissent model, which theorized that an individual's decision to report a questionable act is influenced by perceived seriousness of the issue (seriousness), perceived personal responsibility for reporting (personal responsibility) and perceived personal cost of reporting (personal cost). Seriousness involves an individual's assessment of the act, which is influenced by situational characteristics, others affected, magnitude of harm and frequency of the questionable act. Perceived personal responsibility is an individual's feelings of social responsibility and obligation towards associates, employers and/or the profession, and is also contingent on the individual's ethical values. The final component of the model, the personal cost of reporting a questionable act, is influenced by the potential organizational response to the dissent and the related cost for reporting. Graham (1986) argued that the risk of reprisal from colleagues and management is the primary personal cost of reporting misconduct in organizations.

Therefore, management has a key role to play in addressing the personal costs attached to whistleblowing. They have several options, including either ignoring the report, correcting the wrongdoing or retaliating against the whistleblower (Near and Miceli 1996). Positive responses from management can signal to employees that whistleblowing behaviour is accepted in the organization and demonstrates a willingness to curb the wrongdoing. On the other hand, negative responses in the form of victimization and inaction can serve as a disincentive to whistleblowing. For example, prior research has shown that potential whistleblowers are less likely to report wrongdoing in organizations with a high-perceived retaliatory culture (Keenan 1995; King 1999; Near and Miceli 1996).

Whistleblowing in the Caribbean

While there is a dearth of literature on whistleblowing within the Caribbean, the literature that does exist is congruent with the international literature presented in the previous section. Individuals could be reluctant to blow the whistle due to their lack of confidence in the organization's ethical values and reporting systems, as well as if they perceive there to be high personal costs to reporting wrongdoing (Alleyne 2016; Alleyne and Pierce 2017). Thus, positive responses from management to whistleblowing reports, as well as a willingness to curb corrupt behaviours, will encourage employees to report wrongdoing. If whistleblowers truly believe that something will be done about the corrupt behaviour or practice, they will choose to whistleblow (Trinidad and Tobago Newsday 2012). However, the opposite is also true, especially if victimization or retaliation by management in response to whistleblowing occurs within the organization (Alleyne and Pierce 2017). Thus, as noted by Alleyne and Pierce (2017, 11) "an organization with effective and trusted institutions and practices can signal to employees that they can report wrongdoing with confidence."

Furthermore, whistleblowing legislation, or lack thereof, can also influence the decision of persons to come forward. Within the Caribbean, there is generally a lack of whistleblowing legislation, and subsequently a lack of protection and incentives for potential whistleblowers (Alleyne 2016). Whistleblowing legislation has only been enacted in Jamaica and the Cayman Islands, while Guyana and Trinidad and Tobago have drafted bills to be reviewed by their respective governments. However, despite the implementation of the two legislations mentioned previously, persons within these Caribbean countries still appear reluctant to come forward, possibly due to how those within Caribbean culture perceive whistleblowers. The act of reporting wrongdoing is generally not perceived as an acceptable means of correcting such behaviour (Alleyne 2016), and in fact is perceived negatively by some, who sometimes brand whistleblowers as traitors and snitches (Alleyne 2010). However, whistleblowing should be perceived as a tool that can halt organizational corruption, thus benefiting the entire organization.

Research conducted within the Caribbean has revealed that additional predictors of whistleblowing intentions include age, job level, organizational climate, perceived organizational support, perceived behavioural control, need for approval from others (desired moral approbation), job satisfaction, anonymity of the reporting mechanism, personal benefits, independence commitment and group cohesion (Alleyne 2010), organizational commitment and corporate ethical values (Alleyne 2016; Alleyne et al. 2013). Specifically, trust and confidence in the organization's values (for example, ethical climate) and personal factors (such as organizational commitment), encourage whistleblowing while personal costs and organizational values (such as a poor ethical climate) discourage whistleblowing (Alleyne 2016). Alleyne (2010) also finds that perceived personal responsibility, perceived seriousness of the wrongdoing and perceived personal costs also influence intentions to whistleblow, thus providing support to Graham's (1986) model. With reference to personal costs, in some instances, individuals are threatened with acts of reprisal which include job loss, salary reductions, over-supervision of work tasks, changes in duties and responsibilities, as well as harassment (Alleyne et al. 2013).

Despite these and other influences on whistleblowing, there is no denying the fact that whistleblowing has become of crucial importance to the stability of the global financial market, especially considering the ethical failures that resulted in the global economic collapse in 2008 (Alleyne 2016; Alleyne and Pierce 2017). When the relevant authorities are notified of wrongdoing in an organization, they can put the mechanisms in place to effect action. The importance of whistleblowing in organizations is also highlighted by the various international legislations that have been implemented across the world, such as the Sarbanes-Oxley Act (2002) and the Dodd-Frank Wall Street Reform and Consumer Protection Act (2010) (Alleyne 2016). Additionally, whistleblowing has the capability of eliminating wrongdoing so that benefits are realized both at the employee level and the organizational level. Specifically, whistleblowing can help improve the efficiency

40   *Philmore Alleyne and Marissa Chandler*

of the workplace, especially if it manages to reduce corrupt practices within organizations (Alleyne and Pierce 2017).

Corruption within the Caribbean

Corruption is a major concern in the Caribbean, as its effects on the society are widespread in both direct and indirect ways. This section discusses corruption in the Caribbean first by looking at the current situation by analyzing the 2016 Corruption Perceptions Index, before proceeding to a discussion of some cases of corruption within the region.

Corruption Perceptions Index 2016

Transparency International, a global movement that aims to have a world free of corruption, publishes the yearly Corruption Perceptions Index (CPI), an index that ranks various countries in the world based on corruption. Scores range from 0 (highly corrupt) to 100 (very clean). Table 3.1 presents the rankings of the English-speaking Caribbean islands for the year 2016.

All but two of the Caribbean territories are ranked in the top half of the CPI. While the scores are not phenomenal, six of the nine territories presented here have scores above the global average (43). The table shows that the Bahamas is the least corrupt country in the Caribbean, although its overall score declined from its last entry on the index (2014) while Guyana is ranked as the most corrupt country in the Caribbean with a score of 34, a slight improvement on 2015's score. According to the Heritage Foundation (2017), the most common corruption issue in these territories is government corruption. Lower-ranked countries on the CPI

Table 3.1   2016 Corruption Perceptions Index scores for selected countries in the Caribbean

2016 Rank	Country	2016 Score	2015 Score	2014 Score	2013 Score	2012 Score
24	Bahamas	66	N/A	71	71	71
31	Barbados	61	N/A	74	75	76
35	St. Lucia	60	N/A	N/A	71	71
35	St. Vincent and the Grenadines	60	N/A	67	62	62
38	Dominica	59	N/A	58	58	58
46	Grenada	56	N/A	N/A	N/A	N/A
83	Jamaica	39	41	38	38	38
101	Trinidad and Tobago	35	39	38	38	39
108	Guyana	34	29	30	27	28

Notes: Scores range from 0 (highly corrupt) to 100 (very clean).

Source: Adapted from Transparency International (2017, January 25). *Corruption Perceptions Index 2016*. Retrieved from www.transparency.org/news/feature/corruption_perceptions_index_2016

tend to be "plagued by untrustworthy and badly functioning institutions like the police and the judiciary" (Transparency International 2017), and this is evident in the three countries rated as the most corrupt Caribbean countries. For Jamaica, the ties between elected officials and organized criminals contribute to high levels of corruption, which affects both business and individuals. The situation in Trinidad and Tobago is similar, as the corruption in that country undermines long-term economic development. In Guyana, there is a pervasive corruption, involving officials at all levels within the country, including the police and the judiciary (Heritage Foundation 2017).

The Caribbean's modest resources make fighting corruption a priority. The devastating impact of waste, fraud and inefficiency on these countries' economies, social development and political systems is much greater than in countries with abundant resources. Some Caribbean nations have been more successful than others in establishing and enforcing strict controls on corruption. Jamaica and Guyana are two examples at both ends of the spectrum. As recently as January 31, 2017, the Integrity Commission Bill was approved in Jamaica, which "provides for the establishment of a single body to be known as the Integrity Commission, to promote and strengthen the measures for the prevention, detection, investigation and prosecution of acts of corruption" (Linton 2017). This bill demonstrates the commitment of Jamaica to fighting corruption within the country. On the other hand, Guyana tried to tackle corruption by developing the website "I paid a bribe" which was launched in 2013. It involved persons making reports anonymously to the website, which was then passed on to the relevant agencies for investigation and if necessary corrective action (Campbell 2014). Although this website garnered some level of success in detecting corruption in several government agencies, to date (2017), the website and its Facebook page are both inactive.

Thus, as noted by Hylton and Young (2007), while steps have been taken to combat corruption within the region, many areas of weaknesses exist, specifically lack of enforcement. These authors note that much more needs to be done in order to combat corruption. This point is emphasized by the cases of corruption within the Caribbean, a few of which will be discussed in the following sections.

A closer look at corruption within the Caribbean: selected cases[1]

The previous section has highlighted the overall state of the Caribbean with reference to corruption. With that background, we now turn to a discussion of some of the major cases in the Caribbean that have resulted in some of the poor rankings on the CPI.

The Allen Stanford case: Antigua and Barbuda

In the early 1990s, Stanford established Stanford International Bank in Antigua, which over the years evolved into a multi-billion-dollar bank, culminating in the Stanford Financial Group. This became a massive empire with over 21,000 clients throughout the United States and South America (Shochat and Fionda 2016).

42 *Philmore Alleyne and Marissa Chandler*

However, amidst its rapid growth and development, the U.S. government was keeping tabs on Stanford's operations. Eventually, in 2009, the U.S. Securities and Exchange Commission (SEC) regulators seized Stanford's operations, based on accusations that he and his group of companies had orchestrated a US$7 billion Ponzi scheme (Calkins 2011).

Stanford and two associates were subsequently charged with securities fraud by the SEC on February 17, 2009. The SEC also charged Leroy King, administrator and chief executive officer of Antigua's Financial Services Regulatory Commission (FSRC), for accepting bribes to ignore the Stanford Ponzi scheme and keep Stanford abreast with the SEC investigation by supplying him with confidential information (Clarke 2011). King was later removed from office, and was due to be extradited to the United States (he held dual citizenship in Antigua and the United States) (Clarke 2011; U.S. Securities and Exchange Commission 2009). However, he fought this request for extradition for seven years but eventually lost the fight in April 2017 when a high court ruling paved the way for his extradition (Johnson 2017). Most accounts of this story have speculated that the government of Antigua and Barbuda was reluctant to extradite King over fears that he could possibly implicate other Antiguan officials in this scandal (Clarke 2011).

At Stanford's trial, it was revealed that he (Stanford) "bribed Antiguan officials . . . to run interference and keep his operation from being disclosed to U.S. regulators" (Shochat and Fionda 2016). In addition to bribery, Stanford was allegedly involved in money laundering and political manipulation (Fletcher 2010; Gibson 2010). According to reports, Stanford was also under investigation by the U.S. Federal Bureau of Investigation (FBI) regarding money laundering in connection with the Mexican-based, narco-trafficking Gulf Cartel, one of the most violent criminal organizations in the world (Mendick and Lea 2009; Vulliamy and Harris 2009). In the United States, Stanford allegedly wined and dined members of Congress, Democrats and Republicans and donated over US$1.6 million to both Republican and Democratic national campaign committees in an attempt to obtain political favours (Fitzgerald 2013; Roston 2012). Political manipulation was also evident within the Caribbean, where, for example, in Antigua, Stanford had very comfortable relationships with government officials; his bank made loans to the government, which were then used to award Stanford's companies lucrative construction contracts (Krauss et al. 2009).

Investigations by the SEC also revealed that Stanford had run a massive, two-decade scam centred on the sale of certificates of deposit, where he allegedly misused the money of his clients to fund risky investments and his extravagant lifestyle, including the sponsorship of cricket tournaments (Roan and Nathanson 2016). Stanford's former CFO and right-hand man since the 1980s, James David, pleaded guilty to several felony charges and testified against Stanford, which contributed significantly to Stanford being convicted (Associated Press 2013; Calkins and Harris 2013; Lozano 2012; Sarnoff 2013). Subsequently, a Houston jury found Stanford guilty in 2012 and sentenced him to 110 years of imprisonment (Danner 2015; Krauss 2012; Vardi 2012). However, at the time of writing,

Stanford maintains his innocence and is certain that he will walk out of prison a free man, cleared of all charges against him (Roan and Nathanson 2016; Shochat and Fionda 2016).

As a result of the massive international fraud scheme, the investors who lost money have sued several companies associated with Stanford, including Stanford's auditor, BDO USA LLP, and its parent company, Chadbourne & Parke (the company for which Stanford's former lawyer Thomas Sjoblom worked up to 2006); Adams and Reese; Breazeale, Sachse & Wilson; Proskauer and Rose (Stanford's lawyer went to work for them after leaving Chadbourne & Parke in 2006); Greenberg Traurig and Hunton & Williams LLP (Carlos Loumiet, legal counsel for the Stanford Financial Group of Companies from 1988 to 2009, spent 13 of those years at Greenberg Traurig, before leaving to work at Hunton & Williams where Stanford was also his client) (Calkins 2011; Lodge 2015; National Law Review 2016; Triedman 2016a, 2016b). The number of firms and institutions sued, as a result of this Ponzi scheme, has reached double figures, reflecting the deep-rooted nature of the corruption that characterized this case (Triedman 2016b).

However, these widespread consequences could have been avoided had the words of a whistleblower been heeded. Leyla Wydler, former vice president and financial adviser to the Stanford Financial Group, had approached the SEC and FINRA (the Financial Industry Regulatory Authority, formerly the National Association of Securities Dealers) in 2003 (anonymously) and 2004 (non-anonymously), alleging, "the Stanford International Bank certificates of deposit were a massive Ponzi scheme" (Turk 2009; White 2009). Wydler had been fired in 2002 for refusing to sell the certificates to her clients (White 2009). In the anonymous complaint, Wydler stated potential consequences of Stanford's scheme, noting it "will destroy the life savings of many, damage the reputation of all associated parties, ridicule securities and banking authorities, and shame the United States of America" (Turk 2009; White 2009), while her 2004 disclosure was accompanied by emails and other information (Turk 2009; White 2009). However, she was only contacted by the SEC again in 2009, one month before Stanford Financial Group imploded (White 2009). Thus, it is alleged that the SEC may have in fact covered up Stanford's scheme, possibly due to corruption within that organization itself, as it has been suspected that there was collusion between the SEC and Stanford, which is contradictory to the SEC's claim that their investigation was hindered by Stanford and Leroy King. In her testimony at a congressional field hearing, she expressed her belief "that if the government had acted on her warnings thousands of investors could have avoided the catastrophe they are now confronting" (White 2009).

CL Financial: Trinidad and Tobago

CLICO, founded by Cyril Lucius Duprey in 1936, was the first local insurance firm to be founded in Trinidad and Tobago. It offered "life insurance coverage with premiums that ranged from six cents to 24 cents" per week, allowing the company to gross TT$20,000 in its first fiscal year (Dassrath 2009). The company built on this first-year success and opened numerous branches across the region in Grenada, Guyana, Barbados, St. Vincent, St. Kitts, St. Lucia, Aruba and Tobago by 1953.

By the time Cyril Duprey stepped down and his son Lawrence Duprey was appointed as the chairman of CLICO's board of directors in 1987, the company held several insurance companies in its portfolio. It continued its rapid physical and financial growth and expansion and later became the CL Financial (CLF) Group, the largest privately owned conglomerate in the Caribbean. CLF provided a variety of services: insurance (its core business), financial, real estate development, manufacturing, agriculture and forestry, retail and distribution, energy, media and communication, operated 65 subsidiaries in 32 countries and managed assets that represented 25% of Trinidad's GDP (Sookram 2016; Soverall 2012; Soverall and Persaud 2013).

Thus, the collapse of CLICO took many by surprise and had widespread consequences – locally (unemployment) and regionally (cost 17% of the region's GDP and affected 15 CARICOM states (Gordon 2013; Soverall 2012; Soverall and Persaud 2013). However, this collapse should not have been a surprise, due to the flawed and extremely risky business model employed by the holding group and its subsidiaries. CLICO for example, invested in companies within the conglomerate and sold EFPAs (Executive Flexible Premium Annuities) which offered huge interest rates ranging from as low as 7% to as high as 13%. These practices represented a clear shift away from the traditional long-term insurance business (Hutchinson-Jafar 2010). Money from the sale of the EFPAs was then transferred to CLF to fund risky regional and international investments and acquisitions (Gordon 2013; Hutchinson-Jafar 2010; Sookram 2016). However, the parent company CLF was unable to repay CLICO, and their poor financial situation was compounded by the global financial crisis of 2008. As a result of the subsidiaries channelling funds into the holding company, CLF became heavily reliant on loans and deposits through its subsidiaries, with these and other short-term payables accounting for 65% of its liabilities. This, along with the heavy administrative and operating expenses, meant that CLF was in severe strife.

Furthermore, CLICO broke the law in several instances: "by paying dividends when its statutory fund was in deficit, apparently understated liabilities through the failure to submit acceptable actuarial certificates, and was using policyholders' funds to offer guarantees to affiliates" (Sookram 2016, 11). CLICO's auditors were also deemed to be negligent. In 2005, CLICO's liability composition was as follows: 66% insurance contracts, 7% investment contracts and 27% other. In 2008, KPMG reclassified more than 50% of CLICO's insurance contracts into investment contracts and therefore, the new liability composition became 60% investment contracts, 21% insurance and 19% other (Gordon 2013).

In 2011, it was revealed that someone was willing to come forward about some of CLF's poor practices. As part of the Commission of Enquiry into the collapse of CLF, CLICO and the Hindu Credit Union (HCU), Michael Carballo, the former financial director of CLF, stated in his witness statements that emails were sent from a former employee of CLICO ("the anonymous whistleblower") to the former Central Bank governor, Ewart Williams, regulators, auditors and members of the public, claiming financial impropriety within CLF. These emails included damaging information with reference to regulatory issues, the methods CLICO would employ to circumvent certain compliance requirements and the "acquisitive nature of the CL Financial group [and] the aggressive stature of the CL Financial group especially when it came to investments and spending" (Stabroek News 2011; Trinidad Express Newspapers 2011). However, Carballo stated that these emails were exaggerated, "not 100 per cent true" and were circulated prior to the request for withdrawals from policyholders and depositors (Stabroek News 2011; Trinidad Express Newspapers 2011). Carbello implied that the whistleblower emails helped to trigger the collapse of CLICO, as he noted that the sudden surge of withdrawals was detrimental to CLICO. However, it must be noted that if this or any other whistleblower had come forward sooner, it may have helped mitigate some of the negative consequences on the economy and the public.

The Hindu Credit Union (HCU): Trinidad and Tobago

The HCU was formed in 1985 to serve the Hindu population in Trinidad and Tobago, although its membership was not limited to these persons. Harry Harnarine, who took over as chairman in 1997, and his board decided to "look at a strategic plan to move away from being a traditional credit union to see ourselves as a key player within the financial sector" (Javeed 2008). As such, the HCU Group of Companies was formed which included several types of businesses, such as security, food distribution, insurance, medicine and media entities (Javeed 2008). The formation of these companies further emphasized the exponential growth of the HCU during Harnarine's tenure.

However, Harnarine's vision to move beyond traditional credit union business, despite warnings from the HCU's auditors and its regulatory body, was to the detriment of the HCU (Alexander 2016). The HCU used money that came into the organization as a result in the rapid increase of members to invest in non-traditional credit union activities, which had low profits. These investments completely drained the credit union's resources, and led to the organization resorting to using new members' funds to further finance poor business ventures (Trinidad and Tobago Newsday 2011).

In a detailed report submitted to the Commissioner for Co-operative Development (CCD) prepared by a seven-member inspection team in 2007, it was noted that the HCU engaged in several questionable and corrupt acts including but not limited to:

- Illegal and delinquent loans to several HCU officials (highlighting potential conflicts of interest),
- Mortgages in violation of company by-laws,
- Illegal loans to the HCU subsidiaries,
- Questionable land transactions (for example, the HCU Convention Centre was valued at TT$1 million in November 2001, purchased by an HCU member

in March 2002 for TT$710,000 and then sold seven months later to the HCU for TT$2.5 million) (Javeed 2008), and

- Million-dollar discrepancies in the union's financial statements (Bagoo 2008).

Thus, in her report arising out of the Commission of Enquiry, the prime minster of Trinidad and Tobago at the time, Kamla Persad-Bissessar, called for both civil and criminal action to be taken against the members of the executive management of the HCU who were involved in the corruption, specifically Harry Harnarine (Stabroek News 2014; Trinidad Express Newspapers 2014b). It was also recommended by Persad-Bissessar that the Director of Public Prosecutions (DPP) ascertain if 22 criminal charges of fraud and larceny should be brought against Harnarine for his role in the collapse of the credit union (Stabroek News 2014).

Within this report, further allegations of corruption were brought against Harnarine and the HCU. It was alleged that the former president of the HCU "conspired with Gayndlal Ramnath, Yadwanath Lalchan, Jameel Ali and Ravindra Bachan to defraud members of the HCU and their depositors in HCU. . . by agreeing dishonestly to put at risk the value and recoverability of the members' investments and/or deposits by members and others as evidenced by certain 'reckless actions'" (Stabroek News 2014). Additionally, according to the Trinidad Express Newspapers (2014b), Harnarine made loans to non-members without approval from the CCD and also made loans to members of the board in excessive amounts, many of which were not obtained through the proper application channels. Although many of the loanees did not qualify for these loans, it was stated that loan officers were told to grant approval for these loans via telephone conversations (Bagoo 2008). Harnarine also misappropriated the HCU's funds to finance his wife's, his sister's and his own lifestyle, as well as the lifestyle of some of the members of his board (Trinidad Express Newspapers 2014a). The Commission of Enquiry also presented evidence that the misappropriation of the TT$60,000 a month allowance he was granted to perform chairman duties for the HCU Group of Companies and HCU Financial LLC in Miami and Florida (Trinidad Express Newspapers 2014a) was further evidence of Harnarine's reckless behaviours. The HCU made "payments to Mr Harnarine in 2003, 2004 and 2005 in response to his claims for foreign travel expenses which were not established by vouchers or other contemporary or other evidence to have been incurred for the purposes of HCU" (Trinidad Express Newspapers 2014b).

The corruption even extended to the HCU's auditor Chanka Seeterram. In his testimony to the Commission of Inquiry, Seeterram admitted that he failed to disclose a TT$150 million (approx. US$22 million) consolidated loss at an annual general meeting, concealed a TT$31 million (approximately US$5 million) loss among "prior adjustments" in the previous year's accounts, back-dated audited accounts and rushed preparing accounts – represented as fully audited accounts – upon the request of Harry Harnarine (Bagoo 2012a).

However, amidst the HCU's corrupt dealings, there was someone who was willing to come forward and make a disclosure of unethical conduct. According to Bagoo (2012b), "an anonymous whistle-blower once phoned Anthony

Pierre (former head of the ill-fated Credit Union Supervisory Unit [CUSU]), and remarked, 'the Commissioner for Cooperative Development is a waste of time. He is in conspiracy with Harry.'" Pierre noted that "he got several phone calls from a whistle-blower, whom he felt was possibly a director at the HCU, who informed the CUSU of 'financial impropriety', falsified property valuations and 'secret scholarships'" (Bagoo 2012b). Pierre reported this disclosure to the Permanent Secretary and to the Minister of Finance, Conran Enill. However due to separate claims that Enill was one of "several PNM ministers who failed to act on concerns of money-laundering at the HCU and Clico", and given the fact that Enill was later fired from his post (Bagoo 2012b), it is unlikely that this matter was pursued further. In addition to this, a letter was also written anonymously to the CCD, claiming that the HCU was in fact insolvent (Colman 2014). Thus, if these disclosures had been thoroughly investigated, the collapse and the consequences of the collapse of the HCU could have been avoided.

The impact of whistleblowing on corruption in the Caribbean

As evidenced by the 2016 CPI, countries in the Caribbean continue to be poorly ranked on corruption. It can be said that these rankings have been influenced by the corporate failures discussed in the previous section. Many researchers have posited various recommendations with reference to anticorruption strategies that organizations and countries should employ. However, we posit that the use of whistleblowing as a mechanism for combatting corruption in the region will be extremely beneficial for the Caribbean. As Doig and Riley (1998, 57) note, developing countries should aim to find "the most effective and economical measures to control corruption". However, whistleblowing is not only a cost-effective anti-corruption strategy, but it is one which in the long term can eradicate corruption from society. This is supported by Rachagan and Kuppusamy (2012), who posited that the Enron case highlights that whistleblowers can reduce unethical practices.

With reference to the Caribbean and other emerging economies, Alleyne and Pierce (2017, 2) posited, "whistleblowing can assist in rooting out corruption and wrongdoing in these contexts". This was supported by the results of a survey conducted by Alleyne (2016) on corporate governance and whistleblowing in the financial sector in the Caribbean. The results revealed that 75.1% of respondents believed whistleblowing can root out corruption (Daily Nation [Barbados] 2017). Researchers such as Kreikebaum (2008) and Doig and Riley (1998) have also proposed whistleblowing as a strategy that can be used to combat corruption. Specifically, Doig and Riley (1998) proposed that it could be a means to provide citizen involvement in the anti-corruption process. As an anti-corruption mechanism, whistleblowing will involve persons within organizations coming forward to report unethical and corrupt acts. By bringing corrupt behaviour to the attention of the relevant authorities who can effect action, corruption can be addressed and those involved will be punished. If those involved are dealt with appropriately, this will therefore serve as a deterrent to others in the organization and show employees

48 *Philmore Alleyne and Marissa Chandler*

that they are serious about tackling corruption. Thus, corruption can be reduced by the simple act of whistleblowing.

In each of the three cases discussed in the previous section, there was someone willing to come forward and disclose the corrupt practices within the respective organizations. In the CLICO and the HCU cases, the individuals chose to remain anonymous perhaps due to the fears of what could happen if their names were released (see discussion below). In the case of Allen Stanford, Leyla Wydler's first disclosure was an anonymous one, before she came forward non-anonymously with evidence of the corruption within the Stanford Financial Group. However, each of these cases had something crucial in common – none of the whistleblowers' disclosures were acted upon by those who had the power to do so. Specifically, in the Stanford case, the SEC waited far too long to act on Wydler's disclosure, allowing several years to pass before any action was taken. As Wydler herself noted, the far-reaching consequences of that scandal could have been avoided had some action been taken earlier, and this perspective can also be applied to the other cases. Thus, her comments highlight how whistleblowing, if addressed in the appropriate way, can indeed root out corruption within organizations.

In the cases of CLICO and the HCU, whistleblowing could have eliminated the corruption in those organizations if the disclosures had prompted swift action in the form of internal and external investigations into those corporations' activities. Investigations into the dealings of CLICO and the HCU would have resulted in an uncovering of the corruption and poor corporate governance of those organizations. Thus, had these deficiencies been uncovered, the corruption within the organizations would have been eliminated either through a termination of the services of the perpetrators, a curbing of the corrupt practices or both.

However, the act of whistleblowing can only be effective with the right mechanisms in place to address the disclosures. Thus, there should have been an internal whistleblowing protocol implemented within each of the three organizations discussed. This protocol, which should outline the procedures for making a disclosure and the roles and responsibilities of those in charge of investigating the disclosures, would have provided an internal means for employees to make disclosures of corrupt and unethical conduct. In the cases of CLICO and the HCU, each whistleblower made their disclosure externally, thereby suggesting a lack of internal whistleblowing mechanisms within their organizations. If the disclosures had been made internally, it would have provided the organization with a means of addressing the issue before the scandals resulted in catastrophic consequences and would have given them the opportunity to protect their name and reputation.

While in theory whistleblowing as an anti-corruption mechanism can root out corruption, putting this ideal into practice can be challenging in the Caribbean where persons are reluctant to come forward and when they do come forward, they prefer to do so anonymously. As noted by Deryck Murray, head of the Trinidad and Tobago Transparency Institute (TTTI), probes into corruption in the Trinidad tend to be stifled due to the reluctance of persons to go forward with the cases and risk exposure (Trinidad Express Newspapers 2015). Additionally, as noted by Trinidad and Tobago Newsday (2012) although "one of the most direct methods of exposing corruption is whistleblowing" it is unfortunate that "whistle-blowers commonly face retaliation in the form of harassment, firing, blacklisting, threats and even physical violence, and their disclosures are routinely ignored." This statement sufficiently encapsulates the two most prominent factors that influence the decisions of those in the Caribbean to whistleblow: personal costs and the culture of the region. Persons fear possible reprisals for coming forward, due to the lack of anonymity in small, close-knit societies such as the Caribbean, where "everybody knows everybody". Thus, the consequences described previously, such as loss of jobs, lower salaries and harassment at work, are just a few of the consequences experienced by those who choose to whistleblow within the Caribbean. Additionally, the presence of a culture that reinforces the poor perception of whistleblowers within the Caribbean also plays a role. Currently, the culture of the Caribbean does little to encourage whistleblowing, and in fact serves as a deterrent. Thus, businesses and governments within the region should address these issues in order to make whistleblowing an effective anti-corruption strategy.

Conclusion

Therefore, for the true benefits of whistleblowing as an anti-corruption strategy to be realized, the relevant authorities need to address the two biggest issues in the Caribbean: its culture and the personal costs associated with whistleblowing. Addressing these issues will serve to give potential whistleblowers, and other employees within organizations, the confidence to know that there are concerted efforts towards eliminating corruption at the organizational and national levels.

Thus, we posit a few recommendations that should be implemented throughout organizations to ensure that whistleblowing can become an effective anti-corruption strategy. First, organizations need to implement more protection and support mechanisms in order to encourage staff to come forward and whistleblow. If staff members feel protected, they would be more willing to come forward and report any wrongdoing they witness from their colleagues (Alleyne 2016). Additionally, organizations should look to create a culture and an environment that encourages whistleblowing. This can be done through the provision of training programmes (to help them deal with situations when wrongdoing may occur and also to enhance certain characteristics which influence whistleblowing, for example, organizational commitment), the creation of financial incentives for valid whistleblowing (for example, reward systems) and allow anonymous whistleblowing through the provision of trusted and confidential reporting mechanisms (Alleyne 2016; Rachagan and Kuppusamy 2012). Organizations can also seek to recruit ethically minded individuals who are most likely to report wrongdoing when it is observed. This can be done using personality and integrity tests to ascertain the characteristics that potential employees possess (Alleyne and Pierce 2017). Furthermore, organizations should also seek to implement a comprehensive whistleblowing policy that defines the key terms and outlines the procedures for reporting (who can make a disclosure of improper conduct); procedures for investigating (who will be responsible for investigating the allegations); roles, rights and responsibilities of those involved in the process and the protection that the whistleblower will be afforded under the policy (Rachagan and Kuppusamy 2012).

Regulators can also create a more receptive culture for whistleblowing within the region by strengthening or implementing whistleblowing legislation that protects those willing to come forward. This can also help to combat the potential personal costs and the poor perception of whistleblowers as a result of the region's culture (Trinidad Express Newspapers 2015; Trinidad and Tobago Newsday 2012). Drafting such legislations at the organizational and national levels will send a message to employees and citizens that those in authority are serious about using whistleblowing to combat corruption. Thus, this can be the first step to changing the culture of the Caribbean that is vehemently against whistleblowing, as "positive cultural change must be complemented by laws that reflect a national commitment to such change" (Trinidad and Tobago Newsday 2012). Furthermore, these legislations should have stipulations that protect whistleblowers and punish the wrongdoers, and not the other way around, and should also include punishment for those who seek to retaliate against whistleblowers (Rachagan and Kuppusamy 2012). This will also reduce the personal costs that persons experience as a result of their disclosures. Additionally, such legislations should also include incentives for whistleblowers, so they can be further encouraged to make disclosures and also have a means of potentially combatting any reprisals they may face in the future as a result of their disclosures. Legislations would have been useful in each of the cases discussed previously, as whistleblowers may have been encouraged to make non-anonymous reports if they felt they were going to be adequately protected and rewarded for their actions and if they had confidence that perpetrators of the corrupt behaviours would have been punished.

However, the mere creation of these legislations is not enough. These legislations need to be implemented and enforced within the society, to the extent that persons will be punished if they contravene any of the stipulations within the legislation. Jamaica and the Cayman Islands are the only two Caribbean countries to have implemented whistleblowing legislation. The rest of the Caribbean needs to follow their lead and in the process of doing so, ensure that implemented legislation is sufficiently enforced in society. Any legislation implemented also needs to consider the specific country's culture, instead of blindly applying international best practices hoping that they are effective (Alleyne and Pierce 2017). Additionally, for those preferring to report to an external source, countries can look to create an independent body comprising certain ethical members in society (for example, religious persons) who can act on behalf of those making the disclosures and in the public interest (Alleyne 2016).

Corruption in the Caribbean is a fundamental problem for governments of and organizations within each territory to address. The cases discussed within this chapter have been detrimental to many of the Caribbean nations and their impacts have been multifaceted. Thus, now more than ever, there is a need to develop anti-corruption strategies that seek to address this pervasive problem in the region. One of these strategies should be whistleblowing.

While the instances of whistleblowing in the cases discussed in this chapter did not yield particularly beneficial results to the companies involved, there is

Whistleblowing in the Caribbean's financial sector 51

evidence that suggests that whistleblowing, if properly used, can be an effective tool to combat and eradicate corruption within the Caribbean. However, there is much work to be done within the region. The recommendations provided highlight the need for personal costs to be reduced and a culture of whistleblowing to be created. Crucial to this is the creation of effective whistleblowing policies at the organizational level and whistleblowing legislation at the national level. Such recommendations may not yield immediate results but may lead countries in a direction to reduce corruption in Caribbean society.

Note

1 The information for these cases was compiled using secondary data, primarily from newspaper articles, websites, and academic articles.

References

Akinseye-George, Y. (2000) *Legal System, Corruption and Governance in Nigeria*. Lagos: New Century Law Publishers Limited.

Alexander, G. (2016) Colman report knocks Central Bank in CLICO, HCU fiasco: Regulatory control seriously lacking. *Trinidad and Tobago Guardian*. [Online]. Available from: www.guardian.co.tt/news/2016-06-23/colman-report-knocks-central-bank-clico-hcu-fiasco-regulatory-control-seriously [Accessed 10th July 2017].

Alleyne, P., Hudaib, M. & Haniffa, R. (2016) The moderating role of perceived organisational support in breaking the silence of public accountants. *Journal of Business Ethics*, 1–19.

Alleyne, P. & Pierce, A. (2017) Whistleblowing as a corporate governance mechanism in the Caribbean. In: Bissessar, A. M. & Ryan, S. (eds.) *Snapshots in governance: The Caribbean experience*. Trinidad and Tobago, University of the West Indies, 176–98.

Alleyne, P., Weekes-Marshall, D. & Arthur, R. (2013) Exploring factors influencing whistle-blowing intentions among accountants in Barbados. *Journal of Eastern Caribbean Studies*, 38 (1–2), 35–62.

Alleyne, P. A. (2010) *The influence of individual, team and contextual factors on external auditors' whistle-blowing intentions in Barbados*. PhD thesis School of Management, University of Bradford.

Alleyne, P. A. (2016) The influence of organisational commitment and corporate ethical values on non-public accountants' whistle-blowing intentions in Barbados. *Journal of Applied Accounting Research*, 17 (2), 190–210.

Associated Press. (2013) Aide in Stanford Ponzi case gets 5 years. *The New York Times*. [Online], 22 January. Available from: www.nytimes.com/2013/01/23/business/james-m-davis-top-witness-in-stanford-ponzi-trial-sentenced-to-5-years.html [Accessed 11th July 2017].

Bagoo, A. (2008) HCU officials borrowed millions. *Trinidad and Tobago Newsday*. [online], 27 July. Available from: www.newsday.co.tt/business/0,83317.html [Accessed 10th July 2017].

Bagoo, A. (2012a) Auditor cook the books. *Trinidad and Tobago Newsday*. [Online], 24 October. Available from: www.newsday.co.tt/news/0,168190.html [Accessed 10 July 2017].

Bagoo, A. (2012b) Credit union bobol. *Trinidad and Tobago Newsday*. [Online] 10 July. Available from: www.newsday.co.tt/news/0,163038.html [Accessed 10 July 2017].

52 Philmore Alleyne and Marissa Chandler

Bowling, N. A. & Lyons, B. D. (2015) Not on my watch: Facilitating peer reporting through employee job attitudes and personality traits. *International Journal of Selection and Assessment*, 23 (1), 80–89.

Buscaglia, E. (1999) Judicial corruption in developing countries: Its causes and economic consequences. In *Berkeley program in law and economics, working paper series*. Berkeley, University of California.

Calkins, L. B. (2011) Auditor BDO USA sued by Stanford's investors for $10.7 billion. *Bloomberg*. [Online], 27 May. Available from: www.bloomberg.com/news/articles/2011-05-26/stanford-investors-sue-former-auditor-for-10-7-billion-1- [Accessed 10th July 2017].

Calkins, L. B. & Harris, A. (2013) Allen Stanford's ex-CFO James Davis gets 5 year sentence. *Bloomberg*. [Online], 22 January. Available from: www.bloomberg.com/news/articles/2013-01-22/allen-stanford-s-ex-finance-chief-gets-five-year-prison-sentence [Accessed 10th July 2017].

Campbell, K. (2014) *'I paid a bribe' website successful in detecting corruption in several Gov't agencies*. [Online] Available from: www.inewsguyana.com/i-paid-a-bribe-website-successful-in-detecting-corruption-in-several-govt-agencies/ [Accessed 10th July 2017].

Caribbean360. (2016) *Corruption case: T&T government goes after officials under past administration*. [Online] Available from: www.caribbean360.com/news/corruption-case-tt-government-goes-officials-past-administration-accused-corruption#ixzz4fyH9OK6f [Accessed 10th July 2017].

Cassematis, P. G. & Wortley, R. (2013) Prediction of whistleblowing or non-reporting observation: The role of personal and situational factors. *Journal of Business Ethics*, 117 (3), 615–34.

Clarke, S. (2011) *Antigua and Barbuda: History of corruption and the Stanford case*. [Online] Available from: www.loc.gov/law/help/ag-corruption/stanford.php [Accessed 10th July 2017].

Colman, A. (2014) *HCU report*. [Online] Available from: www.ttparliament.org/documents/2243.pdf [Accessed 10th July 2017].

Crane, A. & Matten, D. (2004) *Business ethics: A European perspective*. New York, Oxford University Press.

Daily Nation Barbados. (2017) *Alarm bell over governance*. [Online] Available from: www.pressreader.com/barbados/daily-nation-barbados/20170224/281857233309691 [Accessed 10th July 2017].

Danner, P. (2015) Accounting firm settles Allen Stanford litigation for $40 million. *Houston Chronicle*. [Online], 15 May. Available from: www.houstonchronicle.com/business/a:rticle/Accounting-firm-settles-Allen-Stanford-litigation-6267109.php [Accessed 10 July 2017].

Dassrath, M. (2009) Clico: A history of growth. *Trinidad and Tobago Newsday*. [Online] 8 February. Available from: www.newsday.co.tt/news/0,94787.html [Accessed 10 July 2017].

Della Porta, D. (2000) Social capital beliefs in government, and political corruption. In: Pharr, S. J. & Putnam, R. D. (eds.) *Disaffected democracies: What's troubling the trilateral counties?* Princeton, Princeton University Press.

Doig, A. & Riley, S. (1998) Corruption and anti-corruption strategies: Issues and case studies from developing countries. In: United Nations Development Programme (eds.) *Corruption and integrity improvement initiatives in developing countries*. New York, United Nations, 45–62.

Elias, R. (2008) Auditing students' professional commitment and anticipatory socialization and their relationship to whistle-blowing. *Managerial Auditing Journal*, 23 (3), 283–94.

Everhart, S. S., Martinez-Vazquez, J. & McNab, R. M. (2009) Corruption, governance, investment and growth in emerging markets. *Applied Economics*, 41, 1579–94.

Figg, J. (2000) Whistleblowing. *Internal Auditor*, 57 (2), 30.

Fitzgerald, A. (2013) Obama campaign pocketed Ponzi schemer cash. *The Huffington Post*. [Online]. Available from: www.huffingtonpost.com/the-center-for-public-integrity/obama-campaign-pocketed-p_b_4109588.html [Accessed 10th July 2017].

Fletcher, P. (2010) U.S. diplomats were leery of Allen Stanford. *Cable*. [Online]. Available from: www.reuters.com/article/us-wikileaks-usa-stanford-idUSTRE6BL2DO20101222 [Accessed 10th July 2017].

Gibson, O. (2010) WikiLeaks cables: US suspected Allen Stanford long before ECB deal. *The Guardian*. [Online]. Available from: www.theguardian.com/world/2010/dec/20/wikileaks-cables-allen-stanford-warning [Accessed 10th July 2017].

Gordon, L. C. (2013) *Colonial Life Insurance Company Limited: From growth to failure: An analysis of reported financial activity 2003–2008*. [Online]. Available from: https://mpra.ub.uni-muenchen.de/58311/1/MPRA_paper_58311.pdf [Accessed 10th July 2017].

Gould, D. J. (1991) Administrative corruption: Incidence, causes and remedial strategies. In: Farazmand, A. (ed.) *Handbook of comparative and development public administration*. New York, Marcel Dekker Inc.

Graham, I. (2002) *Country life: The Caribbean*. Sydney, Franklin Watts Ltd.

Graham, J. W. (1986) Principled organizational dissent: A theoretical essay. *Research in Organizational Behavior*, 8, 1–52.

Heritage Foundation (2017) *Country rankings*. [Online]. Available from: www.heritage.org/index/ranking [Accessed 10th July 2017].

Hooks, K. L., Kaplan, S. E. & Schultz Jr, J. J. (1994) Enhancing communication to assist in fraud prevention and detection. *Auditing: A Journal of Practice & Theory*, 13 (2), 86–117.

Hutchinson-Jafar, L. (2010) CL Financial called a scandal of monumental proportions. *The Gleaner*. [Online]. Available from: http://jamaica-gleaner.com/gleaner/20101008/business/business93.html [Accessed 10th July 2017].

Hylton, M. & Young, G. (2007) Anti-corruption efforts in the Caribbean: Are we doing enough? *Journal of Financial Crime*, 14 (3), 250–63.

Javeed, A. (2008) The fall of the HCU empire. *Trinidad & Tobago Guardian*. [Online]. Available from: http://legacy.guardian.co.tt/archives/2008-08-02/bussguardian1.html [Accessed 10th July 2017].

Johnson, M. (2017) Leroy King loses. *The Daily Observer*. [Online]. Available from: http://antiguaobserver.com/leroy-king-loses/ [Accessed 10th July 2017].

Kaplan, S. E. & Whitecotton, A. M. (2001) An examination of the auditors' reporting intentions when another auditor is offered client employment. *Auditing: A Journal of Practice & Theory*, 20 (1), 45–63.

Keenan, J. P. (1995) Whistleblowing and the first-level manager: Determinants of feeling obligated to blow the whistle. *Journal of Social Behavior and Personality*, 10 (3), 571–84.

King III, G. (1999) The implications of an organization's structure on whistle-blowing. *Journal of Business Ethics*, 20 (4), 315–26.

Krauss, C. (2012) Stanford sentenced to 110-year term in $7 billion Ponzi case. *New York Times*. [Online]. Available from: www.nytimes.com/2012/06/15/business/stanford-sentenced-to-110-years-in-jail-in-fraud-case.html?_r=0 [Accessed 10th July 2017].

Krauss, C., Creswell, J. & Savage, C. (2009) Fraud case shakes a billionaire's Caribbean realm. *The New York Times*. [Online]. Available from: www.nytimes.com/2009/02/21/business/21stanford.html [Accessed 10th July 2017].

54 *Philmore Alleyne and Marissa Chandler*

Kreikebaum, H. (2008) Corruption as a moral issue. *Social Responsibility Journal*, 4 (1–2), 82–8.

Lacayo, R. & Ripley, A. (2002) Persons of the year: Cynthia Cooper, Coleen Rowley and Sherron Watkins. *Time Magazine*. [Online]. Available from: www.time.com/time/subscriber/personoftheyear/2002/poyintro.html [Accessed 10th July 2017].

Linton, L. (2017) *House passes bill to strengthen measures to fight corruption*. [Online]. Available from: http://jis.gov.jm/house-passes-bill-strengthen-measures-fight-corruption/ [Accessed 10th July 2017].

Lodge, B. (2015) Baton Rouge, New Orleans law firms, others agree to $4.9 million Stanford settlement: Law firms, others to pay $4.9 million in claims. *The Advocate*. [Online], 23 May. Available from: www.theadvocate.com/baton_rouge/news/business/article_a159728a-70d9-5027-ac43-dd0c5b2b1458.html [Accessed 10th July 2017].

Lozano, J. A. (2012) James M. Davis, ex-Stanford CFO: Aims to hide Ponzi scheme proved unsuccessful. [Online], 7 February. Available from: www.newster.co/homebodyinmotion.com%3Fnews%3D1207714&sa=U&ved=0ahUKEwjErICW67KAhWHtRoKHWuwAzMQwW4IHjAD&usg=AFQjCNEoRtqCAqD4itdfZA6wglQ1OfC_aA?news=13709#news=13709 [Accessed 20th July 2017].

Lucas, N. & Koerwer, V. S. (2004) Featured interview Sherron Watkins, former vice president of corporate development for Enron. *Journal of Leadership and Organizational Studies*, 1 (1), 38–47.

Mason, A., van Loon, B. & Savage, A. (1989) *The Caribbean (people and places)*. New York: Macmillan Publishers Limited.

Mendick, R. &Lea, R. (2009) FBI investigate Stanford over money laundering for dangerous Mexican drug cartel as cricketing tycoon goes missing. *The Daily Mail*. [Online], 19 February. Available from: www.dailymail.co.uk/news/article-1148984/FBI-investigate-Stanford-money-laundering-dangerous-Mexican-drug-cartel-cricketing-tycoon-goes-missing.html [Accessed 11 July 2017].

Mesmer-Magnus, J. R. & Viswesvaran, C. (2005) Whistle-blowing in organizations: An examination of correlates of whistle-blowing intentions, actions and retaliation. *Journal of Business Ethics*, 62 (3), 277–97.

Miceli, M. P., Near, J. P. & Dworkin, T. M. (2008) *Whistle-blowing in organizations*. New York, Taylor & Francis.

National Law Review. (2016) *Two respected law firms fight claims that they aided Ponzi schemer*. [Online], 20 January. Available from: www.natlawreview.com/article/two-respected-law-firms-fight-claims-they-aided-ponzi-schemer [Accessed 11th July 2017].

Nayir, D. Z. & Herzig, C. (2012) Value orientations as determinants of preference for external and anonymous whistleblowing. *Journal of Business Ethics*, 107 (2), 197–213.

Near, J. P. & Miceli, M. P. (1985) Organizational dissidence: The case of whistle-blowin. *Journal of Business Ethics*, 4 (1), 1–16.

Near, J. P. & Miceli, M. P. (1996) Whistle-blowing: Myth and reality. *Journal of Management*, 22 (3), 507–26.

Peyton, K. & Belasen, A. R. (2012) Corruption in emerging and developing economies: Evidence from a pooled cross-section. *Emerging Markets Finance & Trade*, 48 (2), 21–36.

Rachagan, S. & Kuppusamy, K. (2012) Encouraging whistle blowing to improve corporate governance? A Malaysian initiative. *Journal of Business Ethics*, 115 (2), 367–82.

Roan, D. & Nathanson, P. (2016) *Defiant US fraudster Allen Stanford vows to clear name*. Available from: www.bbc.com/news/world-35283297 [Accessed 11th July 2017].

Roston, A. (2012) Bipartisanship! Republicans and democrats both want to keep Allen Stanford's money. *The Daily Beast*. [Online], 3 July. Available from: www.thedailybeast.

com/articles/2012/03/07/bipartisanship-republicans-and-democrats-both-want-to-keep-allen-stanford-s-money.html [Accessed 11th July 2017].

Sarnoff, N. (2013) Former Stanford officer gets 5 years in prison. *Houston Chronicle*. [Online], 22 January. Available from: www.chron.com/business/article/Former-Stanford-officer-gets-5-years-in-prison-4213549.php [Accessed 11th July 2017].

Schollhammer, H. (1977) Ethics in an international business context. *Management International Review*, 17 (2), 23–33.

Seifert, D. L. (2006) *The influence of organizational justice on the perceived likelihood of whistle-blowing*. PhD thesis College of Business, Washington State University.

Seligson, M. A. (2002) The impact of corruption on regime legitimacy: A comparative study of four Latin American countries. *The Journal of Politics*, 64 (2), 408–33.

Shabbir, G. & Anwar, M. (2007) Determinates of corruption in developing countries. *The Pakistan Development Review*, 46 (4), 751–64.

Shochat, G. & Fionda, F. (2016) Allen Stanford's house of cards: How TD banked the 2nd-largest Ponzi scheme in U.S. history. *Global News*. [Online], 29 January. Available from: http://globalnews.ca/news/2485811/allen-stanfords-house-of-cards-how-td-banked-the-2nd-largest-ponzi-scheme-in-u-s-history/ [Assessed 11th July 2017].

Sims, R. L. & Keenan, J. P. (1998) Predictors of external whistle-blowing: Organizational and intrapersonal variables. *Journal of Business Ethics*, 17 (4), 411–21.

Sookram, R. (2016) Corporate governance in the emerging economics of the Caribbean: Peculiarities, challenges, and a future pathway. *Journal of Values-Based Leadership*, 9 (1), 1–9.

Soverall, W. (2012) CLICO's collapse: Poor corporate governance. *American International Journal of Contemporary Research*, 2 (2), 166–78.

Soverall, W. & Persaud, W. (2013) A study of corporate failure and the political economy of financial regulation in Trinidad and Tobago and the Caribbean. *International Journal of Humanities and Social Sciences*, 3 (16) (Special Issue), 17–28.

Stabroek News. (2011) E-mails from CLICO whistleblower sparked withdrawals, claims witness. *Stabroek News*. [Online], 21 September. Available from: www.stabroeknews.com/2011/archives/09/21/e-mails-from-clico-whistleblower-sparked-withdrawals-claims-witness/ [Accessed 11th July 2017].

Stabroek News. (2014) Criminal charges recommended against head of collapsed Hindu Credit Union. *Stabroek News*. [Online], 19 July. Available from: www.stabroeknews.com/2014/news/regional/07/19/criminal-charges-recommended-against-head-of-collapsed-hindu-credit-union/ [Accessed 11th July 2017].

Taylor, E. Z. & Curtis, M. B. (2010) An examination of the layers of workplace influences in ethical judgments: Whistle-blowing likelihood and perseverance in public accounting. *Journal of Business Ethics*, 93 (1), 21–37.

Transparency International. (2017) *Corruption perception index 2016*. [Online], 25 January. Available from: www.transparency.org/news/feature/corruption_perceptions_index_2016 [Accessed 11th July 2017].

Triedman, J. (2016a) Chadbourne & Parke agrees to settle Stanford Ponzi claims. *The American Lawyer*. [Online], 28 February. Available from: www.americanlawyer.com/id=1202750891836/Chadbourne-Parke-Agrees-to-Settle-Stanford-Ponzi-Claims [Accessed 11th July 2017].

Triedman, J. (2016b) Chadbourne pays $35M in Stanford Ponzi suit; Proskauer faces new class action. *The American Lawyer*. [Online], 2 May. Available from: www.americanlawyer.com/id=1202756535510/Chadbourne-Pays-35M-in-Stanford-Ponzi-Suit-Proskauer-Faces-New-Class-Action?mcode=0&curindex=0&curpage=ALL [Accessed 11th July 2017].

56 *Philmore Alleyne and Marissa Chandler*

Trinidad and Tobago Newsday. (2011) HCU board was 'reckless'. *Trinidad and Tobago Newsday*. [Online], 30 June. Available from: www.newsday.co.tt/crime_and_court/0,143082.html [Accessed 11th July 2017].

Trinidad and Tobago Newsday. (2012) The Whistle blower's dilemma. *Trinidad and Tobago Newsday*. [Online], 30 August. Available from: www.newsday.co.tt/businessday/0,165565.html57233309691 [Assessed 11th July 2017].

Trinidad Express Newspapers. (2011) E-mails from whistle blower sparked withdrawals, claims witness. *Trinidad Express Newspapers*. [Online], 20 September. Available from: www.trinidadexpress.com/news/E-mails_from_whistleblower_sparked_withdrawals__claims_witness-130248153.html [Accessed 11th July 2017].

Trinidad Express Newspapers. (2014a) HCU, first citizens: 'Poor corporate governance'. *Trinidad Express Newspapers*. [Online], 28 May. Available from: www.trinidadexpress.com/business/HCU-First-Citizens-poor-corporate-governance-261029341.html [Assessed 11th July 2017].

Trinidad Express Newspapers. (2014b) The full HCU report. *Trinidad Express Newspapers*. [Online], 18 July. Available from: www.trinidadexpress.com/news/THE-FULL-HCU-REPORT-267722881.html [Accessed 11th July 2017].

Trinidad Express Newspapers. (2015) Murray: We need whistle blower protection, campaign finance laws. *Trinidad Express Newspapers*. [Online], 10 February. Available from: www.trinidadexpress.com/news/Murray-We-need-whistleblower-protection-campaign-finance-laws-291469571.html [Assessed 11th July 2017].

Turk, L. (2009) Stanford whistle blower testifying in BR today. *The Independent*. [Online], 17 August. Available from: http://theind.com/article-4552-stanford-whistleblower-testifying-in-br-today.html [Accessed 11th July 2017].

U.S. Securities and Exchange Commission. (2009) *SEC charges two accountants and Antiguan regulator for roles in Stanford Ponzi scheme*. [Online], 19 June. Available from: www.sec.gov/news/press/2009/2009-140.htm [Accessed 11th July 2017].

Vardi, N. (2012) Allen Stanford convicted in $7 billion Ponzi scheme. *Forbes*. [Online], 6 March. Available from: www.forbes.com/sites/nathanvardi/2012/03/06/allen-stanford-convicted-in-7-billion-ponzi-scheme/ [Accessed 11th July 2017].

Vulliamy, E. & Harris, P. (2009) FBI investigates possible links with Mexico drug gang. *The Guardian*. [Online], 22 February. Available from: www.theguardian.com/world/2009/feb/22/allen-stanford-drugs-trade-mexico [Accessed 11th July 2017].

White, J. (2009) *Federal regulators covered up Ponzi scheme at Stanford bank*. [Online], 19 August. Available from: www.wsws.org/en/articles/2009/08/stan-a19.html [Accessed 11th July 2017].

4 A fish rots from the head

Corruption scandals in post-Communist Russia

Leslie Holmes

Introduction

According to Transparency International's annual Corruption Perceptions Index (CPI), Russia is widely perceived to be the world's most corrupt country relative to its level of economic development; in the most recent (2017) CPI, Russia was perceived to have the same level of corruption as Iran, Kazakhstan, Nepal and Ukraine (all scored 29 out of 100, where higher scores indicate less perceived corruption), and to be slightly worse than Azerbaijan, Djibouti, Honduras, Laos, Mexico, Moldova, Paraguay and Sierra Leone (all scored 30; Transparency International 2017: 3).[1] An official US analysis published shortly after Putin first became president maintained that "Corruption has . . . become the number one political issue in national [Russian – LTH] politics. Hence Putin's election slogan about a 'dictatorship of law' clearly appealed to Russian voters in the recent presidential elections" (Webster *et al.* 2000: 25) Unfortunately, Putin has been unable or unwilling to reduce corruption during his 18 years in office, and Russian sources themselves frequently note how corrupt the country is (e.g. Anishyuk 2009). Indeed, soon-to-be Russian president Dmitry Medvedev stated openly at a meeting of the Economic Forum held in Krasnoyarsk in February 2008 that corruption was "the most serious disease affecting our society" (Medvedev 2008).

There were certainly corruption cases, and occasionally even corruption scandals, during the Soviet era (1917–1991; see Clark 1993; L. Holmes 1993),[2] but they have increased significantly since the collapse of the Communist system.[3] In this chapter, four scandals will be analysed in detail, in part to highlight the wide range of corruption types present in today's Russia, and in part to demonstrate that such scandals have occurred at the highest levels. The four chosen for analysis are:

1 The Yeltsin scandal
2 The 'werewolves in epaulettes' scandal
3 The Sergei Magnitsky case
4 The Medvedev scandal

Before examining these cases, however, a short definitional detour is necessary.

58 *Leslie Holmes*

What is a corruption scandal?

In determining what constitutes a 'corruption scandal', the obvious starting point is to define the two component parts individually. Unfortunately, in attempting to do so, the problematic nature of both words soon becomes obvious. In the early 1980s, Simcha Werner (1983: 147) argued that corruption, like beauty, is in the eye of the beholder. This encapsulates nicely the fact that corruption is a subjective concept: one person's corruption is another person's normal and acceptable way of doing things. Since I have elsewhere elaborated at length the conceptual problems of defining and classifying corruption (e.g. L. Holmes 1993: 63–90; L. Holmes 2006: 17–43; L. Holmes 2015: 1–17), that exercise will not be repeated here. Rather, the simple definition used for the present analysis is the most common one – the abuse of public office for private gain.

According to the Oxford English Dictionary, a scandal is "An action or event regarded as morally or legally wrong and causing general public outrage". This definition requires interrogation. The first problem is that the identity of the person or persons doing the regarding is not clear. Does it have to be the 'general public' referred to later in the definition? Presumably this is not necessarily the case since, if the focus is on *legally* wrong, the judicial system would be the most appropriate location for determining whether an action or event is wrong. However, deciding who is to determine what is morally wrong is far less obvious. Should it be 'public opinion', which is notoriously difficult to gauge accurately, and may be deeply divided anyway? Is it the state? Could it be the mass media? If the last of these, what if they, too, are divided? And is it appropriate to equate morally with ethically, which many analysts do – while others distinguish them? Focusing explicitly on the topic of this chapter – corruption scandals in Russia – is it legitimate for outsiders to be the judge of what constitutes a scandal?

A second problem with this definition of scandal is the requirement that there be 'general public outrage'. Unless there are mass demonstrations concerning a particular action or event, what evidence is required to prove 'general public outrage'? Will a statistically significant public opinion survey result suffice? If so, what percentage of respondents expressing 'outrage' – which would probably have to be inferred from less loaded terms such as 'concern' or 'disappointment' – would be the minimum to assume *general* public anger? If we focus on mass demonstrations, how can we be reasonably confident that a 'mass' protest by 1 million people more or less represents the views of a population of 100 million?

Clearly, there are numerous and significant epistemological and practical difficulties involved in defining corruption scandals and in accurately identifying them in any given country. These general problems are compounded in the case of Russia, which has become increasingly authoritarian under Vladimir Putin, rendering many potentially obvious signs of 'general public outrage' more difficult to detect. Notably, the penalties for participating in unauthorised demonstrations were dramatically increased in June 2012. Given this, we here sidestep these very real problems by arbitrarily defining a corruption scandal in Russia as an action or event that *can* be criticised on ethical grounds and that *should* lead most citizens to consider it morally unacceptable; clear evidence of public outrage will be a bonus.

Before examining our four cases, a final introductory caveat concerning corruption scandals in Russia is that, like corruption scandals elsewhere, many details are hazy or contested, and the stories that follow have to be more heavily reliant on investigative journalism, and sometimes even widespread rumour, than is normal or preferred in social science analysis.

The scandals

1 President Yeltsin

Boris Yeltsin was popularly elected President of the Russian Federation in June 1991, and assumed office on 10 July that year. That date is not as easy to remember as the date on which he resigned – 31 December 1999. One does not have to assume that all leaders are hyper-egocentrics like Donald Trump to accept that most would prefer to be recorded in the history books as being in power at the turn of a millennium. Given this, the timing of Yeltsin's resignation was surprising and noteworthy. In fact, it is now widely accepted that the reason for this timing was that the prime minister at the time, Vladimir Putin, made a deal with the then president that, in return for being granted immunity for a corruption scandal that had blown up earlier that year, Yeltsin would transfer the headship of the Russian state to him (see e.g. Economist 2000; Osborn 2010).

At midday on 31 December, Yeltsin appeared on Russian television and announced that he had resigned that morning, and that Putin was to be the acting head of state until presidential elections could be held in March 2000. Although other factors contributed to Yeltsin's decision – there had been a failed Communist-led second attempt to impeach him in May of that year (the first being in March 1993) – it is widely accepted that Putin had made him an offer of immunity on the condition that it be accepted before the end of the year, century and millennium. In other words, the precise timing of the resignation was almost certainly determined by the corruption charges.

Allegations of Yeltsin's corruption had been made on several occasions over the years, mainly in connection with spending above the permitted maximum in election campaigns. For instance, presidential elections were held in Russia in 1996, and it has been estimated that the Yeltsin camp improperly spent between US$100 million and US$500 million to secure the incumbent's re-election; the maximum official sum they should have spent was a little over US$3 million (Hockstader and Hoffman 1996; see, too, Korzhakov 1997: 10–20).[4] But the 1999 claims were different, in that they related to the president's personal expenditure. In fact, by international standards, the scale and nature of Yeltsin's alleged corruption at the end of the 1990s initially appears to have been rather trivial.

During the 1990s, it was decided to renovate the Kremlin. The contract for the renovation was eventually awarded to a Lugano-based construction company, Mabetex, which had already worked on the reconstruction of the Russian

60   *Leslie Holmes*

parliament building (partly destroyed during the clash between the president and the parliament in late 1993) and was headed by an Albanian Kosovar, Behgjet Isa Pacolli (Willan and Meek 1999).[5] In September 1999, following investigations that began in mid-1998 and were originally led by Swiss attorney general Carla del Ponte, Swiss authorities alleged that Mabetex had been paying off the credit card bills of both Yeltsin himself and his two daughters – as well as of several other senior Russian officials (LaFraniere 1999). In October, the Swiss bank Banca del Gottardo publicly acknowledged that it had been requested to guarantee credit cards allegedly issued to Yeltsin and members of his family (Traynor 1999), although it declared that it had not issued any credit cards to the Yeltsin family (Kenesov 1999).[6] Eventually, details of the payments made by Mabetex were made public, and the sum involved in the case of the Yeltsin family was approximately US$93,000. Compared with the sums allegedly acquired corruptly by Muhammad Suharto in Indonesia (estimated US$15–35 billion), Ferdinand Marcos in the Philippines (estimated US$5–10 billion) or – closer to home for the Russian case – former Ukrainian Prime Minister Pavlo Lazarenko (estimated US$114–200 million), this sum was trivial (all sums from Hodess 2004: 13; replicated in Sandbrook 2016).

On the other hand, it should be noted that there were allegations that Mabetex had also paid other senior Kremlin officials between US$10 million and US$15 million (LaFraniere 1999) to secure various contracts worth in total US$335 million (US$49 million for the Kremlin alone – Bohlen 1999). Moreover, the 1999 allegations against the Yeltsin family were being made at about the same time as a much bigger scandal – in dollar terms at least – broke in the US media. This was the claim, first made publicly in August 1999, that Russian funds amounting to several billion dollars had been laundered through the Bank of New York by Russian organised crime gangs (Dejevsky 1999; Meland 2005; Cullison 2007), and that Yeltsin or people very close to him had been aware of this (Angelo 1999: but note that others disagreed with this inference – see Staff and Wire Reports 1999). Finally, there were also Swiss allegations in 1999 that Pacolli had deposited US$1 million in a Budapest bank for use by Yeltsin (LaFraniere 1999), though Yeltsin denied any knowledge of this. In short, what looks at first sight to have been relatively insignificant sums of money *may* in fact have been much larger and dirtier. Certainly, Desdemona's handkerchief had been dropped into the public's mind.

The lead-up to the December 1999 dénouement reads like a sleazy second-rate novel. In March 1999, there was a less than subtle campaign, said to have been run by senior Russian officials and certain oligarchs, to discredit the Russian chief prosecutor (Procurator-General), Yurii Skuratov. Skuratov had been contacted in 1998 by del Ponte, who informed him that she had evidence of large-scale questionable connections between German and Swiss companies on the one hand, and very high-ranking Russian officials on the other, which had prompted Skuratov to initiate an investigation into alleged corruption among senior politicians and tycoons (Zapodinskaya 1999). Some of these people were part of Yeltsin's inner circle, which the Russian media had been calling 'the Family'. Symptomatic of how blatant the smear campaign against Skuratov was is the fact that a blurry

A fish rots from the head   61

video, allegedly of the Procurator-General naked in bed with two young women – assumed to be prostitutes – was broadcast on the very day (17 March) that the Russian upper house (Federal Chamber) of the legislature was voting whether or not to accept his (forced) resignation – though they opted not to. Such character besmirching is not uncommon at the higher echelons of Russian politics and business: the Russians call it *Kompromat* (i.e. compromising material), and use it to discredit or blackmail both members of the Russian elite and foreigners, especially diplomats (see e.g. Szilágyi 2002; Ioffe 2017; Rainsford 2017).[7]

Even though the scale of Yeltsin's personal corruption *may* have been relatively minor, there were some significant corruption scandals in his immediate entourage (the Family) during his presidency. One of these eventually resulted in a Swiss attempt in 2001 to prosecute Pavel Borodin, who was in charge of the property section of the Department of Presidential Affairs from 1993–2000, for his alleged involvement in large-scale money laundering, primarily in the context of the Mabetex scandal. Although this essentially came to naught – charges were eventually dropped in 2002, largely because the Swiss authorities were from early on unable to secure Russian assistance in investigating the case (Tagliabue 2001) – the Swiss continued to seek to prosecute him, and in 2015 again came close to this with the help of the US Federal Bureau of Investigation (FBI). Once more, however, the attempt failed. Also of significance were the allegations made during 1999 by senior Communist politician Viktor Ilyukin that Yeltsin's daughter and adviser,[8] Tatyana Dyachenko, was, through a third party, holding shares in an Australian company that had received more than US$2 billion in Russian credits during 1998 (Bohlen 1999).

2   *'Werewolves in epaulettes'*

Police corruption has long been a major problem in Russia (see e.g. Altukhov 2001): according to almost all analysts, it has substantially increased in both scale and seriousness under Putin (for the best analysis see Taylor 2011). Some forms of this, while not entirely unique to Russia, are particularly salient there. One is 'roofing' (*kryshevanie*), which is basically where officers of the state, including police officers, run protection rackets. Whereas mainly organised crime gangs ran such rackets during the 1990s, these gangs have been largely replaced by groups of corrupt police officers in the 21st century (Taylor 2011: 164). Another is a form of collusion between either corrupt officials (often politicians) or the police, or between criminals and the police. This is so-called raiding (*reiderstvo*). A typical scenario is where, in return for bribes or kickbacks from criminal groups or on instructions from their political masters, the police raid a well-functioning business and falsely alleges improprieties of one kind or another. The business proprietors will then have to go to court, where – again in many cases – corrupt judges will find them guilty and fine them so much that the owners are compelled to sell off their business at well below its market value; the criminal groups or corrupt politicians, as well as the police themselves, are the purchasers and beneficiaries (on *reiderstvo* see Rochlitz 2014; Shelley and Deane 2016).

62   *Leslie Holmes*

Technically, the 'werewolves in epaulettes' (often rendered as 'werewolves in uniform', though the translation given here is a more accurate rendition of the Russian term *oborotny v pogonakh*) scandal refers to several cases, all of which involve serious corruption by Russian law enforcement officers – and even officers in other states that were once Soviet republics, such as Kyrgyzstan (Huber 2014) and Ukraine (Yegorova 2017). The term was first coined in 2003 by then Russian Minister of the Interior Boris Gryzlov to refer to law enforcement officers engaging in corruption and other criminal acts (Bernstein 2008); it has since been used by Russians themselves to refer *inter alia* to police corruption even during the Soviet era (TVTs 2017).

But the particular scandal to which it is most frequently applied in recent times relates to a case that became public in Russia in 2003–4 and was described in the on-line blurb on a 2005 full-length book on the subject as 'the biggest police scandal of recent years'.[9] It involved a former general in the Ministry of Emergencies (lit. Extreme Situations – MChS) and a gang of at least six police officers from the Moscow Criminal Investigation Department that had engaged in extortion, blackmail, bribery, forging of evidence ('fixing'), *kryshevanie*, *reiderstvo* and other forms of corruption since 1997. The arrest of six of the suspects was made in front of journalists, thus helping to create a media scandal (Favarel-Garrigues 2005–6: 73). The case is also known as the 'Ganeev affair', after the ringleader of the gang, Lieutenant-General Vladimir Ganeev. Their corruption is said to have netted the group 'millions of dollars' – having allegedly generated almost US$1 million a month over many years (Salagaev *et al.* 2006). The case was reported in serial form in the newspaper *Moskovskii Komsomolets* in February 2005, while a book by the lead investigative journalist from this newspaper (as well as being a deputy to Russia's lower house, the *Duma*) was published later that year (Khinstein 2005a).

3   *The Magnitsky affair*

Sergei Magnitsky was a Russian lawyer and auditor who was arrested in November 2008 and imprisoned for purported involvement in alleged tax evasion by the Hermitage Capital Management Company. This company specialises in asset management and investment. But it became well known in Russia from the late 1990s for investigating suspected corruption in major corporations on the grounds that a reputation for corruption reduces a company's share price. One such investigation was of the large Russian corporation Gazprom, which Hermitage examined in 1998–2000.

In November 2005, the head of Hermitage, British citizen William Browder,[10] was blacklisted by the Russian authorities, officially because he represented a security risk. On one level, this was surprising, since Browder was known to be a supporter of Vladimir Putin. But his company's investigations into Russian companies and individuals were causing embarrassment to Russian elites, and this appears to have overridden the support for the president.

Magnitsky himself was charged with tax fraud. This was ironic, because he was accused of having defrauded the Russian state of US$230 million – precisely the sum he claimed Hermitage had attempted to pay in tax, but which officers of the Russian Ministry of the Interior, Tax Office and other official agencies had siphoned off for their personal benefit (i.e. a clear case of corruption). Magnitsky died in November 2009, aged 37, while in custody in a Moscow prison. An independent Russian NGO, the Public Oversight Commission, published a 20-page report in December 2009 in which it claimed that Magnitsky had been subjected to "psychological and physical pressure" (Aldrick 1999), and may even have been murdered (Harding 2009; Kleiner 2012: 17 and 21). Meanwhile, on the orders of President Medvedev, the Kremlin itself also established an investigative commission within a week of Magnitsky's death; while this had not published a report by the time the independent commission published its analysis, it is telling that 20 officers from the prison in which Magnitsky had been held for most of his incarceration (the notorious Matrosskaya Tishina) were suspended in the week following his death (for detailed analyses of all this see Kleiner 2012; Lenta.Ru 2017).

One reason why this case is of direct relevance here is that Magnitsky had been alleging widespread and large-scale corruption (including fraud, embezzlement and cover-ups by the tax office and the police) – and that some official Russian media themselves referred to 'public outrage' about his death (RIA Novosti 2010). Here, then, is clear evidence of the 'public outrage' we are looking for in identifying Russian corruption scandals.[11]

4 Prime Minister Medvedev

It is in many ways ironic that, despite his earlier reputation for being much more genuine than Putin in wanting to combat corruption in Russia,[12] a scandal erupted around Prime Minister Dmitry Medvedev in early March 2017. The best-known independent anti-corruption campaigner in Russia and would-be candidate in the 2018 Russian presidential election, Alexei Navalnyi, uploaded onto the internet a 50-minute video – made largely with the help of drones – of numerous expensive properties allegedly belonging to Dmitry Medvedev, and located in both Russia and Italy.[13] The claim was that this was clear evidence of Prime Minister Medvedev's corruption, allegations Navalnyi had been making for some time. By early June, the video had had over 22 million hits; even allowing for the fact that some of these would have been by non-Russians outside of Russia, there can be no question that the Russian public's interest in the video was considerable (the population of Russia is approximately 143 million.)

On 11 June 2017, the day before planned mass demonstrations across Russia, Navalnyi's video was posted on two government websites – one the regional prosecutor's office in Yaroslavl, the other the St. Petersburg regional administration. In the St. Petersburg case, the video was quickly removed – while the Yaroslavl website was soon down (RFE/RL 2017). The Russian authorities were clearly embarrassed and angered by this display of bureaucratic insubordination.

Impact and outcomes

The most obvious outcome of the Yeltsin scandal was that the president resigned. But analysis of the aftermath of this resignation highlights the fact that President

64 *Leslie Holmes*

Putin has not had a continuously high level of support, at least from politicians, from day one. Thus, there was an attempt in the *Duma* in March 2000 to annul the new president's decree granting immunity to a present or past president: the motion was only narrowly defeated. In many ways, the Yeltsin corruption scandal was only put to bed in February 2001, with a final version of the law on presidential immunity (see next section).

In the case of the 'werewolves in epaulettes', the original case initially had little impact on either legislation or policy within Russia. Following a lengthy indictment of some 2000 pages (Khinstein 2005b), six officers plus Ganeev were eventually found guilty in 2006, and given long prison sentences totalling 121 years (Izvestiya 2006; Shcheglova 2006: for numerous recent examples of 'werewolves in epaulettes' see Vzglyad 2017). Ganeev himself received a 20-year prison sentence plus a 100,000 ruble fine; he was also stripped of his formal title of Lieutenant General (Shcheglova 2006). However, when Dmitry Medvedev became Russian president in 2008, he made the fight against corruption in the law enforcement agencies a top priority; this is considered in the following section. At this juncture, it is worth noting that surveys over recent years reveal that the police have not been and still are not trusted much in Russia (Sergevnin and Kovalyov 2013: 210; Semukhina and Reynolds 2014; Dergachev *et al*. 2017); at least among businesspeople, a major reason for this is the kind of predatory policing typified by 'werewolves in epaulettes'.

Like both the Yeltsin and Magnitsky cases (less so – so far – the Medvedev scandal), the police corruption case examined here had international ramifications. Thus Russian citizens' concerns about 'werewolves in epaulettes' resulted in a case (*Lashmankin and Others v. Russia*) going up to the Council of Europe's European Court of Human Rights, which resulted in the Court finding in favour of the 23 claimants in early 2017 and ordering the Russian authorities to pay them a total of €160,000 in costs and damages (Council of Europe 2017a, 2017b).[14]

As for the Magnitsky case – there was a cover-up by the Russian authorities through 2010 (for detailed evidence see Kleiner 2012: 18–36). However, in July 2011, the president's six-person Human Rights Council published its official report, in which it found that Magnitsky's arrest and imprisonment had been illegal, and that he had been tortured before his death. The findings were immediately endorsed by President Medvedev, though in a rather lukewarm manner. On the other hand, the Ministry of Internal Affairs rejected the findings of the Human Rights Council, declaring on the day following the report's publication that "There was no wrongdoing" (Kleiner 2012: 39) – thus contradicting their own president. In August 2011, the case was re-opened. But the outcome was hardly encouraging. One result of the revived investigation was harassment of Magnitsky's mother. Arguably even sicker was the fact that, despite his death in 2009, Magnitsky was still tried *posthumously* and found guilty of tax evasion in July 2013 (Elder 2013).

One last point to note concerning our third case-study is that eight people involved in the Magnitsky case have died in mysterious circumstances, while others have narrowly escaped death, including one (the Magnitsky family's lawyer, Nikolai Gorokhov) as recently as March 2017 (Engel and Petropoulos 2017). This

A fish rots from the head 65

figure is far too high to be a mere coincidence, while the fact that the Gorokhov case is so recent indicates that there continues to be fallout from the Magnitsky affair.

Finally, with regard to the Medvedev scandal, 2017 saw mass demonstrations in Russia against corruption – once on 26 March, and then again on 12 June. These were the largest anti-government demonstrations in Russia since those protesting alleged vote-rigging (another corruption scandal!) in 2011–12. The March demonstrations have been directly attributed to the Navalnyi video of Medvedev's alleged corruption, 'He is not Dimon to you', and were instigated by Navalnyi – as were the June demonstrations. In Moscow, in both March and June, many of the protesters called for Medvedev's resignation. While the numbers protesting are contested, ranging up to 60,000 according to a Russian source (cited in Walker and Luhn 2017) across more than 80 cities for the March demonstrations, and from 'about 8500' in Moscow and St. Petersburg alone, according to the Russian Ministry of Internal Affairs and Moscow Police (BBC 2017a), to 'tens of thousands' (ABC News 2017) in more than 100 cities for the June protest marches,[15] a representative survey of 1600 respondents across Russia by Russia's most respected pollsters published two days after the March protests – though conducted in early March – suggested that 65% of Russians considered corruption completely unacceptable, and that 79% considered Russia's 'organs of power' to be either completely (32%) or 'to a significant degree' (47%) affected by corruption (Levada-Tsentr 2017a). If we combine these two figures, it cannot be denied that there is widespread 'outrage' about corruption in Russia.

Medvedev called the allegations made against him 'politically motivated nonsense', and Navalnyi a charlatan (ABC News 2017): it could be argued that the charges against Navalnyi of embezzlement, which resulted in him being given a five-year suspended sentence that was heavily criticised by the European Court of Human Rights, are also 'politically motivated nonsense', as were those laid against Magnitsky. It should also be noted that although the Medvedev video was the initial trigger for the 2017 demonstrations, many of the protesters were also strongly critical of Putin, calling him a 'thief' and a 'murderer'.

Large numbers of Russians were arrested in 2017 as a result of their protest activities. Estimates of the number of arrests in March range from 'around 500' in Moscow alone to well over 1000 across Russia, while police announced that approximately 650 were arrested in June in Moscow and St. Petersburg alone, compared with the estimate of a human rights group of at least 1700 across the two cities (Walker 2017). Within days, many of these protestors had been sentenced to 15 days in jail. Navalnyi himself was sentenced to 15 days' imprisonment for unauthorised organisation of the March protests, and 30 days for the June ones.[16]

While many observers have made the point that one of the most significant features of the 2017 protests is that the average age of the demonstrators was much lower than in previous anti-government displays, one Russian commentator writing on the independent Levada Center website has argued that the level of support for Navalnyi's video, even among young Russians, has been greatly exaggerated (Volkov 2017). This said, his analysis was written before the June

66   Leslie Holmes

demonstrations revealed that there was still a lot of anger among many Russians, both young and older.

Even if most Russians did not protest in 2017 against Medvedev's alleged corruption, Navalnyi's allegations do appear to have found *some* resonance among the general public. The most respected Russian opinion-polling organisation, the Levada Center, ran a survey of 1600 respondents in early April 2017 specifically concerning the Russian prime minister. Among the various results published were that 40% had a negative view of Medvedev, while a further 30% were neutral or indifferent towards him; only 31% had a positive view of their premier. These data represent a marked decline in Medvedev's popularity compared with when he first became president: in May 2008, the respective figures were 16%, 15% and 63%. Moreover, by April 2017, 52% of respondents distrusted Medvedev, while 33% still trusted him. But it should be noted that while the distrust figure was the highest ever recorded – across 18 surveys – between March 2006 and April 2017, it was not *markedly* higher. In short, Medvedev has never enjoyed a high level of trust among members of the Russian public. Finally, 45% of the April 2017 respondents were in favour of dismissing Medvedev as prime minister, compared with 33% who were not (all data from Levada-Tsentr 2017b).[17] While more Russians favoured Medvedev's dismissal than did not, perhaps many in the minority simply prefer 'the devil you know'.

Before concluding this section, it should be noted that it was not only members of the general public who reacted angrily to the Medvedev video. Shortly after its release, three Communist Party deputies attempted to pass a motion in the Russian lower house demanding an investigation into Navalnyi's allegations of Medvedev's corruption. This was supported by only 43 members of the *Duma* (Sharkov 2017); however; it would require support from a majority of deputies for such a motion to be carried.

Impact on legislation and policies

The way in which these scandals have been dealt with in Russia, and their wider implications for policy, differs from case to case. It can be argued that the Putin presidency got off to a bad start. Putin's very first act as (acting) president was to pass a decree (No. 1763) on his first day in office granting immunity to any Russian president, past or present, and his family (the decree was published in *Rossiiskaya Gazeta*, 5 January 2000: 3). Had this act still been valid, it might one day have been used to protect Putin himself, who Bill Browder claimed in July 2017 is the world's wealthiest person (Morris 2017). However, there is little doubt that the primary original beneficiary of this was to be Yeltsin. Although this decree can be criticised, it could be argued against this that Putin's action was intended to bring closure, much as the post-Stalin Soviet leadership allegedly engaged in one last show trial (of Stalin's secret police chief and then deputy premier, Lavrentii Beria) to symbolise the end of the Stalin terror regime, or the Chinese leadership did with the trial of the 'Gang of Four' to bring a symbolic conclusion to the Cultural Revolution. This said, while the attempt in the *Duma* to overturn Putin's *de facto* amnesty ultimately failed (see above), Putin appears to have made a concession to critics of his policy in February 2001, when he signed a new law that limited the scope of immunity for former presidents in cases where allegations of serious crimes had been made (EECR 2001: 37; Remington 2003: 114).

The Ganeev case and other forms of police corruption led Dmitry Medvedev to wage a war against police corruption when he was president (2008–12), himself using the term 'werewolves in epaulettes'. Having initiated a series of measures in 2008 designed to combat corruption generally – including organising a survey of 34,000 Russian citizens – he began to focus explicitly on police corruption in late 2009. In December, President Medvedev signed a decree designed to reform the Ministry of Internal Affairs. During 2010, much tougher penalties were introduced for police officers found to have engaged in corruption. At the same time, and echoing Lenin's call for 'Better Fewer, But Better', Medvedev announced that police numbers were to be reduced by 20% by January 2012 and entry standards to the police were to be raised, but also that salaries were to be significantly increased. Finally, one of Medvedev's more original – if questionable – innovations at this time was to instruct the police that they were to interact less with citizens; the idea behind this was that it would reduce the opportunities for bribery.

In many ways, the policy impact of the Magnitsky case has been much greater outside of Russia than within it: no noteworthy policy changes have emanated from Moscow in light of the Magnitsky affair. On the other hand, the US imposed sanctions against Russia – the so-called Magnitsky Act of 2012 – following Magnitsky's death. This act led to the naming of prominent Russians who are said to have been involved in serious human rights abuses, including Magnitsky's death, and who have had assets in the US frozen and are banned from entering the US.[18] Subsequent to this act, Estonia and the UK have introduced essentially similar legislation, in the Amendment to the Obligation to Leave and Prohibition on Entry Act (2016) and the Criminal Finances Act (2017), respectively (Rettman 2016; BBC 2017b; UK Parliament 2017).

In retaliation for the US legislation, Putin banned what had become quite a common and (for some) lucrative practice – namely the selling of Russian infants to Americans for adoption. The impact of the case could still be felt in the US as of mid-2017, when Donald Trump Jr. claimed that the meeting he had had with Russians in June 2016, allegedly hoping to be provided with information that could be used to discredit his father's Democratic competitor in the 2016 presidential race, Hillary Clinton, in fact proved to be an opportunity for the Russians to push for a repeal of the Magnitsky Act. The main person Trump Jr. met with, Nataliya Veselnitskaya, is well known as a lobbyist for the repeal of this act. While Putin's claim that he did not know who she was until she hit the world's headlines in July 2017 may be true (MacFarquhar and Kramer 2017), Veselnitskaya *is* well known to Russia's Prosecutor General, Yurii Chaika, and it may have been him, acting either on direct instructions from Putin or else on an assumption about what his ultimate boss wanted, who encouraged her to set up a meeting with Trump Jr., Jared Kushner and Paul Manafort.

68   *Leslie Holmes*

At the time of writing (mid-2017), the Russian authorities had essentially done nothing about the allegations of Medvedev's corruption; as noted above, an attempt in the lower house to have the case properly examined was thwarted. Whether this situation will continue is difficult to predict. As long as Putin continues to want Medvedev as his trustworthy sidekick, nothing is likely to happen to the prime minister: the partnership – sometimes referred to as a 'tandemocracy', though it seems inappropriate nowadays to describe the current Russian regime as any kind of democracy – is too useful to Putin to allow any undermining of it. However, if Putin should decide that Medvedev has become a liability, or simply wants a change of personnel at the very top, then it is quite feasible that Medvedev will find that the allegations of corruption come back to haunt him.

Conclusions

One of the striking features of several of the corruption scandals in Russia is that they have had international ramifications, especially in the US. Thus the Yeltsin scandal, in its broader sense (i.e. including those in his immediate entourage), was linked to the major Bank of New York money-laundering scandal, while the Magnitsky case not only resulted in the 2012 Magnitsky Act, but continues to resonate in 2017, with Donald Trump Jr.'s claims that his June 2016 meeting with Russians was mostly about repealing that act.[19] But what of the overall impact within Russia itself?

Measuring the scale of corruption accurately in any country is impossible. But perceptions matter in politics, so that it is worth noting that Russians not only continue to see corruption as a major problem, but also that most Russians see the fight against corruption as Putin's joint biggest failing (along with living standards – Levada-Tsentr 2017c).[20] Despite this, most Russians still do not hold Putin particularly responsible for the corruption epidemic in Russia (Levada-Tsentr 2017a). Moreover, a late June 2017 survey indicated that Russians are almost evenly divided on the question of whether or not they approve of people who participated in the June 2017 demonstrations: 39% approved, while 37% disapproved (Levada-Tsentr 2017d). In terms of the requirement that there be 'general public outrage', the evidence on just how *scandalous* the corruption situation is in Russia is unclear.

Many more Russian corruption scandals could be cited and interrogated. But our analysis of just four is illuminating. One point that emerges clearly is that the Putin regime has often talked the talk, but rarely walks the walk. For instance, Putin argued in a 2015 speech to the Federation Council that corruption was hindering Russia's economic development – which is true, since foreign investors are known to be wary of Russia, in part because of its bad reputation for corruption. But Putin went further than this, pointing out that

> 83 percent of entrepreneurs who faced criminal charges fully or partially lost their business – they got harassed, intimidated, robbed and then released. This certainly isn't what we need in terms of a business climate. This is actually the opposite, the direct destruction of the business climate.

(Putin 2015)

In short, Putin was being highly critical of *reiderstvo* and other forms of intimidation of Russian business by corrupt officials. On the surface, this is admirable. But he made these comments at a time when he had been in power for some 15 years; since the Russian system has been described as 'super-presidential' (S. Holmes 1993–4; Clark 1998), Putin can hardly blame others for his inability or unwillingness to curb corruption.

This leads to the big question of whether Putin is *unable* or *unwilling* to curb corruption in his country. He has stated publicly that corruption has been *the* most intractable problem of his presidency – or at least of his first two terms (Putin 2008); when it is borne in mind that he has also had to deal with terrorism, declining life expectancy, economic problems and other serious issues, the significance of such statements comes clearly into focus. This reference to intractability suggests inability, and perhaps weakness.

Counter-intuitively for most Westerners, it has been argued by Yeltsin's daughter (Tatyana Dyachenko – Osborn 2010) that Putin is a shy and nervous person, while Lilia Shevtsova (2017) has long maintained that Putin is actually a weak leader. This could explain the fact that he has done so little in practice to reduce corruption – he fears a backlash from his own bureaucracy. When it is borne in mind that Max Weber argued that the most serious threats to a leader's position come not from the masses but from the 'staffs', turning a blind eye to corruption, particularly high-level corruption and corruption in the security agencies, might appear to be Putin's best course of action – especially given that so many ordinary Russians appear not to be overly critical of their president.

But is this weakness argument persuasive? Is fear likely to be the most convincing explanation for Putin's lukewarm approach to anti-corruption? At least as convincing is the argument that Putin lacks political will to combat corruption among either his entourage or law enforcement officers. The latter might well relate to his KGB and FSB background;[21] a number of analysts have pointed to the fact that Putin has privileged the military–security complex (the so-called *siloviki*) since coming to power, when need be at the expense of the oligarchs, and certainly at the expense of organised crime syndicates. The former – not wanting to cleanse his entourage – is probably best explained by the fact that he has surrounded himself with malleable and apparently loyal officers who appear unlikely to challenge him (though never say never in Russian politics!); Medvedev is the quintessential example of this.

Another reason for questioning the 'weakness' argument is that there is some hard and much circumstantial evidence that the Russian authorities can treat those who investigate and report on corruption very harshly – though the Putin regime appears to be clever at covering its tracks when this seems appropriate. Thus, while it makes no secret of its attempts to undermine Navalnyi – publicly accusing him of embezzlement – others have experienced more draconian fates. Prisoners who have made accusations of corruption against the authorities are often given grossly inadequate medical care, if any at all: Magnitsky is a perfect example. It has been claimed that the then Russian editor of *Forbes* magazine, Paul Klebnikov, was murdered by (still unidentified) contract killers in July 2004 because of his

70 *Leslie Holmes*

investigations into the improperly acquired wealth of some of Russia's wealthiest people. Opinion is divided over who was most likely to have hired the killers. However, while the most commonly cited suspects are Chechen rebels or oligarch Boris Berezovsky, some have also blamed the Kremlin. Anna Politkovskaya was murdered in October 2006, in part because of her investigations into high-level corruption in Russia.[22] Although six people – a police chief and five Chechens – are serving long prison sentences for her murder, it remains unclear who was or were the mastermind(s) behind the killing. But there have been widespread rumours that the killers were paid by the Russian authorities to remove someone who had become a serious thorn in their side. This was certainly the claim of former FSB officer Alexander Litvinenko, who was himself murdered – many allege by the FSB – just a few weeks after Politkovskaya.

In many ways, the notion that Putin's lack of commitment to combating corruption is *either* a function of fear *or* lack of will is misguided: it is a function of both. There is no doubt that Putin has in recent years feared that the factors leading to the so-called 'coloured revolutions' in other former Soviet republics (see Bunce and Wolchik 2009, 2011; Finkel and Brudny 2012; Bunce 2017) could become salient in Russia and endanger his regime. He may also fear unrest among his security agencies. On the other hand, he is sympathetic to those very agencies – and, if the rumours about his enormous personal wealth are even half true, he has no vested interest in mounting too serious a campaign against corruption. After all, people who live in glass houses should not throw stones.

But the fact that Putin is now becoming nervous about the possibility of corruption destabilising his regime can be seen in the fact that he has recently dramatically changed his position, re-framing the whole discourse on corruption. Following the June 2017 mass anti-corruption demonstrations, Putin claimed publicly in a televised call-in ('phone or e-mail') that corruption was not high on the list of ordinary Russians' concerns, and became visibly irritated when asked why punishments of corrupt officials were often so lenient. This has led one analyst to observe:

> Nevertheless, Navalny has done something unprecedented. He has forced the president of Russia to stop pretending that he is against corruption. Others may rail against it, but for Putin, corruption is now officially 'fake news'.
>
> (Sestanovich 2017)

Ultimately, there is insufficient hard evidence to know whether Putin's apparent tolerance pf corruption is a function of weakness, fear, his own corruption, a combination of these or some other factor. Certainly, he is no Lee Kuan Yew, Mikheil Saakashvili or Xi Jinping when it comes to fighting corruption. All we can say is that it was a corruption scandal that brought Putin to power, and that this has, in the long term, contributed to the de-democratisation of Russia. It is also possible that it will be a corruption scandal that will bring the Putin regime down. But if it does, and unless his successor issues a new decree annulling the February 2001 law on presidential immunity or that law is applied for corruption, Putin himself should be safe.

Notes

1 Some of the research for this chapter was generously funded by the Australian Research Council (notably award numbers A79930728 and DP110102854).
2 For a brief but useful overview of anti-corruption legislation during the Soviet era, see Ramazanov (2001).
3 In line with an increasingly popular convention, Communist (i.e. with uppercase) is used here to refer to actual systems ruled by communist parties or the parties themselves; communist (lowercase) would refer to the theoretical end-goal of Marxists.
4 Given the 2017 controversy about alleged Russian involvement in the 2016 US presidential election, it is worth recalling that there were many allegations that the US had poured considerable funds into the 1996 Russian presidential campaign – a case of the pot calling the kettle black?
5 Pacolli was subsequently Kosovo's President (in 2011) and then First Deputy Prime Minister (2011–14). He is reputed to be the world's wealthiest ethnic Albanian.
6 In December 1999, Pacolli contradicted this claim in an interview with *Literaturnaya Gazeta*, stating publicly that the bank had indeed opened credit card accounts for both Yeltsin and his daughters (Webster *et al.* 2000: 31).
7 Yeltsin tried a total of three times during 1999 to remove Skuratov, but the Federation Council thwarted his attempts on each occasion. Skuratov was eventually dismissed by Putin and the Federation Council in April 2000.
8 Donald Trump is not the first president of a major power to have chosen his daughter as a close adviser!
9 Blurb for A. Khinshtein, *Okhota na oborotnei – Opisanie*, www.ozon.ru/context/detail/id/2402975/.
10 Browder was born in the US, and was originally a US citizen. He changed his citizenship in 1998. An interesting fact about him relating to Russia is that his grandfather was once the head of the Communist Party in the US.
11 For Browder's own analysis of the Magnitsky case, see Browder (2015). For his July 2017 testimony before the US Senate Judiciary Committee, go to www.theatlantic.com/politics/archive/2017/07/bill-browders-testimony-to-the-senate-judiciary-committee/534864/.
12 For support for this assumption of a genuine commitment from the head of the Russian chapter of Transparency International see Panfilova (2008).
13 For the video with English subtitles go to www.youtube.com/watch?v=qrwlk7_GF9g. A summary of the claims in English can be found on Navalnyi's Anti-Corruption Foundation website at https://fbk.info/english/english/post/304/.
14 It should be noted that the claims concerned a number of planned peaceful demonstrations, not only one in May 2010 that, ironically, was *in support of* the government's crackdown on police corruption.
15 One major reason why it was impossible to measure the scale of the demonstrations in June was that they were timed to coincide with official demonstrations celebrating Russia Day; separating the two groups, in terms of accurately counting the participants, proved impossible.
16 Navalnyi did have permission to organise peaceful demonstrations in Moscow in June, but in a quiet part of the city; he illegally moved the demonstration to the city centre.
17 Unfortunately, no directly comparable over time results on this question were published.
18 For details of the act, formally 'H.R. 6156 – Russia and Moldova Jackson-Vanik Repeal and Sergei Magnitsky Rule of Law Accountability Act of 2012', go to www.congress.gov/congressional-report/112th-congress/house-report/632/1. The act was signed off by President Obama in December 2012.
19 Although only fleeting reference has been made here (see below) to the Klebnikov and Politkovskaya cases, it is worth noting that the Chair of the Council of Europe Parliamentary Assembly's Sub-Committee on the Media was in 2009 strongly critical of what he saw as half-hearted attempts to find the murderers of 'journalists

72 *Leslie Holmes*

writing against corruption and crime within government' – https://web.archive.org/web/20090528114840/http://assembly.coe.int/ASP/Press/StopPressView.asp?ID=2132.

20 Note that in the 11 surveys between 2004 and 2016 in which Russians were asked to name Putin's biggest failures, corruption topped the list every time (i.e. the living standards issue has only matched it in 2017).

21 The FSB (Federal Security Service) is basically the successor to the Soviet-era KGB (Committee of State Security).

22 A book based on Politkovskaya's notebooks was published posthumously, and includes the word 'corruption' in the subtitle (Politkovskaya 2007).

References

ABC News. (2017) Russian protesters, Putin critic Alexei Navalny imprisoned amid anti-corruption demonstrations. *ABC News*. [Online], 12–13 June, Available from: www.abc.net.au/news/2017-06-12/putin-critic-alexei-navalny-arrested-ahead-of-corruption-protest/8611410 [Accessed 3rd August 2017].

Aldrick, P. (1999) Sergei Magnitsky: Independent investigation into death of lawyer slams Russia. *The Telegraph*, 28 December.

Altukhov, S. (2001) *Prestupleniya Sotrudnikov Militsii*. St. Petersburg, Yuridicheskii Tsentr Press.

Angelo, J. (1999) Bank of New York probers eye Yeltsin Ties. *New York Post*, 27 August.

Anishyuk, A. (2009) Russia leads the world in economic crime, report says. *Moscow Times*, 19 November.

BBC. (2017a) Russia protests: Hundreds detained at opposition rallies. *BBC News Europe*. [Online], 12 June. Available from: www.bbc.com/news/world-europe-40245152 [Accessed 4th August 2017].

BBC. (2017b) Magnitsky bill turns UK into "hostile environment" for kleptocrats. *BBC News UK*. [Online], 21 February. Available from: www.bbc.com/news/uk-39047321 [Accessed 26th July 2017]

Bernstein, J. (2008) Medvedev reportedly set to name an anti-corruption aide. *Jamestown Foundation Eurasia Daily Monitor*, 18 June.

Bohlen, C. (1999) Yeltsin's inner circle under investigation for corruption. *New York Times*, 24 March.

Browder, B. (2015) *Red Notice: How I became Putin's No.1 Enemy*. London, Bantam Press.

Bunce, V. (2017) The prospects for a color revolution in Russia. *Daedalus*, 146 (2): 19–29.

Bunce, V. & Wolchik, S. (2009) Getting real about "real causes". *Journal of Democracy*, 20 (1): 69–73.

Bunce, V. & Wolchik, S. (2011) *Defeating Authoritarian Leaders in Postcommunist Countries*. New York, Cambridge University Press.

Clark, W. (1993) *Crime and Punishment in Soviet Officialdom*. New York, Sharpe.

Clark, W. (1998) Presidential power and democratic stability under the Russian Constitution: A comparative analysis. *Presidential Studies Quarterly*, 28 (3): 620–37.

Council of Europe. (2017a) Russia: Court judgement looms in "right to protest" complaint. *Human Rights Europe*. [Online], 6 February. Available from: www.humanrightseurope.org/2017/02/russia-court-judgement-looms-in-right-to-protest-complaint/ [Accessed 7th July 2017].

Council of Europe. (2017b) Russia: Court makes €160,000 award after backing "right to protest" complaint. [Online], 7 February. Available from: www.humanrightseurope.

org/2017/02/russia-court-makes-e88000-award-after-backing-right-to-protest-complaint/ [Accessed 7th July 2017].

Cullison, A. (2007) Russia Sues Bank of New York over 1990s scandal. *Wall Street Journal*, 18 May.

Dejevsky, M. (1999) Russian mafia laundered $10bn at Bank of New York. *Independent*, 19 August.

Dergachev, V., Okrest, D., Istomina, M. & Vit'ko, S. (2017) Sotsiologi zayavili o znachitel'nom snizhenii doveriya k institutam vlasti. *RBK*. [Online], 29 March. Available from: www.rbc.ru/politics/29/03/2017/58dbb1ed9a7947e4c4de9dcb?from=newsfeed [Accessed 8th August 2017].

Economist. (2000) Putin the great unknown. *Economist*, 8 January.

EECR. (2001) Constitution watch – Russia. *East European Constitutional Review*, 10 (1), 34–7.

Elder, M. (2013) Sergei Magnitsky verdict, most shameful moment since Stalin. *The Guardian*, 11 July.

Engel, R. & Petropoulos, A. (2017) Lawyer probing Russian corruption says his balcony fall was "no accident". *NBC News*. [Online], 7 July 2017. Available from: www. nbcnews.com/news/world/lawyer-probing-russian-corruption-says-his-balcony-fall-was-no-n780416 [Accessed 9th July 2017].

Favarel-Garrigues, G. (2005/6) La police russe en procès. *Le Courrier des Pays de l'Est*, (1052): 66–74.

Finkel, E. & Brudny, Y. (2012) Russia and the colour revolutions. *Democratization*, 19 (1): 15–36.

Harding, L. (2009) Hermitage lawyer's death in Russian jail a crime, say colleagues. *The Guardian*, 19 November.

Hockstader, L. & Hoffman, D. (1996) Yeltsin campaign rose from tears to triumph. *Washington Post*, 7 July.

Hodess, R. (2004) Introduction. In: R. Hodess, T. Inowlocki, D. Rodriguez & T. Wolfe (eds.), *Global Corruption Report 2004*. London and Berlin, Pluto Press and Transparency International, 11–18.

Holmes, L. (1993) *The End of Communist Power: Anti-Corruption Campaigns and Legitimation Crisis*. New York, Oxford University Press.

Holmes, L. (2006) *Rotten States? Corruption, Post-Communism, and Neoliberalism*. Durham, NC, Duke University Press.

Holmes, L. (2015) *Corruption: A Very Short Introduction*. Oxford, Oxford University Press.

Holmes, S. (1993–4) Superpresidentialism and its problems. *East European Constitutional Review*, 2 (4) and 3 (1): 123–6.

Huber, B. R. (2014) Drug trafficking corrupts Kyrgyzstan's politics and underworld. In: *News and Events*. Princeton, NJ, Woodrow Wilson School of Public and International Affairs. [Online], 17 March. Available from: http://wws.princeton.edu/news-and-events/ news/item/drug-trafficking-corrupts-kyrgyzstans-politics-and-underworld, [Accessed 7th July 2017].

Ioffe, J. (2017) How state-sponsored blackmail works in Russia: The art of kompromat. *The Atlantic*. [Online], 11 January. Available from: www.theatlantic.com/international/ archive/2017/01/kompromat-trump-dossier/512891/ [Accessed 5th August 2017].

Izvestiya. (2006) Oborotni v pogonakh. Poluchili 121 god na semerykh. *Izvestiya*, 7 September.

Kenesov, B. (1999) Osada prodolzhaetsya. *Delovaya Nedelya*, 22 October.

74 *Leslie Holmes*

Khinstein, A. (2005a) *Okhota na Oborotnei*. Moscow, Detektiv-Press.

Khinstein, A. (2005b) Brigada-2: Chast' 2. *Moskovskii Komsomolets*, 22 February.

Kleiner, V. (2012) *The Sergei Magnitsky Case: Testimony to European Parliament Subcommittee on Human Rights*. [Online], 28 February. Available from: www.europarl.europa.eu/meetdocs/2009_2014/documents/droi/dv/4-10-magnitsky_/4-10-magnitsky_en.pdf [Accessed 6th August 2017].

Korzhakov, A. (1997) *Boris Yeltsin: Ot Rassveta do Zakata*. Moscow, Interbuk.

LaFraniere, S. (1999) Yeltsin linked to bribe scheme. *Washington Post*, 8 September.

Lenta.Ru. (2017) Magnitskii, Sergei: Konsul'tant investitsionnogo fonda. Hermitage Capital Management, pogibshii v 2009 godu v SIZO "Matrosskaya Tishina". [Online], 6 August. Available from: https://lenta.ru/lib/14202380/ [Accessed 6th August 2017].

Levada-Tsentr. (2017a) Institutsional'naya Korruptsiya i Lichnyi Opyt. *Levada-Tsentr*. [Online], 28 March. Available from: www.levada.ru/2017/03/28/institutsionalnaya-korruptsiya-i-lichnyj-opyt/ [Accessed 27th July 2017].

Levada-Tsentr. (2017b) Dmitrii Medvedev. *Levada-Tsentr*. [Online], 26 April. Available from: www.levada.ru/2017/04/26/dmitrij-medvedev/ [Accessed 8th August 2017]

Levada-Tsentr. (2017c) Vladimir Putin: Otnoshenie i Otsenki. *Levada-Tsentr*. [Online], 24 April. Available from: www.levada.ru/2017/04/24/15835/ [Accessed 11th August 2017].

Levada-Tsentr. (2017d) Protesty i Naval'nyi. *Levada-Tsentr*. [Online], 17 July. Available from: www.levada.ru/2017/07/17/protesty-i-navalnyj/ [Accessed 9th July 2017].

MacFarquhar, N. & Kramer, A. (2017) Natalia Veselnitskaya, lawyer who met Trump Jr., seen as fearsome Moscow insider. *New York Times*, 11 July.

Medvedev, D. (2008) Tochki nad "i" – Dmitrii Medvedev nazval chetyre prioriteta blizhaishego chetyrekhletiya: instituty, infrastruktura, innovatsii, investitsii. *Rossiiskaya Gazeta*, 16 February.

Meland, M. (2005) Bank of New York pays $38M in money laundering case. *Law360*. [Online], 9 November. Available from: www.law360.com/articles/4456/bank-of-new-york-pays-38m-in-money-laundering-case [Accessed 25th July 2017].

Morris, D. (2017) Vladimir Putin is reportedly richer than Bill Gates and Jeff Bezos combined. *Fortune*. [Online], 30 July. Available from: http://fortune.com/2017/07/29/vladimir-putin-russia-jeff-bezos-bill-gates-worlds-richest-man/ [Accessed 7th August 2017].

Osborn, A. (2010) Boris Yeltsin's daughter attacks Vladimir Putin. *The Telegraph*, 23 January.

Panfilova, E. (2008) High stakes in Russia's corruption battle: Interview with Elena Panfilova. *OpenDemocracy*. [Online]. Available from: www.opendemocracy.net/Russia/article/high-stakes-in-Russias-corruption-battle

Politkovskaya, A. (2007) *A Russian Diary: A Journalist's Final Account of Life, Corruption, and Death in Putin's Russia*. New York, Random House.

Putin, V. (2008) Transcript of Annual Big Press Conference. Moscow, Website of the President of Russia. [Online], 14 February. Available from: www.kremlin.ru/eng/speeches/2008/02/14/1011_type82915_160266.shtml [Accessed 19th February 2008].

Putin, V. (2015) Presidential address to the federal assembly. Moscow, Website of the President of Russia. [Online], 3 December. Available from: http://en.kremlin.ru/events/president/news/50864 [Accessed 7th July 2017].

Rainsford, S. (2017) Russia and the art of "kompromat". *BBC News (Europe)*. [Online], 14 January. Available from: www.bbc.com/news/world-europe-38613979 [Accessed 4th August 2017].

A fish rots from the head   75

Ramazanov, G. (2001) Otvetstvennost' za vzyatochnichestvo v sovetskii period. In: P. Panchenko, A. Chuprova & A. Mizeriya (eds.), *Korruptsiya v Organakh Vlasti*. Nizhny Novgorod, Institut Otkrytoe Obshchestvo, 268–71.

Remington, T. (2003) Taming *Vlast*. In: D. Kelley (ed.), *After communism: Perspectives on democracy*. Fayetteville, University of Arkansas Press, 89–118.

Rettman, A. (2016) Estonia joins US in passing Magnitsky law. *Euobserver*. [Online], 9 December. Available from: https://euobserver.com/foreign/136217 [Accessed 26th July 2017].

RFE/RL. (2017) Navalny video accusing medvedev of corruption posted on government websites. *Radio Free Europe/Radio Liberty*. [Online], 11 June. Available from www. rferl.org/a/navalny-video-medvedev-corruption-posted-goverment-websites/28541102. html [Accessed 9th July 2017].

RIA Novosti. (2010) RIA Novosti's choice: The ten major political events of 2009. [Online], 2 January. Available from: https://sputniknews.com/analysis/20100102157444345/ [Accessed 11th July 2017].

Rochlitz, M. (2014) Corporate raiding and the role of the state in Russia. *Post-Soviet Affairs*, 30 (2–3): 89–114.

Salagaev, A., Shashkin, A. & Konnov, A. (2006) One hand washes another: Informal ties between organized criminal groups and law-enforcement agencies in Russia. *Journal of Power Institutions in Post-Soviet Societies*, (4/5). [Online]. Available from: http://pipss. revues.org/449 [Accessed 26th July 2017].

Sandbrook, J. (2016) The 10 most corrupt world leaders of recent history. Rozelle NSW, Integritas 360. [Online]. Available from: http://integritas360.org/2016/07/10-most-corrupt-world-leaders/ [Accessed 5th July 2017].

Semukhina, O. & Reynolds, M. (2014) Russian citizens' perceptions of corruption and trust of the police. *Policing and Society*, 24 (2): 158–88.

Sergevnin, V. & Kovalyov, O. (2013) Policing in Russia. In: G. Meško, C. Fields, B. Lobnikar & A. Sotlar (eds.) *Handbook on Policing in Central and Eastern Europe*. New York, Springer, 191–216.

Sestanovich, S. (2017) Vladimir Putin is suddenly on the defensive against corruption. *Washington Post*, 22 June.

Sharkov, D. (2017) Russian parliament blocks Medvedev corruption probe despite protests against him. *Newsweek*, 6 April.

Shcheglova, T. (2006) Chistye Ruki. Delo "oborotnei v pogonakh" dovedeno do logicheskogo kontsa. *Lenta.Ru*. [Online], 7 September. Available from: https://lenta.ru/articles/ 2006/09/06/werewolf/ [Accessed 9th July 2017].

Shelley, L. & Deane, J. (2016) *The Rise of Reiderstvo: Implications for Russia and the West*. Washington, DC, TraCCC Consulting LLC.

Shevtsova, L. (2017) Bessil'noe vsesilie. *Radio Svoboda*. [Online], 2 May. Available from: www.svoboda.org/a/28459893.html [Accessed 10th August 2017].

Staff and Wire Reports. (1999) Ex-KGB in Russia probe: Russia's prosecutor orders security service to look into money-laundering. *CNN Money*. [Online], 27 August. Available from: http://money.cnn.com/1999/08/27/worldbiz/russia_probe/ [Accessed 4th August 2017].

Szilágyi, Á. (2002) Kompromat and Corruption in Russia. In: S. Kotkin & A. Sajó (eds.) *Political Corruption in Transition: A Skeptic's Handbook*. Budapest, Central European University Press, 207–31.

Tagliabue, J. (2001) Extradited Russian suddenly free after 3-year inquiry. *New York Times*, 13 April.

76 *Leslie Holmes*

Taylor, B. (2011) *State building in Putin's Russia: Policing and coercion after communism.* New York, Cambridge University Press.

Transparency International. (2017) *Corruption perceptions index 2016.* Berlin, Transparency International.

Traynor, I. (1999) Swiss bank hardens Yeltsin sleaze claim. *The Guardian*, 15 October.

TVTs. (2017) Sovetskie Mafii – Oborotni v Pogonakh. *TV Tsentr*. [Online]. Available from: www.tvc.ru/channel/brand/id/1820/show/episodes/episode_id/37328/?page=4 [Accessed 9th July 2017].

UK Parliament. (2017) Criminal finances act 2017. [Online]. Available from: http://services.parliament.uk/bills/2016-17/criminalfinances.html [Accessed 26th July 2017].

Volkov, D. (2017) Effekt ot fil'ma "On vam ne Dimon" pochti proshel. *Levada Tsentr*. [Online], 29 May. Available from: www.levada.ru/2017/05/29/effekt-ot-filma-on-vam-ne-dimon-pochti-proshel/ [Accessed 8th August 2017].

Vzglyad. (2017) Oborotni v Pogonakh. *Vzglyad, Delovaya Gazeta*. [Online]. Available from: https://vz.ru/tags/4050/ [Accessed 9th July 2017].

Walker, S. (2017) Russian courts sentence protesters arrested at anti-corruption rallies. *The Guardian*, 14 June.

Walker, S. & Luhn, A. (2017) Opposition leader Alexei Navalny detained amid protests across Russia. *The Guardian*, 27 March.

Webster, W., Borchgave, A. de, Cillufo, F. & Nelson, T. (2000) *Russian Organized Crime and Corruption: Putin's Challenge*. Washington, DC, Center for Strategic and International Studies.

Werner, S. (1983) New directions in the study of administrative corruption. *Public Administration Review*, 43 (2): 146–54.

Willan, P. & Meek, J. (1999) Yeltsin family "took bribes". *The Guardian*, 26 August.

Yegorova, D. (2017) Ukrainskie bandity v pogonakh – oborotny novogo obraztsa. *Russkaya vesna*. [Online], 12 June. Available from: http://rusvesna.su/news/1497193755 [Accessed 5th August 2017].

Zapodinskaya, Y. (1999) Skuratov ne poletel v Shveitsariyu. *Kommersant*, 24 June.

5 Toa kitu kidogo

When "chai" is not tea – and Kenya's corruption scandals

Stephen Magu

Introduction

Corruption *events* in Kenya are predictable, pervasive, high reaching, of great magnitude, unstoppable and regular as sunrise. Petty corruption, reports of scandals and public procurement anomalies with great financial impact on the exchequer occur every few months. Most Kenyans have taken part in, seen or facilitated "corruption". Many commuters using public transport witness the inevitable slowdown as the matatu approaches the police checkpoints, an imperceptible exchange, and often help pass the Kshs. 50 (US$.50) bribe to the driver, to be handed to the police. Thrice-folding booklets that are drivers' licenses are ready-made to facilitate graft. Despite exhortations inside the matatus urging citizens to report speeding and reckless driving, nothing is said of corruption. Periodic "stings" where "anti-corruption detectives" pounce on police manning roadblocks make a show of finding the loot in pockets and under rocks and arresting the officers, suggesting that the government is combating graft.

This is petty "corruption", and it does not rise to the level of scandals. Volume-wise, there are about 18,000 matatus on Kenyan roads; the National Highway Transportation Authority's (NHTSA's figure is over 100,000), and 95% of Kenyans report using them almost daily (Wangari, 2016). If each of these were to pay this "road tax", Kshs. 5 million daily, almost Kshs. 2 billion (US$20 million) will be lost to traffic police. Civilian vehicles with infractions are generally "taxed" at higher rates. Matatus lose more money depending on the severity of the infraction. Thus, even though the more public corruption covers huge sums of money and fewer beneficiaries, "petty" corruption on Kenya's roads has quite a significant effect.

Corruption becomes scandalous when it is publicly evident, and is different from petty corruption. Garland argues that for a "corruption" anomaly – or other similar event – to be classified as a scandal, three interlinked features must be present. First, they must be 'different from corruption [although] some form of behavior defined as corrupt (whether financial, political or sexual) is often involved'; second, 'scandals are essentially public phenomena wherein hitherto private behavior . . . is publicly revealed and then widely deemed morally outrageous'; and third, 'scandals do not have a fixed content. This varies over time,

78 *Stephen Magu*

and from one location to another' (2007, p. 27). What might have been acceptable before, or not scandalous, may change over time. This research refers to most of the egregious public corruption taking place in Kenya as corruption scandals.

There is a limited history of whistleblowing in Kenya. Some – if not most – major corruption scandals have come into the public realm after exposure by zealous lawmakers (Kenya's are the second highest paid in the world), journalists or civil servants. For civil servants, this reflects the constraints imposed by the Official Secrets Act. Some scandals involve tens of millions of dollars; one of the longest running, best known was the Goldenberg scandal, concocted in the 1990s as a subsidy scheme to export gold from Kenya, with deposits earning dollars at the exchange rate and a further 20% commission. The scandal cost Kenya near Kshs. 158 billion (US$1.58 billion, 2017 rates), or 10% of Kenya's GDP. It roped in everyone from the president to key government officials. Close behind it was the Anglo Leasing scandal with a sum of US$55 million dollars, a hefty Kshs. 5.5 billion. Its ultimate cost on the economy was never accurately calculated.

When Transparency International (TI) releases its Corruption Perceptions Index (CPI), Kenyan elite and the media rush to see Kenya's placement. Despite pushback over TI's report and methodology, the country knows that donors, media, publics and investors consider these reports sacrosanct, thus the concerted attempts to delegitimize TI's CPI reports. In the 2016 ranking, Kenya was 145 of 176 with a score of 26 out of 100 (TI, n.d.); in 2015 it was ranked 139 of 167 with a score of 25 out of 100. Citizens, clergy and political leaders grapple with the problem of corruption and its intractability, while setting up ineffectual commissions that end up prosecuting no one. What, drives corruption in Kenya? What are the opportunities, the constraints, and possibilities for eliminating it? This research seeks to understand corruption processes in Kenya, and practical ways to end it.

Anatomy of Kenya's scandals

Kenya's corruption scandals have dogged its 50-plus years of independence from the British, beginning with disenfranchisement, rather than settlement of African freedom fighters (Mau Mau); instead, the new political class appropriated most of the land. After independence, and despite service to the British as far away as Burma during World War II, land reform programs excluded the freedom fighters; 'this led to the appropriation of large areas of land by chiefs, loyalists and wealthy farmers at the expense of the Mau freedom fighters and the rural poor. The land of the Mau Mau freedom fighters was often reallocated and redistributed while they were in detention' (Amanor, 2008, p. 14).

The first 30 years of Kenya's nationhood solidified one-party rule: successive governments brooked little resistance, jailed dissidents, constrained freedoms of speech and association and expanded and monopolized government control over crucial socio-economic sectors such as infrastructure, telecommunications, power generation and distribution, health and education. Foreign investments were constrained; where foreign investments were allowed, cronyism and graft arose; elsewhere the investment climate was so challenging that investors stayed off.

As state-owned enterprises (SEOs) grew in importance, they were perfect tools for cronyism, nepotism and tribalism, to ensure they "ate". Rather than centers of innovation, such SEOs showed little innovation curiosity; liberalization led to looting and collapse. As competition grew, they became redundant, and new players dominated market segments.

The Cold War raged during Africa's nascent period of statehood; Africa's strategic importance meant that even the west privileged security and capitalism over good governance. When the Cold War ended in 1991, former client states lost their importance to the west: the governance heat turned up. 'African dictators, no longer to useful to their former patrons, were cut adrift. African nations were left with a legacy of looted resources, massive debts, collapsed states and multiple regional wars over the spoils' (Schmidt, 2013, p. 11). Western powers demanded good governance and the oppressor state was pushed to abandon the one-party rule, leading to economic reforms which rather unfortunately resulted in significant political and economic disenfranchisement, as the countries were not ready for the changes. At the same time, resentment by government and marginalized communities bubbled up. Complementing the political changes – 29 African countries, including Kenya, held multi-party elections between 1990 and 1992 (Quinn, 2016, p. 162).

It was not an easy transformation, given that 'during the era of the Cold War, Western bilateral donors often overlooked corruption on the part of African state elites espousing anti-communist views. Thus, for example, despite considerable evidence of extensive high-level corruption in Zaire' (Tangri & Mwenda, 2013, p. 9). These sudden, western-driven reforms did not help much. Requirements for government divesture from the economy pushed by the Bretton Wood Institutions and donors, under the Washington Consensus, Structural Adjustment and Poverty Reduction and Growth Facility (PRGF) strategies saw SEOs sold off for pittance, mostly at no-bid sales, to government officers and their cronies, elites and foreign concerns. For Kenya, many prospects for grand corruption became available with the economic reforms.

The innovation of Kenya's corruption scandals

Kenya's major corruption scandals have fleeced the public coffers of trillions – actual figures are difficult to ascertain given corruption's secrecy. For example, in 2014, the government issued a Eurobond debt instrument for US\$2.7 billion, payable in 5 and 10 years. Reports of a 500% oversubscription circulated; some doubted the wisdom of borrowing Kshs. 176 billion to repay Kshs. 278 billion for public wages, rather than eliminating government waste and decreasing the wage bill (Ochwangi, 2014). On 31 May 2017, the government inaugurated the Standard Gauge Railway (SGR), a Build-Operate-Transfer (5-year BOT) public–private partnership with China Communications Construction Company. The 609-kilometer railway cost US\$3.8 billion (Kshs. 327 billion), financed jointly by China's Exim Bank (90%) and the Kenya Government (10%) (RailwayTechnology.com, n.d.). Accusations surfaced, that the cost was inflated to 300%; that individuals purchased wayleave in anticipation of the railway project and inflated

80   *Stephen Magu*

the price of the land. Economists questioned whether at current prices for goods and passenger services the railway would recoup its costs, therefore saddling the taxpayer with the bill for another white elephant. Whether these are scandals or simply bad investment decisions remains to be seen.

By some estimates, the Goldenberg scandal cost Kenya 'an estimated US$600 million' (Burbidge, 2015, p. 33), while some suggest that the 18 Anglo Leasing–type contracts cost at least $700 million. Donors withholding aid to Kenya to push multi-party politics gave rise to Goldenberg and Anglo Leasing–type scams; they morphed into made-for-patent, innovative and rapidly became a Kenyan-adopted field of entrepreneurship: tenderpreneurship. Tenderpreneurship is defined as 'insider trade deals for state contracts' (Bond, 2015, p. 203), a process by which an individual 'has made an extraordinary sum of money from a contract (usually a national government, provincial government or municipal tender) that has been awarded for some sort of service' (Nyamnjoh, 2015, p. 223). Southall defines tenderpreneurship as 'the parlaying of political position or influence into the award of tenders' (2016, p. 93). Tenderpreneurship may arise from prior work for and employment by government, utilizing insider knowledge and connections to bid for contracts (Southall, 2016, p. 93). In South Africa, 'many of the 1,135 public officials reported by the Public Service commission in 2009/10 as suspended for financial misconduct were accused of involvement in the wrongful allocation of tenders' (2016, p. 93), including collusion, kickbacks or having a direct stake in the awarded tenders. Southall adds to the definition: 'the allocation at all levels of government contracts to friends, relatives and associates of politicians and public officials' (2016, p. 90).

The majority of Kenya's corruption scandals involve procurement of goods and/ or services, billed to the government – except in the case of the National Youth Service (NYS) scandal, where money was directly transferred from a government ministry to pay fictitious contractors and suppliers. They also generally utilize "insider networks" – individuals with knowledge of and access to contracts or ability to manipulate systems: tenders, supply, banking, etc. Some proceeds were used in financing electoral politics, whereas others paid for patronage and access. This chapter next examines two major scandals: the Goldenberg scandal and the Anglo Leasing scandal, which was the first under Mwai Kibaki's government, elected on the promise of transparency and fighting corruption.

Goldenberg: exporting imaginary gold – to imaginary people – and getting paid

The Goldenberg scandal stems from the company founded and run by Kamlesh Pattni and his brother, Vrajlal, which purported to export gold (Kenya has minimal deposits). Facing forex shortage due to suspension of foreign aid, the Central Bank of Kenya offered export firms "export compensation"; the value of compensation equaled the value of the exported goods plus 20%. Goldenberg 'had the only licence issued for gold and jewellery exports by the finance minister and vice-president, George Saitoti' (Anonymous, 1993, p. 38; Brownbridge, Harvey & Gockel, 1998,

p. 95). Rather than 20% compensation, Goldenberg was paid 35% for gold exports, purportedly to two companies in Dubai and Switzerland; however, 'no evidence was provided to confirm that the gold and other precious metal claimed to have been exported and for which compensation was irregularly paid originated and were processed in Kenya' (Anonymous, 1993, p. 38). Using proceeds from the "exports", Pattni founded the Exchange Bank, which was used to invest in the currency market (Anonymous, 1993, p. 38). Central Bank officials persistently queried the payments, but were overruled.

Estimates on Goldenberg's cost to the economy vary widely; Gakuo writes that 'computed figures indicate that as much as US$1 billion could have directly and indirectly been siphoned through Goldenberg networks' (Mwangi 2008, p. 273). Some of the money was paid outside the 'formal clearinghouse mechanism controlled by the CBK' (Mwangi 2008, p. 273), which paid out the export compensation. The monies were paid through banks controlled by the same exporters, often co-owned by individuals in high (KANU, the ruling party) positions, and in government, including the head of the Directorate of the Security Intelligence. Warutere's figure is between $600 million and $1 billion (2005, p. 1). He writes: in 1993, 'transactions associated with Goldenberg networks together accounted for over 10% of Kenya's Gross Domestic Product (GDP)' (2005, p. 1). In 1997, Holman, Steyn and Wrong estimated that 'the scam [that] cost the country $430m (£260m)' (1997, n.p.). Despite the variance, the strategy and impact were clear: Goldenberg was 'a series of frauds estimated to have cost Kenya the equivalent to 10 per cent of the country's annual gross domestic product' and whose 'irregularities drew in Central Bank of Kenya officials, Kenyan businessmen, senior politicians and ultimately two international banks' (1997, n.p.).

Matiang'i notes that the Goldenberg scandal came to light 'when the whistle was blown in parliament by the opposition MPs Anyang Nyong'o and Paul Muite, who had gained information from junior officials in the Central Bank' (2006, p. 73). Pattni held that the fictitious export scheme was carried out to finance the first multi-party election in 1992, which KANU needed to win. Gakuo demonstrates the connection between multiparty politics in Kenya and grand corruption. He contends that with the opening of democratic space, inter- and intra-political party competition increased, requiring vast sums of money to win elections; KANU had never had significant opposition in the one-party state. As competition increased, 'opportunities for corrupt political financing' increased, too (Mwangi, 2008, p. 267). Gakuo holds that both the Goldenberg and Anglo Leasing mega-scandals were sources of 'significant insights into the relationship between corrupt political financing and democracy in Kenya, demonstrating that pursuit and use of illegal campaign funds has negative effects on democratic politics' (2008, p. 267).

Given Kenya's half-century independence, many appointees to government are tainted by working in previous administrations. Several of those implicated in the Goldenberg scandal joined Kenya's third government, Mwai Kibaki's. Kibaki's government seemed to suffer paralysis: attempts to prosecute the perpetrators of the Goldenberg scandal went nowhere a quarter century after the scandal broke. In part, the paralysis arose from networks developed through "javelin throwing"

82 *Stephen Magu*

and other connections. Where the new government might pursue incidences of corruption and persecute perpetrators, Southall holds that 'too many of the new ruling elite are out to get rich, rather than govern'. Members of Parliament, in a country where the average annual income is a modest $400, have awarded themselves an annual salary and allowances of $169,625 and 'new patronage networks are replacing the old ones, as the well-connected appoint their, chums and relatives to plum public posts' (2005, p. 143).

Anglo Leasing scandal

The Anglo Leasing scandal, derisively referred to as Anglo Fleecing, extruded upon the Kenyan scene in 2003/2004, during the early years of Kibaki's government. In total value, Anglo Leasing ranked fourth behind Goldenberg, the Silverson Establishment tender to provide 900 security vehicles for the police and security services, and the Infotalent Systems Private Limited tender, a contract to build a forensic lab for the Criminal Investigations Department (CID), computerize Kenya's police force (e-Cop) and install security cameras in Nairobi (Marango, 2010, pp. 123–4). Rather ironically and predictably, the founders of companies that were awarded the contracts were significant players in the Anglo Leasing scandal. The scandal's import is primarily due to the government's reaction, protecting ministers and other politicians implicated, in addition to being run by the same people and entities involved in previous procurement scandals.

Despite non-delivery of goods, Kenya continues to make payments. In 2014 the government made a US$14 million payment to First Mercantile Securities Corporation and Universal Satspace Corporation in "Anglo Leasing–type contracts" after a court ruling in London against the Kenyan government, requiring the payment of the arrears; it sheds light on the process of tendering and procurement of the security equipment that aborted and led to the scandal and continuing obligations. According to Maina, 'Anglo Leasing involved government tenders – many linked to security contracts – with some involving inflated costs, ghost companies and payments made for work that had not been done' (Maina, 2015, n.p.). State House Spokesperson Manoah Esipisu provided clarity on Anglo Leasing and similar contracts; the genesis of the scandal 'was the contracting of a loan in December 2003 by the Department of Immigration . . . to enhance security by modernising the issuance of secure passports and purchase of security equipment for use at Kenya's borders' (Esipisu, 2014, n.p.). Endemic of these type procurement-driven corruption scandals, '"Anglo Leasing and Finance Company Ltd" was awarded the tender and Ksh. 93.0 million [~US$1 million] paid up-front' (Esipisu, 2014, n.p.). What was perhaps illuminating and descriptive of this model of corruption, was that after the suspect contracts were revealed in the press in 2003 and an audit carried out, 'in the external public debt database, there were a total of 18 contracts similar to the one arranged by the Anglo Leasing and Finance Company Ltd' (Esipisu, 2014, n.p.).

This account is supported in other literature, but there are inconsistencies in the value of the contracts and amounts paid. For example, Bachelard argues that the 18 contracts signed under the Anglo Leasing–type procurement practices 'had been signed between August 2001 and January 2004, to a total value of approximately US$721 million' (2010, p. 191). Shimoli notes that by 2005, the contracts had 'already cost taxpayers Sh17.5 billion' (2006, n.p.), but were worth 'a staggering Sh56.8 billion' (2006, n.p). Manson writes of '18 allegedly grossly overpriced state security contracts worth a combined $770m' (2015, p. 6). In a report published by BBC by Ethics and Governance Permanent Secretary (PS) John Githongo, instrumental in exposing the Anglo Leasing scandal, in addition to the Kshs. 90 million down payment (3% of the contract), by 4 May of 2004, the Kenyan government through the Central Bank, was planning to pay a €3.7 million "commitment fee" (Githongo, 2006, p. 2).

The Anglo Leasing scandal's malfeasance was exposed by a government-employed "junior servant", and later, by parliament's Public Accounts Committee chair, MP Hon. Maoka Maore, late 2004. On reaching John Githongo, the start of investigations, offers, counter-offers and threats were made to bury the investigation. Blanchard writes that Githongo 'was offered the opportunity to have his father's private debt cancelled. On 17 May, Finance Minister Mwiraria warned Githongo that a businessman called Wanjigi had sworn to kill him' (2010, p. 191). Ultimately, several of the principal procurement officers lost their government positions, although given the pressure and threats, PS Githongo went into exile into the UK, and his redacted report to the president was published. As of 2017, the prosecution of some principal actors was ongoing in Kenyan courts. Even after the discovery of the fraud, the government's actions and responses suggested that it was bound by the terms of the contracts, despite flouting tender procedures.

The scandals revolved around the same actors who did business with previous governments; even the new Mwai Kibaki government, elected on promises of ending endemic corruption, did not cancel or renegotiate the contracts; indeed, it signed new, more no-bid contracts. The shadowy nature of the companies that won the tenders, and sub-contracting that saw the tender winners inflate their tenders, but then sub-contract the work to other (losing) bidders was breathtaking. In the secure passports printing portion of the Anglo Leasing scandal, Anglo Leasing would print the passports and provide equipment at £20m million, but subcontract the Parisian François Charles Oberthur – also identified as a supplier of Visa and Mastercard – who would do the work for less than 10% of the Anglo Leasing unsolicited tender quote.

Salient features of Kenya's corruption scandals

Expansive literature on corruption shows the global pervasiveness of graft; its persistence, blatancy and lack of successful prosecution is more widespread in developing countries. Western donors and international financial institutions (IFIs) acknowledge as much: Williams-Elegbe notes the World Bank's admission that 'about 30 per cent of Bank funds has been lost to corruption. Subsequent evidence shows that many Bank-financed projects are still subject to corruption and that approximately 10–15 percent of contract value goes to bribery' (2012, pp. 68–9).

84 *Stephen Magu*

Even in developed and potentially better governed countries in Europe, 'public procurement is [. . .] the government activity most vulnerable to waste, fraud and corruption due to its complexity, the size of financial flows, and the close interaction between the public and private sectors' (Neamtu & Dragos, 2015, p. 156). This is true in the tendering process in Kenya. 'Bribery in public procurement is estimated to be adding 10%–20% to total contract costs' and 'the overall share of budgets lost to corruption tends to be higher in smaller projects than in larger projects' (Neamtu & Dragos, 2015, p. 156).

Major corruption scandals in Kenya approximate scandals elsewhere; according to Rose-Ackerman and Palifka, they include where 'basic parameters of the deal – both cost and characteristics – are known ahead of time, and bribes are used to give firms a greater share of the net gains' (2016, p. 99). Others provide quotes excessively over-budget to compensate for the bribe, while some modify projects midway – including cost-overruns, and others push competitors out of the sector leaving virtual monopolies (2016, pp. 100–1). Some companies seeking tenders pay off businesses and high-level officials with decision-making powers, assuring inflated tenders that function as "incentive" for public officials. Some companies and officials pay bribes significantly less than taxes, reducing their tax burden and increasing their profit margins (Rose-Ackerman, 1999, p. 18) or in the issuance of licenses and in the performance of other regulatory government oversight activities (1999, p. 18) Other strategies include making purchases 'with little or no macroeconomic rationale' (1999, p. 29), such as the construction of the Eldoret International Airport at an estimated cost of US$25 million at 2017 forex rates.

Although inexhaustive, features of major Kenyan corruption scandals have included: contracting for goods and/or services (usually never delivered); inflated project costs, supplies or equipment; single-sourcing, or blatantly flouting the tender process; selective disqualification of bidders; last-minute inclusion of well-connected bidders; "sizeable kickbacks" from the tendering firms; insider trading; sale of secrets or technical information to specific bidders; multiple bidding on the same or similar contracts under different companies; pre-payment prior to the supply of the equipment, making the customer the true buyer; and litigation in foreign jurisdictions more likely to uphold contract laws even where the tender winner may have failed to deliver the procured materials (akin to hostage-taking, threatening default and limiting the government's ability to obtain credit, investment or sovereign bonds). For the Anglo Leasing and Goldenberg scandals, many of these features were present. Other strategies include *quid pro quo* offers, and if corruption is uncovered, bid winners litigate, tying up the courts for such a long time that the cases fade into memory or some of the accused die (e.g. Kenya's former Finance Minister and Anglo Leasing–linked David Mwiraria) without defending themselves and/or clearing their names.

Domestic impacts of corruption scandals

Although corruption has many outcomes, some affect the public most. Corruption deprives the exchequer of funds for development projects. It deprives communities of 'much needed resources that would have added value to service delivery at those levels, thus entrenching poverty' (Waswa et al., 2014, p. 134). Paolo Mauro's analysis and findings, articulated by Lipset & Lenz, show 'a 2.4 decline in the corruption index . . . is associated with a four-percentage point in the per capita growth rate' (2000, pp. 114–15); and 'the effect of corruption on growth seems to result in part from reduced levels of investment' (Lipset & Lenz, 2000, p. 115). Corruption increases investment risk and reduces public spending on key social sectors such as education and health. Grand corruption also led to withholding money for critical, internationally funded projects, for example the World Bank–funded Urban Infrastructure Project undertaken by KUTIP, stopping the construction of major roads in urban areas after the disbursement of more than US$21.67 million of a US$100 million loan (Anassi, 2004, p. 242).

Regarding corruption's impact, businesses rank corruption as the third top major or severe business constraint, after tax rates and access to finances (Iarossi, 2009, p. 19). Infrastructure was ranked fourth – including transportation and irregular electricity supply. One of Kenya's earliest scandals in the late 1980s was the Turkwell Hydro-Electric Power (HEP) project, built at three times the budgeted cost (Hornsby, 2012; Kibwana, Wanjala & Okech-Owiti, 1996). Hope argues that corruption 'has also stifled initiative and enterprise in Kenya. Rent-seeking activities tend to have the effect of inflating the cost of doing business, and thereby destroying investor confidence and driving them away' (2012, p. 117). Investors favor countries where the cost of doing business is predictable, the rule of law is supreme and business competition is fair. More importantly, Hope reiterates the finding that 'the amount of money lost through . . . – the Goldenberg Affair – . . . had this money been used instead to provide antimalarial nets, the entire Kenya population would have been provided with these nets', preventing 34,000 annual deaths (2012, p. 117).

A more long-term outcome of corruption is distrust in public institutions, especially those providing essential services to citizens (police, judiciary, immigration, health and lands). This is reflected in periodic citizen surveys; an Ethics and Anti-Corruption Commission (EACC) survey showed that perception of 'corruption among Kenyans nationally was at 74 per cent, which has increased from 67.7 per cent . . . in 2012' (Karanja, 2016, n.p.). The Ministry of Interior and Coordination of National Government, also in charge of internal security and police, was perceived corrupt by 40.3% of respondents (the police department was deemed most corrupt in the ministry; Karanja, 2016, n.p.). An earlier Anti-Corruption Commission report 'said that 80% of new police recruits had either paid bribes or used their connections to get jobs' (BBC News, 2006, n.p.).

In the previous (2012) survey, 60% of respondents had voted the police most corrupt, a 20% improvement. Among the departments, traffic police were perceived corrupt by 18% of respondents – 90% of the population uses public transportation. Chiefs and local administrators, who citizens meet frequently, applying for permits, identity cards, support letters or verification of residence, ranked corrupt by 6.2% of respondents (Karanja, 2016). The cost to report a crime (Occurrence Book entry) was Kshs. 4,430 (US$44) – for a service that is free, while bail for an

86 *Stephen Magu*

arrested individual cost Kshs. 3,725 (US$37) (Karanja, 2016). Access to hospitals, in addition to user fees, costs Kshs. 1,866 (US$19) (Karanja, 2016).

Citizens have limited personal interaction and/or participation in mega-scandals such as Anglo Leasing, Goldenberg or the 2015 Kshs. 691 million (US$6.91 million) NYS scam through siphoning funds from the "tamper-proof" Integrated Financial Management Information System (IFMIS) used for government expenditure management. But they do interact with rent-seeking government officers (police, chiefs, doctors) in their everyday lives. Nationally, they rue interactions with judges, Lands Offices, the Immigration Department, police, NYS, or armed forces recruitment, for the bribes rise exponentially. With each interaction, confidence in institutions erodes; knowledge that government service may not be obtained without "incentivizing" civil servants grows. For systems *designed* to extort, for example, the inexplicable roadblocks whose highest purpose is to collect Kshs. 50 from every passing motorist, the denial of services, the "missing files" and other code words such as "chai" or "buying lunch", corruption's impact and institutional decay continues.

Corruption threatens public safety: violent non-state actors (VNSAs, terrorists) can use corrupt networks to gain access or IDs necessary to facilitate their activities. Corruption undermines the sanctity of official documents; the possibility of terrorists acquiring documents and using them to travel, for example, to the US, as bona-fide Kenyan citizens, increases. The Anglo Leasing–type contracts involved acquisition of security-related equipment and service, such as secure passports and police communication gear. Corruption in the secure passport tender process left Kenya with older passports; the ease in acquiring fake travel documents and committing crimes becomes more prescient. Thus, secure passports and older, booklet-type driver licenses continue to illustrate how little consideration is given to national – and global – security.

International impacts of corruption scandals: ODA, foreign aid and loans

During the Cold War, autocratic, non-democratic or quasi-democratic countries in the Global South, Kenya included, escaped scrutiny of regime types. The end of the Cold War quickly illuminated the future of Kenya's relationship with donors in the early 1990s. Under pressure internally from pro-democracy reformists and from suddenly pro-good–governance western governments led by the vocal "Rogue (US) Ambassador" to Kenya, Smith Hempstone, Kenya implemented modest political changes deemed insufficient; the changes came 'just two weeks after Western donors meeting in Paris decided to suspend $328 million in new commitments of fast-disbursing aid until Kenya adopted political and economic liberalization measures' (Haugerud, 1997, p. 25; Kpundeh, 2004, p. 264; Tangri & Mwenda, 2013, p. 19).

In 1997, citing insufficient progress and delays in the privatization of telecommunications and power sectors, the IMF and the Paris Club of donors suspended assistance to Kenya again, resuming in 2000 (Holman, 2006). 'In 1997, Kenya

Toa kitu kidogo 87

faced another aid embargo when it failed to comply with donor conditions such as maintaining sound public finances and reducing corruption' (Tangri & Mwenda, 2013, p. 19), although some scholars argue this was insufficient to ensure that corruption was eliminated. Despite the rhetoric and public pronouncements, the continued provision of foreign aid continued to provide 'ample scope for rent-seeking opportunities' (Fletcher & Herrmann, 2016, p. 48).

Foreign governments and institutions watch donors' signaling behavior prior to deciding to continue or withhold aid. Mutonyi notes that 'the Danish, British, Swedish, and Norwegian governments have either withdrawn or scaled down their aid to Kenya, while aid from multilateral agencies such as the World Bank and International Monetary Fund (IMF) has been unsteady and lacking in continuity' (2005, p. 69). The donors and their signals can be inconsistent, even downright confusing. For example, Sperling notes that despite the Bretton Woods institutions' promotion of good governance, they still lends to Kenya, including finances to fight graft. For example, 'the World Bank announced a new \$145 million loan to the government in January 2006, \$25 million of which was designated for anti-corruption work' (2009, p. 72).

Investigating and prosecuting corruption scandals: legislation and agencies

Although Kenya's anti-corruption legislation dates back to 1956, before Kenya independence, the debate over defining corruption and prosecution of individuals accused of corruption began in the late 1980s and the 1990s, as donors and western countries emphasized good governance and democratization as conditions for foreign aid and loans. Burbridge records the 1956 Prevention of Corruption Act as the first legislation, criticized as insufficiently definitive of corruption; as one legislator argued, incapable preventing "that which it does not define" (2015, pp. 84–5). In the 1980s, some anti-graft initiatives were established by the Police Service – ironic, given the demonstrated public perception of the Police Service as the most corrupt government department in Kenya.

After the suspension and resumption of aid before the 1992 multi-party elections, donor pressure led to cosmetic changes and some arrests of officials linked to corruption. In 1997, facing another round of punitive measures, the government updated the 1956 law, to establish the Kenya Anti-Corruption Authority (KACA) (Byrnes & Munro, 2016). But KACA faced hostility and lack of support; in parliament, there was talk of forming a Parliamentary Select Committee on corruption, whereas others questioned KACA's request for manpower, stating: 'they have not really sat down and put their authority into practice. But they have come up with corruption cases' (Government of Kenya, 1998, p. 1076). In December 2000, KACA's existence was found by the High Court to be in violation of the prosecutorial powers of the Attorney General and the Commissioner of Police, leading to its disbanding, and passing the anti-corruption mantle to the Anti-Corruption Police Unit (ACPU) in 2001 (AfriMAP, 2015, p. 20).

88 *Stephen Magu*

In 2003, the new anti-corruption crusading NARC government quickly enacted the Anti-Corruption and Economic Crimes Act of 2003; among other things, it defined corruption to include 'bribery; fraud; embezzlement or misappropriation of public funds; abuse of office; breach of trust; or an offense involving dishonesty' (Burbidge, 2015, p. 84), but failed to include the use of public office for private gain as corruption. The Kenya Anti-Corruption Commission (KACC) was established (Burbidge, 2015; Hope, 2012; OECD, African Development Bank, 2012); perhaps it would find success. Along with the act, public officers were required to declare wealth, but the declaration was to remain private, only obtained under court orders. The mechanisms to trigger audits of wealth that would uncover incidences of corruption were not clear. Other failures of the KACC included the lack of 'political and administrative commitment and the efficiency of the agency's leadership' (Okoth, 2014, p. 222), apathy and lack of desire to grant the institution prosecutorial powers. After the 2010 constitution was promulgated, the KACC was dissolved.

In 2011, the independent Ethics and Anti-Corruption Commission (EACC) was established, with a four-prong mandate: educate the public on its mandate, prevent corruption and unethical measures, initiate investigations and complaints and mediate/negotiate (AfriMAP, 2015, p. 22). EACC was one of the constitutional commissions entrenched in law; yet, there remains a general paralysis in the prosecution of corrupt officials. Okoth argues that after the creation of EACC 'the legislatures [parliament and senate] made sure that the new agency does not have the powers that might make the lawmakers vulnerable to any future investigations for alleged corrupt practices' (2014, p. 222). The zeal of public officials to forestall credible investigations saw the first director and his team removed less than a year in office. The agencies also fail to execute their mandate, arguing that less than 2% (of 36,000) cases reported fell under its mandate. There has been no conviction in 6 years from 84% of cases accepted for prosecution (Okoth, 2014, p. 223).

Kwaka and Mutunga note that corruption in Kenya persists because of the lip-service to fighting corruption and disempowered anti-corruption agencies, which lack funding, governmental support or are ruled to contravene existing laws. Especially pertinent is whether anti-corruption agencies have the power to prosecute. Today, prosecutorial powers remain with the police and Director of Public Prosecutions (2011, p. 16). Anti-corruption laws and a constitutional commission were created in the 2010 constitution; however, 'despite the unearthed big corruption scandals, no senior government officer or politician has ever been prosecuted and convicted of corruption' (2011, pp. 16–17). The government strives to appease disparate publics – especially the donors – with the right institutions, but with no intention of allowing the institutions freedom to function, and actively throttles their independence, thus subverting their very *raison d'être*.

Some international conventions and mechanisms potentially addressing corruption in Kenya

In the era of globalization, corruption often is transnational, as Kenya's major corruption scandals have shown. In the Goldenberg Scandal, given the absence of gold deposits in Kenya, the company resorted to exporting smuggled gold (smuggled from the Democratic Republic of the Congo), and alleged that the exports were sent to two companies in Switzerland and Dubai, UAE (Anonymous, 1993), thus bringing in an international dimension. In the Anglo Leasing scandal, the supplier of the passports was French; in the Euromarine scandal, the naval ship was sourced from Spain; the Eurobond "scandal" had international and American connections in the brokerage. Considering this, perhaps, too, in pursuit of good governance, a number of East African countries, including Kenya, Uganda, Tanzania, Rwanda and Burundi, under the auspices of the new East African Community (EAC), formed in 2007 the East African Association of Anti-Corruption Authorities (EAAACA) (Republic of Kenya, 2009, p. 118; Odhiambo & Chitiga, 2016, p. 24).

Kenya is a signatory to regional, continental and global anti-corruption agreements and conventions. It participated in the African Regional Ministerial Workshop on Organized Transnational Crime and Corruption in Dakar, Senegal, in 1997, which approved the Dakar Declaration on the Prevention and Control of Organized Transnational Crime and Corruption (Roth, 2012, pp. 82–3). It is a signatory to the

> African Convention on Preventing and Combating Corruption and the African Union Anti-Corruption Convention, which requires African government officials to declare their assets, adhere to ethical codes of conduct, provide citizens access to government information about budget spending, and to protect those who blow the whistle on state fraud.
>
> (Persson et al., 2010, p. 7)

Kofele-Kale notes that in the AU Anti-Corruption Convention corruption is an extraditable offense (2016). Despite the convention being adopted on 11 July 2003 and entering into force on 5 August 2006, as of 2011, it had 43 signatories and 27 ratifications (Adeyeye, 2012, p. 113). Per Nicholls, Daniel, Bacarese and Hatchard, by 2011, 31 AU countries had ratified the convention (2011, p. 517). Regionally, the East Africa Community (EAC) collaborates with the 15-member Southern African Development Community (SADC) and the Common Market for Eastern and Southern Africa (COMESA) in trade and anti-corruption initiatives; efforts have been made to launch a tripartite cooperation initiative to culminate in the COMESA-EAC-SADC Free Trade Area (FTA) (SADC, n.d.).[1]

Kenya became a signatory to the UN Convention against Corruption (UNCAC) on 9 December 2003 (UNODC, 2014, p. 2), but its compliance with UNCAC's provisions is poor. A 2014 review of Kenya's implementation of UNCAC's convention found nine agencies that deal with corruption, showing institutional and legal frameworks have been enacted. On criminalization and law enforcement, specifically bribery and trading in influence, dealt with by articles 15, 16, 18 and 21 of UNCAC, Kenya's legislation did not cover third-party, or indirect, bribery of public officials; had not criminalized bribery of foreign officials; omitted dimensions of trading in influence through intermediaries; and did not address bribery

90 *Stephen Magu*

in the private sector (UNODC, 2014, pp. 3–4). Difficulties in reporting corruption in Kenya are well chronicled: 'there are no comprehensive measures to protect whistleblowers' (UNODC, 2014, p. 6). Kenya also ratified the United Nations Convention against Transnational Organized Crime (or the Palermo Convention), which entered into force on 29 September 2003, with 147 signatories and 188 parties (Hatchard, 2014). Article 9 requires parties to 'ensure effective action by its authorities in the prevention, detection and punishment of corruption of public officials, including providing authorities with adequate independence to deter the exertion of inappropriate influence on their actions' (Hatchard, 2014, p. 25).

Kenya participated in the Africa Peer Review Mechanism (APRM), described as 'a Specialized Agency of the African Union (AU)' and which was 'initiated in 2002 and established in 2003 by the African Union in the framework of the implementation of the New Partnership for Africa's Development (NEPAD)' (APRM, n.d., n.p.). Kenya's reviews occurred in 2006 and 2011 (Ouendji, 2015). The APRM process through NEPAD was made into an African process over Nigeria's objection that if it was carried out by the United Nations Economic Commission for Africa it would be too western oriented (Murray, 2004, p. 41). The outcome was the near-separation from NEPAD of APRM, leading to according the review attracting far fewer states than NEPAD (Yusuf, 2017, p. 316). Notably Kenya has volunteered twice for the NEPAD review on good governance.

Outside institutional arrangements, Kenya's fight against corruption has been aided in novel ways. The contract to print Kenya's ballot papers for the 2010 constitutional referendum was awarded by the Independent Electoral Boundaries Commission (IEBC) to Smith & Ouzman (S & O) of Eastbourne, Sussex, England. S & O is a security printer, supplying ballot papers and other documents since 1991. 'In October 2013, Britain's Serious Fraud Office brought charges against British Company Smith and Ouzman Limited, a supplier of Kenyan ballot papers, for corruptly winning tenders totaling nearly half a million pounds, contrary to the Prevention of Corruption Act' (Makulilo & Ntaganda, 2016, p. 99). In the court's judgment against the accused, for bribery of up to 500,000 pounds, in December 2014 the firm was ordered to pay £2.2 million restitution. The Sales and Marketing manager, Nicholas Smith was sentenced to 3 years in jail and the chairman, Christopher Smith, to 18 months, 250 hours of unpaid work and a 3-month curfew (Harrison & Ryder, 2017, p. 1989). It was in the process, and after the UK convictions, that Kenyans became aware of their country's involvement in the "chickengate", leading to the arrests and prosecution of the then-IEBC CEO, the Deputy Commission Secretary for support services, the Finance and Procurement Director and the Procurement Manager (Makulilo & Ntaganda, 2016, p. 100). There is need for Kenya to work with foreign governments to not only unearth corruption, but also punish the perpetrators and repatriate stolen taxpayer funds.

Avenues for prevention and elimination of corruption

Corruption is a part of the Kenyan landscape, and it permeates all levels: the local chief, police, doctor to the military, and up to a globally connected web of connected networks, countries, companies, banks and shady deals. Kenya has enacted some legislation; also, the international community has been active, pushing for better governance through a bevy of threats, coercion and incentives. Among others, the World Bank, the IMF, bilateral and multilateral donors, institutions such as TI, and, to some extent, domestic sources of *angst* against runaway corruption have staunchly advocated on the public's behalf. Kenya has ratified regional, continental and international conventions against corruption; however, Kenya's ratification of these instruments is simply to save face, rather than to implement a concerted program of reducing graft, despite empirical evidence linking good governance and economic development with reduced corruption.

There is lack of will, administratively and politically, to address corruption. Those accused of corruption, for example, Nicholas Biwott, who was linked to Goldenberg, or former Ministers Murungaru and Mwiria, steadily and gradually find their way back into government. Anti-corruption agency leaders and the bodies themselves are often entrenched within the graft networks, or considered deeply compromised, as was the recent case of the resignation of EACC Chairman Philip Kinisu, after accusations that a company ran by his wife was awarded a tender by the NYS, which was at the time embattled, particularly due to the unexplained and fraudulent loss of Kshs. 691 million [US$6.91], through the IFMIS system.

Although the tender in question was awarded in 2008, long after the chairman had reportedly resigned from running his company, parliament approved a motion to investigate him (Simiyu, 2016). Perhaps the new chairman, Rtd. Archbishop Dr. Eliud Wabukala, will have better luck. Suffice to say, between the lack of confidence and the corruption in the very anti-corruption agencies, investigators and associated agencies such as the police force, investigations and prosecutions are often scuttled through judicial action, or the anti-corruption agencies by design lack the necessary authority to prosecute perpetrators. As such, there has never been successful prosecution of individuals implicated in corruption scandals dating back to 1956.

The opacity of the tendering process and the deep rot from within led to scandals such as the "chickengate" ballot tender only coming to light after prosecution of S & O principals in the UK. Even then, those accused of receiving bribes are still walking the streets of Kenya. Where the government has taken steps to automate and computerize systems, for example, the IFMIS system, required to be used by all government agencies for financial management, loss of public funds has not been successfully stanched, as was evident with the loss of $6.91 million from the NYS. Thus, it is not clear that there are loss-prevention processes, and if such processes exist, how they can so easily be bypassed without triggering alarms.

Introduction of electronic citizen services, or e-Citizen, is a step to curb graft. Although some such systems work flawlessly, requirements for submission of physical documents to the national (or regional) headquarters is still problematic. The unpredictability of the length of time during which government services must be provided still proffers opportunity for graft. One recent development in Kenya occurred through devolution, where the national government devolved powers to county governments. The national government retained significant

92 Stephen Magu

centralized functions, such tax collection, business licensing and vehicle registration, areas that have traditionally provided avenues for rent-seeking by public servants. The lack of computerized land and property records offers perfect avenues for some public officials to continue corruption. Yet even these measures will not end the runaway corruption that approaches scandal proportions; an all stakeholders' approach must be implemented, together with robust checks and balances, eliminating loopholes in such areas as contracting and tenders, and the recognition of the benefits of good governance to economic development and prosperity.

Note

1 Some scholars refer to the African Union Convention on Preventing and Combating Corruption as the AU Convention.

References and further reading

Adeyeye, A., 2012, *Corporate Social Responsibility of Multinational Corporations in Developing Countries: Perspectives on Anti-Corruption.* New York: Cambridge University Press.

African Peer Review Mechanism (APRM), n.d., "History." Available from: http://aprm-au.org/pages?pageId=history [Accessed 16 July 2017].

AfriMAP, 2015, *Effectiveness of Anti-Corruption Agencies in East Africa: Kenya, Tanzania and Uganda.* Cape Town: African Minds/OSF.

Amanor, K., 2008, "Introduction: Land and Sustainable Development in Africa." In Amanor, K. & Amanor, S. (eds.). *Land and Sustainable Development in Africa.* New York: Zed Books, pp. 1–34.

Anassi, P., 2004, *Corruption in Africa: The Kenyan Experience: A Handbook for Civic Education on Corruption.* Victoria: Trafford Publishing.

Anonymous, 1993, "Kenya: Riches all round." *The Economist,* August 14, 328 (7824): 37–38. [Accessed 16 July 2017].

Bachelard, J., 2010, "The Anglo-Leasing corruption scandal in Kenya: The politics of international and domestic pressures and counter-pressures." *Review of African Political Economy,* 37 (24): 187–200, DOI: 10.1080/03056244.2010.483903 [Accessed 16 July 2017].

BBC News, 2006, "Graft claims rock Kenyan cabinet." BBC News Online. Monday January 23. Available from: http://news.bbc.co.uk/2/hi/africa/4638728.stm [Accessed 14 July 2017].

Bond, P., 2015, "Marikana's Meaning for Crisis Management: An Instance of South Africa's Resource Curse." In Schuerkens, U. (ed.) *Global Management, Local Resistances: Theoretical Discussion and Empirical Case Studies.* New York: Routledge, pp. 192–219.

Brownbridge, M., Harvey, C. & Gockel, A., 1998, *Banking in Africa: The Impact of Financial Sector Reform Since Independence.* Trenton, NJ: Africa World Press, Inc.

Burbidge, D., 2015, *The Shadow of Kenyan Democracy: Widespread Expectations of Widespread Corruption.* New York: Routledge.

Byrnes, W. & Munro, R., 2016, *Money Laundering, Asset Forfeiture and Recovery and Compliance – a Global Guide.* New York: LexisNexis.

Toa kitu kidogo   93

Commonwealth Secretariat, 2003, *Commonwealth Public Administration Reform 2004.* Norwich: The Stationery Office.

Esipisu, Manoah, 2014, "Government statement on settlement of Anglo Leasing debts." *Nation Media.* (Web). Available from: https://mobile.nation.co.ke/news/1950946-2316374-format-xhtml-spelwuz/index.html [Accessed 16 May 2017].

Fletcher, C. & Herrmann, D., 2016, *The Internationalisation of Corruption: Scale, Impact and Countermeasures.* New York: Routledge.

Garrard, J., 2007, "Scandals: A tentative overview." Moore, J, & Smith, J (eds), *Corruption in Urban Politics and Society, Britain 1780–1950.* Burlington: Ashgate.

Githongo, John. "Kenya: Githongo Report." Available from: http://news.bbc.co.uk/2/shared/bsp/hi/pdfs/09_02_06_kenya_report.pdf [Accessed 13 July 2017].

Government of Kenya, 1998, *Kenya National Assembly Official Record (Hansard) Jul 8, 1998.* Nairobi: Government Printer.

Harrison, K. & Ryder, N., 2017, *The Law Relating to Financial Crime in the United Kingdom,* 2nd Edition. New York: Routledge.

Hatchard, J., 2014, *Combating Corruption: Legal Approaches to Supporting Good Governance and Integrity in Africa.* Cheltenham, UK: Edward Elgar.

Haugerud, A., 1997, *The Culture of Politics in Modern Kenya (African Studies).* Cambridge: Cambridge University Press.

Holman, M., 2006, "IMF loan closes donors' three-year Kenyan rift: [London edition]." *Financial Times*; London (UK) published: 29 July 2000.

Holman, M., Steyn, G. & Wrong, M., 1997, "Scandal undermines investors' confidence in Moi: International doubts about Kenya are as much to do with the Goldenberg affair as with recent demonstrations." *Financial Times*; London (UK) published: 18 July 1997.

Hope, K., 2012, *The Political Economy of Development in Kenya.* New York: Continuum.

Hornsby, C., 2012, *Kenya: A History since Independence.* New York: I.B. Tauris.

Iarossi, G., 2009, *An Assessment of the Investment Climate in Kenya.* Washington, DC: The World Bank.

Karanja, S., 2016, "Interior, health ministries most corrupt, EACC survey shows." *Daily Nation*, Wednesday March 16 2016. Available from: www.nation.co.ke/news/Nkaissery-ministry-the-most-corrupt-says-EACC-survey/1056-3118708-8687ea/index.html [Accessed 14 July 2017].

Kibwana, K., Wanjala, S. & Okech-Owiti, A., 1966, *The Anatomy of Corruption in Kenya: Legal, Political and Socio-Economic Perspectives.* Nairobi: Claripress.

Kofele-Kale, N., 2016, *The International Law of Responsibility for Economic Crimes: Holding State Officials Individually Liable for Acts of Fraudulent Enrichment.* New York: Taylor & Francis.

Kpundeh, S., 2004, "Process Interventions Versus Structural Reforms: Institutionalizing Anticorruption Reforms in Africa." In Brian Levy, B. & Kpundeh, S. (eds.). *Building State Capacity in Africa: New Approaches, Emerging Lessons.* Washington, DC: IBRD/The World Bank, pp. 257–282.

Kwaka, J. & Mutunga, T., 2011, "Contemporary Kenya and Its Leadership." In Okoth-Okombo, D., Kwaka, J., Muluka, B., & Sungura-Nyabuto, B. (eds.). *Challenging the Rulers: A Leadership Model for Good Governance.* Nairobi: East Africa Educational Publishers, pp. 1–37.

Lipset, S. & Lenz, G., 2000, "Corruption, Culture and Markets." In Harrison, L. & Huntington, S. (eds.). *Culture Matters: How Values Shape Human Progress.* New York: Basic Books, pp. 112–125.

94   *Stephen Magu*

Maina, S., 2015, "Ex-ministers among 15 to be charged with masterminding scam." *Daily Nation*, February 28 2015. Available from: www.nation.co.ke/news/Anglo-Leasing-Suspects-Arrests-EACC/1056-2639160-10q2rii/index.html [Accessed 13 July 2017].

Makulilo, A. & Ntaganda, E., 2016, *Election Management Bodies in East Africa: A Comparative Study of the Contribution of Electoral Commissions to the Strengthening of Democracy*. Cape Town: African Minds/OSI.

Manson, K., 2015, "Kenya renews efforts to target architects of Anglo Leasing corruption scandal: Crime." *Financial Times*; London (UK) published: March 16 2015.

Marango, M., 2010, *A Different Path: The Story of an Army Family*. Bloomington: Xlibris.

Matiang'i, F., 2006, "Case Study on the Role of Parliament in the Fight against Corruption: The Case of the Kenyan Parliament." In Stapenhurst, R., Johnston, N., & Pelizzo, R. (eds.). *The Role of Parliament in Curbing Corruption*. Washington, DC: The World Bank, pp. 69–79.

Munda, C., 2017, "Public debt doubles to Sh3.77tn in five years." *The Star*, January 26 2017. Available from: www.the-star.co.ke/news/2017/01/26/public-debt-doubles-to-sh377tn-in-five-years_c1494609 [Accessed 15 July 2017].

Murray, R., 2004, *Human Rights in Africa: From the OAU to the African Union*. Cambridge: Cambridge University Press.

Mutonyi, J., 2005, "Fighting Corruption: Is Kenya on the Right Track?" In Rick Sarre, R., Das, D., & Albrecht, H. (eds.). *Policing Corruption: International Perspectives*. Lanham: Lexington Books.

Neamtu, B. & Dragos, D., 2015, "Fighting Corruption in Central and Eastern European Countries through Transparency: Regulatory and Institutional Challenges." In Zhang, Y. & Lavena, C. (eds.). *Government Anti-Corruption Strategies: A Cross-Cultural Perspective*. Boca Raton: Taylor & Francis Group/CRC Press, pp. 136–166.

Nicholls, C., Daniel, T., Bacarese, A. & Hatchard, J., 2011, *Corruption and Misuse of Public Office*. Oxford: Oxford University Press.

Nyamnjoh, F., 2015, "South Africa: Hopeful and Fearful." In Ribeiro, G. & Dwyer, T. (eds.). *Social, Political and Cultural Challenges of the BRICS*. Bamenda: Langaa RPCIG & ANPOCS, pp. 217–254.

Ochwangi, D., 2014, "Eurobond scandal: For Ksh. 176 billion borrowed, Kenya will pay 278 billion shillings; was this necessary?" *Kenya Today*, July 3 2014. Available from: www.kenya-today.com/news/eurobond-scandal-ksh-176-billion-borrowed-kenya-will-pay-278-billion-shillings-necessary [Accessed 13 July 2017].

Odhiambo, M. & Chitiga, R., 2016, *The Civil Society Guide to Regional Economic Communities in Africa*. Cape Town: African Minds/OSF.

OECD, African Development Bank, 2012, *Stocktaking of Business Integrity and Anti-Bribery Legislation, Policies and Anti-Bribery Efforts in Africa*. Paris: OECD Publishing, http://dx.doi.org/10.1787/978926416586-en

Okoth, S., 2014, "Prosecute and Punish: Curbing Political and Administrative Corruption in Kenya." In Mudacumura, G. & Morçöl, G. (eds.). *Challenges to Democratic Governance in Developing Countries*. Geneva: Springer, pp. 211–226.

Oscar Gakuo Mwangi. "Political corruption, party financing and democracy in Kenya." *The Journal of Modern African Studies*, 46, No. 2 (June, 2008): 267–285. Accessed 10 November 2017. https://doi.org/10.1017/S0022278X08003224

Ouendji, N., 2015, "Kenya: Launching of the second country review mission." *African Union*, April 17 2015. Available from: http://aprm-au.org/viewNews?newsId=18 [Accessed 16 July 2017].

Pallister, D., 2004, "Scandals cast shadow over Kenya's government." *The Guardian*, July 5. Available from: www.theguardian.com/world/2004/jul/06/kenya.davidpallister [Accessed 13 July 2017].

Persson, A., Rothstein, B. & Teorell, J., 2010, "The failure of anti-corruption policies: A theoretical mischaracterization of the problem." *The Quality of Government Institute*. QoG Working Paper Series 2010. Available from: http://qog.pol.gu.se/digitalAssets/1350/1350163_2010_19_persson_rothstein_teorell.pdf [Accessed 16 July 2017].

Quinn, J., 2016, *Global Geopolitical Power and African Political and Economic Institutions: When Elephants Fight*. Lanham: Lexington Books.

RailwayTechnology.com, n.d., "Mombasa-Nairobi standard gauge railway project, Kenya." *Railway Technology*. Available from: www.railway-technology.com/projects/mombasa-nairobi-standard-gauge-railway-project/ [Accessed 14 July 2017].

Republic of Kenya, 2009, *The Kenya Gazette*, January 9 2009. Vol. 111, No. 4. Nairobi: Government Printer.

Rose-Ackerman, S., 1999, *Corruption and Government: Causes, Consequences, and Reform*. Cambridge: Cambridge University Press.

Rose-Ackerman, S. & Palifka, B., 2016, *Corruption and Government: Causes, Consequences, and Reform*. Cambridge: Cambridge University Press.

Roth, V., 2012, *Defining Human Trafficking and Identifying Its Victims: A Study on the Impact and Future Challenges of International, European and Finnish Legal Responses to Prostitution-Related Trafficking in Human Beings*. Leiden: Martinus Nijhoff Publishers.

SADC, n.d., "Tripartite Cooperation." *SADC*. Available from: www.sadc.int/about-sadc/continental-interregional-integration/tripartite-cooperation/ [Accessed 16 July 2017].

Schmidt, E., 2013, *Foreign Intervention in Africa: From the Cold War to the War on Terror*. New York: Cambridge University Press.

Shimoli, E., 2006, "Kenya: Revealed: Secrets of Sh58 Billion deals." *All Africa.com*, April 20 2006. Available from: http://allafrica.com/stories/200604190646.html [Accessed 13 July 2017].

Simiyu, O., 2016, "Kenya: Kinisu Bows to pressure, resigns as EACC chairman." *AllAfrica. com*, August 31 2016. Available from: http://allafrica.com/stories/201608310947.html [Accessed 16 July 2017].

Southall, R., 2005, "The Ndungu report: Land & graft in Kenya." *Review of African Political Economy*, 32 (103), Imperialism & African Social Formations, pp. 142–151. Available from: www.jstor.org/stable/4006915. [Accessed 13 July 2017].

Southall, R., 2016, *The New Black Middle Class in South Africa*. Johannesburg: James Currey.

Sperling, V., 2009, *Altered States: The Globalization of Accountability*. Cambridge: Cambridge University Press.

Tangri, R. & Mwenda, A., 2013, *The Politics of Elite Corruption in Africa: Uganda in Comparative African Perspective*. New York: Routledge.

Trading Economics, n.d., "Kenya Government Debt to GDP." *Trading Economics*. Available from: https://tradingeconomics.com/kenya/government-debt-to-gdp [Accessed 15 July 2017].

Transparency International. *Kenya*. Available from: www.transparency.org/country/KEN [Accessed 15 July 2017].

Transparency International, n.d., *Table of Results: Corruption Perceptions Index 2015*. Available from: www.transparency.org/cpi2015/#results-table [Accessed 12 July 2017].

96 *Stephen Magu*

UNODC, 2014, "Country review report of Kenya." *United Nations Office on Drugs and Crime.* Available from: www.unodc.org/documents/treaties/UNCAC/CountryVisitFinalReports/2015_09_28_Kenya_Final_Country_Report.pdf [Accessed 16 July 2017].

Wangari, N., 2016, "Safety in Kenya's public transport vehicles (Matatu)." November 11 2016. Available from: http://blog.geopoll.com/violence-against-women-in-kenyas-public-transport-vehicles-matatus-an-escalation-from-insults [Accessed 14 July 2017].

Warutere, P., 2005, "The Goldenberg conspiracy: The game of paper, gold, money and power." *Institute for Security Studies, Paper 117.* Available from: https://issafrica.org/research/papers/the-goldenberg-conspiracy-the-game-of-paper-gold-money-and-power [Accessed 13 July 2017].

Waswa, F., Kilalo, C., Mwasaru, D. & Kennedy, A., 2014, *Sustainable Community Development: Dilemma of Options in Kenya.* New York: Palgrave Macmillan.

Williams-Elegbe, S., 2012, *Fighting Corruption in Public Procurement: A Comparative Analysis of Disqualification or Debarment Measures.* Portland: Hart Publishing.

Yusuf, A., 2017, "Unconstitutional Change of Government and the Public Law of Africa: Outlawing *Coups d'états* in Africa." In Maluwa, T., et al. (eds.). *The Pursuit of a Brave New World in International Law: Essays in Honour of John Dugard.* Leiden: Koninklijke Brill NV.

6 Campaign donation and extradition of the connected in Jamaica

Omar E. Hawthorne

Introduction

Corruption scandals have been a common characteristic of Jamaican politics. Each scandal is often seen as a nine-day wonder; essentially a dime-a-dozen event considering the rate and frequency at which scandals occur. Corruption scandals have shaken politics in Jamaica and across the Caribbean. Politics, political campaigns and government contracts all have a common recipe – scandals of impropriety. Jamaica is not new to corruption scandals; in fact, it has a 'rich' history of corruption scandals over several decades. Jamaica's political system follows the Westminster parliamentary system and, as Mills (1997: 40), argues, "cult of secrecy and confidentiality in government." The Protected Disclosures Act 2011 (Whistleblower Law) in a heightened culture of retaliation, often with death for perceived informers, is yet to be utilized. In that, there are no accompanying regulations and the legislation, while in theory it protects an individual from being dismissed, it does not provide an incentive for potential whistleblowers. It is also notable that the Official Secrets Act is still in existence.

The relevance of corruption and corruption scandals in Jamaica cannot be overstated. Repeated public opinion surveys reiterate that corruption is amongst the most pressing issues. The perception that corruption has increased is seemingly validated by numerous scandals. Cognizant that as a society we only become aware of corruption when it becomes a sandal, the frequency of scandals has undoubtedly produced high concerns about corruption. Jamaica has some well-written legislation on corruption but what is often lacking is regulation and reform. Furthermore, there is a lack of public education and sensitization as it relates to informing citizens of anti-corruption legislation and how to utilize the law. With over 50 years of independence, and more than 40 years of anti-corruption legislation, corruption is still a major problem in Jamaica. The state of investigations, charges and convictions of alleged perpetrators remains relatively low. In recent years, only three senior public officials have been successfully convicted for acts of corruption (Hawthorne 2017). From as early as 1973 Jamaica has a growing number of institutional efforts aimed at improving administrative processes and reducing corruption. A few of these are: the Office of the Contractor General (1983), the National Contracts Commission (1999), the Public Management Accountability

98 *Omar E. Hawthorne*

Act 2002; codes of conduct for public officials and politicians (1973) and government ministers (2002), the Commission for the Prevention of Corruption (2003) and the Integrity Commission (2016), among others. Nonetheless, despite these anti-corruption institutions, the public perception is that corruption is endemic, and this view is supported by numerous local public polling statics as well as Transparency International's Corruption Perceptions Index (CPI). Corruption exists in Jamaica; it is understood and can be identified in every society. The DaCosta Commission, from as early as 1972, identified political corruption in the form of venality, graft, sale of office, kickbacks from state contracts and theft of public largess (Jones 1992b: 40).

This chapter presents an overview of the growth and tenacity of corruption and corruption scandals in Jamaica; despite the surfeit of anti-corruption policies and institution initiatives, corruption scandals have seemingly become the norm. Jamaica has had several corruption scandals, but this chapter will focus primarily on the corruption scandal of the international entity Trafigura Beheer, which is still ongoing. Additionally, this chapter examines the corruption scandal surrounding the extradition of drug kingpin Christopher Coke by the United States. The scandals differ; one examines an alleged international bribe, the other a drug kingpin and his level of political influence. The chapter concludes that resolution, political will and a change in political culture are required to complement institutional responses, as corruption scandals will continue to be the norm, as there have been rarely any ramifications for alleged participants.

The media plays an important role in modern democracies. It is the bastion of hope for democratic countries and the means of keeping government honest and forcing the issue of transparency. Another view holds that corruption scandals actually signal a healthier democracy where misdeeds are exposed and eventually punished. Other, more pessimistic views contend that more scandals arise simply from more corruption. The emergence of corruption scandals (Balán 2011: 459) indicates growing levels of corruption. Furthermore, government insiders leak damaging information about other political actors as part of intra-government political competition for power and resources. By examining the politics of corruption scandals, the present analysis shows that scandals are more likely to occur under specific configurations of inter-party and intra-party or coalition competition. Denouncers (Balán 2011: 459) are generally government insiders. Corruption scandals are a consequence of the way in which political systems channel conflict and dissent within government coalitions. Scandals are a by-product of political competition. They also are a by-product of watchdog journalism.

Catalogue of corruption scandals

Corruption is a symptom of something gone wrong in the management of the state. Institutions, designed to govern the relationships between citizens and the state, are used instead for the personal enrichment of public officials and the provision of benefits to the corrupt (UNDP 1997). Osei (2007: 168) highlights that historically there has been a significant increase in the perception of corruption in Jamaica by referring to Mills' (1997) work that "from the end of the 1930s to the 1950s [before independence] – public service corruption was negligible. When cases came to light we were horrified." This contrasts with later years (the 1980s to the present) where there is no doubt whatsoever that the incidence of unethical behaviour and corrupt practices has risen significantly, becoming so prevalent that it has become almost the norm; we now take it almost for granted. This changing historical perception, Osei citing Mills' 1997 work argues, seems to strengthen the case that in Jamaica corruption has become a perennial problem of public administration in the particular circumstances of the post-Independence period. Osei's 2007 work on corruption scandals provides a good analysis as it relates to the work of the anti-corruption institution-building interventions in Jamaica. Osei, in highlighting the frequency of corruption scandals, notes that the perception amongst the Jamaican people that corruption has increased is validated by numerous scandals and acts of corruption recorded in the last 15 years. In a number of the cases, the reasons for mismanagement and waste of tax dollars were attributed to: cost overruns, overpayments for work not done, budgeting difficulties, lack of oversight, due diligence, misjudgements and failure of respective portfolio ministers to heed warnings that led to the loss of billions of tax dollars over an extended period. The following are merely some of the corruption scandals which have occurred in Jamaica: the 1980s Spring Plain scandal (JMD 270 million); the Rollins Land Deal scandal (1989); the JMD 500 million zinc scandal (1990); the furniture scandal (JMD 10.6 million) (1991); the Shell waiver scandal (JMD 29.5 million) (1991); the motor vehicle importation scandal (1992); the Public Sector Salary "Fat Cat" scandal (JMD 60 million) (1998); the NetServ Jamaica scandal (JMD 220 million) (2001); NHDC and Operation Pride (JMD 5.5 billion) (2002); the NSWMA scandal (JMD 2 billion) (2004); the Sandals Whitehouse scandal (USD 43.3 million) (2005); the Trafigura scandal (2006); the Cuban Light Bulb Scandal (JMD 114 million) (2007); the Dudus extradition debacle (2009); the transport minister house purchase/upgrade scandal (JMD 50 million) (2009); the NHT Outameni scandal (JMD 180 million) (2014);[1] the Mombassa grass scandal (2016); and the De-bushing scandal (JMD 800 million) (2016).

In 2002, one corruption scandal cost nearly JMD $6 billion. In 2005, cost overruns on government projects cost an estimated JMD $8 billion. Nearly JMD $1 billion was spent in the 2016 de-bushing and drain cleaning scandal that occurred a month prior to the announcement of local government elections. The volume of the corruption scandals is relevant as 70 cents on every dollar of the Jamaican government revenue goes towards servicing the debt of the country. The highlighting of these scandals shows the frequency of occurrence in Jamaica, and it also speaks to the seemingly 'nine-day wonder' culture in the country. The lack of accountability and perceived poor governance contributes to the view that corruption is rampant in Jamaica. There have been few instances of individuals being fired or released from a job because of a corruption scandal, and the charge and prosecution rates have been very low. In fact, in Jamaica's history only three senior public officials have been charged and sentenced for acts of corruption.

100   *Omar E. Hawthorne*

The causes of corruption in Jamaica, as Osei (2007: 168) argues, have been linked to different factors, inclusive, but not limited to, the failure of successive administrations to deliver development and improved human welfare which aggravates the lack of trust in politicians. Jones (1992a) includes material scarcity that generates social demands for a limited supply of valued resources, such that some clients often pay to cut red tape in order to transform the aloof public administrator into a friendly patron. Stone (1980) connects Jamaica's corruption with the legacy of the Westminster system in the Caribbean, and the evidence for Stone represents bureaucratic clientelism within, more broadly, a system of political clientelism. This, Jones (1992b: 41) argues, created a degree of social acceptance of unethical behaviour rooted in strong partisan feelings that judge conduct according to partisan persuasion. To be sure, the public policy process is also embedded in a culture in which anti-corruption deterrence is mainly symbolic and weak.

Campaign finance

Early literature on campaign finance is that it enhances governance by fostering competition and reducing incumbent advantage (Mayhew 1974; Abramowitz, Alexander, and Gunning 2006). Bonica 2014 suggests that campaign finance can also create a pro-elite bias. In many new democracies, campaign finance is intermeshed with corruption. Thus, the relationship between campaign finance and malfeasance scandals requires more analysis. Scandals affect citizens' trust in institutions (Bowler and Karp 2004) and in democracy more generally (Canache and Allison 2005). As argued by Parker (2004), politicians care greatly for their reputational capital, which is why legislators spend so much time and energy building it. Politicians use different strategies to avoid blame for involvement in corruption scandals; some features of scandals are more salient than others.

One of the longest political corruption scandals in Jamaica, the Trafigura Beheer scandal, is linked to campaign finance. This corruption scandal is pivotal for many reasons, including the involvement of a trans-national corporation governed under the Organization for Economic Cooperation and Development Anti-Bribery Convention and a Jamaican politician and political party. More importantly, this alleged bribery incident occurred in 2006. It is currently 2017, and the legal wrangling is still ongoing, with no clear end in sight. Recently, on June 23, 2017, the Jamaica Court of Appeal denied the People's National Party PNP members the request to appear in chambers to answer questions rather than in open court.

The role of the media in modern democracies is important. It provides a large proportion of the information with which policymakers and voters make decisions, as well as analysis and editorial content that may influence the conclusions reached by potential voters. The Trafigura scandal of 2006 undoubtedly contributed to the defeat of the PNP at the polls in the general elections of 2007. This scandal dominated the news for an extended period of time. *The Gleaner* and other media houses had no shortage of articles or cartoons related to the Trafigura scandal, as Figures 6.1 and 6.2 illustrate.

Figure 6.1 PM Portia Simpson Miller mum on Trafigura scandal

Figure 6.2 Painting the Trafigura scandal

102 *Omar E. Hawthorne*

One of the compelling distinguishing features with the Trafigura matter is that it also led to the amendment of Jamaican law. In November 2006, Mr. Bruce Golding, in his capacity as Leader of the Opposition, and being dissatisfied with the explanation offered by the PNP officials, wrote a letter to the Kingdom of the National Investigation Unit of the Netherlands requesting that an investigation be carried out into the circumstances in which the payment was made to a bank account CCOC – Colin Campbell Our Candidate. Golding's reason for requesting the investigation, as declared in his letter to the Office of the Contractor General OCG, was that "the explanation for the payment by Trafigura, and that given by the PNP were clearly contradictory and irreconcilable and raise issues of corruption, kickback and bribery."[2]

Trafigura's history with Jamaica

Trafigura is one of the world's largest oil and metal traders, with multiple subsidiaries on almost every continent. Trafigura has been linked to several international scandals, including, but not limited to, toxic waste dumping in the Ivory Coast, oil smuggling in Iraq and bribing politicians in several countries. On October 4, 2006, Jamaica's Leader of the Opposition, Bruce Golding, and the Jamaica Labor Party JLP raised concerns about the propriety and legality of payments to the PNP government by Trafigura. The payment appeared to be an act of corruption – being a kickback or bribery to the government in the amount of JMD $31 million.

Why and how was Trafigura involved with Jamaica and making political contributions to the PNP government? Context is needed to better understand the scandal. In December 1978, Jamaican Prime Minister Michael Manley and President Olusegun Obasanjo of Nigeria negotiated a bilateral agreement in which earnings from the oil trade would be used for development projects for Jamaica's energy security. This contract with the Nigerian National Petroleum Corporation (NNPC) was scheduled to be renewed on a yearly basis. Since the Petroleum Corporation of Jamaica (PCJ) lacked the capacity to process crude oil from Nigeria, the first of the lifting arrangements that PCJ had with the NNPC was for the crude to be delivered to the Shell plant in Curacao for refinement. The sale of the Curacao Shell plant in 1984 resulted in the cancelling of the agreement. Up until 1993, when the newly elected president of Nigeria cancelled all concessionary contracts, Vitol SA Inc. was contracted by the PCJ to lift and sell the crude on the international market on Jamaica's behalf. With a change in Nigerian government in 2000, the NNPC reinstated the contract. Both Vitol SA Inc. and Trafigura Beheer lifted Nigerian crude on behalf of the PCJ.[3] In 2001 the PCJ, dissatisfied with the profit-sharing arrangement, invited other accredited companies to bid. Of the three bidders, Vitol SA, Trafigura and Glencore, Trafigura was contracted as it was deemed the most responsive bid at the time (OCG 2010a: 32). The Office of the Contractor General (2010a: 38) report indicates that between October 2000 and April 2006, there were six contracts, and Trafigura lifted and traded 34,354,660 barrels of oil, with concession payments of US $2,443,381 earned by the PCJ.

The timeframe of the alleged bribery is key. Trafigura was a contractual party with the Government of Jamaica for oil lifting. The contract expired in 2005. In 2006, Trafigura continued to lift oil by virtue of an interim arrangement with the government. This interim arrangement was in place although the National Contracts Commission (NCC) had *recommended* at the time that Glencore Energy UK Limited be awarded the new contract. It was during the time that the interim arrangement was in place that three payments, totalling (466,000 euros), were made by wire transfer to the CCOC account. The allegation by Bruce Golding, Leader of the Opposition, was that these payments represented an attempt by Trafigura to influence the Jamaican government's decision to award the contract to them for the continued lifting of oil. Trafigura continued to lift oil after the payments were made, and the PNP continued to maintain that those payments were made as a donation to its political campaign with no strings attached.

Punishing your opponents?

Trafigura, an international firm, gave Golding the remit to seek assistance from the country in which Trafigura is registered, in particular, an investigation into whether, and the extent to which, the payment made by Trafigura contravenes the Dutch Penal Code, principally the provisions of the Convention on Combating Bribery of Foreign Public Officials and the OECD Guidelines for Multinational Enterprises. However, the Kingdom of the Netherlands had not been declared by the relevant Jamaican Minister of Justice as a foreign state to which the act applied for mutual assistance in criminal matters. Subsequently, in September 2007, there was a change in government following the general election. The JLP formed the government and Mr. Golding became prime minister. On November 9, 2007, two months after forming the government, the JLP-appointed Minister of Justice declared the Mutual Assistance (Criminal Matters) (Foreign States) Order 2007 ("The Foreign States Order"), making the provisions of the MACMA applicable to the Kingdom of the Netherlands. By this change, the Kingdom of the Netherlands was included in the list of countries that could obtain assistance from Jamaica in the investigation of criminal matters. The Minister of Justice listed the Office of the Director of Public Prosecution (DPP), as the Central Authority. With the change in the law, on December 3, 2007, the Kingdom of the Netherlands made the request to the Director of Public Prosecutions (the DPP) of Jamaica for assistance in the investigation of the Trafigura matter.

Claimants' constitutional rights

Of interest, the claimants' (PNP individuals) argued that their constitutional rights would be breached if they were made to attend court to publicly answer questions under oath concerning the Trafigura affair. They argued further that the DPP, when she procured the order to compel them to appear in court and to give evidence on oath, in essence was treating them as persons accused of a crime rather than as persons being asked questions to further an investigation about breach of Dutch

104 *Omar E. Hawthorne*

law. The claimants further argued that they were subject to inequitable and inhumane treatment by the DPP as a public authority based on the political influence by functionaries of the JLP. Additionally, because in the affidavit of the DPP, the claimants were referred to as 'defendants' as opposed to the proper term of 'respondents,' they had been treated as persons accused of a crime rather than as persons furthering the course of an investigation. But, based on the synopsis of the Supreme Court ruling this does not equate to inhumane treatment for the purpose of alleging a constitutional breach.

The Trafigura case brings to the fore the vexing issues of political campaign finance and why there should be reform in the way political campaigns are financed. As Strauss (1994: 1369) argues; one objective of reform is to reduce corruption, in that, without reforms, donations to a political party are understood as the implicit exchange of campaign contributions for legislators' votes or other government action; essentially rent-seeking. The other objective is to promote equality, and since persons who are willing and able to spend more money, it is said, should not have more influence over who is elected to office. Furthermore, it is far from clear that campaign finance reform is about the elimination of corruption at all. That is because corruption, understood as the implicit or explicit exchange of campaign contributions for official action, is a derivative problem. Those who say they are concerned about corruption are actually concerned about two other things: inequality and the nature of democratic politics. If somehow an appropriate level of equality were achieved, much of the reason to be concerned about corruption would no longer exist. And to the extent the concern about corruption would persist under conditions of equality, it is a concern about certain tendencies inherent in any system of representative government that are, at most, only heightened by quid pro quo campaign contributions; specifically the tendency for democratic politics to become a struggle among interest groups (Strauss 1994: 1370).

Corruption: a derivative evil?

For Strauss (1994), corruption can be seen as a derivative evil when individuals and corporations promise contributions explicitly contingent on a legislator voting in a certain way; explicitly rewarding legislators for past votes; punishing legislators by reducing contributions for legislative actions that the contributors opposed; making contributions during campaigns with the intention of reminding the candidate to whom they contributed of their support and redeeming their 'IOU'; and so on. This is the anti-corruption nightmare scenario (Strauss 1994: 1372). The payment by Trafigura to CCOC can lead to the inference that the company made the payments to win the contract. This would be an act of bribery of a public official; illegal under Dutch law.

Trafigura maintains that the money lodged to the CCOC account at First Caribbean International Bank (FCIB) was in pursuance of an alleged 'commercial arrangement.' As previously mentioned, the CCOC is a political campaign account bearing the signatures of Colin Campbell and Norton Hinds, the Chairman of the Jamaica Urban Transit Corporation and the Transport Authority. The organization,

CCOC, and its bank account were initially established as a political support group for Campbell when he first entered politics in 1992. But, with the caveats that Trafigura cannot admit to 'donating' to a political party because it would be illegal and the PNP, at the same time, cannot admit that the JMD $31 million was based on a commercial arrangement, as that would implicate the PNP as diverting state funds to the party, leaves the PNP and Trafigura in a dilemma. Media reports have quoted Campbell as saying "donors were typically hesitant to write cheques in the names of the political parties because of Jamaica's volatile political climate."[4] If Campbell's account is true, then Trafigura knowingly gave campaign donations to the PNP, which is a violation of the OECD's Anti-bribery Convention. On the other hand, Trafigura's pronouncements that the payments were made under the terms of a 'commercial agreement' as part of its business development objectives in Jamaica would leave the PNP in jeopardy. Additionally, if Trafigura's account is true, as vague as it is, the PNP diverted and or changed the 'regular' method of payment for a 'commercial agreement' to the PNP party via CCOC account, which is illegal. Campbell denies that the funds were for oil lifting and trading. In responding to the OCG, Campbell stated, "The Trafigura contribution was not linked to the Nigerian Oil trading agreement. It was a straight political contribution."[5]

The deposit to CCOC implies that a direct relationship between Trafigura and Campbell existed. Campbell, a Government Senator, member of the PNP Cabinet and General Secretary for the PNP, later resigned due to the scandal. The timeframe of the deposits and Trafigura's representatives' visit to Jamaica and meeting with Prime Minister Simpson Miller is all but 'too coincidental' and highlights political representatives' direct and indirect involvement with corruption and alleged bribery. Based on the documentation by the OCG – the JMD $31,256,744.93 deposits were as follows: on September 6, 2006, JMD $10,648,316.05 was lodged to the CCOC account at First Caribbean International Bank; six days later JMD $10,161,516.72 and JMD $10,410,911.62 were deposited to the same account. Consequently, three cheques were subsequently drawn on the account – two in the amount of JMD $30 million payable to SW Services, an account, which, according to the OCG's report, had several signatures, including Campbell and Phillip Paulwell, the former Minister of Industry, Commerce and Technology, and one for JMD $465,000 payable to Campbell.

For many Jamaicans, the PNP, instead of investigating the serious allegations of bribery, appeared more concerned of presenting a united front to the people of the country. Many of the senior and high-level members of the PNP kept insisting it was merely a donation and not a kickback. In addition, the PNP subsequently made the decision to return the funds. According to scholars such as Della Porta and Vannucci (1999), this specious blind support of party members is indicative of the role that political parties play in socializing corruption among its members. At present, without a completed investigation, there is no available evidence of which a Trafigura representative authorized the payments or the entire list of Trafigura representatives who visited Jamaica. Media reports revealed that Claude Dauphin, the co-founder of Trafigura, and other executives had visited Jamaica in August 2006 to meet with PNP officials. This event took place a few days before the wire transfers were made; so, there is probable cause that they had been given the necessary authorizations.

Subsequently, the talking points of the PNP changed from donation to a consultancy agreement based on Portia Simpson-Miller. In postulating answers to the relations and transaction for the financial activity, Prime Minister Portia Simpson-Miller, the leader of the PNP, disclosed in parliament some of the details about the relationship between the trans-national corporation and the CCOC, stating that:

> Trafigura Beheer contributed to the People's National Party in September 2006. The contribution was paid into an account in the name of CCOC Association and was facilitated by a document signed by the donors and a representative of CCOC Association. The document was described as a Service Agreement, the subject of which was ostensibly a Consultancy Agreement, whereby CCOC undertook to do a study of the Bauxite Industry.
>
> (*Jamaica Gleaner*, 2007)

The variance in the explanation for the funds raises more questions than answers. Trafigura, as a commodity trader, deals with metals, oil and minerals. Thus, while it is plausible that Trafigura would be interested in the bauxite industry in Jamaica, it is highly questionable as to why the alleged 'commercial agreement' was developed with CCOC instead of the government of Jamaica. Furthermore, CCOC was listed as a political fundraising account – thus, for it to 'suddenly' transition to a consulting firm to undertake a study of this nature is questionable. It has been over a decade and the PNP has yet to put forward answers in this regard. Furthermore, no study has been made public as it relates to the stated consultancy agreement. Since the case is still ongoing and the terms of reference for the alleged consultancy agreement have not been made public – one can only speculate as to the motives behind Trafigura being negligent in paying payments of a commercial agreement into a political account. Or, based on Campbell's initial answer – it was a 'straight political donation.' Two cheques, amounting to JMD $30 million being made payable to SW Services, a PNP fundraising entity, and a portion of the balance to Campbell seems to substantiate Campbell's claim that the funds were a political contribution. This discredits Trafigura 'commercial agreement' and Simpson-Miller's 'consultancy agreement' claims. The individual payment to Campbell, it can be deduced, bears the appearance of a facilitation fee, since Campbell was not a candidate during the 2007 elections yet he was paid.

Within any political system, but especially a democratic system, the real problem of 'corruption' through campaign contributions is not the problem of conventional corruption; the problem is that representatives sell their offices and betray the public's trust for personal financial gain. In the Trafigura case, since it is still ongoing, and the investigation is yet to be completed – there is not a clear case of who coerced who or if any coercion occurred. Campbell's insistence that the funds from Trafigura were a 'straight political contribution,' he [Campbell] inferred as if it was Trafigura, not him or any other PNP members, who had approached the party offering donations to assist with the upcoming elections.[6] The general attitude during the initial breaking of the scandal and commencement of investigation by the Office of the Contractor General (OCG) was met with defiance from Campbell and other PNP members. The sense of disdain in how the PNP members handled the allegations gave the impression that they were either not knowledgeable of illegality of the transaction, indifferent because the law at the time of the alleged bribe did not facilitate corporation with The Netherlands or the political party appraised the scandal as just another nine-day wonder that Jamaicans are used to and will forget about in short order. But, it did serve to highlight corruption in campaign finance.

In at least one respect, corruption in campaign finance cannot be reduced to a problem of inequality or interest group politics. In a system in which campaign contributions are freely exchanged for official action, there is a danger that representatives may coerce potential contributors; in effect extorting contributions by the threat that they will act against the contributor's interests. Although some such extortion might be possible if the currency were votes, instead of campaign contribution dollars, votes are cast in secret and can go only to one side; the dangers of extortion are therefore far greater when contributions are allowed. To the extent this danger exists, contributors, instead of being predators, as they are in the usual anti-corruption story, become the victims. Instead of the contributor working her will on the representative, who feels obligated to comply with the contributor's request to obtain money, the representative forces an unwilling citizen to contribute (Strauss 1994: 1380).

While the PNP party proffered that the opposition party leader Bruce Golding's action to make public the CCOC and Trafigura transaction was purely political, it was highly effective. With an election expected around November 2006 and the corruption scandal involving senior PNP members, it was an opportune time for Golding and the JLP to gain traction with the electorate. The Jamaica Labour Party had been in opposition for over 18 years – the PNP had survived several corruption scandals – but the Trafigura scandal struck a chord with the Jamaican public, and some wanted a change in the political party leading the country. Politics in Jamaica is highly competitive, and thus the public embarrassment of the new leader of the PNP, Simpson Miller, garnered favour with the public.

Trafigura scandal and legislative amendment

The Trafigura affair resulted in an amendment of Jamaica's law, which facilitated The Netherlands in formally requesting investigative services. There are two ways to examine this legal amendment; on one hand, Golding's action can be lauded as him adhering to his campaign promise to be tough on corruption. Thus, shortly after winning the 2007 election one of the first policy changes for the Golding-led JLP government was the amendment of the law to facilitate the Dutch government's criminal investigation. A seemingly strong sign that corruption will not be tolerated, the amendment of the law now gives the PNP the right (in the future) to request foreign assistance in investigations if there is probable cause for concern

108   *Omar E. Hawthorne*

in JLP functionaries engaging in acts of corruption or bribery. On the other hand, some will argue that Bruce Golding's amending the law is a sign of vindictiveness to his outgoing opponents. On this note, the PNP members implicated have consistently argued that Golding violated their constitutional rights by amending the law in 2007 to facilitate an investigation by a foreign government. Golding's 2006 letter initiated the investigation process of making The Netherlands government aware of the alleged kickback and bribery. But, it introduced a new element in Jamaican politics – where a rival once elected can amend the law to punish his former opponent. In a twist of fate, in 2011, Golding, who was elected in 2007 on an anti-campaign platform, was 'forced' to resign from political office amidst corruption allegations over his handling of the Christopher 'Dudus' Coke extradition request with the United States; another corruption scandal that will be examined later in this chapter.

Whistleblower or political activist

The question of how Bruce Golding obtained the private bank records of the transaction of the CCOC account can be assessed from either an act of whistleblowing or that it was the handy work of a political activist working at the FCIB. It was reported that, Sonia Christie, a FCIB employee responsible for anti-money–laundering and risk management within the bank, was the source of the leak. Subsequently, it was revealed that Sonia Christie was the wife of a former JLP deputy mayor from the parish of Trelawny. Christie, some reports alleged, was a JLP activist. The leak of FCIB financial records was instrumental to the JLP's campaign strategy and subsequent defeat of the PNP, ending its 18 years of continued government.

The FCIB placed Christie and other staffers on leave while they conducted an internal investigation, FCIB did not divulge who was being investigated. The bank was obliged, under the Money Laundering Act of 1998, to make a report to the Designated Authority (the Financial Investigations Division of the Ministry of Finance) of any cash transaction involving US $8000 or more. The three transactions of the Trafigura 'donation/gift' to the PNP via the CCOC account were several times above the amount that required the bank to make a report to the Designed Authority. By law, the bank would have been penalized if it had not – referencing sub-section (5) of the act which states that failure to comply is an offence for which the bank can be convicted and fined JMD $400,000. The PNP members implicated are all lawmakers except for Norton Hinds. Even if the transactions were merely a 'gift/donation' to the PNP – they ought to have known the law as it relates to wire transfers and that the monies would have been reported.

While some Jamaicans viewed the alleged actions of Christie as a good act of whistleblowing, PNP supporters viewed the actions as a partisan attack and a crime against privacy laws. With the JLP's election victory and with Mrs Christie no longer employed to the FCIB, her appointment as Executive Director of the Government's Social Development Commission, a political appointment, further fuelled speculations that disclosure of the banking information was politically motivated.[7] FCIB in its review of the disclosure noted that the action by the employee, though highly inappropriate but apparently not illegal, breached the bank's internal policies and procedures as well as its Employee Code of Conduct and Employment Agreement. Campbell eventually sued FCIB and its senior executive Sonia Christie, claiming the bank had breached confidentiality agreements by leaking account information to the JLP.[8] The lawsuit eventually ended out of court but without the public knowledge of the out-of-court settlement.

The Court of Appeal

On June 23, 2017, Jamaica's Court of Appeal, with a unanimous decision, dismissed the appeal brought by former PNP president, Portia Simpson Miller, and four other party functionaries, Robert Pickersgill, Phillip Paulwell, Colin Campbell and businessman Norton Hinds, to answer questions in open court about a JMD \$31 million donation made to the PNP by the Dutch firm Trafigura more than a decade ago. The PNP attorneys, K.D. Knight and Patrick Atkinson, declined to comment. Likewise, the DPP, whose office acts on behalf of the Dutch authorities, declined to provide comments. It is currently a wait and see situation. Will the PNP representatives pursue the case to the Privy Council or adhere to Justice Lennox Campbell's[9] ruling that they should give answers in open court? Under the MACMA regime, an obligation on states to provide mutual legal assistance is now an accepted feature of several international instruments in the global battle against trans-national criminality and corruption. Legally, while the PNP has one final option, the Privy Council, the Trafigura case has put the PNP officials in a predicament. If public officials attempt to use the Privy Council to 'block' an open testimony in an open court, they are going against the principle of accountability in a democratic society. The PNP officials had many opportunities to 'come clean' on the matter – and as the OCG reports indicate – the PNP ignored every opportunity to cooperate with the office.

The extradition of Christopher Coke and political corruption

Political corruption, economic stagnation and limited opportunities to improve one's standard of living, in addition to social norms, have created and fostered an environment susceptible to development of networks facilitating crimes in Jamaica. Individuals like Christopher 'Dudus' Coke have caused significant havoc with his extradition process and subsequent political issues. The view that party comes before country is a mentality that is seen across the political aisle. This political culture has its roots in the clientelist relationships that emerged in the pre-Independence period as a means of attracting votes to the two dominant political parties. The 'party before the country' attitude has significantly contributed to the intense partisanship and authoritarian tendencies in Jamaica's democracy. And, the 2010 extradition controversy between the United States and Jamaica which resulted in Prime Minister Bruce Golding resigning from office amidst the scandal is pivotal.

Powerful kingpins such as Coke dominate poor urban neighbourhoods. The sub-culture and sub-system within a formalized system rendered Coke the most important non-state actor in the system and perhaps even the country in 2010. Coke, being the head of the Shower Posse drug cartel in Tivoli, the political constituency of Western Kingston, arguably Jamaica's most powerful garrison, and within the context of partisan structure of garrisons, provides the impetus as to why Coke could dominate and develop strategic and interconnecting relationships with citizens, the state and business community. The May 2010 Tivoli incursion to extract Mr. Coke led to significant unrest, as an armed conflict between the military and police forces and 'gunmen' and the people of Tivoli loyal to Mr. Coke ensued. As Figure 6.3 shows, he was likened onto Jesus, "Jesus died for us, and we will die for Dudus." And the people of Tivoli paid dearly. By the end of the extradition saga, a total of 73 civilians had died, over 40 were injured and more than 500 arrests were made; four security forces personnel were also killed as the security forces battled with the people of Tivoli, a stronghold of Mr. Coke and the constituency of the then Prime Minister Bruce Golding. Massive protests and civil unrest by the people of Tivoli brought the country to a standstill in 2010 when the Jamaica Defence Force had to intervene to assist the Jamaica Constabulary Police in efforts to capture Coke for extradition. This came on the heels of the then Prime Minister Bruce Golding having spent a month resisting the extradition order.

Figure 6.3 Protesters in support of Mr. Christopher 'Dudus' Coke

Extraditing a drug kingpin

The premise by which Prime Minister Golding injected himself in the United States' extradition request of Christopher Coke is amongst the highest level of political corruption the country of Jamaica has witnessed from a government official and the prime minister of the country. Coke was indicted by a grand jury in the United States on charges relating to narcotics, arms and ammunition trafficking. The structure of the extradition law requires that there be a procedural check by the minister with responsibility for justice, but matters regarding the quality of justice should be dealt with by the court, as well as the legality of evidence. For clarification, Senator Dorothy Lightbourne was the Attorney General and Minister of Justice, which means the prime minister at no point needed to comment on Mr. Coke's extradition. In fact, prior to the prime minister's intervention and since the JLP government assumed office in September 2007 the Minister of Justice signed off on 16 of the 26 extradition requests. Mr. Golding made no public comments on the processing of the evidence obtained against any of the previous 16 Jamaicans extradited. However, in the case of Mr. Coke, the prime minister assumed the position, many have argued, of the head defence for Mr. Coke. Noting, that on Tuesday, March 2, 2010, in the honourable House of Representatives, the prime minister publicly launched his government's defence for Mr. Coke stating that the Jamaican government would not extradite one of its citizens without being provided with a stronger case and it would suspend all other pending US extradition requests. This marked a drastic change in the country's commitment to its international obligation in the cooperation of extradition.

On March 16, 2010, opposition member Dr. Peter Philips made reference to a contractual arrangement between the government and the US law firm Manatt, Phelps & Phillips to lobby the US government. Through the US Department of Justice Foreign Agents Registration Act (FARA), the lobby firm revealed it had secured a contract worth US $400,000 to represent the Government of Jamaica in the treaty dispute. Bruce Golding denied such claim, despite the lobby firm registering itself as the agent of the Government of Jamaica through Harold Brady, Brady and Company. Golding stated, "Let me make it quite clear. The Government of Jamaica has not engaged any legal firm, any consultant, any entity whatsoever, in relation to any extradition matter other than deploying the resources that are available within the Attorney General's Department, who has a duty and a responsibility to guide the Government in these matters."[10] Nonetheless, Karl Samuda, Minister of Industry, Investment and Commerce, made a statement in which he noted that unnamed members of the JLP approached Harold Brady to see whether he could assist in facilitating the opening of discussions between the US authorities and the Government of Jamaica, and thereby seek to resolve what had become a treaty dispute between the United States and Jamaica.

In what can be described as political maneuvering, Golding remained resolute that it was the JLP, through Brady, which hired the lobby firm and not the Government of Jamaica. A subsequent release by the prime minister to quell the issue

112   *Omar E. Hawthorne*

raised more questions than answers in that Mr. Golding, in retracting his earlier denial admitted that

> Mr. Brady, from as far back as September (2009), had contacted the Solicitor-General to discuss issues relating to the extradition request. Subsequently, 'the Solicitor-General and other government officials who went to Washington in December for a meeting with officials of the State and Justice Departments met with representatives of Manatt, Phelps & Phillips at the invitation of Mr. Brady.' Furthermore, 'in discussions between the Solicitor-General and Manatt, Phelps & Phillips following the meeting with the State and Justice Departments, it was suggested that a draft release be prepared on the outcome of the meeting. Email correspondence ensued between the Solicitor-General and Manatt, Phelps & Phillips on the contents of the release but the issuing of the release was eventually not pursued.' . . . Additionally, 'Manatt, Phelps & Phillips has relied on these meetings between its representatives and government officials and the email correspondence to which I have referred as authentication that it was acting on behalf of the government of Jamaica.' Furthermore, 'The Solicitor-General was not aware that Manatt, Phelps & Phillips had already been retained by Mr. Brady when he met with their representatives, only that their services were available should the government wish to retain them. Had he been so aware, he would not have entertained any such meeting.'[11]

In the Westminster parliamentary model the party president is the prime minister, thus Bruce Golding, trying to separate the JLP from the government leads to the question: how did the JLP, if not the government, become knowledgeable of the extradition request by the United States to then solicit Mr. Brady to lobby the US government on behalf of Mr. Coke?

Golding accused the US government of using illegally intercepted telephone conversations for the basis of drug and weapons trafficking charges against Mr. Coke. As Mr. Golding stated:

> I know that perhaps it is politically expedient to say it is Coke. Or it could have been Matthews Lane strongman Zekes [Donald Phipps PNP strongman] . . . Or it could be any of these. I am not defending the wrongdoing of any person but, if I have to pay a political price for it, I am going to uphold a position that constitutional rights do not begin at Liguanea [the US Embassy is based in Liguanea, Kingston].[12]

For Prime Minister Golding, "'the Interception of Communications Act makes strict provisions for the manner in which intercepted communications may be obtained and disclosed,' he posits further 'the evidence supporting the extradition request in this particular case violated those provisions.'"[13] For Golding, under these circumstances the Attorney General and Justice Minister Dorothy Lightbourne had a duty to protect the constitutional rights of Coke and not extradite

Campaign donation and extradition in Jamaica   113

him. With an even more forceful position, Prime Minister Golding insisted: "If the Minister, having examined it, recognizes that it is supported by evidence that was illegally obtained, disclosed or used, but still proceeds to sign it, she should immediately sign one other document – her resignation."[14] By most assessment, and public record, this was the first time in Jamaica's history a sitting prime minister had publicly intervened and essentially publicly challenged an Attorney General and Minister of Justice – it should be noted that the prime minister is not learned in constitutional law, nor was he an attorney by profession. On some level, Prime Minister Golding's insinuation that the Attorney General should sign her resignation letter if she signed off on the extradition document is tantamount to abuse of power.

Golding's action in the extradition matter was a breach in the separation of powers and thereby implied mistrust of the judiciary. In that, if Jamaicans are to exercise faith in the authorities, then due process must be observed. The prime minister did not interfere in the process of the previous Jamaicans extradited, but when the drug kingpin from his political constituency was facing extradition he intervened. He seemingly breached the public trust by launching what is tantamount to a defence of Mr. Coke from the House of Parliament. Golding, in whom many Jamaicans had placed their hope and faith when he declared years earlier that he had turned his back on garrison politics, seemed false. But, at the first instance to demonstrate that he believed in the rule of law and due process, the prime minister decided to be head spokesperson for Mr. Coke and now an added profession, without any legal training, a constitutional lawyer. It can be argued that the prime minister's interference in the legal proceeding contributed to the security uprising that occurred in the preceding months when the military and police tried to extract and arrest Mr. Coke. This action resulted in the death of over 70 Jamaicans and is a stain on the political history of the country where political corruption triggered a deadly standoff between the security forces and citizens of West Kingston. With Mr. Coke's capture by the security forces and his decision to waive all legal proceedings and to be extradited to the United States where he eventually entered a guilty plea to the charges provides serious questions as it relates to politicians and their activities with trans-national criminals and the misuse and abuse of political office. On the surface, Prime Minister Golding was seemingly more concerned about what he perceived to be a breach of the Interceptions Act, without respecting due process and allowing the judicial system to take its course and allow Mr. Coke's legal team to review and challenge the extradition and for the courts to determine if Mr. Coke's constitutional rights were violated.

Prime Minister Golding miscalculated by assuming Jamaicans would have sided with him that the United States did not obtain the intercepts legally – calculated to his own peril. Coke is from one of the most organized criminal families in the country. After the 1991 extradition request of Dudus' father, Lester 'Jim Brown' Coke, who died in a Jamaican prison under mysterious circumstances while waiting to be extradited to the United States for drug trafficking and other related crimes, Dudus inherited the 'Shower Posse' from his father. The Shower Posse is an infamous international organized crime group known for the number

114   *Omar E. Hawthorne*

of bullets it 'showered' on its victims. The prime minister's perceived abuse of power by interfering with the judicial process was of greater concern to the people. This was the first extradition request that a prime minister decided to publicly inject him or herself into, rather than allowing the justice system to take its course. Furthermore, the prime minister's decision to on the floor of the Houses of Parliament state that Dudus was not wanted and or charged with any crimes in Jamaica incensed many Jamaicans. Bruce Golding became prime minister denouncing the Trafigura corruption scandal of the Portia Simpson–led government. Ironically, the political corruption scandal of Mr. Coke's extradition led to Mr. Golding's resignation from office in November 2011. Golding's successor, Andrew Holness, called an election in late December; the JLP suffered a bruising loss to Portia Simpson's PNP government which won a two-thirds majority of the parliamentary seats.

Political, economic and social factors have influenced corruption and expansion of illicit activities across Jamaica. It further explains how these factors have influenced the persistence of crime, violence and corruption in the country. These factors have it made possible for different types of informal alliances to emerge for the purpose of pursuing illicit ends, political and economic gains through illicit means and overcoming some of the weaknesses of the state, among other objectives.

The role of the Office of the Contractor General in corruption scandals

The Office of the Contractor General (OCG), despite its efforts in investigating and reporting irregularities in the procurement of government contracts, is undoubtedly weakened by its inability to prosecute individuals. The 2011 OCG report indicates that 64 contracts were awarded to Incomparable Enterprises Limited between 2006 and 2010 totalling JMD \$222.16 million;[15] an entity in which Mr. Coke was a majority shareholder. In that, many suspected Justin O'Gilvie's status as Director was merely a cover for the company. Noting that another of Christopher Coke's entity, Bulls Eye Security Coke, changed his status from Director to majority shareholder to satisfy the mandates of Public Security Regulatory Agency.[16] Specifically, in order to be a director and operate a security company in Jamaica, the fingerprinting of Coke was required for a background check clearance. In the Trafigura case, Colin Campbell, the PNP Senator and Minister, proved to be uncooperative. As the OCG noted, it found Mr. Colin Campbell's responses to be severely lacking in respect of the information sought and requested of him by the OCG. In fact, the responses from Mr. Campbell did not lend themselves to further interrogatories.[17] The OCG, upon its receipt of the written correspondence from the Netherlands National Police Agency KLPD, believed it would have access to information that would shed light on the link, if any, between the payments which were allegedly made by Trafigura Beheer to the PNP, and the award and/or potential award of a Government of Jamaica contract.

With the passage of new legislation to merge corruption entities, the Integrity Commission is still weak in many areas. Two major flaws inherent in the newly passed legislation reside with, firstly, Clause 32

> (5) where a difference of opinion exists between the Director of Corruption Prosecution and the Director of Public Prosecutions in relation to a matter referred to the Director of Public Prosecutions pursuant to the subsection (4), the opinion of the Director of Public Prosecutions shall prevail and be binding.

The Director of Corruption Prosecution is not independent; the final decision as it relates to prosecuting an individual would still reside with the DPP. The DPP's failure to charge and prosecute Hanover parish Councillor and Mayor Shernette Haughton for corruption highlights why the DPP must be independent. The Contractor General, Mr. Dirk Harrison (former senior deputy DPP), in 2015 appealed the decision of the DPP to not prosecute Haughton; the OCG was successful. The DPP had to retract the former position and then charge and prosecute Ms. Haughton (case is still ongoing). The Director of Corruption Prosecution should have full independence in prosecuting – assuming that an independent, qualified and competent person holds the position.

Secondly, as it relates to the Director of Investigation, Clause 50(2)c is an issue of contention: 50(2)a & b have been law since 1983 in the Contractor General Act in Section 15(2) and Section 19, respectively. Instead of repealing and/or limiting these clauses the government kept both and added 50(2)c, which opens the door even wider for corruption. Without legislation relating to campaign finance reform, companies and individuals that donate to a political party can receive contracts but it will kept out of the public domain. This is very worrying. There is a lack of trust in the government. Thus, if any Jamaican government is given the ability to limit the ability of the Director of Investigation, in that the director "shall not, without approval of the Secretary of the Cabinet acting on the direction of Cabinet" investigate, is very troubling. This broad and general "any government contract which Cabinet determines" is tantamount to the government 'legally' creating a backdoor for corrupt activities and preventing the Director of Investigation from investigating contracts awarded. In plain English, it is essentially a blank cheque for cabinet to determine the awarding of government contracts without accountability to the taxpayers of Jamaica. Hence, under no circumstances should any Jamaican cabinet be given such a blank cheque. There is no sense of fairness and transparency and no provision for accountability to the Jamaican people. The 'November de-bushing' just weeks before an election and cabinet selecting/instructing the National Water Commission as to which contractors to use is a perfect case of why such power must never be given to political representatives.

Conclusion

The public perceptions of corruption and corruption scandals continue to be a phenomenon in Jamaica. The political system within the country and the commingling of personal and political relationships, coupled with political tribalism,

116 *Omar E. Hawthorne*

continues to undermine the efforts of offices such as the OCG in its efforts to fight corruption. Within the last 15 years, there have been several legislative and organizational reforms to compliment anti-corruption regulations. The legislation to create the Integrity Commission was passed in 2016, but there are weaknesses within the legislation which seeks to put the power in the hands of politicians; in this respect, the cabinet can determine which government contracts can be investigated or not. In an era of countries getting stronger on corruption, the legislative thrust of the Jamaican government is not one of openness, accountability and transparency, but one shrouded in legislative protection for cabinet decisions. The volume of corruption scandals over the years and lack of accountability for individuals involved does not reveal a country that is serious about corruption reform but more like a governments scoring political points against its rival instead of focusing on the development of the country over political party. Jones' (1992b: 40) statement that programmatic leadership will ultimately determine the effectiveness of institution-building processes is pointed. Consequently, institutional problem-solving capacity, indeed, institutional survival, will therefore relate to the provision of human, financial, informational and technological resources, as well as political support. The leadership from both political parties is lacking and to some extent has contributed significantly to the lack of accountability and poor governance structure within Jamaica.

Notes

1 Marvin Williams, "Jamaicans Nine-Day Wonder Mentality – the Source of our Failure," *Jamaica Observer*, www.jamaicaobserver.com/columns/J-can-s-nine-day-wonder-mentality-the-source-of-our-failure_18349483 (Accessed May 20, 2017).
2 See Supreme Court of Jamaica documents reference, *The Hon. Mrs. Portia Simpson-Miller et al v the Attorney General and the Director of Public Prosecutions*, [2013] JMFC FULL CRT. 4. Claim No. 2011 HCV07019.
3 Office of the Contractor General, Special Report of Investigation, "Conducted into the Oil Lifting Contracts between Petroleum Corporation of Jamaica (PCJ) and Trafigura Beheer," in *General* (Kingston: Office of the Contractor General of Jamaica, 2011), 2010, p. 32.
4 See Olivia Leigh Campbell, "I'm Not Involved, Says Norton Hinds," *Jamaica Observer*, October 6, 2006, www.jamaicaobserver.com/news/113711_I-m-not-involved-says-Norton-Hinds (Accessed May 12, 2017).
5 For full text, see OCG, PCJ/Trafigura Beheer Investigation, 2010. 53.
6 See Balford Henry, "Nothing Shady," *Jamaica Observer*, October 5, 2006, *Jamaica Observer*, www.jamaicaobserver.com/news/113678_Nothing-shady (Accessed June 11, 2017).
7 Mrs. Christie eventually resigned as Head of the SDC due to illness (she later died May 18, 2009). See media report on Mrs. Christie's Appointment, "Government Defends Appointment of SDC Director," http://rjrnewsonline.com/local/govt-defends-appointment-of-sdc-director (Accessed July 12, 2017).
8 See "Campbell Ends Trafigura Battle with First Caribbean," *Jamaica Gleaner*, October 23, 2009, www.jamaica-gleaner.mobi/20091023/lead/lead2.php (Accessed July 11, 2017).
9 Justice Lennox Campbell has since retired.
10 See "Opposition, Gov't Lock Horns Over Brady Contract," *Jamaica Gleaner*, http://jamaica-gleaner.com/gleaner/20100317/lead/lead4.html (Accessed July 11, 2017).

11 See "Statement by Prime Minister Bruce Golding on Manatt Affair," *Jamaica Gleaner*, May 11, 2010, http://jamaica-gleaner.com/power/19232 (Accessed July 11, 2017).
12 See "Dudus Defence," *Jamaica Gleaner*, March 3, 2010, http://jamaica-gleaner.com/gleaner/20100303/lead/lead1.htmlIbid (Accessed July 11, 2017).
13 Ibid.
14 Ibid.
15 Office of the Contractor General of Jamaica, *The Twenty-Fourth Report of the Office of the Contractor General* (Kingston: Office of the Contractor General of Jamaica, 2011).
16 See Tyrone Reid, "Presi's Power," *Jamaica Gleaner*, http://jamaica-gleaner.com/gleaner/20100620/lead/lead3.html (Accessed July 11, 2017).
17 For full text, see OCG, PCJ/Trafigura Beheer Investigation, 2010, p. 61.

References and further reading

Abramowitz, A. I., Alexander, B. and Gunning, M. (2006) Incumbency, Redistricting, and the Decline of Competition in US House Elections. *The Journal of Politics*, 68 (1) 75–88.

Balán, M. (2014) Surviving Corruption in Brazil: Lula's and Dilma's Success Despite Corruption Allegations, and Its Consequences. *Journal of Politics in Latin America*, 6 (3) 67–93.

———. (2011) Competition by Denunciation: The Political Dynamics of Corruption Scandals in Argentina and Chile. *Comparative Politics*, 43 (4) 459–478.

Basinger, S. J. (2013) Scandals and Congressional Elections in the Post-Watergate Era. *Political Research Quarterly*, 66 (2) 385–389.

Bonica, A. (2014) Mapping the Ideological Marketplace. *American Journal of Political Science*, 58 (2) 367–386.

Bowler, S. and Karp, J. (2004) Politicians, Scandals, and Trust in Government. *Political Behavior*, 26 (3) 271–287.

Canache, D. and Allison, M. (2005) Perceptions of Political Corruption in Latin American Democracies. *Latin American Politics and Society*, 47 (3) 91–111.

Charles, C. and Beckford, O. (2012) The Informal Justice System in Garrison Constituencies. *Social and Economic Studies*, 61 (2) 51–72.

Della Porta, D. and Vannucci, A. (1999) *Corrupt Exchanges: Actors, Resources, and Mechanisms of Political Corruption*. New York, Aldine de Gruyter.

Former National Security Minister and Key Opposition Figure Slams PM as 'Indecisive' in 'Dudus' Extradition Request. September 17, 2009. https://wikileaks.org/plusd/cables/09KINGSTON695_a.html

Jamaica Gleaner. Lightbourne Biased in Handling 'Dudus' Extradition Case – KD. *Jamaica Gleaner*, March 11, 2011. http://jamaica-gleaner.com/gleaner/20110311/lead/lead4.html [Accessed 12 June 2017].

———. Crushing Coke – How the Security Forces Conquered 'Dudus' Fortress. *Jamaica Gleaner*, May 30, 2010. http://jamaica-gleaner.com/gleaner/20100530/lead/lead1.html [Accessed 10 June 2017].

———. Diehards Defend 'Dudus'. *Jamaica Gleaner*, May 21, 2010. http://jamaica-gleaner.com/gleaner/20100521/lead/lead2.html. [Accessed 12 June 2017].

———. Trafigura Questions Answered. *Jamaica Gleaner*, March 26, 2007, http://old.jamaica-gleaner.com/gleaner/20070326/business/business1.html [Accessed June 12, 2017].

Jamaica Observer. How Did 'Dudus' Get Extradition Papers? 'Dudus' Abandoned Fighters in Tivoli, Say Security Officials. *Jamaica Observer*, May 30, 2010. www.jamaicaobserver.com/news/dudus-papers [Accessed 11 July 2017].

118   *Omar E. Hawthorne*

————. Bank Sends Top Exec on Leave. *Jamaica Observer*, October 7, 2006. www.jamaicaobserver.com/news/113733_Bank-sends-top-exec-on-leave [Accessed 11 July 2017]. Sonia Christie, 14.

————. I'm Not Involved, Says Norton Hinds. *Jamaica Observer*, October 6, 2006. www.jamaicaobserver.com/news/113711_I-m-not- involved-says-Norton-Hinds [Accessed 11 June 2017]. Norton Hinds, 10.

Jones, E. (1992a) *Development Administration: Jamaican Adaptations*. Kingston, Caricom Publishers.

Jones, E. (1992b) "Maladministration and Corruption: Some Caribbean Realities", in Ryan, S. V. and Brown, D. R. (eds.), *Issues and Problems in Caribbean Public Administration*. Trinidad and Tobago, ISER, The University of the West Indies, 39–41.

Juca, I., Melo, M. and Renno, L. (2016) The Political Cost of Corruption: Scandals, Campaign Finance, and Reelection in the Brazilian Chamber of Deputies. *Journal of Politics in Latin America*, 8 (2) 3–36.

Harriott, A. and Katz, C. (2015) *Gangs in the Caribbean: Responses of State and Society*. Kingston, University of the West Indies Press.

Hawthorne, O. (2017) Light on Corruption | Until Jamaicans Start to Demand Change, it will continue to be Business as Usual. *Jamaica Gleaner*, http://jamaica-gleaner.com/article/news/20170601/ [Accessed 11 June 2017].

Maier, J. (2011) The Impact of Political Scandals on Political Support: An Experiment Test of Two Theories. *International Political Science Review*, 32 (3) 283–302.

Mayhew, D.R. (1974) *Congress: The Electoral Connection*, Yale: Yale University Press.

Mills, G. (1997) *Westminster Style Democracy: The Jamaican Experience*. Grace, Kennedy Foundation Lecture 1997. Kingston, Stephenson's Litho Press Ltd.

Office of the Contractor General. (2011) *The Twenty-Fourth Report of the Office of the Contractor General*. Kingston, Office of the Contractor General of Jamaica. www.ocg.gov.jm/ocg/sites/default/files/annual_report/annual_report_2010_0.pdf

————. (2010a) *Special Report of Investigation Conducted into the Oil Lifting Contracts between the Petroleum Corporation of Jamaica (PCJ) and Trafigura Beheer, Part 1*. Kingston, Office of the Contractor General of Jamaica. www.japarliament.gov.jm/attachments/496_OCG%20Investigation%20Rep ort%20-%20Trafigura%20Beheer%20Part%201.pdf

————. (2010b) *Special Report of Investigation Conducted into the Oil Lifting Contracts between the Petroleum Corporation of Jamaica (PCJ) and Trafigura Beheer, Part 2*. Kingston, Office of the Contractor General of Jamaica. www.japarliament.gov.jm/attachments/496_OCG%20Investigation%20Rep ort%20-%20Trafigura%20Beheer%20Part%202.pdf

Osei, P. (2007) "Corruption Scandals and Anti-Corruption Institution Building Interventions in Jamaica", in Bracking, S. (ed.), *Corruption and Development: The Anti-Corruption Campaigns*. New York, Palgrave Macmillan.

Parker, G.R. (2004) *Self-policing in Politics: The Political Economy of Reputational Controls on Politicians,* Princeton, NJ: Princeton University Press.

Stone, C. (1980) *Democracy and Clientelism in Jamaica*. New Brunswick and London, Transaction Books.

Strauss, D. (1994) Corruption, Equality and Campaign Finance Reform. *Columbia Law Review*, 98 (4) 1369–1389.

Trafigura Scandal May Affect Timing of General Elections. October 12, 2006. https://wikileaks.org/plusd/cables/06KINGSTON2020_a.html

UNDP (1997) *Corruption and Good Governance: Discussion Paper 3*. New York: UNDP.

USA v Christopher Michael Coke. *Declaration in Connection with the Sentencing of Christopher Michael Coke, a/k/a "Duddus," a/k/a "Shortman"*. Case No. 1:07-cr-00971-RPP. Southern District of New York, May 23, 2012.

———. *C5M9COK1*. Case No. 1:07-cr-00971. Southern District of New York, May 22, 2012.

———. *Sentencing Letter Addressed to Judge P. Patterson from Christopher Coke*. Case No. 1:07-cr-00971-RPP. Southern District of New York, September 7, 2011.

———. *Statement of the Honourable Dorothy Lightbourne, CD, QC, Attorney General and Minster of Justice*. Case No. 1:07-cr-00971-RPP. Southern District of New York, January 26, 2011.

WikiLeaks. *A Trafigura Scandal Primer*. October 12, 2006. https://wikileaks.org/plusd/cables/06KINGSTON2021_a.html

7 Big, bigger, biggest

Grand corruption scandals in the oil sector in Nigeria

Sope Williams-Elegbe

Introduction

The pervasiveness of corruption in Nigeria has been explained, denigrated and ridiculed (Hope 2017; Smith 2009; Sherk 2005; Okonjo-Iweala 2012). In 2016, the then prime minister of the UK, David Cameron, was overheard telling Queen Elizabeth II that Nigeria and Afghanistan were "fantastically corrupt", a statement that was not refuted by President Muhammed Buhari of Nigeria (BBC 2016).

Many explanations have been given for the nature and scale of corruption in Nigeria, which will not be reproduced here (Smith 2015); suffice it to say that in 2017 the first national survey on corruption produced by the Nigerian National Bureau of Statistics (NBS) and the United Nations Office on Drugs and Crime (UNODC) highlighted that Nigerians consider corruption to be the third most important problem in the country (after the high cost of living and unemployment) (UNODC 2017, 6). The Global Corruption Barometer for 2015 also paints a similar picture, and Nigerians were one of three countries in sub-Saharan Africa to perceive that corruption had increased in the 12 months prior to the survey (Afrobarometer and Transparency International 2015, 5).

Corruption in Nigeria is systemic, collective and pervasive (Persson et al. 2013, 449; Marquette and Peiffer 2015), and there are problems with petty as well as grand corruption Okonjo-Iweala 2012), which are often mutually reinforcing (Poeschl and Ribeiro 2016, 59–60). Whilst petty corruption is problematic and affects the lives of ordinary citizens, often acting as a tax on (sometime free) public goods and often denying the poorest and most vulnerable access to these goods, it is grand corruption in Nigeria that makes national and international headlines and commands the most attention.

Grand corruption is defined by Transparency International (2016) as occurring when

> A public official or other person deprives a particular social group or substantial part of the population of a State of a fundamental right; **or causes the State or any of its people a loss greater than 100 times the annual minimum subsistence income** of its people; as a result of bribery, embezzlement or other corruption offence.
>
> (emphasis added)

Another definition describes grand corruption as "the capture of high offices of government by elites and the use of these offices for private gain" (Rowley and Schneider 2004, 126). Nicholls et al. (2011, 3) also characterize grand corruption in terms of "size, immediacy of its rewards and mystification: the more technical and complicated a transaction the less likely that questions will be asked". With grand corruption, its manifestations are often as multiple as the manifestations of other forms of corruption. It has been said that it may include highly placed officials receiving bribes from transnational corporations, arms dealers, drug barons and the like, who appropriate significant payoffs from contract scams, or who simply transfer money from the public treasury into private (usually overseas) bank accounts (Doig and Theobald 2000, 3). As will be seen below, these manifestations occur in the context of Nigeria as well, the one constant factor being the very large payoffs for the perpetrators.

This chapter will consider several high-profile grand corruption scandals that occurred in the oil sector in Nigeria between 2007 and 2017. In examining these scandals, we will use certain parameters to filter the scandals under consideration. First of all, the scandals that will be examined here will be those that relate to Nigeria's oil industry. Nigeria is the world's 15th largest producer of crude oil and the largest producer of petroleum products in Africa (EIA 2016)[1], and many grand corruption scandals relate to the oil industry, which is managed by state-owned corporations, and characterized by high levels of fraud and corruption. Second, we will restrict this chapter to the consideration of scandals where the amount implicated in the scandal was $1 billion and greater. This amount may seem outrageous, but the amount provided in Transparency International's definition (losses greater than 100 times the annual minimum subsistence income)[2] is too low to be used in the context of grand corruption in Nigeria, and is not a suitable enough filter. In addition, owing to constant fluctuations in the Nigerian naira, the relevant sums will be denominated in US dollars, as appropriate. Third, we will also aim to look at the more complex or seemingly complex occurrences that involved several actors.

Finally, it should be noted that consideration will be limited to scandals that occurred in the last decade. However, note that the year attributed to the scandal in this chapter will be the year that the corruption scandal was first discovered and reported by the media or the authorities, even though the transactions underlying the scandal may have occurred at an earlier point in time.

This chapter will be structured as follows: it will commence with a brief analysis of the problems with grand corruption more generally, and in Nigeria in particular, then it will examine several grand corruption scandals in the oil sector over the last decade, highlighting the kind of corruption, the actor(s) involved and the consequences that followed the particular scandal, if any. The chapter will then conclude with a look at the approach to anti-corruption under the Buhari administration and the successes recorded by his regime.

Problems with grand corruption

It is generally accepted that all corruption has a negative impact on development (Lambsdorff 2006, 22–36). However, grand corruption is particularly insidious, as it is more likely to undermine the rule of law and reduce public trust, and also creates unequal access to public services, thereby exacerbating inequalities (Uslaner 2015). It also reduces public spending on important sectors such as education, health and infrastructure (Schwindt-Bayer and Tavits 2016, 7–8). For instance, in Nigeria, grand corruption in the defence sector was responsible for crippling the ability of the Nigerian army to repel Boko Haram insurgents. Grand corruption also often results in political instability (Schwindt-Bayer and Tavits 2016, 6–7), and can be used as fodder for terrorist or insurgent groups as part of their narrative to win public support and delegitimize a government (Transparency International 2017). Grand corruption also reinforces and perpetuates itself. In Nigeria, it has been said that "the grand corruption of political leaders and top functionaries led to the impoverishment of lower-level officials, who now embraced the same practices without any fear of sanctions" (Enweremadu 2012, 10).

The greatest risk posed by grand corruption, however, is the inability of domestic law enforcement to address it. This is a problem with grand corruption generally, and this problem is exacerbated in developing countries with systemic corruption and inadequate legal and law enforcement infrastructure. Nigeria has problems with corruption in the police and the judiciary. In the 2017 survey mentioned earlier, police officials were signaled as the most common public official to whom bribes were paid (UNODC 2017, 7). The same survey highlighted that the likelihood of paying a bribe to public officials was highest with the police, followed by prosecutors and then the judiciary (UNODC 2017, 8).

However, beyond the problems engendered by corruption in law enforcement and the administration of justice; grand corruption does not inherently easily lend itself to domestic law enforcement. According to Transparency International (2016), "domestic authorities are often unable or unwilling to bring the grand corrupt to justice." There are a few reasons for this: in the first place, grand corruption is by definition carried out by the high-ranking, the powerful, the connected and the wealthy, who in highly corrupted societies are able to influence law enforcement outcomes and the administration of justice. In speaking to former investigators in Nigeria's primary anti-corruption body, the Economic and Financial Crimes Commission (EFCC), the author was informed that very often investigations of high-profile officials were halted by "orders from above". In cases where investigators persisted with inquiries, despite calls to desist from investigating connected individuals, such officials were suddenly promoted or transferred to other roles, which often meant the termination of the investigation. As grand corruption usually involves the accumulation of vast amounts of wealth by the perpetrators, this wealth is also available to be used in societies with systemic and collective corruption to make corruption investigations and prosecutions "disappear".

Secondly, judicial corruption may affect the outcomes of grand corruption prosecutions. There is also anecdotal evidence by Nigerian lawyers of cases being stalled or dismissed by judges in cases where the lawyers refused to pay demanded bribes. The scale of this kind of activity is unknown, as it has not been mapped, but it is clear that this type of situation will cripple the prosecution of grand corruption, and may be one reason for the slow pace of the few grand corruption trials, and the negligible number of corruption convictions. In Nigeria, the manipulation of the judiciary presents particular challenges to anti-corruption enforcement. In October 2016, nine high-ranking judges were arrested for corruption (two judges were from the Supreme Court, which is the highest court in the country, two from the Court of Appeal and five from the High Court) (Sahara Reporters 2016a). These arrests brought into the limelight the fact that judicial corruption had reached the highest levels. Of the arrested judges, seven were charged to court, including one Supreme Court judge charged with money-laundering offences to the value of US$1.7 million (ENCA 2016).

Third, we had discussed that grand corruption may involve the capture of offices of government by elites for their own gain. In Nigeria, this has occurred, if one considers that in many respects the same people, networks and families have been involved in high political and judicial office since Nigeria's independence in 1960. The consequences of this capture is that high-ranking officials are often connected to each other and are able to use the machinery of office to ensure that the status quo is maintained.[3]

Fourth, it may be noted that the Nigerian Constitution grants immunity from arrest and prosecution in civil and criminal matters to the president, the vice-president, state governors and deputy governors whilst in office (section 308). This has meant that grand corruption committed by these holders of political office cannot be addressed unless and until those office holders leave office or are impeached, or are prosecuted overseas (Okonjo-Iweala 2012, 81–84). In many cases, by the time these office holders are out of office, they are not investigated for several reasons; they often metamorphose into "elder statesmen", continue to operate as "political godfathers" (Human Rights Watch 2007) and enjoy the support of their successors, meaning that investigations against them will be unlikely.

Fifth, in some cases, the "mystification" surrounding grand corruption scandals and the complex and technical nature of the scandals, especially as they occur in large procurement contracts or in the extractive sector can be bewildering for under-funded investigators and prosecutors. In the words of Enweremadu (2012, 5), "in Nigeria . . . the necessary administrative capacity (adequate funds, quality manpower, strong laws, and efficient judicial systems) and strong political support are often lacking" in law enforcement. Add to this the abuse of power by the corrupt, and law enforcement in Nigeria struggles to address incidences of grand corruption.

Grand corruption scandals in the oil sector in Nigeria: 2007–2017

As was stated in the introduction, this chapter will analyse grand corruption scandals in the oil sector occurring between 2007 and 2017, filtering these scandals by the amount of money involved and the complexity of the corruption scheme. The section will also highlight the consequences that resulted from the particular scandal, if any.

124   *Sope Williams-Elegbe*

1   *Kerosene subsidy scam: 2009–2011*

Nigeria is one of the world's largest producers of crude oil, but paradoxically, it is also a net importer of refined petroleum products (Centre for Public Policy Alternatives and International Institute for Sustainable Development 2012, 4). For a variety of reasons, Nigeria lacks the capacity to refine a sufficient quantity of petroleum for domestic consumption and so imports refined petrol and kerosene (International Institute for Sustainable Development 2016, 1). In 1977, owing to rising international oil prices (International Institute for Sustainable Development 2016, 1), and the relatively weak strength of the Nigerian currency, the government of Nigeria introduced a policy of subsidizing the prices of refined petroleum products, namely premium motor spirit (PMS) or gasoline and household kerosene (HHK).

Energy subsidies are often politically and economically motivated and can take many forms, but in Nigeria they take the form of price controls and direct cash transfers to importers (Centre for Public Policy Alternatives and International Institute for Sustainable Development 2012, 7). In relation to both kerosene and petrol, the government[4] sets the retail price for both products and then pays marketers/importers the difference between the market price, referred to as the "expected open market price" (which covers the sum of landing costs; all costs incurred up until product purchase, including production in foreign refineries, shipping and port charges, the cost of distribution in Nigeria and the various actors' profit margins, plus taxes) (Centre for Public Policy Alternatives and International Institute for Sustainable Development 2012, 8).

The expected open market price fluctuates with the international oil prices (Centre for Public Policy Alternatives and International Institute for Sustainable Development 2012, 9), and when the Nigerian currency weakens relative to the US dollar or international oil prices rise, the subsidy payments will increase to marketers and importers of kerosene (International Institute for Sustainable Development 2016, 1).

In Nigeria, the total annual cost of the kerosene subsidy is calculated by taking the subsidy amount per litre of kerosene and multiplying it by the amount of kerosene that is imported annually. However, there have been ongoing allegations that the amount of subsidy paid to marketers and importers is greatly exaggerated and is in excess of the amounts of kerosene actually imported. As will be seen, in the case of kerosene (and gasoline) subsidies, the amount of subsidy paid by the government is often more than what is anticipated and provided for by the budget (Centre for Public Policy Alternatives and International Institute for Sustainable Development 2012, 11).

According to a report by the Centre for Public Policy Alternatives and the International Institute for Sustainable Development 2012, 14):

> it has been alleged that import figures have been significantly inflated and the associated expenditure captured by corruption. There is also controversy over the exact status of the payments from August 2009 to December 2011. In

2009, a directive from the president ordered the Nigeria National Petroleum Corporation (NNPC) to discontinue HHK subsidies that were not reaching the intended beneficiaries. The NNPC discontinued its claim for funds to pay for the subsidy until February 2011, when it claimed arrears for kerosene subsidies during the period the policy had been suspended. The house committee probe into subsidy payments has ordered that NNPC refund the sum of ₦310billion (US$1.9 billion) it claimed. It also recommended that the previous directive be withdrawn and the subsidy restored.

What essentially occurs is that kerosene importers fraudulently claim to have imported more kerosene than they actually did and are paid the subsidy amounts claimed on the non-existent imports. This fraud took the form of the presentation of false documentation and the double-counting of cargo. Apart from the fraud, by 2009, inflation and devaluation of the naira served to increase the subsidy budget to over a third of the recurrent budget, until it became unsustainable (International Institute for Sustainable Development 2016, 1).

It has been claimed that the Nigerian government was spending about $2 billion annually on this kerosene subsidy payments (Vanguard 2011). However, according to International Institute for Sustainable Development 20162016, 9), the total subsidy payment for all refined petroleum payments (including gasoline) was US$14 billion in 2011 and $5.3 billion in 2013. In November 2016, the vice-president claimed that $1 billion was spent on kerosene subsidy in 2015 (Vanguard 2016a). To put it into context,

> an analysis of the 2013 budget, for example, shows that allocation for fuel subsidy amounted to about 20 per cent of the entire budget. It was also 10 times more than the allocation for agriculture and rural development (NGN81.4 billion), three times that of health (NGN279.2 billion), and twice that of education (NGN426.5 billion).
>
> (International Institute for Sustainable Development 2016, 9)

In an audit into the state-owned oil company, the Nigerian National Petroleum Corporation (NNPC), by Pricewaterhouse Cooper (PwC) (Auditor-General for the Federation 2015, 28), it was stated that:

> Our examination of the PMS and DPK import verified by PPPRA revealed that some discharges were apparently verified and subsidy advised to NNPC more than once. The repeated subsidy for PMS amounted to ₦3,709,879,190 ($23,954,796). The repeated subsidy for DPK amounted to ₦6,169,502,266 ($39,836,652).

In addition, despite the subsidized cost of kerosene it was never retailed at the government mandated price of NGN50.00 per litre, and the lower income groups that generally rely on kerosene for cooking and lighting were paying between 100–300% more than the subsidized price (Ohaeri and Adeyinka 2016, 1).

In January 2016, the government realized that the retail price was above the expected open market price and that, as a result, no subsidy payments were due to marketers, although these payments were still being made. As a result, the government officially announced the end of the subsidy policy on kerosene in Nigeria (Sahara Reporters 2016b), and increased the retail price from NGN50.00 per litre to NGN83.00 per litre. In August 2016, a further increase was announced to increase the price form NGN83.00 to NGN150.00 per litre (International Institute for Sustainable Development 2016, 1).

The kerosene subsidy scandal has been one of the most problematic to assess in terms of the exact amounts of money lost and the exact identity of the participants in the scheme. This is due in part to the lack of transparency in the oil industry in Nigeria, and collusion between oil importers and the public officials responsible for the payment of the subsidy. The corruption scheme was a joint criminal enterprise by the officials of the Petroleum Products Pricing Regulatory Agency (PPPRA),[5] a subsidiary of the NNPC, and the other public agencies responsible for the assessment and payment of the subsidy amounts, as well as the oil importers and marketers. It was a fraud both on the Nigerian government who paid out billions of US dollars in fictitious subsidy payments over several years, and on the Nigerian people who were unable to buy kerosene at the subsidized prices.

The corruption thus operated at multiple levels, the first being the fraudulent claims, and the repeated fraudulent claims on the same cargo (or the same non-existent cargo), and secondly, the fraudulent subsidy claims were often made in excess of the difference between the expected open market price and the government mandated price,[6] and finally, the kerosene was not retailed to consumers at the subsidized rates.

The consequences of this scam were the official removal of the subsidy and investigations by parliament into the scam, but there have been no indictments to date.

2 Petrol (gasoline) subsidy scam: 2012

It was discussed in relation to the kerosene subsidy scam that Nigeria maintains a subsidy regime on petroleum products, including on what is referred to as "premium motor spirit" (PMS/ gasoline). Subsidies on gasoline operate in the same way as subsidies on kerosene.

In 2012, the news of an extensive scam in relation to PMS subsidies was revealed. The scheme operated similar to the kerosene subsidy scheme and subsidies were being paid to PMS importers for 59 million litres of PMS a day, whilst domestic consumption did not exceed 35 million litres per day. This fraud allegedly cost Nigeria $6.8 billion over three years (Reuters 2012).

Public knowledge of the scandal emerged at the beginning of 2012, when the then president, Goodluck Jonathan, removed the subsidy on PMS on 1 January 2012, increasing the price of gasoline from NGN65 to NGN140 per litre and sparking mass riots and social upheaval. The reason given by the president for the removal of the subsidy was that Nigeria could no longer afford the increasing amounts for the payment of the subsidy.

As a result, the House of Representatives set up an ad hoc committee to "verify and determine the actual subsidy requirements and monitor the implementation of the subsidy regime in Nigeria" (House of Representatives 2012). The committee decided to investigate the gasoline subsidy regime between 2009 and 2011, and its report revealed mass-scale fraud and corruption in relation to the gasoline subsidy regime in Nigeria. The report found that the "subsidy regime, as operated between the period under review (2009 and 2011), were fraught with endemic corruption and entrenched inefficiency. Much of the amount claimed to have been paid as subsidy was actually not for consumed PMS" (House of Representatives 2012, 5).

In addition, whilst the official figure given by NNPC, the state-owned oil corporation, for the subsidy payments up to 31 December 2011 as NGN1.3 trillion, the committee found that the true amount was NGN2.5 trillion, and this was possible because the NNPC was able to withdraw sums directly from the Excess Crude Account, without such sums being appropriated in the budget (House of Representatives 2012, 6). Other problems were that the PPPRA often recovers excess subsidy payments from marketers, but these recovered amounts could not be found in the official accounts for the agency. In 2009, "NGN5.27Billion was established as over recovery in 2009 however, there was no evidence that this money was credited to the PSF Account" (House of Representatives 2012, 11).

In facilitating the fraudulent payments, the Accountant General of the Federation was found to have authorized payments of equal instalments of NGN999 million for a record 128 times within 24 hours on the 12th and 13th of January 2009, totaling NGN127.872 billion (House of Representatives 2012, 7). Furthermore, the beneficiaries of these payments could not be identified by the committee (House of Representatives 2012, 7).

The committee recommended the prosecution of the parties identified to have been involved in this scam and also "recommended the refund to the treasury the sum of N1,067,040,456,171.31" (House of Representatives 2012, 12).

The investigation of the fuel subsidy scam set in motion a number of events. In the first place, in June 2012, the sadly ironic news broke that the head of the ad hoc committee that investigated this scam, Farouk Lawan, requested bribes to the tune of $3 million dollars from Femi Otedola, the head of Zenon Oil, a company that was implicated in the ad hoc committee's report (Premium Times 2012). It is said that the bribe was to have Zenon Oil redacted from the report. In response, Femi Otedola apparently reported to the security forces and the first tranche of the bribe given to Farouk Lawan was marked US dollar bills worth $620,000.00 ($500,000 went to Lawan and $120,000 to Boniface Emenalo, the secretary to the ad hoc committee). After the news of the bribery scandal broke, Femi Otedola's companies were relisted in the report (Premium Times 2014). Farouk Lawan and Boniface Emenalo were charged to court in February 2013 (BBC 2013), but their case is yet to be concluded.

The second consequence of the fuel subsidy scam was that several individuals and companies were charged to court. For instance, in the most high profile

128 *Sope Williams-Elegbe*

of the cases, Ontario Oil and Gas is charged with receiving unearned subsidy payments to the tune of NGN1.9 billion (EFCC Press Release 2014a); Axenergy Limited is charged with fraud of NGN2.6 billion in unearned subsidy (EFCC Press Release 2014b); Yanaty Nigeria Limited was also charged with fraud to the tune of NGN1.8 billion. The company claimed subsidy payments for importation of 42.7 million litres of PMS, whilst the records showed it only imported 13.9 million litres. These cases are all ongoing (EFCC Press Release 2017k).

3   Central Bank of Nigeria and the "missing" $20 billion: 2013–2017

In September 2013, Nigeria received the shocking news that the then governor of the Central Bank, Lamido Sanusi II, had alleged that that $49 billion had not been remitted from the state petroleum company, NNPC, to the Central Bank. In a swift response, the governor was suspended in February 2014 for "financial recklessness and misconduct" (Aljazeera America 2014) and later retired by the then president Goodluck Jonathan (Forbes 2016). NNPC countered that it used about $10 billion for petroleum subsidy payments and only failed to remit $6 billion. In 2014, Sanusi testified before the Senate Finance Committee that $20 billion was still unaccounted for by the NNPC.

In response to the allegations, a Reconciliation Committee was set up comprising representatives of the Central Bank, the NNPC, the Ministry of Finance, the Ministry of Petroleum Resources, the Budget Office and the Auditor-General's Office (Auditor-General for the Federation 2015, 9–10). This committee estimated the unremitted funds to be $10.8 billion, whilst the CBN maintained it was $12 billion.

In June 2014, the Auditor General of the Federation hired PricewaterhouseCoopers "to investigate any and all crude oil revenues generated by the Nigerian National Petroleum Corporation ('NNPC') that was withheld or unremitted to the Federation Accounts between 1 January 2012 and 31 July 2013" (Auditor-General for the Federation 2015, 8).

This report highlighted that $69.34 billion was received as revenue during the period under consideration and $50.81 billion was remitted to the Federation Account, leaving a shortfall of $18.53 billion, and that of this sum, $2.81 billion was incurred as operational costs by NNPC and $3.38 billion was incurred as subsidy payment on kerosene products, although there was no appropriation for this in the budget, as in October 2009, the then president, Musa Yaradua had issued a directive to discontinue the payments of kerosene subsidy.

According to the report

> the accounting and reconciliation system for crude oil revenues used by Government agencies appear to be inaccurate and weak. We noted significant discrepancies in data from different sources. The lack of independent audit and reconciliation led to over reliance on data produced from NNPC. This matter is further compounded by the lack of independence within NNPC as

the business has conflicting interests of being a stand-alone self-funding entity and also the main source of revenue to the Federation account.

(Auditor General for the Federation, 18)

Unfortunately, the unreliable nature of the data relied on by PwC adversely affects the veracity of the report as PwC could not independently confirm the documents presented. Despite this however, the fact remains that there has been a misappropriation and misapplication of billions of dollars and that the true scale of this fraud may never be uncovered.

4 Dan Etete, Malabu Oil & Gas, Shell Oil and ENI: 2011–present

In what must arguably be one of the biggest bribery scandals in the world (Global Witness 2017a), a former Nigerian minister of petroleum, Dan Etete, a former minister of justice, Mohammed Bello Adoke, and three international oil companies, Shell, ENI and Nigeria Agip Exploration (owned by ENI), apparently defrauded Nigeria of $1.2 billion in a scandal that has seen prosecutions take place in Italy, the Netherlands and Nigeria (Faull et al. 2017).

This scandal has a long and complicated history over the most lucrative oil field in Nigeria and arguably West Africa (Global Witness 2017a).[7] It is claimed that the oil field, known as Block 245, (over which an oil mining licence [OML] had been issued, making it OML 245), was wrongly and in breach of due process allocated to an oil company known as Malabu Oil & Gas, which was owned by Nigeria's former minister of petroleum, Dan Etete, who was in office between 1995 and 1998.

According to the scandal chronology, in April 1998, Etete, as the minister of petroleum awarded a license to work this oil field to his company, Malabu Oil & Gas, a company that had no assets or employees (Sotubo 2017). The directors of the company were Mohammed Sani Abacha (the son of the then president General Sani Abacha), Dan Etete (using the pseudonym Kweku Amafagha) and Hassan Hindu (allegedly the wife of a former High Commissioner to the UK). The license fee was a paltry $20 million, of which only $2 million was paid (Global Witness 2017a).

In 2000, Shell Ultra Deep (a Shell subsidiary formed for this purpose) bought a 40% stake in the oil field from Malabu, and soon after Shell bought its stake in the oil field; in July 2001, the license given to Malabu was revoked by the Nigerian government, then led by Olusegun Obasanjo. At the time, Shell Ultra Deep and Malabu challenged the revocation in court.

However, in an odd turn of events, Shell Nigeria and Exxon Mobil were invited to bid for an oil prospecting license (OPL) over Block 245, after which the highest bidder would obtain the OPL. After the bidding process in May 2002, OPL 245 was awarded to Shell Nigeria as the successful bidder, and in December 2003 Shell Nigeria entered into a production-sharing contract with NNPC (the state-owned oil company and the lease holder of Block 245).

Following the conclusion of the challenge by Malabu of its earlier revocation in the Nigerian Supreme Court, a settlement judgement was entered into between

130 *Sope Williams-Elegbe*

Malabu and the government, which saw the government re-awarding OML 245 to Malabu in 2006, thereby vitiating the production sharing agreement between NNPC and Shell Nigeria.

As a result, in 2007, Shell Nigeria (through Shell Ultra Deep) took the Nigerian government to international arbitration under the Netherlands-Nigeria Bilateral Investment Treaty (BIT), claiming that the Netherlands-Nigeria BIT had been breached and that NNPC should be declared the valid leaseholder of Block 245 and that Shell Nigeria should be allowed to fulfil the production-sharing contract with NNPC (*Shell Nigeria Ultra Deep Limited v Federal Republic of Nigeria* 2007).

In 2011, whilst the arbitration was on-going, the parties decided to the withdrawal of the arbitration and the conclusion of a resolution agreement with all the interested parties. We know now that this was a part of the grand bribery scheme (Global Witness 2017a). In the resolution agreement, the arbitration was discontinued, and it was agreed between the parties that the government would pay Malabu off for it to waive its rights in OML 245 so that the government could re-allocate the field. Shell Nigeria would reimburse Shell Ultra Deep to the tune of $335 million and the government would reallocate Block 245 to Shell Nigeria and Nigeria Agip Exploration (wholly owned by ENI) (LeVine 2012).[8]

The resolution agreement contained several bizarre and incomprehensible provisions, which with the benefit of hindsight were clearly included in furtherance of the corrupt scheme. For instance, it was agreed that the money paid by Shell and ENI for Block 245 would be given to Malabu to waive all its rights in the Block, and Malabu would settle any outstanding claims by Shell Ultra Deep from that amount (*International Legal Consulting v Malabu Oil and Gas Ltd* 2012). It also stated that the signature bonus due to the government from Shell Nigeria and Nigeria Agip would be given to Malabu, but this sum could be deducted as recoverable costs by Shell and NAE. The government waived its right to acquire any interest in the Block, except the payment of taxes and royalties, and then gave Shell Nigeria and Agip a "full and unconditional exemption" from the payment of any taxes under the resolution agreement (Obaje 2011).

In April 2011, the then Director of Petroleum Resources in the Ministry of Petroleum Resources, Andrew Obaje, wrote a letter to the Attorney-General of the Federation (Obaje 2011), advising him against the resolution agreement and advising that the arbitration should not be discontinued as the outcome would be in Nigeria's favour, given than Shell Ultra Deep was simply requesting that the arbitral tribunal to declare NNPC as the rightful leaseholder of OML 245.

In the letter, Obaje stated that the resolution agreement was "highly prejudicial to the interests of the government" for several reasons, including the fact that Malabu had never paid the initial signature bonus of $210 million, which was part of the settlement judgment it entered into with the government, and the government paying Malabu to relinquish its rights in OML 245 would be paying Malabu for an asset it did not yet legally own. Also, Obaje highlighted that the grant of Block 245 to Shell Nigeria and Nigeria Agip was not done in a transparent way, and Nigeria Agip was hitherto not a party to any of the prior transactions, and also that the agreement also excluded the government from any rights in the Block for the duration of the OPL

Big, bigger, biggest 131

(10 years) and the OML derived afterwards (20 years) and the government "would be throwing away an enormous amount of financial resources" (Obaje 2011).

Despite these reservations, the resolution agreement went ahead in May 2011 (*International Legal Consulting v Malabu Oil and Gas Ltd* 2012), and it was agreed that $1.1 billion would be paid by Shell ($110 million) and Nigeria Agip ($980 million) to a Nigerian government escrow account with JP Morgan Chase for OPL 245. Shell also paid the signature bonus of $207 million to the Nigerian government. It was also agreed that the $1.1 billion paid by Shell and ENI (on behalf of Nigeria Agip) would go to Etete, through his company, Malabu.[9] The idea being that Etete would be responsible for ensuring the distribution of the money to the government officials concerned, including President Goodluck Jonathan, who oversaw and approved this deal (Global Witness 2017a). Of the $1.1 billion paid, $800 million was transferred to two accounts controlled by Malabu, and $520 million of this was paid to AA Oil, owned by Nigerian businessman Aliyu Abubakar, (also said to be a close friend of the then Attorney General, Mohammed Adoke Bello) and later converted to cash to be given to the relevant public officials. The balance of $280 million was spent by Etete (Global Witness 2017a).

In 2011, the bribery scam came to light when Adnan Edgaev, Etete's Russian lawyer, sued Etete for $65.5 commission in a New York court, and some of the money was frozen in this regard (*International Legal Consulting v Malabu Oil and Gas Ltd* 2012. In 2014, the Nigerian House of Representatives voted to cancel the deal, and in 2016 the offices of Shell in the UK were raided by investigators and prosecution against Shell and ENI commenced in Italy (Global Witness 2017b).

In January 2017, the Federal High Court ordered the interim forfeiture of Block 245 to the government (Financial Times 2017; EFCC Press Release 2017i). In 2017, Shell confessed that it knew that Etete was involved in the transaction (Global Witness 2017b). The Nigerian courts have charged Shell, Eni, Dan Etete, Aliyu Abubakar and Mohammed Adoke Bello with money laundering and corruption offences (EFCC Press Release 2017a), although the cases have been stalled as Etete and Adoke are out of the country and have not been extradited.

5   *Deziani Madueke, Kola Aluko and Jide Omokore, the high life at Nigeria's expense: 2015–present*

In 2015, the world woke up to the news of yet another scandal in the oil industry in Nigeria. The central characters were the immediate past minister of petroleum, Deziani Allison-Madueke, as well as two prominent Nigerian businessmen, Kola Aluko and Jide Omokore. Madueke was the minister of petroleum resources from 2010–2015, appointed by Goodluck Jonathan, former president of Nigeria.

The known chronology of this scandal is that sometime in 2010 (Sahara Reporters, 2015), Kola Aluko, together with Jide Omokore, formed two oil companies known as Atlantic Energy Drilling Concepts Nigeria Ltd, and Atlantic Energy Brass Development Ltd. It is now known that these were shell companies formed for the purpose of a corruption scheme. It is alleged that in return for payments in cash and in the form of millions of dollars worth of real estate in London and

132   *Sope Williams-Elegbe*

Lagos, as well as luxury furniture and art work, Madueke abused her position as minister to award strategic alliance agreements (SAAs) to Aluko and Omokre's companies between 2011 and 2013 (Sahara Reporters, 2015).

By way of background information, it may be noted that in 2010, President Jonathan signed the Nigerian Oil and Gas Industry Content Development Act (known as the Local Content Act) into law, aimed at increasing the participation of local oil and gas firms in the oil industry, which was hitherto dominated by foreign companies. Under the act, local companies are to be awarded "first consideration" in the award of oil and gas contracts and be given exclusive consideration for oil and gas service contracts. There was thus a legal requirement for NNPC to engage with domestic companies, and the Local Content Act set the scene for the award of lucrative contracts to Aluko and Omokore's companies.

Under the SAAs, which were a venture between the exploration arm of the NNPC, the Nigerian Petroleum Development Company (NPDC), and the Atlantic companies, the Atlantic companies were required to finance the exploration and production operations of eight on-shore oil and gas blocks (African Press Organisation 2013). In return for financing these operations, the companies expected to receive a portion of the oil and gas produced. However, as part of the corruption scheme, the companies provided only a fraction of the agreed upon financing or, in some instances, failed entirely to provide it, leaving a situation where the NPDC financed the operations under the SAAs. The Atlantic companies also failed to meet other obligations under the SAAs, including the payment of the "entrance" fee, which was set in respect of OML 30 (the largest of the oil blocks at $50 million) (The Senate, Federal Republic of Nigeria Notice Paper 2013).[10] Nevertheless, according to the allegations, the companies were permitted to lift and sell more than $1.5 billion worth of Nigerian crude oil. The money that was due to the Nigerian government was used instead to bribe public officials, contributed to a slush fund for electioneering in 2015, and funded a lavish lifestyle for Madueke, Aluko and Omokore. Despite the non-payment of amounts due under the SAA, the Atlantic companies had taken loans which were outstanding with two Nigerian banks (Sahara Reporters, 2015).

The corruption scandal came to the fore in 2015, after Jonathan lost the presidential elections. In May 2015, NPDC wrote to Atlantic Energy (just days before President Buhari was sworn in as president) requesting the payment of just over $1.8 billion that was due to it under the SAA. This letter revealed the sham that was the SAA with the Atlantic companies and alerted the Nigerian society that there had been irregular transactions with the Atlantic companies.

In October 2015, Madueke was arrested in London by the UK National Crime Agency, but no charges were brought against her (BBC 2015), although a court order was obtained to seize GBP27,000 from her (Reuters 2015).

In 2016, the Nigerian government took Madueke, Aluko, Omokore and several public officials to court to recover their assets for the money owed (EFCC Press Release 2016). Thus, in January 2016, the Federal High Court in Lagos, ordered the forfeiture of NGN32.4 billion and $5 million, which were sums that were siphoned by Madueke from the state oil corporation, during her tenure as minster (EFCC Press Release 2017f).

Big, bigger, biggest 133

It is alleged that of these monies, NGN23 billion (initially $115 million and later converted to Nigerian naira) was a slush fund created by Madueke to be used in bribing officials of the Independent Electoral Commission (INEC) to ensure that President Goodluck won the 2015 general elections (EFCC Press Release 2017h; EFCC Press Release 2017l). She also forfeited a properties in Nigeria valued at $58.8 million and various sums found in accounts linked to her (EFCC Press Release 2017b; EFCC Press Release 2017c; EFCC Press Release 2017e).[11] Similarly, Omokore was charged with fraud to the tune of $1.6 billion in the Federal High Court in Abuja (EFCC Press Release 2017a).

In July 2017, the US Department of Justice (DOJ) initiated civil proceedings for the forfeiture and recovery of $144 million dollars in assets that were the proceeds of corruption in Nigeria and were laundered through the United States. According to the DOJ (US Department of Justice Press Release 2017):

> from 2011 to 2015, Nigerian businessmen Kolawole Akanni Aluko and Olajide Omokore conspired with others to pay bribes to Nigeria's former Minister for Petroleum Resources, Diezani Alison-Madueke, who oversaw Nigeria's state-owned oil company. In return for these improper benefits, Alison-Madueke used her influence to steer lucrative oil contracts to companies owned by Aluko and Omokore. The complaint alleges that the proceeds of those illicitly awarded contracts were then laundered in and through the U.S. and used to purchase various assets subject to seizure and forfeiture, including a $50 million condominium located in one of Manhattan's most expensive buildings – 157 W. 57th Street – and the *Galactica Star*, an $80 million yacht.

It is clear that others were involved in this scheme, although no others have been indicted as a result. However, in an unrelated but highly coincidental incident, on 3 February 2017, the sum of $9.7 million and GBP74,000.00 was recovered in cash from the home of the former General Managing Director (GMD) of the NNPC, Mr. Andrew Yakubu, who was GMD between 2012 and 2014, when these SAAs were signed. He later claimed this money was a gift to him from unnamed persons (Sahara Reporters 2017a). He was indicted on money laundering charges in March 2017 and his case is still ongoing (EFCC Press Release 2017j; The Guardian 2017). In addition, several members of the Nigerian bar as well as staff of Nigeria's electoral body were implicated in the bribery scandal that attended Madueke's attempts to secure Jonathan Goodluck's victory in the 2015 general elections in Nigeria (EFCC Press Release 2017h).

This corruption scandal is far from over, as none of the criminal prosecutions in Nigeria have been completed and Madueke and Aluko have not been formally charged in any jurisdiction.

6 $25 billion NNPC contracts?: 2017

Just as this chapter was being concluded, a new scandal erupted in the Nigerian media, relating to the authorization of oil contracts without due approvals. It is not

134 *Sope Williams-Elegbe*

clear at the time of writing whether there is any corruption involved, or whether this is a case of maladministration, or is merely based on political differences and power plays between the parties concerned, as the events are still unfolding and the facts available are still sketchy. Nevertheless, this latest scandal will be examined.

On 3 October 2017, Nigerian media was awash with the news that the Minister of State for Petroleum,[12] Dr. Ibe Kachikwu, had alleged that the current GMD of NNPC, Dr. Maikanti Baru, had awarded oil and oil-related contracts worth $25 billion without recourse to him as the minister and without following due process (Vanguard Newspapers 2017b). The allegations were contained in a letter to the president, dated 30 August 2017, which was leaked to the press by unknown persons.[13]

In the letter, Kachikwu made three different complaints. First, Kachikwu alleged that the GMD had unilaterally awarded

> $10 billion crude term contracts; $5 billion direct sales direct purchase (DSDP) contracts and $3 billion AKK pipeline contract. He also said $3 billion was awarded as a contract for various financing allocation funding contracts and another $3–4 billion NPDC production service contracts.
>
> (Premium Times 2017c)

The allegation being that these contracts were awarded without recourse to the minister and the board of the NNPC. There had earlier been controversy over the AKK contract (the Ajaokuta-Kaduna-Kano gas pipeline) contract awarded to a Chinese company in 2017 (Daily Trust 2017), and over the oil lifting contracts to Duke Oil Limited (a company incorporated in Panama), which has obtained several contracts from NNPC, despite being ill-equipped to handle the contracts and sub-contracting to a third party (Senate of the Federal Republic of Nigeria 2017; Premium Times 2017a). However, Duke Oil is a wholly owned subsidiary of the NNPC,[14] and is by extension owned by the government of Nigeria. It was apparently "established to serve as a vehicle for bringing NNPC directly in contact with the international oil market for strong internal competence and value adding to its oil and gas business" (NNPC 2012).

The other complaint made by Kachikwu in the letter pertained to insubordination and disrespectful conduct by Baru towards Kachikwu. Finally the letter addressed the internal reorganization of the NNPC that was undertaken by Baru without recourse to the ministry or the board of NNPC and requested that the president intervene "to save the NNPC and oil industry from collapse".[15]

In a response to the allegation, the NNPC stated that there was no impropriety in relation to the award of contracts and there is no requirement for the NNPC to consult with the minister or the board on contractual matters, and what is required is

> the processing and approval of contracts by the NNPC Tenders Board, the President in his executive capacity or as Minister of Petroleum, or the Federal Executive Council (FEC), as the case may be . . . There are therefore situations where all that is required is the approval of the NNPC Tenders Board

Big, bigger, biggest   135

while, in other cases, based on the threshold, the award must be submitted for presidential approval. Likewise, in some instances, it is FEC approval that is required.

(Point Blank News 2017)

The NNPC also refuted the allegations that Kachikwu had not been consulted with regard to the crude oil term contracts (Point Blank News 2017).

In response to the allegations, on 12 October 2017, the vice-president, Yemi Osinbajo, asserted that in July 2017, in his capacity as acting president, he gave approval to the NNPC for two contracts worth NGN640 billion ($1.8 billion) (Premium Times 2017b).

As of 12 October 2017, the president had yet to comment on the allegations and the story was still unfolding; however, what is clear is that despite Buhari's anti-corruption agenda, all is still not well at the NNPC and the Ministry of Petroleum Resources, and that does not bode well for Nigerians. Nigerians will have to wait for the outcome of the ad hoc committee established to investigate the allegations and a statement from the presidency on the matter.

Anti-corruption approaches and successes under the Buhari administration: 2015–present

President Buhari was elected on an anti-corruption platform, and it was expected that his personal frugality, historical intolerance of corruption, no-nonsense style and distaste for the establishment was exactly what was needed to turn Nigeria around.

Although the jury is still out on the success of his anti-corruption campaign, there has been severe criticism of the lack of a coherent or coordinated approach and the resulting slow pace of reform and the lack of momentum, especially the lack of criminal convictions (Obaze 2017, 347), after more than two years in office. However, there are a number of institutional and organizational changes that Buhari established after his inauguration in May 2015 which have assisted corruption enforcement in Nigeria.

Perhaps the most significant achievement in relation to anti-corruption was that Buhari's administration was able to block the financial loopholes that had been used by public sector officials to misappropriate public funds. For the first time, the government required all public entities to put public money in what is known as a Treasury Single Account (TSA). The TSA is not peculiar to Nigeria, and it is used by many countries to consolidate all public sector inflows into a single account (Pattanayak and Fainboim 2010), in this case, in the Central Bank of Nigeria (CBN). As defined by the CBN, the TSA is "the operation of a unified structure of Government Bank Accounts, in a single account or a set of linked accounts for ALL Government payments and receipts" (CBN 2016). The idea of the TSA was to "eliminate the fragmented systems for handling government receipts and payments . . . and provide a unified view and centralized control over government's cash resources" (Pattanayak and Fainboim 2010, 4).

136   *Sope Williams-Elegbe*

The TSA was first introduced in 2012 as a pilot test by the Jonathan administration (Oyedokun 2016, 5) but it was not fully implemented by all public agencies. However, on 9th of August 2015, Buhari gave an order that all public entities must transfer their funds to the TSA by the 15th of September 2015, or face sanctions (Premium Times 2015). This order applied to all public agencies and was fully complied with, and by the first quarter of 2016 the government had received an inflow of over NGN3 trillion into the CBN (Vanguard Newspapers 2016b), which had hitherto been deposited into commercial banks. Prior to the implementation of the TSA, it was the norm for public officials to put public funds in commercial banks and obtain the interest for their personal account and in other cases they would misappropriate the money for their own use, with the complicity of bank officials (Oyedokun 2016).

The TSA has thus blocked a loophole that enabled public officials to treat public funds as if they were personal funds. There were however several challenges to the implementation of the TSA by several politicians, with allegations that the money collected by the CBN was used to sponsor elections by the ruling party, the All Progressives Congress (The Pulse 2016).

The second major achievement of the Buhari administration was the institution of a whistleblower programme, and the creation of a Whistleblower Unit within the Ministry of Finance. There have been earlier unsuccessful attempts to pass whistleblower protection legislation in Nigeria. The first attempt at passing legislation in 2008 (Whistleblower Protection Bill SB233 2008) was eventually abandoned, and the most recent attempt in 2017 (Whistleblower Protection Bill 2017) has also not yet been passed into law. In response to the delays in passing the Whistleblower Bill into law, the government, in December 2016, through the Federal Ministry of Finance, announced a whistleblower policy (The Punch 2016).

According to the government, "the Federal Ministry of Finance (FMF) whistleblowing programme is designed to encourage anyone with information about a violation of financial regulations, mismanagement of public funds and assets, financial malpractice, fraud and theft to report it" (Federal Ministry of Finance).

The main thrust of the policy was to provide reporting channels for corrupt acts and to offer a reward of between 2.5% and 5% of recovered funds if the reports led to the recovery of government funds (Quartz 2016). There was also a provision that whistleblowers would be protected if they were adversely treated as a result of reports made. It must be noted of course that the policy falls short of legal protection, and is in any event a stop-gap measure until the current Whistleblower Protection Bill becomes law.

In terms of the success of the whistleblower programme, it was reported that by June 2017 the Nigerian government had recovered about NGN11.6 billion ($32.3 million) in stolen funds and paid whistleblowers rewards to the tune of NGN375.8 million ($1.04 million) (Sahara Reporters 2017b). Although there have not been any convictions, it is still early days, and the recovery of looted public funds is still a step in the right direction.

The third most significant action taken by the Buhari administration is the creation of a system for prioritizing corruption trials. One of the complaints against his administration's anti-corruption campaign is the dearth of convictions. There are many reasons for this, but the slow pace of judicial activity is one of the factors that affects the speedy conclusion of corruption trials. To this end, in September 2017, the Chief Justice of Nigeria, Justice Walter Onnoghen, ordered all the heads of courts to compile a list of all corruption and financial crime cases within their remit and to further designate one court as a special court for hearing corruption cases, in order to reduce the "inexplicable and seemingly intractable delays" in the prosecution of such cases. He also stated that an Anti-Corruption Cases Trial Monitoring Committee would be constituted to monitor the progress of high-profile corruption cases (Vanguard Newspapers 2017a).

This is certainly a welcome development, and if properly implemented may have the potential for changing the time it takes to prosecute corruption cases and the low conviction rate.

Another significant achievement in relation to anti-corruption is that Nigeria joined the Open Government Partnership (OGP) in July 2016, as the 70th member.[16] Nigeria also submitted its National Action Plan for 2017–2019, which is focused on fiscal transparency, anti-corruption, access to information and citizen engagement.[17] The OGP is an international platform, formed in 2011 to assist domestic reformers in making their governments more open, accountable and responsive to citizens.[18]

Whilst there have been other successes recorded, such as the prosecution of highly placed Nigerians and his support to the anti-corruption agencies, these four mentioned above are institutional reforms that have the potential to affect public sector organization and management in Nigeria.

Conclusion

This chapter has attempted to examine the high-profile grand corruption cases that occurred in Nigeria's oil sector between 2007 and 2017. It can be seen that grand corruption in the oil sector has robbed the Nigerian people of billions of dollars in the last decade and is one reason why Nigeria remains an under-developed country with a poverty rate of 62.2% in 2016 (UNDP 2015).

There is a mutually reinforcing relationship between poverty, corruption and politics in Nigeria, and for the grand corrupt, state resources are the only way in which they can retain the political power necessary to remain wealthy and powerful (Human Rights Watch 2007). Oil resources are the single largest source of public wealth in Nigeria, and unless there are changes in the structure and nature of Nigeria's political organization and system, it is always going to be the case that Nigeria's oil wealth will be plundered by Nigeria's elite.

The scandals examined in this chapter show that despite Buhari's best efforts, Nigeria still has a long way to go before the oil sector is free of corruption scandals.

138 *Sope Williams-Elegbe*

Notes

1 See EIA, "Total Petroleum and Other Liquids Production 2016". Available at https://www.eia.gov/beta/international/index.cfm?view=production. Accessed 2 March 2018
2 The *annual* minimum wage in Nigeria as of October 2017 is the equivalent of $600 per annum. One hundred times this is only $60,000.
3 For instance, in the Dan Etete and Malabu Oil case discussed further below, it has been said that Dan Etete used to be ex-president Jonathan Goodluck's employer.
4 Through a state-owned enterprise known as the Petroleum Products Pricing Regulatory Authority (PPPRA).
5 The PPPRA's mandate is to determine the price for petroleum products and regulate the supply and distribution of these products in Nigeria. See http://pppra.gov.ng/mandate/
6 In the Auditor General's report, it was stated that "By selling DPK to marketers at N40.90 and claiming subsidy at an Ex-depot price of N34.51 without adjusting the Landing Costs for the extra costs borne by the marketers, NNPC had over deducted subsidies to an estimated amount of N31,522,234,881.06 ($204 million)."
7 It is asserted that the oil field contains 9 billion barrels of crude oil and is the most valuable oil field in West Africa.
8 Nigeria Agip appeared on the scene after Etete hired a Russian lawyer in 2009, Ednan Agaev, to act for him on the deal, given that he had been convicted in 2007. Agaev found ENI as a willing participant in this oil deal. Other international oil companies wanted nothing to do with Etete.
9 This was done, despite the fact that Etete had been convicted in 2007 in France, in absentia, for laundering $10 million, and was a convicted felon at the time. However, Etete/Malabu worked through Ednan Agaev, a Russian lawyer, who acted as his agent.
10 In 2013, the Nigerian Senate queried the "shady transactions" between Atlantic Energy and NPDC.
11 For a list of all Madueke's known assets in Nigeria, see EFCC, "Diezani Madueke: What an Appetite," 9 August 2017. Available at https://efccnigeria.org/efcc/news/2706-diezani-alison-madueke-what-an-appetite
12 As part of his plans to eradicate corruption in the oil sector, President Muhammadu Buhari appointed himself the minister of petroleum resources. Dr Kachikwu is the operational head of the ministry, but his designation is Minister of State, a junior ministerial post. He is also the Chairman of the Board of the NNPC.
13 The full text of the letter is available at http://dailypost.ng/2017/10/03/kachikwu-reacts-leaked-memo-buhari-nnpc-boss-baru/
14 See http://nnpcgroup.com/NNPCBusiness/Subsidiaries/DukeOil.aspx
15 See full text at http://dailypost.ng/2017/10/03/kachikwu-reacts-leaked-memo-buhari-nnpc-boss-baru/
16 See "Open Government Partnership, Nigeria." Available at www.opengovpartnership.org/countries/nigeria
17 See "Nigeria: National Action Plans 2017–2019." Available at www.opengovpartnership.org/documents/nigeria-national-action-plan-2017-2019
18 See www.opengovpartnership.org

References and further reading

African Press Organisation. (2013) *Atlantic Energy Co-CEO, Kola Aluko Predicts Indigenous Companies to Account for Over 30% of Oil and Gas Production in Nigeria within 5 Years*. [Online] Available from: https://appablog.wordpress.com/2013/12/09/atlantic-energy-co-ceo-kola-aluko-predicts-indigenous-companies-to-account-for-over-30-of-oil-and-gas-production-in-nigeria-within-5-years/ [Accessed 12th October 2017].

Big, bigger, biggest   139

Afrobarometer and Transparency International. (2015) *People and Corruption: Africa Survey 2015 – Global Corruption Barometer*. Berlin, Germany.

Aljazeera America. (2014) *Nigeria Fires Official Who Uncovered Billions in Missing Oil Money*. [Online] Available from: http://america.aljazeera.com/articles/2014/2/20/nigeria-fires-officialwhouncoveredbillionsinmissingoilmoney.html [Accessed 9th August 2017].

Auditor-General for the Federation. (2015) *Investigative Forensic Audit into the Allegations of Unremitted Funds into the Federation Accounts by the NNPC*. Pricewaterhouse Coopers, Lagos, Nigeria.

BBC. (2013) *Nigerian Farouk Lawan Charged Over $3m Fuel Scam Bribe*. [Online] Available from: www.bbc.com/news/world-africa-21294154 [Accessed 17th August 2017].

BBC. (2015) *Nigeria's Ex-oil Minister Arrested in London*. [Online] Available from: www.bbc.com/news/world-africa-34430597) [Accessed 5th October 2017].

BBC. (2016) *David Cameron Calls Nigeria and Afghanistan "Fantastically Corrupt"*. [Online] Available from: www.bbc.com/news/uk-politics-36260193 [Accessed 30th September 2017].

CBN. (2016) *Guidelines for the Operation of Treasury Single Account (TSA) by State Governments in Nigeria*. [Online] Available from: www.cbn.gov.ng/out/2016/bpsd/guidelines%20for%20the%20operations%20of%20tsa%20by%20state%20governments%20in%20nigeria.pdf [Accessed 12th October 2017].

Center for Public Policy Alternatives and International Institute for Sustainable Development. (2012) *A Citizens' Guide to Energy Subsidies in Nigeria*. International Institute for Sustainable Development, Manitoba, Canada.

Constitution of the Federal Republic of Nigeria, Act No. 24, 5 May 1999.

Daily Trust. (2017) *NNPC Awards Ajaokuta-Kaduna-Kano Gas Pipeline Contract to Chinese Company*. [Online] Available from: https://dailytrust.com.ng/news/business/nnpc-awards-ajaokuta-kaduna-kano-gas-pipeline-to-chinese-firm/196839.html [Accessed 12th October 2017].

Doig, A., & Theobald, R. (eds.). (2000) *Corruption and Democratisation*. London.

EFCC. (2017) *Diezani Madueke: What an Appetite*. [Online] Available from: https://efccnigeria.org/efcc/news/2706-diezani-alison-madueke-what-an-appetite [Accessed 5th October 2017].

EFCC Press Release. (2013) *Absence of Adoke, Etete Stalls OPL 245 Fraud Trial*. [Online] Available from: https://efccnigeria.org/efcc/news/2587-absence-of-adoke-etete-stalls-opl-245-fraud-trial [Accessed 30th September 2017].

EFCC Press Release. (2014a) *N1.9bn Subsidy Scam, Wagbatsama, Others Have Case to Answer-Court*. [Online] Available from: https://efccnigeria.org/efcc/news/1017-n1-9b-subsidy-scam-wagbatsama-others-have-case-to-answer-court-rules [Accessed 10th October 2017].

EFFC Press Release. (2014b) *N2.6bn Subsidy Scam: Court fines Abdulahi Alao for Counsel's Absence in Court*. [Online] Available from: https://efccnigeria.org/efcc/news/998-n2-6bn-subsidy-scam-court-fines-abdulahi-alao-for-counsel-s-absence-in-court [Accessed 10th October 2017].

EFCC Press Release. (2016) *EFCC Docks Omokore, Ex-NNPC Chiefs*. [Online] Available from: https://efccnigeria.org/efcc/news/2019-efcc-docks-omokore-ex-nnpc-chiefs [Accessed 5th October 2017].

EFCC Press Release. (2017a) *$1.6 Billion Fraud: Court Refuses to Quash Charges against Omokre and Others*. [Online] Available from: https://efccnigeria.org/efcc/news/2614-1-6bn-fraud-court-refuses-to-quash-charges-against-omokore-others [Accessed 5th October 2017].

140 *Sope Williams-Elegbe*

EFCC Press Release. (2017b) *Court Orders Final Forfeiture of Diezani's N7.6 Billion to FG*. Available from: https://efccnigeria.org/efcc/news/2720-court-orders-final-forfeiture-of-diezani-s-n7-6billion-to-fg [Accessed 6th October 2017].

EFCC Press Release. (2017c) *Court Orders Final Forfeiture of Diezani's $37.5 Million Banana Island Property*. [Online] Available from: https://efccnigeria.org/efcc/news/2703-court-orders-final-forfeiture-of-diezani-s-37-5m-banana-island-property [Accessed 6th October 2017].

EFCC Press Release. (2017d) *Court Orders Final Forfeiture of Diezani's 56 Houses*. [Online] Available from: https://efccnigeria.org/efcc/news/2810-court-orders-final-forfeiture-of-diezani-s-56-houses-2 [Accessed 6th October 2017].

EFCC Press Release. (2017e) *Court Orders Temporary Forfeiture of Another Set of $21.3 Million Diezani Properties*. [Online] Available from: https://efccnigeria.org/efcc/news/2716-court-orders-temporary-forfeiture-of-another-set-of-21-3m-diezani-properties [Accessed 6 October 2017].

EFCC Press Release. (2017f) *Diezani Alison Madueke Loses N34 Billion to FG*. [Online] Available from: https://efccnigeria.org/efcc/news/2329-diezani-alison-madueke-loses-n34-billion-to-fg [Accessed 6th October 2017].

EFCC Press Release. (2017g) *EFCC Arraigns Belgore, Ex-Minister for Money Laundering, February 2017*. [Online] Available from: https://efccnigeria.org/efcc/news/2304-efcc-arraigns-belgore-ex-minister-for-money-laundering [Accessed 5th October 2017].

EFCC Press Release. (2017h) *INEC Director Faces Prosecution for N16M Scam*. [Online] Available from: https://efccnigeria.org/efcc/news/2361-inec-director-faces-prosecution-for-n16m-scam [Accessed 4th October 2017].

EFCC Press Release. (2017i) *Malabu Oil: Court Defers Ruling to March 17*. [Online] Available from: https://efccnigeria.org/efcc/news/2388-malabu-oil-judge-defers-ruling-to-march-17 [Accessed 21st September 2017].

EFCC Press Release. (2017j) *Money Laundering: EFCC Arraigns Ex-NNPC GMD, Yakubu for $9.8m*. [Online] Available from: https://efccnigeria.org/efcc/news/2394-money-laundering-efcc-arraigns-ex-nnpc-gmd-yakubu-for-9-8m [Accessed 5th October 2017].

EFCC Press Release. (2017k) *N1.8bn Subsidy Fraud: S Court to Decide Yanaty's Appeal Dec 15*. [Online] Available from: https://efccnigeria.org/efcc/news/2801-n1-8bn-subsidy-fraud-s-court-to-decide-yanaty-s-appeal-dec-15 [Accessed 10th October 2017].

EFCC Press Release. (2017l) *N23bn Diezani Bribe: INEC Staff Plead Guilty, Two Others to Face Trial*. [Online] Available from: https://efccnigeria.org/efcc/news/2446-n23bn-diezani-bribe-inec-staff-plead-guilty-two-others-to-face-trial [Accessed 5th October 2017].

ENCA. (2016) *Nigeria Supreme Court Judge Charged with Corruption*. [Online] Available from: www.enca.com/africa/nigeria-supreme-court-judge-charged-with-corruption [Accessed 30th September 2017].

Enweremadu, D. U. (2012) Anti-Corruption Campaign in Nigeria (1999–2007): The Politics of a Failed Reform. In: *West African Politics and Society Series*, 1. African Studies Centre, Leiden.

Faull, L., Jeory, T., Mathiason, N. & Doward, J. (2017) The oil deal, the disgraced former minister and $800m paid via a UK Bank. *The Guardian*. [Online] Available from: www.theguardian.com/business/2017/mar/05/the-oil-deal-the-disgraced-minister-and-800m-paid-via-a-uk-bank [Accessed 6th October 2017].

Federal Ministry of Finance. (n.d.) *FMF-Whistleblowing Programme Frequently Asked Questions*. [Online] Available from: https://whistle.finance.gov.ng/_catalogs/masterpage/MOFWhistle/assets/FMF%20WHISTLEBLOWING%20FREQUENTLY%20ASKED%20QUESTIONS.pdf [Accessed 11th October 2017].

Big, bigger, biggest   141

Financial Times. (2017) *Shell and ENI to Temporarily Forfeit Nigerian Oil Prospect*. Available from: www.ft.com/content/fcd50330-e491-11e6-8405-9e5580d6e5fb?mhq5j=e5 [Accessed 21st September 2017].

Forbes. (2016) *The Pain of the Banker Who Investigated the Missing $20 Billion*. [Online] Available from: www.forbesafrica.com/my-worst-day/2016/07/01/pain-banker-investigated-missing-20-billion/ [Accessed 9th August 2017].

Global Witness. (2017a) *Shell Knew*. [Online] Available from: www.globalwitness.org/en/campaigns/oil-gas-and-mining/shell-knew/ [Accessed 3rd October 2017].

Global Witness. (2017b) *We Exposed What Shell Knew: Here's What Happened Next*. [Online] Available from: www.globalwitness.org/en/blog/we-exposed-what-shell-knew-heres-what-happened-next/ [Accessed 3rd October 2017].

The Guardian. (2017) *Court Grants Yakubu Leave to Travel to the UK for Medical Treatment*. [Online] Available from: https://guardian.ng/news/court-grants-yakubu-leave-to-travel-to-uk-for-medical-check-up/ [Accessed 2nd October 2017].

Hope, K. R., Sr. (2017) *Corruption and Governance in Africa: Swaziland, Kenya, Nigeria*. New York.

House of Representatives. *Report of the Ad-Hoc Committee: To Verify and Determine the Actual Subsidy Requirements and Monitor the Implementation of the Subsidy Regime in Nigeria*. Resolution No. (HR.1/2012), laid on Wednesday 18th April, 2012.

Human Rights Watch. (2007) *Criminal Politics: Violence, "Godfathers" and Corruption in Nigeria* 19, No. 16(A).

International Institute for Sustainable Development. (2016) *Compensation Mechanisms for Fuel Subsidy Removal in Nigeria*. International Institute for Sustainable Development, Manitoba, Canada.

International Legal Consulting v Malabu Oil and Gas Ltd. (2012) NY Slip Op 50546(U). Decided on 15 March 2012, Supreme Court, New York County.

Lambsdorff, J. G. (2006) Causes and Consequences of Corruption. In: Rose-Ackerman, S. (ed.) *International Handbook on the Economics of Corruption*. Cheltenham.

LeVine, S. (2012) *How to Do an Oil Deal in Nigeria: A Tale of Middlemen and Millions*. [Online] Available from: https://qz.com/27938/how-to-do-an-oil-deal-in-nigeria-a-tale-of-middlemen-and-millions/ [Accessed 3rd October 2017].

Marquette, H. & Peiffer, C. (2015) Collective action and systemic corruption. Paper presented at the ECPR Joint Sessions of Workshops, University of Warsaw. [Online] 29 March–2 April 2015. Available from: https://ecpr.eu/Filestore/PaperProposal/b5944a31-85b6-4547-82b3-0d4a74910b07.pdf

Nicholls, C. Q. C., Daniel, T., Bacarese, A. & Hatchard, J. (2011) *Corruption and Misuse of Public Office*, 2nd ed. Oxford.

NNPC. (2012) *Duke Oil*. [Online] Available from: http://nnpcgroup.com/NNPCBusiness/Subsidiaries/DukeOil.aspx [Accessed 6th October 2017].

Obaje, W. A. *Re: Resolution Agreement between FGN, Shell Nigeria Ultra Deep, Malabu Oil and Gas Limited, NNPC, Nigeria Agip Exploration and Production Company Nigeria Limited, SNEPCO, in Respect of OPL 245- NNPC's Directives*. [Online] 1st April 2011. Available from: www.globalwitness.org/en/campaigns/oil-gas-and-mining/shell-knew/

Obaze, O. H. (2017) *Prime Witness: Change and Policy Challenges in Buhari's Nigeria*. Ibadan.

Ohaeri, V. & Adeyinka, T. (2016) Policy brief: Kerosene subsidy reform and the burden of supply. *Gender and Energy Policy* 1, No. 1.

Okonjo-Iweala, N. (2012) *Reforming the Unreformable: Lessons from Nigeria*. Cambridge, MA.

142 Sope Williams-Elegbe

Open Government Partnership. (2016) *Nigeria*. [Online]. Available from: www.opengovpartnership.org/countries/nigeria [Accessed 12th October 2017].

Open Government Partnership. (2017) *Nigeria: National Action Plans 2017–2019*. [Online] Available from: www.opengovpartnership.org/documents/nigeria-national-action-plan-2017-2019 [Accessed 12th October 2017].

Oyedokun, G. E. (2016) Imperative of the Treasury Single Account (TSA) in Nigeria. *SSRN*. [Online] Available from: https://papers.ssrn.com/sol3/papers.cfm?abstract_id=2910315 [Accessed 12th October 2017].

Pattanayak, S. & Fainboim, I. (2010) *Treasury Single Account: Concept, Design and Implementation Issues*. IMF Working Paper WP/10/143. IMF Fiscal Affairs Department. Availbale from: https://www.imf.org/external/pubs/ft/wp/2010/wp10143.pdf

Persson, A., Rothstein, B. & Teorell, J. (2013) Why anticorruption reforms fail – systemic corruption as a collective action problem. *Governance* 26, 449.

Poeschl, G. & Ribeiro, R. (2016) Everyday Opinions on Grand and Petty Corruption: A Portuguese Study. In: Teixeira, A. A. C., Pimenta, C., Maia, A. & Moreira, J. A. (eds.) *Corruption, Economic Growth and Globalization*. Abingdon, UK.

Point Blank News. (2017) *$25 Billion Contract: You Are Wrong, NNPC Tells Kachikwu*. [Online] Available from: http://pointblanknews.com/pbn/exclusive/25billion-contract-wrong-nnpc-tells-kachiukwu/ [Accessed 12th October 2017].

Premium Times. (2012) *House of Reps Blasts Otedola as Farouk Lawan Says He Will Be Vindicated*. [Online] Available from: www.premiumtimesng.com/parliament-watch/5699-i_will_be_vindicated_farouk_lawan.html [Accessed 9th October 2017].

Premium Times. (2014) *Alleged $620,000 Bribe Farouk Lawan Didn't Act Alone Says Otedola*. [Online] Available from: www.premiumtimesng.com/news/5630-farouk_lawan_didn_t_act_alone.html [Accessed 12th October 2017].

Premium Times. (2015) *Buhari Orders Federal Ministries, Agencies to Open Treasury Single Account, 9th August 2015*. [Online] Available from: www.premiumtimesng.com/news/headlines/188074-%e2%80%8ebuhari-orders-federal-ministries-agencies-to-open-treasury-single-account.html [Accessed 9th October 2017].

Premium Times. (2017a) *Buhari Keeps Mum as N9trillion Scandal Rocks NNPC*. [Online] Available from: www.premiumtimesng.com/news/headlines/245094-buhari-keeps-mum-n9-trillion-contract-scandal-rocks-nnpc.html [Accessed 12th October 2017].

Premium Times. (2017b) *Osinbajo Admits Approving $640 Billion Oil Contracts for NNPC*. Available from: www.premiumtimesng.com/news/headlines/245881-osinbajo-admits-approving-n640-billion-oil-contracts-for-nnpc.html [Accessed 17th October 2017].

Premium Times. (2017c) Senate probes NNPC GMD. *Baru over Allegations of Corruption, Insubordination*. [Online] Available from: www.premiumtimesng.com/business/business-news/245024-senate-probes-nnpc-gmd-baru-allegations-corruption-insubordination.html [Accessed 17th October 2017].

Pulse. (2016) *Fayose- We won't Accept Your TSA Policy, Governor Tells Buhari*. [Online] Available from: www.pulse.ng/news/local/fayose-we-wont-accept-your-tsa-policy-governor-tells-buhari-id4708980.html [Accessed 13th October 2017].

Punch. (2016) *Nigeria's Whistle-Blower Policy*. Available from: http://punchng.com/nigerias-whistle-blower-policy/ [Accessed 13th October 2017].

Quartz. (2016) *Exposing Corruption is About to become a Lucrative Gig in Nigeria*. [Online] Available from: https://qz.com/870190/nigeria-wants-to-start-paying-people-who-report-corruption/ [Accessed 13th October 2017].

Reuters. (2012) *Factbox, Nigeria's $6.8 Billion Fuel Subsidy Scam*. [Online] Available from: www.reuters.com/article/us-nigeria-subsidy-graft/factbox-nigerias-6-8-billion-fuel-subsidy-scam-idUSBRE84C08N20120513 [Accessed 3rd October 2017].

Reuters. (2015) *UK Crime Agency Authorized to Seize Cash from Nigeria Ex-Oil Minister-Court*. [Online] Available from: http://uk.reuters.com/article/uk-britain-nigeria-arrests/uk-crime-agency-authorised-to-seize-cash-from-nigeria-ex-oil-minister-court-idUKKCN0RZ1XN20151005 [Accessed 3rd October 2017].

Rowley, C. K. & Schneider, F. (2004) *The Encyclopedia of Public Choice*. Dordrecht.

Sahara Reporters. (2015) *Between Diezani, Jide Omokore and Kola Aluko: Inside the Oil Deals That Cost Nigeria Billions*. [Online] Available from: http://saharareporters.com/2015/07/27/between-diezani-jide-omokore-and-kola-aluko-inside-oil-deals-cost-nigeria-billions [Accessed 3rd October 2017].

Sahara Reporters. (2016a) *Names of Nigerian Judges Under Investigation Revealed*. [Online] Available from: http://saharareporters.com/2016/10/16/names-nigerian-judges-under-investigation-revealed [Accessed 2nd October 2017]

Sahara Reporters. (2016b) *Nigerian Government Removes Kerosense Subsidy*. [Online] Available from: http://saharareporters.com/2016/01/25/nigerian-government-removes-kerosene-subsidy [Accessed 29th September 2017].

Sahara Reporters. (2017a) *How EFCC Recovered $9.8 Million from Ex-NNPC GMD Andrew Yakubu*. [Online] Available from: http://saharareporters.com/2017/02/10/how-efcc-recovered-98million-ex-nnpc-gmd-andrew-yakubu [Accessed 9th October 2017].

Sahara Reporters. (2017b) *Nigerian Government Pays Whistleblowers N375.8 Million*. Available from: http://saharareporters.com/2017/06/07/nigerian-govt-pays-20-whistleblowers-n3758million [Accessed 6th October 2017].

Schwindt-Bayer, L. A. & Tavits, M. (eds.). (2016) *Corruption, Accountability, and Clarity of Responsibility*. Cambridge.

Senate of the Federal Republic of Nigeria. (2013) *Notice Paper Tuesday, 24th September, 2013*. Abuja.

Senate of the Federal Republic of Nigeria. (2017) *Order Paper Wednesday, 4th October, 2017*. Abuja.

Shell Nigeria Ultra Deep Limited v. Federal Republic of Nigeria ICSID Case No. ARB/07/18. Available from: http://investmentpolicyhub.unctad.org/ISDS/Details/257

Sherk, D. R. (2005) The Cultural Dimensions of Corruption: Reflections on Nigeria. In: Johnston, M. (ed.) *Civil Society and Corruption: Mobilizing for Reform*. Lanham, MD.

Smith, D. J. (2009) The Paradoxes of Popular Participation in Corruption in Nigeria. In: Rotberg, R. I. (ed.) *Corruption, Global Security and World Order*.Washington, D.C.

Smith, D. J. (2015) The Contradictions of Corruption in Nigeria. In: Heywood, P. M. (ed.) *Routledge Handbook of Political Corruption*. Abingdon, UK.

Sotubo, J. (2017) Malabu Oil Scam: 12 Things you should know about the controversial deal. *Pulse News*. [Online] Available from: www.pulse.ng/news/local/malabu-oil-scam-12-things-you-should-know-about-controversial-deal-id6519987.html [Accessed 29th September 2017].

Transparency International. (2016) *What Is Grand Corruption and How Can We Stop It?* [Online] Available from: www.transparency.org/news/feature/what_is_grand_corruption_and_how_can_we_stop_it [Accessed 9th August 2017].

Transparency International. (2017) *Weaponising Transparency: Defence Procurement Reform as a Counterterrorism Strategy in Nigeria*. Berlin, Germany.

144 *Sope Williams-Elegbe*

United Nations Development Program. (2015) *National Human Development Report: Human Security and Human Development in Nigeria.* Nigeria.

United Nations Office on Drugs and Crime. (2017) *Corruption in Nigeria: Bribery – Public Experience and Response.* Vienna.

US Department of Justice Press Release. (2017) *Department of Justice Seeks to Recover over $100 Million Obtained from Corruption in the Nigerian Oil Industry.* [Online] Available from: www.justice.gov/opa/pr/department-justice-seeks-recover-over-100-million-obtained-corruption-nigerian-oil-industry [Accessed 9th October 2017].

US Energy Information Association. (2016) *Country Analysis Brief: Nigeria.* [Online] Available from: www.eia.gov/beta/international/analysis_includes/countries_long/Nigeria/nigeria.pdf [Accessed 29th September 2017].

Uslaner, E. (2015) The Consequences of Corruption. In: Heywood, P. M. (ed.) *Routledge Handbook of Political Corruption.* Routledge, Abingdon, UK.

Vanguard. (2011) *Kerosene to Gas: A Cleaner, Healthier Living.* [Online] Available from: www.vanguardngr.com/2011/11/kerosene-to-gas-a-cleaner-healthier-living/ [Accessed 2nd October 2017].

Vanguard. (2016a) *FG Spent $1bn on Kerosene Subsidy in 2015 – Osinbajo.* [Online] Available from: www.vanguardngr.com/2016/11/fg-spent-1bn-kerosene-subsidy-2015-osinbajo/ [Accessed 9th October 2017].

Vanguard. (2016b) *TSA- FG records N3 Trillion Inflow.* [Online] Available from: www.vanguardngr.com/2016/05/tsa-fg-records-n3trn-inflow-q1-agf/ [Accessed 10th October 2017].

Vanguard. (2017a) *Anti-Graft War: CJN Okays Special Courts, Judges to try Alleged Looters.* [Online] Available from: www.vanguardngr.com/2017/09/anti-graft-war-cjn-okays-special-courts-judges-try-alleged-looters/ [Accessed 9th October 2017].

Vanguard. (2017b) *NNPC Appointments Tear Kachikwu, Baru Apart.* [Online] Available from: www.vanguardngr.com/2017/10/nnpc-appointments-tear-kachikwu-baru-apart/ [Accessed 11th October 2017].

Whistle Blower Protection Bill [HB. 17.06.1073]. (2017) Nigerian House of Representatives. Available from: http://nass.gov.ng/document/download/8725

Whistle Blower Protection Bill [SB. 233]. (2008). Nigerian Senate. Available from: http://www.nass.gov.ng/document/download/904

8 A spoonful of laws doesn't help the bribery go down

Persistent contributing factors of corruption in the US pharmaceutical and medical device industry

Mikhail Reider-Gordon

In recent years, OIG and the Department of Justice (DOJ) have investigated cases involving industry physician financial relationships in both the pharmaceutical and medical device areas. In these cases, we have seen medical device manufacturers offering physicians lucrative consulting agreements to acquire new business and to maintain physician loyalty. We have also seen instances in which the physicians, in turn, have signaled to the industry that their loyalties and business are for sale to the highest bidder. In some cases, it comes down to how much each company is willing to pay for a physician's business, which is often being simultaneously solicited by multiple competing companies.

(Demske 2008, p. 4)

Introduction

The US has led in legislating and enforcing laws against corruption perpetrated abroad between private and public actors. The US Foreign Corrupt Practices Act of 1977 (as amended, 15 U.S.C. §§ 78dd-1, et.seq) places legal constraints on a broad swathe of business activities, not only upon US companies (FCPA, ss. 78dd-2) but also on those entities traded on US exchanges (FCPA, ss. 78dd-1), or with a nexus to or through the US (FCPA, ss. 78dd-3). This confers significant extra-territoriality to the act. However, violations of the act are enforced only when breaches occur abroad. Within the domestic medical–industrial complex, the story is different. The US domestic pharmaceutical industry in 2016 exceeded $333 billion in sales (Department of Commerce, International Trade Administration 2016). Globally, it is a multi-trillion-dollar sector (Pharmaceutical Online 2017). The US medical device market is the largest in the world, representing nearly 40% of the entire global market (Department of Commerce, International Trade Administration 2017), with a market size of approximately $150 billion. Collectively, the manufacturers of drugs, devices, biological, and medical supplies (hereinafter referred to as "MDBS" or "the Industry") are heavily regulated in the United States when it comes to safety, control of their respective supply chains, development of new products, and the testing of the said. Additionally, the US has a number of domestic laws (discussed in this chapter), partially designed to address

146　*Mikhail Reider-Gordon*

potential corruption and fraud in the Industry. This chapter identifies behaviors by MDBS in the US domestic market that closely mirror activities they engage in in other countries. In these foreign situations, US regulators have prosecuted these same Industry companies criminally and civilly. The chapter focuses on where US domestic laws have failed to curb corruption in the US industry, examining what has been tried and demonstrating its failure. With no irony, the current culture of corruption in the domestic Industry pervades the entire country's health system, whilst federal prosecutors year after year indict similar crimes of bribery abroad by the very same companies. Significant prohibitions that would seek to severely curtail what is presently an entire industry culture rife with corruption are proposed.

US laws

The FCPA prohibits the giving of "anything of value" to a foreign official in order to obtain or retain business. The mere promise of giving something of value that would induce said official to act in such a manner as for the company to gain any form of "business advantage" is sufficient to trigger a violation of the act. The act emphasizes the concept of *quid pro quo* and takes a very expansive view of "anything of value" (US Department of Justice and US Securities & Exchange Commission, A Resource Guide to the U.S. Foreign Corrupt Practices Act 2012). "Anything of value" includes not just cash and gifts, but amongst many other forms of value, hospitality, travel, education, charitable contributions, grants, discounts or reductions in fees, taxes, etc. Yet whilst these forms of inducements are recognized for the bribes that they are and forbidden in relationships between the private sector and government officials abroad, these very same mechanisms are categorized as "marketing" methods domestically and are still legal.

The US does have a number of domestic laws aimed at combating fraud and corruption in the healthcare industry. Some of these laws are aimed at MDBS and others intended for healthcare providers, "HCPs." Throughout this article, "HCP" refers only to physicians, and does not include other types of providers. US laws that address private domestic bribery include those that involve acts such as money laundering. The Sarbanes-Oxley Act of 2002 (15 U.S. Code § 7201) imposes certain requirements on companies that can trigger violations related to corrupt acts if underlying compliance is not met. The US Travel Act (18 U.S.C. § 1952 (1976))[1] contains provisions that address bribery in general (Travel Act, ss. (b)). Travel or use of "the mails"[2] in furtherance of violations of state commercial bribery laws can be used by the US Department of Justice for federal-level prosecutions. Larger US states have laws prohibiting commercial bribery[3] (i.e., bribery which does not involve government officials), but there is no federal statute that directly addresses bribery and corruption domestically.

The False Claims Act (31 U.S.C., § 3729–3733) is the federal government's primary civil enforcement tool for investigating and prosecuting instances of fraud. Any person or entity who "knowingly and willfully makes or causes to be made any false statement or representation of a material fact in any application for any benefit or payment under a Federal health care program" to the federal government

Spoonful of laws doesn't help the bribery go down   147

under the act risks substantial penalties if successfully prosecuted (False Claims, ss. 3722). The FCA is a federal anti-kickback statute, making it a criminal offense to "knowingly and willfully solicits or receives any remuneration (including any kickback, bribe, or rebate) directly or indirectly, overtly or covertly, in cash or in kind" (42 U.S.C., § 1320a-7b). If an otherwise lawful arrangement includes even a portion of an inducement for a referral of a federal healthcare program business, a violation of the FCA is likely. In cases where a device manufacturer has paid an HCP to induce or incentivize the HCP to recommend the MDBS's device for use in a hospital procedure, the claim submitted to the government is not made by the HCP or the MDBS. Rather, it is via the third-party hospital, which gains nothing from the financial arrangement. The FCA allows for civil monetary penalties (42 U.S.C. § 1320a-7a (a)(7)) to be imposed on the MDBS and HCP for having made the arrangement[4] in the first place (Demske 2008, p. 4). However, these laws are only applicable when government-funded reimbursements are claimed under Medicare (42 U.S.C. § 1395) and Medicaid (42 U.S.C. § 1396). Additional laws known as "Stark Laws" (42 U.S.C. 1395nn) address self-dealing in prohibiting HCPs from

> making referrals for certain designated health services (DHS) payable by Medicare to an entity with which he or she (or an immediate family member) has a financial relationship (ownership, investment, or compensation), unless an exception applies; and also prohibits the entity from presenting or causing to be presented claims to Medicare (or billing another individual, entity, or third party payer) for those referred services.

However, there are a number of exceptions for financial relationships that pose no risk to patients or the program.

The private insurance market and private health care are not covered by these laws. Kickbacks, bribery, or other forms of inducements perpetrated in private health care are exempt from the FCA. Both HCPs and MDBS can be barred from participating in these federal programs if they are found to have engaged in violations of the FCA. However, having been booted out of the federal programs, these same bribe-givers and takers can engage in the same behaviors in private settings with no repercussions (Habibi, et.al. 2016).

Detailing

When an MDBS sales representative visits an HCP, at their practice, in a hospital, or at a medical school, the process of their visit and the sales inducements are referred to as "detailing." Marketing to HCPs can take a myriad of forms. MDBS understand that once a patient has been put on a specific brand medication it can be challenging to persuade a physician to change the patient's prescription. Detailing doesn't just allow a rep to pitch the virtues of their company's product as being somehow superior and thus worthy of prescribing, but in winning that physician over to the brand, *and the company* (Marketing to Professionals, 2017). Hospitality

148 *Mikhail Reider-Gordon*

in the form of bringing in free meals to a clinic; hosting expensive outside lunches and dinners; hosting continuing medical education (CME) seminars in enticing locations that include high-end comestibles; providing grant monies for minimal research or nebulous projects; funding labs; paying for medical equipment; paying for luxury travel to conferences; free samples (so the HCP can pass these along to grateful patients); outings and entertainment such as theatre or professional sporting events; branded and unbranded gifts ranging across the spectrum from pens to pricey sporting gear; outright cash; and more all fall under the purview of detailing. One former detailer for Pfizer described his favorite approach to gaining entre and establishing a relationship with an HCP. He would offer food and drink – free bagels, lunches, and coffee coupons coupled with gifts. The gifts ranged from pens to bottles of wine to "unrestricted educational grants" worth thousands of dollars; "we did all sorts of crazy stuff in the industry . . . the regulation hadn't caught up with us" (Oldani quoted in Lewis 2014).

Wazana (2000) reviewed 16 studies of US HCPs published between 1982 and 1997 and estimated that, on average, physicians met with industry representatives four times per month and residents accepted six gifts per year from industry representatives. One 2001 survey (Kaiser Family Foundation 2002) evidenced 92% of physicians having received free drug samples from MDBS. Sixty-one percent of the HCPs had received meals, tickets to events, or free travel. Another 13% had received financial or other kinds of benefits, and 12% received incentives for participation in clinical trials. In 2007, a national survey (Campebell, Gruen, Mounford, et al. 2007) evidenced that the overwhelming majority of HCPs (94%) reported they had some form of relationship with MDBS. Predominantly, the relationships these HCPs held involved "receiving food in the workplace (83%) or receiving drug samples (78%). More than one third of the respondents (35%) received reimbursement for costs associated with professional meetings or continuing medical education ('CME'), and more than one quarter (28%) received payments for consulting, giving lectures, or enrolling patients in trials" (Campbell, et al. 2007, p. 1742).

MDBS purposely create financial relationships with HCPs in order to influence their prescribing habits. When an HCP prescribes more of a particular MDBS's drug, or inserts more of their devices, they are rewarded by the company. Rewards and influencing incentives can largely be seen via three primary categories: (1) kickbacks (for adopting an MDBS's drug onto a hospital formulary, purchasing drugs, switching to a particular MDBS's brand, prescribing in volume), enrolling patients into clinical trials – irrespective of whether the device or drug is right for the patient, authoring scholarly articles that promote the use of an MDBS's drug or device, issuing practice guidelines in specialty fields that support the use of a particular drug/device; (2) gifts; and (3) financial support for professional activities (Rodwin 2011, p. 662).

Gifts from the Industry are awarded HCPs who perform benefits for the MDBS, from providing advisement to the US Food and Drug Administration (FDA), one of the primary regulators of the Industry, to serving as "key opinion leaders" who draft practice guidelines, provide guidance to insurance and health plans on what

Spoonful of laws doesn't help the bribery go down 149

drugs and devices to cover, and provide their names to articles for journals, oftentimes partially ghostwritten by MDBS.

In theory, the FCA and Stark Laws would tamp down kickbacks. Coupled with industry codes of conduct (voluntary), the ethical and legal landscape is most restrictive on the payment of kickbacks. However, "wide latitude on gifts" is indulged, and generally (laws) "permit drug firms to fund professional activities and associations. Consequently, to avoid legal liability, drug firms often replace kickbacks with gifts, grants and 'donations' categorized as charitable contributions" (Rodwin 2011, p. 662). Gifts can include "cash; gift certificates; invitations to resorts; entertainment such as theatre, golf, or sporting events; computers; cases of wine; artwork; consumer goods; meals; medical and office supplies; assistance on literature reviews and research; and help with personal errands" (Rodwin 2011, p. 662). HCPs in turn are often flattered by the attention and the opportunity to burnish their reputation that support from MDBS provides. Running clinical trials, authoring studies, and speaking engagements all lend credibility to a physician's reputation. Pham-Kanter (2014) points out, "Receiving money for recruiting patients for a trial, even a trial that has minimal research validity and in many cases whose validity the patient would not be in a position to evaluate, may be viewed as a signal of being a very good doctor and not a very bad or unethical one."

The FDA is responsible for monitoring and oversight of how MDBS promote their products to HCPs (as well as to patients and others). "The 'Bad Ad Program' is an FDA outreach program designed to educate healthcare providers about the role they can play in helping the agency make sure that prescription drug advertising and promotion is truthful and not misleading" (US Food & Drug Administration). The FDA publishes admonishments it has made to MDBS that have overstepped the marketing mark, and has at its disposal a number of civil remedies against companies engaging in deceptive marketing practices, but enforcement is minimal (US FDA Enforcement Actions 1998–2017). The FDA Office of Prescription Drug Promotion published 9 warning letters to MDBS in 2015, 11 in 2016, but only 2 in 2017. However, the FDA has been exceptionally slow to take any greater steps in both clarifying acceptable marketing behaviors and in enforcing the rules; perhaps because the nebulous nature of the regulations leaves considerable latitude for MDBS. The DOJ has filed a number of FCA enforcement actions for promotion by MDBS of off-label use of their various drugs and devices. Several of these marketing tactics included direct payments of cash to HCPs (Gibbons & Katchery Levy 2017). These actions have not seemingly mitigated said strategies of MDBS toward HCPs. MDBS have honed their advertising and marketing techniques with respect to HCPs over more than 50 years. The Industry now utilizes predictive analytics, psychologists, sociologists, and data analysis that leaves little to chance in terms of manipulating how HCPs will respond to their rep's detailing efforts. As one article on the PharmaExec website recounted:

To get an idea of how well the detail piece will perform, companies can do predictive modeling. In order to assess the effectiveness of a detail piece before it gets handed to sales reps, companies can build predictive models that utilize data collected from physician reactions to the tested detail piece. This data can then be analyzed against actual changes in prescribing once the detail piece is submitted to physicians. Historic data is used to create models that benchmark the underlying aspects of a detail piece to give marketers a sense of whether a detail piece will affect prescribing trends. First, it's important to evaluate the physician-sales rep interaction. This can be accomplished by surveying thousands of physicians about their interactions with sales reps, and inputting their feedback into a database. These answers then can be correlated to actual changes in prescribing. By benchmarking and analyzing all of the underlying aspects of a detail piece (e.g., appealing colors, appropriate images, compelling graphs and charts, useful text), as well as physician reactions to the detail piece (e.g., reps' persuasiveness, believability, and whether the messages easily communicate the advantages of the product), companies can predict the performance of a new detail piece with confidence.

(PharmExec.com)

As evidenced from hundreds of foreign bribery enforcement actions under the FCPA, bribes come in a wide range of formats. Ceresney (2015) observed those made under the guise of charitable giving are of particular risk in the pharmaceutical industry. These forms of bribery are no different than that which is seen in the MDBS's domestic detailing approach – cash, gifts, travel, charitable contributions, awards created specifically for an HCP, etc. Gift-taking by HCPs may start innocently, even lack of awareness of the free pens or lunch brought in to the clinic viewed as a time-saver is anything other than helpful. Perceptions by HCPs of the relationship with a rep or an MDBS can alter quickly to a "two-way street of bribery and extortion" (Mansfield 2003). Henry, quoted in Mansfield (2003, p. 8), noted "it is increasingly common for doctors to ask for and receive 'research funding' from drug companies, despite publishing little or no real research."

Mansfield (2003) interviewed MDBS reps as part of a study in medical ethics, recounting, "Drug company staffs have told me that they resent having to pay bribes. They would prefer to live in a world where medical care for their families depended on the merits of therapies rather than the power of bribes."

To the US Senate, the Assistant Inspector General for Legal Affairs testified,

> in an environment where physicians routinely receive substantial compensation from medical device companies through stock options, royalty agreements, consulting agreements, research grants, and fellowships, evidence suggests that there is a significant risk that such payments will improperly influence medical decision-making.

(Demske 2008)

Conflicts of interest

The EU Serious and Organized Crime Threat Assessment (SOCTA) (2013) states that corruption can appear in "many forms" including conflicts of interest (COI) and trading in influence. Catchick (2014) defines a COI as existing "where an

Spoonful of laws doesn't help the bribery go down 151

individual *could* abuse their position for private gain," but corruption occurring only when "an individual *does* abuse their position for private gain. Thus while a conflict of interest doesn't always lead to corruption, corruption always requires a conflict of interest . . . the corrupt act is committed after the individual decides to put private interests ahead of official obligations or duties" (Catchick 2014).

Let's call the gifts/cash/rewards/etc. showered by MDBS upon HCPs what they are, bribes. Primarily, the giving of a bribe is enforced in the US against the giver, not the taker. But accepting a bribe is also a form of corruption. Corruption does not occur in a vacuum, and is never a unilateral act. By its very nature, a corrupt act is made possible by an inherent conflict. A COI occurs when an individual abrogates their responsibility under a role of trust. HCPs hold a role of trust that goes significantly beyond fiduciary; their duty is Hippocratic and ethical as well. A corrupt act takes place when an HCP betrays that trust by engaging in a COI that places the advantage of that conflict in their favor. General and even industry-specific COIs are addressed in both administrative and criminal law in many jurisdictions, including the US. Transparency International (2016) calls attention to the fact that oversight mechanisms for COI rules in general are frequently weak, thereby undermining any effectiveness such controls may have in identifying and preventing them. TI includes in its definition of COI, "any situation whereby an individual is confronted with choosing between the duties and demands of their position and their own private interests" (TI 2016)

Conflicts of interest are given suprisingly less attention as it relates to corruption and the international regime dedicated to combating it. The OECD Convention on Combating Bribery of Foreign Public Officials in Interantional Business Transactions, the United Nations Convention against Corruption (UNCAC), and the United Nations Office on Drugs and Crime (UNODC) Guidebook on anti-corruption in public procurement and the management of public finances all neglect to make any mention, or meaningful mention, of conflicts of interests, despite COI's being central to so much of nation-level anti-bribery and corruption regime. Arguably, the entire medical industry is institutionally corrupt. Whilst this chapter does not attempt to tackle the institutional corruption of the Industry as a whole, it does examine a core element of it. COIs and the culture of gifting and paying to HCPs by MDBS have resulted in dozens of enforcement actions[5] for exactly these same activities in foreign countries, yet the US has failed to draft comprehensive legislation to address these same behaviors at home. Hypocrisy and inconsistent application of laws (FCA, etc.), when set against the volume of evidence of bribes paid to HCPs domestically, underscores the disparity between policy abroad and action at home. "The term *bribe* has the advantage of accuracy but the disadvantage of eliciting defensive reactions. Consequently there are strategic reasons for continuing to call bribes 'gifts'" (Mansfield 2003, p 47). Addressing COIs in the context of HCPs and their relationship to the Industry makes the issue one of urgent public policy, and less about the individual actions of HCPs.

Choudhry, Stelfox, and Detsky (2002) observed in their research on COIs and the role conflicts play in HCP attitudes and bias in medical research that transparency in procedures was critical. The risk of substantive bias was far greater

152   *Mikhail Reider-Gordon*

when an HCP had a COI as it related to determining prescribing guidelines and the outcome data from which the guidelines were derived than the level of bias driven by over marketing by MDBS. Their study documented a substantial number of (medical) experts serving on practice guidelines committees who held financial ties to pharmaceutical companies. More than half of the experts surveyed had financial relationships with companies whose drugs had been considered in a practice guideline authored by the expert. Such ties raise valid questions about the credibility of a guideline. These same COIs exist when MDBS fund research performed by HCPs, as continued access to funding holds, unsurprisingly, a strong influence on the HCP, who then influences the results of the outcomes of the research (Relman & Angell 2002; Psaty & Rennie 2003; Lo & Grady 2017).

Physicians in denial

> *Although most physicians believe that free lunches, subsidized trips, or gifts have no effect on their medical judgment, the research has shown that these types of perquisites can affect, often unconsciously, how humans act. For example, physicians who request additions to hospital drug formularies are far more likely than their peers to have accepted free meals or travel funds from drug manufacturers. Similarly, a device company's largess may influence a physician to favor the company's products. As the American Academy of Orthopaedic Surgeons observed, "[w]hen an orthopaedic surgeon receives anything of significant value from industry, a potential conflict exists which should be disclosed to the patient."*

> (Demske 2008)

The strategic largesse MDBS bestow upon HCPs is not passive advertising. Many of the MDBS knowingly spend more on sales and marketing efforts than they do on developing their drugs (Demske 2008). Why? They understand that providing even the cheapest of meals (less than $20) alters the prescribing habits of HCPs (Kurtzman 2016). HCPs who received even one meal paid for by a MDBS were up to *twice as likely* to prescribe the MDBS's promoted brand-name drug than HCPs who received no meals. HCPs who were the beneficiaries of more than one meal from a MDBS were *three times as likely* to prescribe their host's promoted drug (Waldman 2017). "The effect of *de minimis* favors cannot be isolated from the effects of MDBS's other marketing efforts" (Kurtzman 2016). Okogbule (2006) describes corruption as "a device or strategy usually employed to sway people away from the right course of action, duty or conduct either in the performance of their official duties or in activities relating to economic or political matters." MDBS understand that "generosity" garners tangible benefits far beyond just increased sales of their products.

Zhang and Grouse (2013, p. 712) posit "There is a line between taking a bribe with no expressed agreement or contract as to the performance of the physician who has taken it and the taking of a bribe when there is a specific *quid pro quo* agreed upon." But as multiple studies have evidenced over the years,[6] the smallest of gifts, even an inexpensive meal, can influence an HCP's prescribing habits. There is a *quid pro quo*, even if it is not fully understood by the HCP at the time. GSK, one of

Spoonful of laws doesn't help the bribery go down   153

the larger pharmaceutical companies, settled federal charges of violating the FCPA for having provided lavish meals, gifts such as watches, and other items of value to HCPs, in order to "improperly influence them and increase sales of GSK products in China. The funds used for the improper inducements were frequently obtained under the guise of, and falsely recorded in GSK's books and records as, legitimate travel and entertainment expense, marketing expense, speaker payments, medical association payments, and promotion expense" (SEC 2016, Release 79005). The significant difference in this enforcement action opposed to a MDBS in the US providing items for the same purposes of influence is that in the US, speaker payments and promotional expenses are recorded as just that. HCPs are public officials and thus instrumental in adding GSK's products to PRC hospital formularies. They are really no different from American physicians induced to add an MDBS's product to their formulary or that of a hospital/clinic where they wield the same decision-making ability. The form the bribes take and the outcomes were and are the same. US prosecutors charge bribery if it happens abroad, but not in the US.

In May 2017, *JAMA*, the medical journal, devoted an entire issue to COIs. Whilst all of the articles discussed COIs in a range of settings related to the medical profession (patient care, interactions with Industry, research, scholarly publications, academia, etc.), overwhelmingly, the authors came to similar conclusions. Disclosure of the incentives received from the Industry was fine, but that is as far as responses should go. Many HCPs seemingly do not want to recognize themselves as biased, or influenced by the financial patronage they accept from MDBS. This leaves the realm of law and enters into human psychology. The industry purports to place patient care first, but acts intentionally or unintentionally in its own best interests. More than a dozen psychological and sociological studies[7] evidence the impact gifting (in whatever forms it arrives in) has on creating positive bias and influencing HCP behaviors.

Industry guidelines

The Industry has sustained criticism for their marketing practices in the US over quite a number of years. The pharmaceutical industry's trade association, PhRMA, came under pressure as far back as the 1980s. PhRMA issued a guideline document. However, 19 of their own members then urged the federal government not to make the guidelines the "minimum standard" (Arnold & Porter, referenced in Rodwin 2011). They told the Feds they shouldn't prosecute PhRMA members under the FCA so long as they adhered to the weaker guidelines. The HCP professional organization, the American Medical Association (AMA), issued similar guidelines with respect to HCPs accepting gifts from MDBS, and together the two organizations sought to preclude further restrictions on their marketing activities. These guidelines "discouraged" (not forbade) certain gift-giving and gift-taking practices, whilst leaving the federal laws unchanged, thus allowing HCPs to easily violate the Industry recommendations without recourse. The guidelines (PhRMA 2008) helpfully suggested HCPs shouldn't accept kickbacks, as if this unethical practice should ever have been up for deliberation by an HCP. The guidelines continue to

154 *Mikhail Reider-Gordon*

allow gifts with a value up to $100 to be dispensed by MDBS to HCPs. At the time, $100 easily covered the cost of medical textbooks, certain lab tests, and even small equipment such as stethoscopes. Moreover, no cap was set on cumulative totals an MDBS could give to any one HCP. PhRMA had already opposed including restrictions on funding CME and research in the guidelines. "Twenty-five major professional medical organizations opposed all restrictions. Several specialty societies asked the OIG to allow all drug firm grants to medical societies" (Rodwin 2011). The guidelines also allowed for MDBS to fund residents, interns, and medical fellows (PhRMA 2008). Meals, events, speaker fees (for an HCP lecturing on the benefits of an MDBS's product), honoraria, tickets to entertainment events, trips to resorts (to attend trainings, of course), seats on boards, consulting roles, were all considered acceptable (bribes) (PhRMA 2008). However, by the early 2000s, both PhRMA and the AMA had to admit that the respective associations were incapable of enforcing their own guidelines. Nonetheless, they continued to argue to the government to be allowed to self-regulate (Demske 2008).

> In 2005, the orthopedic device market for hips and knees witnessed domestic sales in excess of $5.1 billion.[8] From 2002 through 2006, four manufacturers (which controlled almost 75 percent of the hip and knee replacement market) paid physician consultants over $800 million under the terms of roughly 6,500 consulting agreements. Although many of these payments were for legitimate services, others were not. The Government found that sometimes industry payments to physicians (were not) related to the actual contributions of the physicians, but instead (were) kickbacks designed to influence the physicians' medical decision-making. These abusive practices are sometimes disguised as consulting contracts, royalty agreements, or gifts . . . physician ownership of medical device manufacturers and related businesses appears to be a growing trend in the medical device sector. These business ventures raise substantial concerns that a physician's return on investment from the venture may influence the physician's choice of device. In some cases, physicians could receive substantial returns while contributing little to the venture beyond the ability to generate business for the venture. As we cautioned in a widely-disseminated letter to a medical device trade association, "[g]iven the strong potential for improper inducements between and among the physician investors, the entities, device vendors, and device purchasers, we believe these ventures should be closely scrutinized under the fraud and abuse laws.
>
> (Demske 2008, p. 2)

PhRMA introduced an updated code to its members in 2002. The code again *discouraged* HCPs accepting tickets to theatre/entertainment/sports events, sporting equipment, and other gifts that didn't "convey primary benefit to patients." But as Dr. Bob Goodman (2003) observed,

> The AMA distinguishes between gifts that benefit patients and gifts that do not, the former being acceptable, the latter not. While I am not an ethicist, I

Spoonful of laws doesn't help the bribery go down 155

fail to see the moral distinction between a $100 golf bag and a $100 stethoscope that frees up physician income so he or she can buy the $100 golf bag. It's not as if the physician is telling patients, "Come back in a month – hopefully a drug company will have bought me a stethoscope by then, and I'll be in a better position to auscultate your heart."

As both federal regulators and the public became more aware of the "generosity" of MDBS toward physicians (often made known by whistleblowers, investigative reporters, and academic researchers), some states made cash inducements illegal. At the federal level, the FCA forbade cash inducements for prescriptions covered by Medicare/Medicaid. However, these efforts have yielded little results in combating the levels of bribery in the Industry. A study by Eric Campbell of Harvard Medical School found that among a random sample of doctors, the share of those who said they had received gifts from Industry fell from 83% in 2004 to 71% in 2009. The share for those acknowledging payments for services such as consulting or public speaking dropped from 28% to 14% over the same period. However, in 2009 nearly 84% of respondents reported some form of financial relationship with Industry (Campbell quoted in Lewis 2014). Company transparency regarding lobbying and marketing is generally low. There is continuing cause for concern regarding companies' apparently weak enforcement of compliance with laws and codes of conduct.

The Sunshine Act

This growing concern over the influence of physician COIs relating to the inducements made by the Industry, and heightened awareness of impacts to patient care and rising healthcare costs, resulted in the US enacting in 2013 the Sunshine Act (Patient Protection and Affordable Care Act, 42 U.S.C. § 6001 (2010)). The act's Final Rule requires MDBS operating in the US to annually report to the US federal government (Open Payments 2017) certain categories of gifts and payments they make to HCPs. In introducing the proposed act in 2007, Senator Charles Grassley specifically cited luxury travel to exotic locales, speaking and consulting fees, honoraria, and research funding as examples of why the transparency law was needed. (155 Cong. Rec. 2, 319–20 (2009)) During the course of the provision making its way through Congressional committee, Grassley referenced many of these "marketing" avenues as perhaps having an improper influence over the physicians who received them and that patients may not be receiving the best treatment because of it (154 Cong. Rec. 2, 319–320 (2008)). He keenly observed that MDBS wouldn't spend the billions they do in marketing to HCPs if it wasn't effective (153 Cong. Rec. 11, 218 (2007)).

There was little support for the act until it was included in the ACA as part of larger reforms aimed at US healthcare. MDBS are required to categorize transfers of value (ToVs) into one of several categories,[9] including payments made to consulting firms or other third parties who would, in turn, provide the payments in part or in full to an HCP (Open Payments 2017, FAQs). Whilst it is a lengthy

156   *Mikhail Reider-Gordon*

list of transferred values that must be reported, the exceptions carved out of what is nothing more than a centralized reporting system is breathtaking: educational materials *and items* that directly benefit patients, or are intended to be used by or with patients are not reportable. These can include MDBS covering the "overhead expenses" of printing and developing patient "educational materials." Neither are payments or ToVs to providers of CME so long as the provider didn't pass along payments or ToVs to other physician speakers (defined at 42 U.S.C. § 403.902).[10] Payments or ToVs by MDBS to HCPs' immediate family members who hold "an ownership or investment interest in an applicable (MDBS)" are exempt from reporting (42 U.S.C. § 403.906(b)).[11] Buffet meals, snacks, or coffee provided to physicians at a "large annual conferences" or any "settings where it would be difficult to establish the identity of the physicians who partook in the meal or snack" need not be reported (78 Fed. Reg. 9479). MDBS that provide free repairs, services, and/ or additional training in association with contractual warranties need not report providing these valuable benefits (Congressional Record 154).

Yet despite the act not prohibiting vast categories of ToVs from MDBS to HCPs, merely that MDBS must report the giving on an annual basis, efforts in 2016 were made to repeal the act. Members of the US Congress (backed by 100 US national and state medical societies) (Silverman 2016b) attempted to insert a provision into another piece of healthcare legislation, an exception that would have exempted MDBS from reporting payments they made to HCPs covering CME, medical journals, and textbooks. After sustaining significant public approbation the provision was abandoned. However, it underscores the fragility of the transparency law. It is a tenuous law so long as it remains tied to the ACA under which it was passed. The entire ACA continues to be at risk, lacking permanence as the Republican Party in the US has attempted over the past 7 years to repeal it on numerous occasions. If the ACA were to be repealed, so, too, would the Sunshine Act be abolished. Limited in efficacy, it is at least a starting point.

Several individual US states have over the past two decades attempted to force reporting of MDBS's ToVs to HCPs, or even proscribed certain types of value transfers. In 2002, Vermont required pharmaceutical firms to report physician gifts worth over \$25. By 2007, five states required reporting gifts. However, state-level legislation has also proven unstable and prone to repeal depending on states' political climate or challenges through the federal courts.

Recent FCPA cases involving the Industry

In a 2015 speech to a pharmaceutical industry conference, then head of enforcement for the SEC, Andrew Ceresney, told the companies in attendance:

> The pharma industry is one on which we have been particularly focused in recent years. A few factors combine to make it a high-risk industry for FCPA violations. Pharmaceutical representatives have regular contact with doctors, pharmacists, and administrators from public hospitals in foreign countries. Those people often are classified as foreign officials for purposes of the FCPA,

Spoonful of laws doesn't help the bribery go down 157

and they often decide what products public hospitals or pharmacies will purchase. This influence over the awarding of contracts is true for virtually every country around the globe . . . There have been three types of misconduct that we have seen arise most often in our pharma FCPA cases. One is "Pay-to-Prescribe"; another is bribes to get drugs on the approved list or formulary; and the third is bribes disguised as charitable contributions. In "Pay-to-Prescribe" cases, we see public official doctors and public hospitals being paid bribes in exchange for prescribing certain medication, or other products such as medical devices. Some of our cases involve simple cash payments to doctors and other medical officials. But we have also seen some more innovative schemes created for the purposes of rewarding prescribing physicians . . . . Let me turn to a second form of bribery, which is aimed at getting products on a formulary. Of course, getting your company's drugs on formularies is important to success in this industry. But the FCPA requires that you do this without paying bribes, and we have taken action where companies have crossed that line.

(Ceresney 2015)

Little heed appears to have been taken to Mr. Ceresney's speech. Of the top 19 MDBS in 2016 during the period of analysis, only 4 were *not found* to have been the subject of settlements related to corruption and/or unethical marketing (Access to Medicine 2016). The MDBS are now exporting the US marketing strategies that have proven so effective. The significant difference is that they are now suddenly running afoul of anti-bribery laws, of both the FCPA and foreign regulations. The sole difference being the HCPs in other countries are considered foreign officials because they work for state-owned hospitals and clinics. SEC FCPA enforcement actions (SEC 2017) evidence a continuous pattern of violations by MDBS year after year. In 2017, Orthofix International (a US-based company) paid fines to settle charges that one of its subsidiaries in Brazil used inducements to government-employed HCPs to use Orthofix products. Biomet, another US-domiciled corporation, paid $30 million to resolve Department of Justice and SEC investigations for similar violations. In 2016, GlaxoSmithKline agreed to over $20 million in penalties for pay-to-prescribe schemes in China. Teva Pharmaceutical, AstraZenaca, Novartis AG, and SciClone Pharmaceuticals also settled for similar violations that year. Bristol-Myers Squibb, Mead Johnson Nutrition paid to settle cases involving improper payments in 2015. Since 2004 to present day, with the exception of one year, at least one major anti-bribery enforcement action has been taken against a MDBS. In fact, 2013 saw no fewer than seven MDBS settle foreign corruption charges (SEC 2017). The penalties for these patently fabricated avenues by which to pass cash to HCPs in return for higher volumes of sales for their devices were minor to the companies in question. As with so many other instances of corporate corruption the Department of Justice allowed the companies to avoid criminal prosecution and enter into Deferred Prosecution Agreements (DPAs) (Eisinger 2017).

A series of civil actions by the US Attorney's Office in New Jersey into hip and knee device manufacturers (US DOJ 2007)[12] found the medical device companies

158 Mikhail Reider-Gordon

providing a range of financial inducements to orthopedic surgeons which included expensive trips and highly lucrative consulting contracts (all ostensibly for legitimate services) "derived little value beyond the acquisition of increased sales of artificial hip and knee implants used by the consulting surgeons" (Demske 2008). The surgeons would bill for having "worked" when in fact, they had engaged in no work or minimal amounts. When work was billed, the activities for which compensation was claimed was minimal, or some consultanting surgeons earned (typically) $5,000 for submitting quarterly reports which were found to contain duplicative information quarter after quarter and provided meaningless information to the paying company, or the reports would have been drafted by device company sales reps. Provider consultants billed for training sessions that involved sales representatives observing the surgeon while in the operating room. These training sessions lasted for 1 to 2 hours, but the HCPs billed for an 8- to 10-hour workday. Some companies entered into product development agreements providing annual payments in the hundreds of thousands or millions of dollars for up to 20 years with consultant physicians, offering them royalty payments once the products were launched. The companies sponsored physicians to attend CME events at resort locations and reimbursed the HCPs for travel expenses. These meetings would only be held for a few hours each day. The presenting HCPs spoke sometimes for as little as 10 minutes, but were compensated $5,000 for a full day of work (Demske 2008).

Stryker was charged with FCPA violations for having allowed bribes to be paid in order to obtain business (SEC 2014). "In Greece, the Company's subsidiary made a donation of nearly $200,000 to a public university to fund a laboratory that was the pet project of a public hospital doctor. In return, the doctor agreed to provide business to Stryker" (SEC 2014). It is difficult to see a true difference between the Stryker actions in Greece when compared to similar circumstances in the US where MDBS have donated to medical schools at the behest of a particular surgeon, or funded a US surgeon's lab, clinic, or research project. As one MDBS sales representative told a research group, "In the eyes of the stock market and the financial markets, if you don't hit your numbers, you're dead. There are no prizes for being the most honest company" (David-Barrett, et al. 2017, p. 28).

The limits of transparency

We don't find it morally, ethically, or legally acceptable for a sports referee to accept some form of value to call the game as anything other than it is. We would not find it acceptable for lawyers to pay a judge prior to rendering a decision in a case. Financial advisors are precluded by law from holding COIs relative to their clients. Yet despite the prohibition, Lowenstein, Sah and Daylian (2012) illustrated that advisors confronted with their own COIs subsequently provided more biased advice when it involved more than one recipient. The human subconscious reasoning that controls intuitive, automatic and largely unconscious decision-making has also been found to control ethical decisions. "As a result, most unethical conduct is likely to be committed unconsciously by people who believe that their intentions

Spoonful of laws doesn't help the bribery go down 159

and actions are ethical" (Feldman, Gauthier & Schuler 2013). Compounding this impact on ethical judgements, some studies have found that if financial incentives are added into the mix, "moral considerations are less likely to play a role in decision making" (Fehr quoted in Feldman, Gauthier & Schuler 2013).

Tackling the pathways to corruption in this industry with volunteer practices and mere reporting rather than acknowledging the underlying drivers to be psychological and sociological in nature has left laws inadequate to mediate individuals' subconscious. In the face of documented human tendencies to misjudge how easily influenced someone can be, merely requiring the reporting of some of the influencing tactics is doomed to fail. Combating conflicts of interest and an industry corrupted requires a complete rethink in the structures and organization of that industry.

The Sunshine Act places the burden on patients to seek out COIs their physicians may hold. The public at large does not appear to know that Open Payments datasets exist, let alone how to interpret what they are reading. Moreover, in many instances individuals have little to no choice in selecting their HCP. Assuming they know about the site, have access to the Internet, the time to learn how to locate data within it, and then learn that their treating HCP is accepting money from MDBS, then what? Factors from their geography to their insurance network will likely constrict their ability to easily move to another HCP. If specialists are involved, or if the HCP found to be on the take is treating a family member (aging parent), it may be nearly impossible to disengage from that HCP in favor of one who is not being bribed. Of course, the individual has to then start the process of looking up the potential replacement HCP to determine if they, too, are on the take. As 71% of HCPs in 2009 were found to have received some form of gift/compensation from an MDBS, the likelihood of finding an HCP in their immediate geographical region with the requisite qualifications to treat whatever ails the said individual and who accepts the person's insurance coverage, and has not been the recipient of MDBS largess, is ludicrously low. As LaFrance (2006) notes, the physician–patient relationship is one where there is a power imbalance, and whilst the patient must place a great deal of trust in the HCP, the HCP has a fiduciary as well as ethical obligation to the patient.

Moreover, the maximum fines[13] under the Sunshine Act are negligible compared to the billions MDBS spend in an average year on marketing and the additional amounts they pay in fines for other transgressions. Under the act, there is no potential loss of operating license, no debarment, and no chance anyone will go to prison. Whilst there have not been a large number of civil claims by patients against HCPs for violating their fiduciary duties to them, and few courts have asserted physicians should be held accountable under this theory, at least one court did find an HCP owed a fiduciary duty to disclose to the patient their financial interests that related to the patient's care and treatment plan.[14]

The Sunshine Act was expected to make public the financial inducements used by firms to persuade doctors to favor their commercial products; and to make these transactions public, reducing firms' influence on doctors (US Senate 2007). But it isn't clear that transparency necessarily equates to positive changes in behavior,

160   *Mikhail Reider-Gordon*

particularly as there is little true recourse by patients in learning of their physician's acceptance of MDBS's inducements. It also isn't evident that by exposing the ToVs that HCPs make meaningful changes to their current biased behaviors, recalling that many of them are resistant to the very idea they could be subconsciously influenced despite the plethora of evidence. "A study of physician prescribing habits in four states (Maine, Massachusetts, Minnesota, and Vermont) that adopted Sunshine rules before the act, found no statistically significant decline in prescribing of expensive branded statins when compared with doctors in states without such rules" (Lenzer 2016).

Additionally, in light of the greater push toward transparency, there is some statistical evidence (Waldman 2017) that MDBS are changing the means by which they transfer value to HCPs. The substantive value amounts are not changing, but adjusting the classifications of types of payments better obfuscates the nature of the bribes. Patient surveys suggest that when the term "consulting" is used as a euphemism for cash given to HCPs, patients are less inclined to view them with suspicion or understand a that a provider COI exists (Pham-Kanter 2014). The positive of the act has been the variety of payments that must now be reported by the MDBS.

It has been extensively studied and documented in social science as well as medical journals[15] that physicians prescribe far greater volumes of drugs from a paying MDBS, eschewing generics and even rival brands from companies that have not provided direct benefits to that provider (Engelberg, Parsons & Tefft 2014, pp. 12–13). "Rationalizations that are rejected at a conscious level may still help justify behavior that doctors would usually find unacceptable. Humans have a strong capacity to rationalize whatever benefits them" (Sah 2012, p. 484). If "gifts" from the Industry remain legal and culturally tolerable, in the provider's eyes, there is no harm in accepting them (Sah 2012, p. 484). This is not unlike the recent past when certain countries allowed the payment of bribes to be deducted on a company's annual tax; foreign bribery in business was legally and culturally acceptable. As awareness has grown around the damage corruption inflicts at so many levels of society, not only has the tax deductibility of bribes been removed, foreign bribery itself has been outlawed.

The AMA has not had a particularly good track record of enforcing ethical standards on its members, particularly as it relates to rejecting kickbacks, eschewing joint ventures with MDBS, and refusing ToVs from the Industry. It has been far more successful in resisting government regulations of said activities and promoting self-oversight (Rodwin 2011). The MDBS form an industry that knows the psychology and effectiveness of their bribery and has waged sustained lobbying efforts to combat meaningful efforts to thwart their ability to legally pay said bribes. According to the Center for Responsive Politics (2013), the pharmaceutical industry ranked first among industries in lobbyist spending. Big Pharma is the largest lobbyist at the federal level, spending in excess of $248 million in 2016 alone. The pharmaceutical/health products industry has outspent every other industry in lobbying for the past 5 years, increasing the amount spent every year since 2010. As pointed out by Pham-Kanter (2014), "tacit collusion could occur

Spoonful of laws doesn't help the bribery go down   161

if firms submit initial payment reports to Open Payments that omit items or that under-approximate the original payment amount," whilst physicians would likely contest figures that are higher than what they genuinely received from an MDBS, they are unlikely to challenge amounts that are reported lower than what they truly received, another weakness of the Sunshine Act.

Lessig (2013b) defines institutional corruption as the consequence "of an influence within an economy of influence." Fields observes, if there is sufficient influence, an industry can gain control over the very rules and laws that regulate it. Institutional corruption or regulatory capture is not marked by one specific act, but rather is an evolving process that allows the internalization of corrupt to embed itself into the very fabic of industry or greater organization. It is highly unusual for institutional corruption to violate any specific laws, as the institution set the bevioural norms that are now accepted. Light, Lexchin, and Darrow (2013) observe

> the concept of institutional corruption highlights numerous distinctions – between what is legal and illegal; between good people doing bad things, not bad people doing bad things; between influences, not money, affecting decisions. These are the ends of continua, and there is a need to recognize degrees of corruption in between.

Physician commitment to better health is compromised as the industry spends billions to create what Lessig calls a "gift economy" of interdependent reciprocation. New research finds that "truly innovative new drugs sell themselves in the absence of such gift-economy marketing" (Light, Lexchin, & Darrow 2013). So, despite mandatory reporting via Open Payments, the Industry has found workarounds to continue to transfer value that engenders institutional corruption. The effects may be more subtle – difficult to detect even as they do not necessarily require disclosure under the act – but they can continue to assert influence on HCPs.

A 2013 study that examined data on federal convictions of corruption-related crime (Glaeser & Saks 2006) as a proxy for the corruption rate of each US state found startling results. The researchers compared the least corrupt states (e.g., Minnesota, Oregon, Nebraska) to the most corrupt (e.g., Louisiana, Mississippi, Illinois), and then compared the results against the amounts of payments HCPs in these states received relative to their prescribing patterns. They found the most corrupt states (often also the poorest) prescribed the highest ratio of branded-to-generic drugs, whilst the less-corrupt states prescribed half as many branded drugs (Engelberg, Parsons & Tefft 2014, p. 6).

According to analysis of data from the Open Payments Program, since the Sunshine Act went into effect, MDBS have given increasing amounts of value, not less:

2013 $4.9 billion[16] paid to 481,000 HCPs by 1,413 MDBS
2014 $7.86 billion paid to 625,000 HCPs by 1,614 MDBS
2015 $8.09 billion paid to 632,000 HCPs by 1,579 MDBS
2016 $8.18 billion paid to 631,000 HCPs by 1,481 MDBS

162 *Mikhail Reider-Gordon*

These figures do not include 12 separate types of payments, including free samples of MDBS products, discounts, rebates (kickbacks), many types of CME, and of course all cumulative payments that fell below the $100 annual threshold. Nor do these amounts include all marketing and advertising costs MDBS have spent over these same periods. Forms of payment shifted slightly, with an uptick of charitable contributions in 2015, whilst payments for travel, meals, and consulting remained consistent, or dropped only marginally. The only categories that fell that year were payments for honoraria (down 50%) and gifts (cheaper, but not less plentiful). Additionally, HCPs and their family members were found in 2015 alone to hold over $1 billion in ownership or investment in the same MDBS (Silverman 2016a). Despite the figures reported, a Senate investigation in 2016 (US Senate Committee on Finance 2016) found that very few surgeons, particularly those who implant medical devices, reported their ownership interests in distributorships for said. This included failing to disclose to their own patients, as well as to hospitals they sold to where they also held privileges. No other industry would be allowed to engage in these behaviors and expect not to be prosecuted for bribery.

In 2013, the US Government Accountability Office auditors examined financial COIs and what impact those conflicts had on HCPs. Included in their findings, was that between 2004 and 2010, urologists who owned radiation therapy centers increased their prescriptions for radiation therapy 356%. Those urologists with no ownership interests in radiation centers reduced their prescription rate of the same treatment by 5%.

Implementing a ban

The Organisation for Economic Co-operation and Development (2005) states: "Conflict of interest occurs when an individual or a corporation (either private or governmental) is in a position to exploit his or their own professional or official capacity in some way for personal or corporate benefit." But transparency is not the sum total of the OECD requirements. Rather, it is the implementation of laws *prohibiting* bribery and corruption (OECD Convention), and the implementation and enforcement of penalties commensurate with violations of these domestic laws, that signatories to the convention are obliged to meet.

The United Nations Convention against Corruption (adopted in 2003, see article 21) agreed that Member States "shall consider adopting" measures outlawing bribery in the private sector, but did not go so far as to make the provision mandatory. "In examining institutional corruption, [Thompson] counsels that discussion should move beyond a focus on bribery, extortion, and simple personal gain and explore the world of implicit understandings, ambiguous favors, and political advantage" (Thompson quoted in Fields 2013).

The World Health Organization's (WHO) 1988 Ethical Criteria for Medicinal Drug Promotion provides a set of guidelines to help national governments regulate promotional activities, encourage rational prescribing, and protect public health. However, incorporation of the Ethical Criteria into national regulation remains imperfect in most countries (Habibi, et.al. 2016). In one of its own reports on managing COI disclosure of financial interests, the WHO stated it deemed it necessary for identifying (COI's) but that it believed disclosures to be insufficient to manage *or prevent* COIs, stating that emphasis should be "put on prevention of COI, rather than management (of them)." In a recent of issue of *JAMA*, HCPs from many of the most renowned US medical centers, outraged and distressed by the studies that have repeatedly demonstrated the adverse impact these COIs and MDBS ToVs have on not only physician ethics, but on the integrity and quality of medical research and study outcomes, and on patient health and safety, called for the elimination of "common practices related to gifts, drug samples, continuing medical education, speakers bureaus, and consulting and research contracts" (Demske 2008). Some facilities, such as the University of Pittsburgh Medical Center and Schools of the Health Sciences have taken matters into hand and banned all faculty, staff and students from accepting any and all gifts, regardless of value, from MDBS (Demske 2008). The US should take heed of these HCPs and facilities that have called for or instituted outright bans. The country led the global anti-corruption effort by launching the FCPA in 1977. It then contributed to the OECD's efforts to draft the OECD Convention on Combating Bribery of Foreign Public Officials in International Business Transactions, and has been the most aggressive enforcer of private to public bribery in the world. It is time for the US to clean up its own house (dare it be said, "physician, heal thyself").

This article has not provided information that has not been written about before. The undue influence and outright engagement in bribery by the Industry in the US is well documented. Many scholars, researchers, investigative reporters, policymakers, and citizen groups have detailed at length the forms this Industry corruption has taken, and the negative impact it has had on HCPs and the healthcare landscape (from medical schools to the costs of medications) (Pham-Kanter 2014). Little has changed despite decades of mounting evidence. It is time to act. To address this endemic corruption in US medicine, a federal law that stands alone and does not depend on the success of failure of any other act should be enacted. Such a law would ban all forms of ToV – gifts, cash, hospitality, sponsorships, grants, reimbursements, trainings, CME, funding patient advocacy organizations, funding medical research, interpreting the results of clinical trials, shaping medical school training, all of it – from MDBS to HCPs (including nurses, physician assistants, and ancillary providers). Force the Industry to reform how they compensate their sales and marketing teams. MDBS are not going to change their winning formulas willingly. To do so would conflict with their primary goal of maximizing profitability. The fines by regulators are but a proverbial drop in the bucket. However, if the legality of their behavior is changed then the stakes become much higher. Potential loss of operating license or debarment from federal contracts or as suppliers under Medicare/Medicaid and more then become real and meaningful risks. Banning all forms of payment by MDBS to HCPs doesn't just relieve the HCPs of undue influence and COI dilemmas; it would substantially alter how the Industry responded in the marketplace. Telling shareholders it is illegal for the company to engage in any *quid pro quo* provides the answer to cease engaging in the practice, and elevates the penalties for those who dare to flaunt the law.

164   *Mikhail Reider-Gordon*

The US insurance industry is an equally powerful lobby that could lead the initiative for a legislative policy shift to banning all forms of compensation from MDBS to HCPs. If insurers determined to reimburse only doctors who do not accept payments because those who do accept them may have prescribing habits that are too costly, a powerful and strong economic incentive to encourage the adoption of such a law would be formed (Pham-Kanter 2014). Already keenly aware of the state-level burden of healthcare costs, many state governors and state-level lawmakers could put their support behind this ban as part of greater strategies to reduce medical care costs and healthcare-related fraud. Extending the FCA to apply to all kickbacks in healthcare – private insurers, medical care financed through employers, and self-funded benefit plans – would be an important first step (Rodwin 2011, p. 668). Were anti-corruption civil society groups to weigh-in and underscore the hypocrisy between US domestic laws and enforcement of MDBS activities abroad and remind lawmakers of the obligations of the US under the OECD Convention sufficient weight could be found to counterbalance the sway of MDBS over the US Congress.

Investigations are expensive and time-consuming. There are too many HCPs and too few prosecutors to possibly undertake the number of investigations that could be justifiably launched just from the Sunshine Act. The more direct approach, and one which dispenses with threshold amounts for gifts and payments, is to just ban all forms of value transfer from MDBS to HCPs. States could enforce as well under a blanket ban. As Demske (2008) testified,

> Criminal, civil, and administrative enforcement is an important facet of an overall strategy to discourage financial arrangements that distort physicians' professional judgment. However, it would be both inappropriate and impractical to rely solely on Government enforcement to address an issue of this complexity. The health care industry, medical community, and the Government must develop and implement additional approaches to reduce the risks raised by these arrangements.

The first approach would be to proscribe accepting ToVs from the Industry: "Corruption is like adultery: ninety percent of it is a matter of opportunity. If you eliminate the opportunities, you eliminate the crime" (Salbu 2000).

Notes

1 The Travel Act, 18 U.S.C. § 1952 (1976): Whoever travels in interstate or foreign commerce or uses the mail or any facility in interstate or foreign commerce, with intent to – (1) distribute the proceeds of any unlawful activity; or (2) commit any crime of violence to further any unlawful activity; or (3) otherwise promote, manage, establish, carry on, or facilitate the promotion, management, establishment, or carrying on, of any unlawful activity. Subsection (b) specifies activities under the act, including bribery.
2 Includes email, phone, wire transfer, fax, and other electronic communications, as well as physical delivery mechanisms.

Spoonful of laws doesn't help the bribery go down   165

3 Not a comprehensive list, but examples include: Cal. Penal Code§ 641.3; Rhode Island Gen. Laws § 11-7-3-5; Ala Code Ann 13A-11–120(b); Alaska Stat Ann § 11.46.670(b); Ga Code Ann § 16-22-33.

4 Any offer, solicitation, payment, inducement, or remuneration.

5 See US DOJ (www.justice.gov/criminal-fraud/related-enforcement-actions/a), US SEC (www.sec.gov/spotlight/fcpa/fcpa-cases.shtml), and TRACE Compendium (https://www.traceinternational.org/compendium (see under Industry: Pharmaceuticals/Medical Devices/Health).

6 See Madhaven, et al. (1997); Coste (1999); Wazana (2000); Coyle (2002); Mehta (2008); Katz, et al. (2003); Sah (2012); Sah and Fugh-Berman (2013); Engelberg, Parsons and Tefft (2014); Tringale, et al. (2017); Larkin, et al. (2017); Kurtzman (2016); Yeh et al. (2016); and ProPublica, "Dollars for Doctors," 2016. For the effects of general gift exchange have on human tendencies to feel reciprocal obligations, see: Mauss (1954); Gouldner (1960); Levi-Strauss (1969); Cialdini (1993).

7 See Madhaven, et al. (1997); Coste (1999); Wazana (2000); Coyle (2002); Mehta (2008); Katz, et al. (2003); Sah (2012); Sah and Fugh-Berman (2013); Engelberg, Parsons and Tefft (2014); Tringale, et al. (2017); Larkin, et al. (2017); Kurtzman (2016); Yeh et al. (2016); and ProPublica, "Dollars for Doctors," 2016. For the effects of general gift exchange have on human tendencies to feel reciprocal obligations, see: Mauss (1954); Gouldner (1960); Levi-Strauss (1969); Cialdini (1993).

8 Demske Testimony 2.

9 Categories are: compensation for services other than consulting, including serving as faculty or as a speaker at an event other than a continuing education program; honoraria; gifts; entertainment; food and beverage; travel and lodging; education; research; charitable contributions; royalties or licenses; current or prospective ownership or investment interests; compensation for serving as faculty or as a speaker for an unaccredited and non-certified continuing education program; compensation for serving as faculty or as a speaker for an accredited or certified continuing education program; grants; and space rental or facility fees (teaching hospital only).

10 This form of payment or other transfer of value would not be reportable because it does not meet the definition of an indirect payment as defined at 42 U.S.C. § 403.902.

11 According to 42 C.F.R. § 403.906(b), applicable manufacturers and applicable group purchasing organizations must report the dollar amount invested by a physician or a physician's immediate family member, but for payments or other transfers of value they are only required to report those to a physician owner/investor (not to an immediate family member of a physician who has an ownership/investment interest). Note that there are two exceptions: (1) when an applicable manufacturer or applicable group purchasing organization gives a payment/other transfer of value to an immediate family member of a physician on behalf of or at the request of a physician owner or investor (i.e., a third-party payment to the family member) or (2) when the payment is provided to the immediate family member of a physician as an indirect payment to be passed through to the physician. In those two scenarios, the payment or transfer of value to the immediate family member of a physician owner/investor must be reported, regardless of whether or not the immediate family member is also an owner/investor.

12 In September 2007, four major medical device manufacturers – Zimmer, Inc., DePuy Orthopaedics, Inc., Biomet Inc., and Smith & Nephew, Inc. – entered into civil settlement agreements with the government collectively totaling $311 million to resolve allegations under the False Claims Act.

13 $1,150,000 combined maximum annual penalty per reporting entity.

14 *Moore v. Regents of the Univ. of Cal.,* 51 Cal. 3d 120, 125 (1990).

15 See Madhaven, et al. (1997); Coste (1999); Wazana (2000); Coyle (2002); Mehta (2008); Katz, et al. (2003); Sah (2012); Sah and Fugh-Berman (2013); Engelberg, Parsons and Tefft (2014); Tringale, et al. (2017); Larkin, et al. (2017); Kurtzman (2016);

166 *Mikhail Reider-Gordon*

Yeh et al. (2016); and ProPublica, "Dollars for Doctors," 2016. For the effects of general gift exchange have on human tendencies to feel reciprocal obligations, see: Mauss (1954); Gouldner (1960); Levi-Strauss (1969); Cialdini (1993).

16 $1.2 billion of this was the value of ownership interests in the paying PMDC. Additionally, 2013 data are incomplete as the Sunshine Act was phased-in for reporting purposes during this year.

References and further reading

153 CONG. REC. 11, 218 (2007) Government Publishing Office.

154 CONG. REC. 2, 319–20 (2008) Government Publishing Office.

155 CONG. REC. 787–88 (2009) Government Publishing Office.

Access to Medicine Index, Market Influence & Compliance. (2016) [Online] Available from: https://accesstomedicineindex.org/subrankings/market-influence-compliance/

Campbell, E., Russel, L., Gruen, M. D., Mounford, J., Lawrence, G. M., Cleary, P. D. & Blunenthal, D. (2007) A national survey of physician-industry relationships. *New England Medical Journal* 356 (17): 1742–1750.

Catchick, P. (2014) Conflict of interest: Gateway to corruption. *Association of Certified Fraud Examiners European Fraud Conference*. Amsterdam, 23–25 March.

Center for Responsive Politics. (2013) [Online] Available from: www.opensecrets.org/lobby/indusclient.php?id=H04&year=2013. [Accessed 14th July 2017].

Ceresney, A., Director, Division of Enforcement, U.S. Securities and Exchange Commission. (2015) *Remarks at CBI Pharmaceutical Compliance Congress*. Washington, DC.

Choudhry, N., Stelfox, H. & Detsky, A. (2002) Relationships between authors of clinical practice guidelines and the pharmaceutical industry. *JAMA* 287(5): 612–617.

Cialdini, R. B. (1993) *Influence: The Psychology of Persuasion*. New York, HarperCollins.

Coste, J. (1999) How drug promotion affects physician pre-scribing behaviour. *eBMJ* 319:69.

Coyle, S. L. (2002) Physician–industry relations. Part 1: Individual physicians. *Ann Intern Med.* 136: 396–402. [Online] Available from: doi: 10.7326/0003-4819-136-5-200203050-00014

David-Barrett, E., Yakis-Douglas, B., Moss-Crown, A. & Nguyen, Y. (2017) A bitter pill? Institutional corruption and the challenge of antibribery compliance in the pharmaceutical sector. *Journal of Management Inquiry* 26(3): 326–347, ISSN 1056–4926.

Demske, G. E. (2008) *Testimony- Examining the Relationship between the Medical Device Industry and Physicians: Hearing before Senate Special Committee on Aging*. United States Senate, 110d Cong. 2.

Eisinger, J. (2017) *The Chicken Shit Club: Why the Justice Department Fails to Prosecute Executives*. New York, Simon & Schuster.

Engelber, J., Parsons, C. & Tefft, N. (2013) *First, Do No Harm: Financial Conflicts in Medicine*. [Online] Available from: http://citeseerx.ist.psu.edu/viewdoc/download?doi=10.1.1.410.1064&rep=rep1&type=pdf

Engelberg, J, Parsons, C. & Tefft, N. (2014) Financial conflicts of interest in medicine. *SSRN*. [Online] 26 January. Available from: https://ssrn.com/abstract=2297094 or http://dx.doi.org/10.2139/ssrn.2297094

European Union. (2013) Europol Serious and Organized Crime Threat Assessment (OCTA), Public Version. [Online] Available from: https://www.europol.europa.eu/activities-services/main-reports/eu-serious-and-organised-crime-threat-assessment-socta-2013

Feldman, Y., Gauthier, R. & Schuler, T. (2013) Curbing misconduct in the pharmaceutical industry: Insights from behavioral ethics and the behavioral approach to law. *Journal of Law, Medicine & Ethics* 41(3): 620–628. [Online] Avaliable from: doi: 10.1111/jlme.12071.

Fields, G. (2013) Parallel problems: Applying institutional corruption analysis of congress to big pharma. *Journal of Law, Medicine & Ethics* 41(3): 556–560.

Francer, J., Music, T., Narsai, K., Nikids, C., Simmonds, H., Woods, P. & Zamarriego, J. (2014) Ethical pharmaceutical promotion and communications worldwide: Codes and regualtions. *Philosophy, Ethics and Humanities in Medicine* 9: 7. [Online] Available from: https://doi.org/10.1186/1747 5341 9[7]

Gibbons, D. & Katchery Levy, D. (2017) Slower than Molasses in January, FDA Moves to Provide Guidance on Product Communications by Pharmaceutical and Device Manufacturers. *FDA Law Blog, Advertising and Promotion (DDMAC)*. [Online] 2 March. Available from: www.fdalawblog.net/fda_law_blog_hyman_phelps/advertising-and-promotion-ddmac/

Glaeser, E. & Saks, R. (2006) Corruption in America. *Journal of Public Economics* 90: 1053–1107.

Goodman, B. (2003) All rationalizations large and small. *American Journal of Bioethics* 3(3): 57–58.

Gouldner, A. W. (1960) The norm of reciprocity: A preliminary statement. *American Sociological Review* 25: 161–178.

Habibi, R., Guenette, L., Lexchin, J., Mint, B., Reynolds, E. & Wiktorowicz, M. (2016) Regulating information or allowing deception? Pharmaceutical sales visits in Canada, France, and the United States. *Journal of Law, Medicine and Ethics* 44: 602–613. [Online] Available from: http://journals.sagepub.com/doi/abs/10.1177/1073110516684803?journalCode=lmec#articleCitationDownloadContainer

Henry, D. (2017) Good, bad and sometimes ugly: The complexities of industry funding of research. *JAMA, Conflict of Interest* 317(17): 1705–1812.

Kaiser Family Foundation. (2002) *National Survey of Physicians, Part II: Doctors and prescription drugs, Highlights & Chartpack*. [Online] March. Available from: https://kaiserfamilyfoundation.files.wordpress.com/2002/03/nhp022-physician-survey-part-ii-rx-drugs-final-4-15-02.pdf

Katz, D., Caplan, A. & Merz, J. (2003) All gifts large and small: Toward an understanding of the ethics of pharmaceutical industry gift giving. *American Journal of Bioethics* 3(3): 39–46.

Kurtzman, L. (2016) With a free meal from pharma, doctors are more likely to prescribe brand-name drugs. *Study Shows*. UC, San Francisco, 20 June.

LaFrance, A. (2006) *Bioethics: Health Care, Human Rights and the Law* (2nd ed.), 691 Newark, NJ, LexisNexis.

Larkin, I., Ang, D., Steinhart, J., Chao, M., Patterson, M., Sah, S, Wu, T., Schoenbaum, M., Hutchins, D., Brennan, T. & Loewenstein, G. (2017) Association between Academic Medical Center pharmaceutical detailing policies and physician prescribing. *JAMA* 317(17): 1785–1795. [Online] Available from: doi:10.1001/jama.2017.4039 [Accessed 25th October 2017].

Lenzer, J. (2016) Two years of sunshine: Has openness about payments reduced industry influence in healthcare? *The BMJ* 354: i4608.

Lessig, L. (2013a) Institutional corruption "defined". *Journal of Law, Medicine & Ethics* 41(3): 553–555.

Lessig, L. (2013b) *Institutional Corruptions, Edmond J. Safra Center for Ethics*. Working Papers, No. 1. [Online] 15 March. Available from: http://ssrn.com/abstract=2233582

Lichter, A. (2017) Conflicts of interest and the integrity of the medical profession. *JAMA* 317(17): 1725–1726.

168   *Mikhail Reider-Gordon*

Levi-Strauss, C. (1969) *The Elementary Structures of Kinship*. Boston, Beacon Press.

Lewis, A. (2014) Should drug firms make payments to doctors? *BBCNewsMagazine.com*. [Online] 17 April. Available from: http://www.bbc.com/news/magazine-26890072 [Accessed August 4, 2017]

Light, D, Lexchin J & Darrow J. (2013) Institutional corruption of pharmaceuticals & the myth of safe and effective drugs. *Journal of Law, Medicine & Ethics* 41(3): 590–600.

Lo, B. & Grady, D. (2017) Payments to physicians: Does the amount of money make a difference? *JAMA* 317(17): 1719–1720.

Lowenstein, G., Sah, S. & Daylian, C. (2012) The unintended consequences of conflict of interest disclosure. *JAMA* 307(7): 669–670.

Madhavan, S., Amonkar, M. M., Elliott, D., Burke, K. & Gore, P. (1997) The gift relationship between pharmaceutical companies and physicians: an exploratory survey of physicians. *Journal of Clinical Pharmacy and Therapeautics* 22(3): 207–215.

Mansfield, P. (2003) Bribes for doctors: A gift for bioethicists? *American Journal of Bioethics* 3(3): 47–48.

Marketing to Professionals: Detailing, PharmExec.com. (n.d.) [Online] Available from: www.pharmexec.com/marketing-professionals-detailing [Accessed 26th July 2017].

Mauss, M. (1954) *The Gift: The Form and Reason for Exchange in Archaic Societies*. [Eng. Ed.] London, Routledge.

McCoy, M. & Emanuel, E. (2017) Why there are no "potential" conflicts of interest. *JAMA* 317(17): 1721–1722.

McKinney, R. & Pierce, H. (2017) Strategies for addressing a broader definition of conflicts of interest. *JAMA* 317(17): 1727–1728.

Mehta, R. (2008). Why self-regulation does not work: Resolving prescription corruption caused by excessive gift-giving by pharmaceutical manufacturers. *Food and Drug Law Journal* 63(4): 799–821.

OECD. (2009) *Convention on Combating Bribery of Foreign Public Officials in International Business Transactions and Related Documents*. Paris, OECD Publishing. [Online] Available from: www.oecd.org/daf/anti-bribery/ConvCombatBribery_ENG.pdf.

OECD. (2005) *Managing Conflict of Interest in the Public Sector: A Toolkit*. Paris, OECD Publishing. [Online] Available from: http://dx.doi.org/10.1787/9789264018242-en

Okogbule, N. S. (2006) An appraisal of the legal and institutional framework for combating corruption in Nigeria. *Journal of Financial Crime* 13(1): 94.

Oldfield, J. (2017) Overview of conflict of interest and related offences. *Transparency International Anti-Corruption Helpdesk*, 8 March.

Open Payments. (2017) Baltimore, MD, Centers for Medicare & Medicaid Services. [Online] Available from: https://openpaymentsdata.cms.gov/dataset/

Ornstein, C. (2017) Pharma money reaches guideline writers, patient groups, even doctors on Twitter. *ProPublica*, 17 January.

Pham-Kanter, G. (2014) Act II of the Sunshine Act. *PLoS Med* 11(11): e1001754. [Online] Available from: doi: 10.1371/journal.pmed.1001754

Pharmaceutical Online. (2017) *Pharmaceutical & Medical Device Infographic Shows Industry Growth*. [Online] 21 February. Available from: www.pharmaceuticalonline.com/doc/pharmaceutical-medical-device-infographic-shows-industry-growth-0001

Pharmaceutical Research and Manufacturers of America (PhRMA). (2008) *Code on Interactions with Healthcare Professionals*. [Online] Available from: http://phrma-docs.phrma.org/sites/default/files/pdf/phrma_marketing_code_2008.pdf

Psaty, B. & Rennie, D. (2003) Stopping medical research to save money: A broken pact with researchers and patients. *JAMA* 289(16): 2128–2131.

Relman, A. & Angell, M. (2002) America's other drug problem: How the drug industry distorts medicine and politics. *New Republic* 227(25): 27–41, PMID:12561803.

Rhodes, R. (2003) The invisible influence of industry inducements. *American Journal of Bioethics* 3(3): 65–66.

Rodwin, M. (2011) Reforming pharmaceutical industry-physician financial relationships: lessons from the United States, France, and Japan. *Journal of Law, Medicine & Ethics* 39(4): 662–670. [Online] Available from: doi: 10.1111/j.1748-720X.2011.00633.x

Sah, S. & Fugh-Berman, A. (2013) Physicians under the influence: Social psychology and industry marketing strategies. *Journal of Law, Medicine & Ethics* 41(3): 665–672.

Sah, S. (2012) Conflicts of interest and your physician: Psychological processes that cause unexpected changes in behavior. *Journal of Law, Medicine & Ethics* 40(3): 482–487.

Salbu, S. (2000) A delicate balance: Legislation, institutional change, and transnational bribery. *Cornell International Law Journal* 33(657): 676.

Silverman, Ed. (2016a) Drug and device makers paid $6.5 billion to docs and teaching hospitals last year. *Stat.* [Online] 30 June. Available from: www.statnews.com/pharmalot/2016/06/30/doctors-payments-drug-firms-device-makers/

Silverman, Ed. (2016b) Medical groups push to water down requirements for disclosing industry ties. *Stat.* [Online] 21 July. Available from: www.statnews.com/pharmalot/2016/07/21/ama-cms-payments-to-doctors/

Sismondo, S. (2013) Key opinion leaders and the corruption of medical knowledge: What the Sunshine Act will and won't cast light on. *Journal of Law, Medicine & Ethics* 41(3): 635–643.

Stamatoglou, A. (2012) The physician payment Sunshine Act: An important first step in mitigating financial conflicts of interest in medical and clinical practice. *The John Marshall Law Review* 963(45).

Strong, C. (2003) Lunch with Lilly: Who pays? *American Journal of Bioethics* 3(3): 62–63.

Terry, S. (2003) Banning pens and pads misses the main point. *American Journal of Bioethics* 3(3): 63–64.

Tett, G. (2017) Lawyers circle America's opioid crises. *Financial Times*, 4 August.

TRACE: Compendium. (n.d.) *Pharmaceuticals, Medical Devices, Healthcare Industry Enforcement Actions.* [Online] Available from: www.traceinternational.org/compendium#results [Accessed 20th August 2017].

Transparency International. (2016) *Corruption in the Pharmaceutical Sector: Diagnosing the Challenges.* June.

Tringale, K. R., Marshall, D., Mackey, T. K., Connor, M., Murphy, J. D. & Hattangadi-Gluth, J. A. (2017) Types and distribution of payments from industry to physicians in 2015. *JAMA* 317(17): 1774–1784. [Online] Available from: doi:10.1001/jama.2017.3091

United Nations Convention against Corruption. (2003) *G.A. Res. 58/4, U.N. Doc, A/58/4.* [Online] 21 November. Available from: www.unodc.org/documents/treaties/UNCAC/Publications/Convention/08-50026_E.pdf

United States Centers for Medicare and Medicaid Services. (n.d.) *Open Payments.* [Online] Available from: www.cms.gov/openpayments/

United States Dept of Commerce, International Trade Administration. (n.d.) *Medical Technology Spotlight.* [Online] Available from: www.selectusa.gov/medical-technology-industry-united-states [Accessed 28th July 2017].

United States Dept of Commerce, International Trade Administration. (2016) *Top Markets Report: Pharmaceuticals.* [Online] Available from: http://trade.gov/topmarkets/pdf/Pharmaceuticals_Executive_Summary.pdf

170 *Mikhail Reider-Gordon*

United States Dept of Justice. (n.d.) *Face Sheet: Significant False Claims Act Settlements & Judgments Fiscal Year 2009–2016*. [Online] Available from: www.justice.gov/opa/press-release/file/918366/download [Accessed].

United States Dept of Justice. (2007) *Press Release*. [Online] 27 September. Available from: www.justice.gov/sites/default/files/usao-nj/legacy/2013/11/29/hips0927.rel.pdf [Accessed].

United States Dept of Justice and US Securities and Exchange Commission. (2012) *A Resource Guide to the U.S. Foreign Corrupt Practices Act, 14–19*. [Online] Available from: www.sec.gov/spotlight/fcpa/fcpa-resource-guide.pdf

United States Food & Drug Administration. (n.d.a) *Office of Prescription Drug Promotion, Enforcement Actions 1998–2017*. [Online] Available from: www.fda.gov/Drugs/GuidanceComplianceRegulatoryInformation/EnforcementActivitiesbyFDA/WarningLettersandNoticeofViolationLetterstoPharmaceuticalCompanies/ucm2007055.htm

United States Food & Drug Administration. (n.d.b) *Truthful Prescription Drug Advertising and Promotion*. [Online] Available from: www.fda.gov/drugs/guidancecomplianceregulatoryinformation/surveillance/drugmarketingadvertisingandcommunications/ucm209384.htm

United States General Accounting Office, GAO Highlights. (2013) Higher use of costly prostate cancer treatment by providers who self-refer warrants scrutiny. *GAO*, 13–525. [Online] Available from: www.gao.gov/assets/660/656027.pdf

United States Securities and Exchange Commission. (2017) *SEC Enforcement Actions: FCPA Cases*. [Online] Available from: www.sec.gov/spotlight/fcpa/fcpa-cases.shtml [Accessed 4th August 2017].

United States Securities and Exchange Commission. (2016) *Administrative Order, Release No. 79005*. [Online] 30 September. Available from: www.sec.gov/litigation/admin/2016/34-79005.pdf

United States Securities and Exchange Commission. (2013) *Press Release, SEC Charges Stryker Corporation with FCPA Violations*. [Online] 24 October. Available from: www.sec.gov/news/press-release/2013-229

United States Senate Committee on Finance. (2016) *Physician Owned Distributorships: an Update on Key Issues and Areas of Congressional Concern*. [Online] Available from: www.finance.senate.gov/chairmans-news/hatch-releases-updated-report-on-physician-owned-distributorships

United States Senate, Special Committee on Aging. (2007). [Online] 7 September. Available from: www.aging.senate.gov/press-releases/grassley-kohl-say-public-should-know-when-pharmaceutical-makers-give-money-to-doctors

Waldman, A. (2017) Big pharma quietly enlists leading professors to justify $1,000-per-day drugs. *ProPublica*, 23 February.

Wazana, A. (2000) Physicians and the Pharmaceutical Industry Is a Gift Ever Just a Gift? *JAMA* 283(3): 373–380. [Online] Available from: doi:10.1001/jama.283.3.373

World Health Organization. (2015) *Addressing and Managing Conflicts of Interest in the Planning and Delivery of Nutrition Programmes at Country Level: Report of a Technical Consultation Convened in Geneva, Switzerland*. 8–9 October.

World Health Organization. (1988) *Ethical Criteria for Medicinal Drug Promotion*. Geneva, Switzerland. [Online] Available from: http://apps.who.int/medicinedocs/documents/whozip08e/whozip08e.pdf

Yeh, J. S., Franklin, J. M., Avorn, J., Landon, J. & Kesselheim, A. S. (2016) Association of industry payments to physicians with the prescribing of brand-name statins in Massachusetts. *JAMA Internal Medicine* 176(6): 763–768.

Zhang, W. & Grouse, L. (2013) Physician bribes in the US and China. *Journal of Thorac Disease* 5(5): 711–715. [Online] Available from: doi: 10.3978

9 The Foreign Corrupt Practices Act in the US and extra-territorial enforcement of an international anti-bribery regime

Jeffery Raymond Mistich

The evolution of anti-bribery law

The 1970s present a unique moment in American history that shaped American views on bribery and corruption in politics. The civil rights movement and the Vietnam War brought renewed vigor to the US public in terms of political activism. Kennedy had been assassinated, and Johnson had failed to pull the US out of the highly unpopular Vietnam War. Nixon followed these two presidents with a string of controversies that eventually led to his resignation. Understanding the historical context in which the Foreign Corrupt Practices Act, and later the Organization of Economic Cooperation and Development (OEC) Anti-Bribery Convention, is situated will be the goal of this chapter. The competing domestic interests that formed the factions for and against an anti-bribery regime are central to the micro-foundations of the theoretical argument forwarded here.

While watching the Watergate hearings, Stanley Sporkin, at the time a Securities and Exchange Commission (SEC) staff member, started an investigation into how the money was accounted for by the companies that made the illegal contributions throughout the duration of Nixon's presidency.[1] He noticed the secret slush funds used by Nixon to employ the Watergate plumbers and pay other nefarious political actors, and began to question how many companies filed with the SEC had similar, undisclosed, funds. This initiated an investigation by the SEC into a series of scandals that became known as the Lockheed scandals (Koehler, 2012). The Lockheed scandals were big news. They were featured at least six times in *Time* magazine in 1976, and once on the cover.[2] These corporate scandals led the US government to adopt a new law that criminalized the bribery of foreign officials by US firms operating abroad (Larson, 1980; Adler, 1982; Erbstoesser, Sturc, and Chesley, 2007). The highest-profile corporations in these scandals included Lockheed Aircraft Corporation, Gulf Corporation, United Brands Company, Northrop Corporation, Ashland Oil, and Exxon Corporation. The bribery scandals came to light just after Nixon's resignation and during the course of the investigation by the Office of the Special Prosecutor (Koehler, 2012). The most shocking of these bribes were made by Lockheed to Japanese Prime Minister Kakuei Tanaka and Prince Bernhard of Belgium in 1976, hence the colloquial reference to them as the "Lockheed scandals."[3]

172 *Jeffery Raymond Mistich*

Stanley Sporkin became the Director of Enforcement at the SEC in 1974 and subsequently discovered secret slush funds that were used for political payments that were not properly disclosed (SEC Historical Society, 2015). This came at an important time for the SEC because they were under attack for their lack of independence in regards to the Watergate scandal (Sierck and Watson, 1976). Al Somner, commissioner of the SEC from 1973–1976, worked to restore the reputation of political independence that it lost because of its association with Watergate (White, 2013). In 1975, the SEC submitted a report to Congress through the Church Committee headed by Democratic senator Frank Church from Idaho, asking how to proceed due to the foreign policy ramifications of public hearings (Koehler, 2012).[4]

At this point, the revelations about the bribery of foreign officials had not yet been made public. US business interests abroad were already meeting resistance from foreign domestic audiences at the time. As US preeminence as a military and economic power became more apparent, the citizens of many European states developed a sentiment of anti-Americanism. In France, this was especially pronounced. In 1967, Jean Jacques Servan-Schreiber published a best-selling book, *Le Défi Américain*, which was very influential not only in France, but across Europe. Servan-Schreiber warned the French public that France and French values were deteriorating because of American influence, technology, culture, and wealth (Schreiber, 1967). This sentiment was not contained only to France, but was gaining traction all over Europe. Members of the Church Committee were concerned that when this story became public in the US it would only serve to bolster that resistance, which would be damaging to US interests and the US economy in general. These concerns were especially salient because of Lockheed's relationship with the US government and the US military.

It is important to note that at the time that the payments were made by Lockheed the company had been bailed out of bankruptcy by the US government with a federally guaranteed loan in the amount of $250 million (Koehler, 2012). Because the company would not have existed without the government bailout, there was an international impression that Lockheed was actually an extension of the US government (*Washington Post*, 1976).[5] Because Lockheed had a special relationship with the US government for the sale of military equipment, this was a great reason for concern for Congress while evaluating the extent of the foreign policy ramifications of these foreign payments.

There were also concerns about the impact these revelations would have on American public opinion. The long string of scandals in the US was eroding the public's trust in the government. The no contest plea and subsequent resignation of Spiro Agnew, followed by the Watergate scandal and then the corporate bribery scandals all coalesced to create an atmosphere of contempt for corruption among the US domestic audience. According to NES data, public trust of the government plummeted from 61% of Americans trusting government just about always/most of the time when Nixon took office in 1968 to just 34% in 1976 following the news of the corruption scandals. Since this string of rapid-fire scandals came to light during the 1970s, public trust in government has not risen above 50% except for the 9/11 spike. This decrease in the public's trust in the government put pressure on government officials to take a hardline stance against corruption. It also created political space for policy entrepreneurship.

Though these are simply descriptive data, and corruption alone certainly does not tell the entire story of public trust in government, they do make a convincing case that the US domestic audience was becoming highly critical of political corruption. The general decrease in public trust generated a stronger reaction to corrupt behavior of elite actors, whether politicians or influential corporate executives. The Foreign Corrupt Practices Act (FCPA) was at least, in part, a response to public pressure calling for the prosecution of corruption. The general public sentiment was that corporations and people in positions of power should be subject to the same laws as the rest of society; a sentiment echoed in US political discourse still today.

Senator Frank Church, a candidate for the 1976 Democratic presidential nomination, wanted to capitalize on this change in public sentiment. He headed the Senate Select Committee to Study Governmental Operations with Respect to Intelligence Activities. This positioned him to gain from the pursuit of a high-profile corporate corruption case just before an election in which an administration that had just been disgraced by a corruption scandal was to be replaced. At this point in time, there was no legal framework in any country regarding the bribery of foreign officials abroad for economic advantage by domestic firms. The visibility of the Watergate hearings and political maneuvering by Senator Church created strong political pressure on the US government to pursue anti-bribery legislation. When considering US firms' competitive advantage, however, a law restricting such activity would have negative consequences because foreign firms faced no such restrictions.

Another important component of the Congressional conversation on foreign payments was whether or not the US was being scapegoated for payments that were actually quite common, and not necessarily considered unethical in many other countries in the world (Koehler, 2012). In response to the Lockheed Scandals, the Peruvian government expropriated the property of Gulf Corp, the Costa Rican government publicly considered expropriations of American investments, and the Communist Party's standing in Italy was bolstered (Koehler, 2012). Senator Church, while addressing Congress on behalf of the Senate Select Committee on Foreign Relations, argued that these foreign payments damaged the credibility of US foreign policy initiatives by undermining the fragile democratic regimes the US was actively trying to foster and support, such as in Italy, (South) Korea, and Libya (Koehler, 2012).

In response, between 1975 and 1977, nearly 20 bills were introduced regarding illegal foreign payments. Multiple angles were taken in an attempt to deal with the problem. The first attempt was blanket criminalization of almost all foreign payments to government officials with penalties of one year in jail and/or a $10,000 fine (Koehler, 2012). Another attempt wanted to require insurance companies to drop coverage for firms that engaged in bribery abroad (Koehler, 2012). The common theme that ran through these legislative initiatives was to take one of two approaches; either incentive-based discouragement of bribery abroad or its criminalization. In fact, the Ford administration favored incentive-based legislation that required full disclosure of foreign payments, but when Carter took office the policy changed, with support from congressional leadership, toward criminalization.

174 *Jeffery Raymond Mistich*

In 1977, the Foreign Corrupt Practices Act (FCPA) was passed into law. The FCPA was fairly narrow in scope, and criminalized payments to foreign government officials to obtain or retain business. It only applied to domestic companies that owned securities traded on the US Stock Exchange and companies that were created in the US or by any US citizen, national or resident. During the floor debates over the FCPA, concerns were raised about the competitiveness of US firms in markets where bribery was commonplace. The argument was made that the US should not be legislating morality in other states (Koehler, 2012). These views were not able to stop the passing of the bill.

The restrictions imposed by the FCPA increased the costs of compliance for US firms, and made it harder to "get things done" in states where bribery was commonplace. For this reason, business interests contested the FCPA almost immediately, but the issue did not gain enough saliency to be discussed in Congress until 1982. From 1982 through 1988, several versions of a foreign trade bill went to Congress to be voted down (Richardson, 1993). The FCPA was just a small part of the congressional conversation on trade in the 1980s. The US appetite for foreign goods, combined with it's propensity to save less than the Japanese or Europeans, led to a massive trade deficit that grew rapidly throughout the 1980s. The conversation in the 1980s was dominated by this growing trade deficit. Following the GATT ministerial meetings in 1982, the US Congress began to insert itself into trade policy more than it had in the previous decade (Richardson, 1993). There was a significant amount of concern about the US losing competitive advantages in trade because it was unilaterally liberalizing while other countries maintained trade restrictions. Historically, one of the hallmarks of US trade policy and an open international system was reciprocity. Liberalization works best when other members of the international community carry it out as well. Because the FCPA did not require reciprocity from US trade partners, it put US firms at a competitive disadvantage. This disadvantage became a prominent talking point about the FCPA in Congress.

Incorporating the competitive position of US firms into the discussion about corruption moved the conversation about the FCPA into a larger congressional conversation about trade. In 1988, in response to the Uruguay Rounds, Congress passed the Omnibus Foreign Trade and Competitiveness Act (OFTCA), which finally addressed the problems created by the FCPA (Richardson, 1993).

The OFTCA is important to this story because it specifically directed the President of the United States to pursue an international anti-bribery regime within the OECD (Title V, OFTCA, 1988). Negotiations over an anti-bribery regime went on for 10 years, and during that time three major events took place which altered the structure of international economic power. First, the Cold War ended with the dissolving of the USSR. Second, in 1993, the EU was officially transformed from a community into an economic union, and finally, in 1999, years of work and international negotiations culminated in the creation of a single European currency and the associated integration of monetary policy. These events led to a period of US hegemony, as well as the need for economic policy coordination among EU members.

In the decade between the passing of the OFTCA and the OECD Anti-Bribery Convention, a long debate occurred between OECD member states over anti-bribery legislation that was initiated by the US. Many states had to make major domestic legislative adjustments, in addition to changing the domestic business culture. For example, Australia, Austria, Belgium, France, Germany, Luxembourg, Netherlands, Portugal, New Zealand, and Switzerland allowed bribes of foreign officials to be written off as tax deductions prior to a 1996 OECD anti-corruption recommendation. Four more states, Denmark, Iceland, Norway, and Sweden, were slightly more restrictive, only allowing bribes to be written off as tax deductions if bribery was a normal custom in the state in which the transaction occurred (Crotty, 1997; Milliet-Einbinder, 2000). The US wanted policy coordination and had a window to exert its power to lead the international regime as the EU was in its infancy.

As economic interdependence increased dramatically from the late 1970s through the late 1990s, the lack of policy coordination on anti-bribery legislation led to policy discrepancies between states that were problematic for many practical reasons, in addition to the normative concerns associated with bribery. The lack of coordination in bribery policy among OECD members pre-1998, reflected the very different normative perceptions of bribery across member states (Abbott and Snidal, 2002).

Finally, in 1997, after a decade of international negotiations, an international anti-bribery regime was created among the OECD members. A great majority of the OECD members and the majority of states that ratified did so by 2001 (See Figure 9.1).

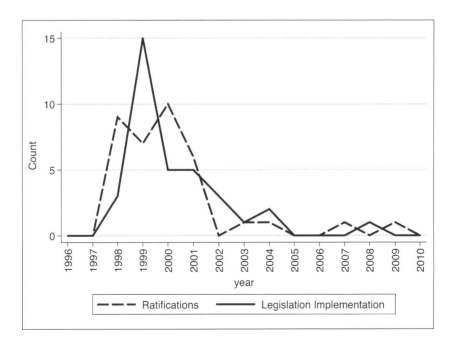

Figure 9.1 Number of ratifications/legislation implemented by year

176 *Jeffery Raymond Mistich*

What gave the regime teeth was a US amendment to the FCPA with an extra-territoriality clause. Knowing that this revision to the FCPA was moving through the US Congress is one of the things that encouraged the OECD member states to finalize the agreement. Congress passed this amendment in 1998. It extended the jurisdiction of the FCPA to include all firms registered with the SEC. This meant that foreign firms that do business with the US were now subject to penalties if they violated US law, even if the transaction had no US nexus. A recent, 2010, example involves the prosecution of Daimler AG for their bribery of foreign officials in at least 22 countries, but not in the US. Daimler AG is a German firm, and their corrupt activities took place in countries other than the US, but they were none the less fined $93.6 million and agreed to a disgorgement of $91.4 million of profits related to these activities (DOJ News Release, 2010).[6]

The extra-territoriality clause was signed into law in 1998, but the issue of extra-territoriality faced domestic and international opposition almost immediately after the passing of the FCPA. Lynne Lambert, an investment advisor for the US Mission to the OECD, from 1981–1985, stated in an interview that there was opposition in the OECD to extra-territorial issues spearheaded by Great Britain and Canada. The issue first arose in the banking industry.

> Oh, yes. The US, during the time I was in Paris, launched a major anti-bribery initiative, which the OECD finally did something about. In my day, however, the attitude of almost every other country was "bribery happens, we are not the policeman of the world, and we can't legislate morality." The other issue that pitted the US against everyone else was extraterritoriality [ET]. All other countries, led by the Brits and Canadians, objected to the extraterritorial reach of US law. Let me explain: US law subjects branches, which legally fall under headquarters, to US law, regardless of where they are located. Subsidiaries, which are legally incorporated in another country, are usually not subject to US law. Banks, to take an example, operate abroad with both subsidiaries and branches. Usually a bank's decision on what form the presence takes in a given country depends on the amount of business expected (more business would mean a subsidiary) and the laws of the host country, including tax laws. Banks that have a major global presence would usually have more branches than subsidiaries. The branch is considered a "US citizen," whereas the subsidiary is considered a "citizen" of the country where it is incorporated. Often a branch in a foreign country would be subject to two conflicting laws, one the US law and the other the law in the country where the branch is located. We fought the ET battle the whole four years I was at the OECD there without much resolution. I think we all agreed on comity but not much else.
>
> (Lynn Lambert, OECD Archives, 1986)

The building of an international regime to combat bribery and corruption took over two decades. In that time, the OECD released only four statements about combatting bribery. On May 27, 1994, the OECD countries made their first official announcement that they had made an agreement to combat bribery (OECD

Archives, 1994). This began official negotiations within the OECD over the development of the Anti-Bribery Convention. In March of 1995, at a Symposium on Corruption and Good Governance, several OECD states expressed interest in approaching non-members about cooperating with the tentative Anti-Bribery Convention (OECD Archives, 1996). All of the states that are members of the OECD are wealthy countries, but a distribution over relative wealth within the OECD still exists. Also, though there are many similarities between the economies of OECD member states, there are also distinct differences. Not all OECD states had the same level of exposure to Latin America or the transitional economies of Eastern Europe, where bribery was still commonplace. This was an attempt to incorporate the most important non-OECD trade partners of OECD states into the agreement.

In 1996, significant headway was made within the OECD that paved the way for the Anti-Bribery Convention to be adopted in 1998. First, the Working Group on Bribery in International Business Transactions

> completed an examination of measures that could be used to combat bribery in international business transactions. The examination covered participating countries' criminal, civil, and commercial laws, administrative laws, accounting requirements, banking and financial provisions and laws and regulations relating to public subsidies and contracts.
>
> (OECD Archives, 1996)

Second, and even more importantly, the OECD countries had come to an agreement that would actually change domestic laws in member states to combat bribery. The OECD made a recommendation to member countries to harmonize their tax codes so that bribery was not tax deductible. As mentioned earlier, payments made in the form of bribes to foreign officials was tax deductible in 14 OECD member states. The summary given in an official OECD press release in 1996 reads as follows:

I.   RECOMMENDS that those Member countries which do not disallow the deductibility of bribes to foreign public officials reexamine such treatment with the intention of denying this deductibility. Such action may be facilitated by the trend to treat bribes to foreign officials as illegal.
II. INSTRUCTS the Committee on Fiscal Affairs, in cooperation with the Committee on International Investment and Multinational Enterprises, to monitor the implementation of this Recommendation, to promote the Recommendation in the context of contacts with non-member countries and to report to the Council as appropriate.

> (OECD Archives, 1996)

In May of 1997, the OECD constructed a formal agreement to be agreed upon by the end of 1997 and enacted into force by the end of 1998 (OECD Archives, 1997). This agreement harmonized international domestic regulation among OECD member states to criminalize bribery.

178   *Jeffery Raymond Mistich*

Policy coordination between states and cooperative institutions have long been studied under a rational choice framework. Bribery is a complex issue, and combating it requires coordination across social, political, and economic actors. To add to this complexity, each of these elements varies across space and time. Tracing the process of a piece of US domestic anti-bribery legislation through to the international anti-bribery institution that exists today will clarify critical aspects of institutional formation. Special attention will be given to the historical context the legislation was crafted in, and how domestic arrangements in the US were able to shape international regulatory arrangements (Farrell and Newman, 2014).

The Foreign Corrupt Practices Act (FCPA) was signed into law in 1977 under the Carter administration.[7] This was a landmark piece of legislation because it was the first time a state regulated a domestic firm's behavior while conducting operations in another state. The FCPA specifically applies to multinational corporations, and what makes the FCPA particularly interesting is that at the time it was signed into law it put US firms at a competitive disadvantage compared to foreign firms. Not allowing American firms to bribe while firms from foreign states had no such restrictions allowed foreign firms to gain advantage over American firms in the international marketplace. The first states to follow and adopt similar legislation would place their firms at the same disadvantage in the international market place that American firms were now in.

However, 25 years later, similar anti-bribery legislation was adopted in most of the OECD states, and today, all 34 OECD member states as well as 7 other states have passed similar domestic laws. Why would other states agree to an international anti-bribery regime? The lack of an international bribery regime was a collective action problem that was overcome by the US through the economic and political power that the US wielded when the institution was formed (Mistich, 2017).

Theoretical argument

The OECD Anti-Bribery Convention is a case in which clustered decision making is apparent. Elkins and Simmons (2005) are clear to distinguish this type of clustered decision making from policy diffusion processes. The determining factor in this story is that for policy diffusion to occur, we must observe uncoordinated interdependence. Though the adoption of anti-bribery legislation designed after the US FCPA is a "transition that increases the probability of another transition," we do not observe a lack of "collaboration, imposition, or otherwise programmed effort on the part of any of the actors" (Elkins and Simmons, 2005, 33, 36). Though this type of uncoordinated interdependence may explain the factors that allowed the US to convince other states to go along with an anti-bribery regime, it certainly does not explain the creation of the OECD anti-bribery convention. Title V of the Omnibus Foreign Trade and Competitiveness Act of 1988 lays out a plan for an international anti-bribery agreement in some detail. This short excerpt clearly places this regime in Elkins and Simmons'

The Foreign Corrupt Practices Act in the US 179

(2005) coordination category of clustered decision-making processes as opposed to diffusion processes.

> It is the sense of the Congress that the President should pursue the negotiation of an international agreement, among the members of the Organization of Economic Cooperation and Development, to govern persons from those countries concerning acts prohibited with respect to issuers and domestic concerns by the amendments made by this section. Such international agreement should include a process by which problems and conflicts associated with such acts could be resolved.
>
> (H.R. 4848–318, 1988)

Directing the President of the United States to pursue an international anti-bribery regime through legislation is clearly not uncoordinated interdependence. Instead, the theory forwarded here will argue that the US made a strategic decision to pursue an international regime in order to appease competing domestic interests.

Despite the normative concerns the general public in the US had concerning corruption, the FCPA was ardently contested by business interests because it resulted in US firms occupying a less competitive position in relation to foreign firms in the global marketplace. This competitive positioning can be explained as a simple prisoner's dilemma (see Figure 9.2) between a domestic firm (Player 1) and a foreign firm (Player 2). Each player operates a firm in a state that imposes anti-bribery legislation (Can't Bribe), or a state that does not (Bribe). In this formulation of the problem, each firm would strictly prefer to bribe foreign officials while the other firm does not so that they will have a competitive advantage over their competitor. Their second-best position would be that neither firm is able to bribe foreign officials for business favor. Bribery is an additional cost of business that firms would like to avoid as it drives the bottom line up and reduces profitability. If a competing firm can improve their market position in comparison to yours through bribery, however, you would also prefer to bribe. The third-best position then is both firms being able to bribe. Finally, the worst competitive position to be in is one in which your competitor has the ability to bribe, and you do not. The resulting preference structure would be: {(B, CB) > (CB, CB) > (B, B) > (CB, B)} where B = Bribe and CB = Can't Bribe. Thus the game is as follows where 1–4 are simple ordinal preference rankings, where 4 is the best payoff and 1 is the worst payoff.

The Nash equilibrium outcome in the absence of an anti-bribery institution is both players engaging in bribery to secure international business deals. When the FCPA was enacted, the US government effectively forced US firms into the

		Player 1	
		Bribe	Can't Bribe
Player 2	Bribe	2 , 2	4 , 1
	Can't Bribe	1 , 4	3 , 3

Figure 9.2 The bribery game

180 *Jeffery Raymond Mistich*

bottom-left quadrant of the game. They were now prohibited from bribing while their foreign competitors continued to bribe, and this left them in their worst possible competitive position. In the rational choice approach to political interaction, this should imply one of two responses. First, the US could abandon the FCPA, thereby no longer disadvantaging its firms, or second, the US could push for the internationalization of an anti-bribery regime. The domestic political climate in the US would not allow for a reversal of the FCPA. Using the prisoner's dilemma to conceptualize the strategic interaction of the US also implies that a cooperative institution would yield higher collective payoffs (greater efficiency) than abandoning the FCPA and allowing US firms to continue to bribe.

Business interests wanted to maintain competitiveness in rapidly globalizing markets, and the electorate wanted to know that corruption would not be tolerated. This sets up two powerful and opposing political forces at the domestic level. The argument presented here is that in situations where competing interests are at play in the domestic policy process, finding a solution at the international level can be a way to appease them both. Making the assumption that the US legislature is a strategic actor that is responsive to multiple competing demands, this is exactly what happened. Because the US had competing preferences internally, there was an incentive for elected lawmakers to look outside of the US for a solution. If they could solve the international collective action problem that existed, they could shift blame to the international community while the issue was resolved.

Recent work by Singer (2007) shows that domestic regulators play an important role in international regulatory policy. Regulators will typically play a balancing game between the interests of business, and not allowing society to be affected by the negative spillover effects that risky business practices can induce. If the economy crashes, the regulators who failed to prevent it lose their jobs, and the legislature steps in and interferes in the regulatory environment. These pressures cause regulators to initiate harmonization of practices with regulators in other countries (Singer, 2007). In the case of the FCPA there were no other regulators to harmonize policy with, so the SEC brought the problem to Congress for fear of the foreign policy implications of the scandals that prompted it. In the decade following the FCPA, regulators found it difficult to maintain the competitiveness of US firms while also enforcing the FCPA. In the end, the US Congress decided to pursue an international institution to appease competing domestic political interests.

At the international level, there are private goods to be had from an international anti-bribery regime. When the FCPA was enacted, a real monetary advantage was provided to foreign competitors. If US firms were not actively losing from the legislation, they would have no incentive to expend capital on lobbying for changes to it. States that have agenda-setting power, or the ability to manipulate choice sets, are "able to use international institutions to transfer wealth from foreign to domestic producers" (Oatley and Nabors, 1998). This chapter will assume that in this time period and concerning this issue, relative market size is the key source of international power (Strange, 1987; Simmons, 2001). International networks of policy actors also tend to reflect the interests of powerful actors (Verdier, 2009). US legislators knew that they had to intervene to please the electorate while restoring the competitiveness of US firms.

To achieve a new equilibrium outcome so that each firm's best response is to not bribe, all states must, at the very least, apply some prohibitively high penalty to the bribery of foreign officials, if not prohibit it outright. As Abbott and Snidal (2002) show, the US Congress faced pressure regarding the FCPA along multiple dimensions. Transforming the payoffs of this game through the creation of international institutions has been long understood (Stein, 1982). Likewise, Keohane (1982) highlights positive transaction costs in his analysis of the conditions necessary for fostering international cooperation.

These costs exist in the form of monitoring and enforcement costs. Monitoring and enforcement is expensive, and is especially expensive without international cooperation. The US had to stiffen its end-of-year reporting requirements, as well as add staff in the SEC and the Department of Justice to handle the implementation of the FCPA. Institutionalizing bribery as a crime at the international level could reduce these expenses. By dispersing the cost of monitoring and enforcement across many states, the public good of a corruption-free market is provided. Every state on its own however has an incentive to free ride. The marketplace and the democratic system would be better in all states for firms and citizens alike if bribery did not occur. However, if this can be achieved without having to incur any of the enforcement costs, each state individually would be better off. Consider a state that does not pass legislation prohibiting bribery. Remembering the actors' preference ordering in the prisoners dilemma elaborated above, each state could on its own, through defection, achieve a better payoff for its firms than those of competing states. This is an example of a classic collective action problem in public goods provision. To provide the good, some institution must be put into place in order to constrain individual state behavior; in this case, the OECD Anti-Bribery Convention.

The US stood to gain from this reduction in monitoring and enforcement costs in addition to it being a politically convenient option. Because the problem at hand is economic in nature, it fell under the scope of the OECD. Additionally, the members of the OECD comprise the large majority of international trade and foreign direct investment (FDI) flows, meaning a deal there would level the playing field for US firms where it mattered most. A deal in the OECD would also have the biggest impact on providing a corruption free international market place as a public good.

Enforcement problems have been shown to be a critical component of institutional design (Koremenos, Lipson, and Snidal, 2001). Prior to the anti-bribery convention being ratified by the OECD member states, the FCPA was riddled with enforcement problems. First, the obvious problem with the enforcement of a no bribery policy is that firms do not admit to this type of behavior willingly. In fact, the Department of Justice offered a period of time in which firms could report instances of bribery without fear of punishment while they were investigating the extent of the bribery problem prior to the passing of the FCPA. Second, the end-of-year reporting required by the SEC did not have the scope nor the granularity needed to identify foreign bribery. Third, a political incentive existed for non-enforcement of the FCPA as long as the US was the only state that required such behavior from its firms. Some provision needed to be included that would ensure enforcement capability at the international level. This was secured with the US extra-territoriality amendment to the FCPA that coincided with the OECD anti-bribery convention.

As Kaczmarek and Newman (2011) show, states are more likely to enforce their own domestic anti-bribery laws if the US has prosecuted one of their firms under the extra-territorial provision of the FCPA. The US, as a purposive and strategic actor, knew that this provision was necessary during the crafting of the regime. It is interesting to consider how states would have responded to US enforcement of an extra-territorial clause in the FCPA before the ratification of the OECD agreement. This is a counter-factual that obviously can't be empirically explored, but one can imagine that it would not go unnoticed. The US had to convince other states to agree to this provision to ensure its enforcement capability.

To manage the political complexity associated with corruption at all three levels of analysis, the US wanted an international anti-bribery regime.[8] It took 20 years for the FCPA to gain institutionalized support within the OECD. The US had to convince states that allowed bribery to be written off for tax purposes to shift to the other side of the spectrum and criminalize it (Abbott and Snidal, 2002). In addition to this process, the US had to use its economic hegemony to gain support. At the time of the signing of the OECD anti-bribery convention, the US had FDI volumes, both in and out, that tripled the next highest country in the OECD, the UK. The anti-bribery law most affected US industries that were rapidly globalizing their production and value chains. FDI constitutes a large portion of this process and therefore gave the US significant leverage in shaping this particular institution.

With the institutionalized support of the OECD Anti-Bribery Convention, the US began to take seriously the crime of bribery. Enforcement powers were granted to the Department of Justice and the SEC. There is a great deal of overlap in the jurisdictions of both agencies, and there is also a great deal of cooperation between the two on FCPA-related cases. Between 1978, when the first charges were brought under the newly minted law, and 2000, after 26 OECD states had actually implemented domestic laws in accordance with the convention, the SEC prosecuted a total of nine cases. The Department of Justice prosecuted 38 in this time, for a total of 47 cases. From 2001–2014 however, there was a combined total of 333 cases; 212 of these were prosecuted by the Department of Justice and 121 by the SEC. Not only has the number of prosecutions increased dramatically since the creation of the OECD Anti-Bribery Convention, but also the size of the penalties has increased dramatically. The top 10 cases issued $4.65 billion in fines and penalties. Seven of those cases have been against foreign firms whose actions had no US nexus whatsoever. But because they were filed with the SEC, they fell under the jurisdiction of the law.

Recent cases and outcomes

The US is the most aggressive anti-bribery enforcer, but it is not alone in prosecuting bribery related offenses. Sixteen additional states have also carried out prosecutions under the OECD Anti-Bribery Convention. In all, between 1999 and the end of 2015, 397 individuals and 133 entities had been prosecuted under the guidelines of the convention. Of those cases, 115 individuals have been sentenced

The Foreign Corrupt Practices Act in the US 183

to prison terms in 11 different countries (OECD, 2015, 17). The largest cases in terms of fines and penalties involved firms from Germany, France, the US, the UK, Japan, Holland, and Italy. The details of these cases illuminate extensive corruption by some of the world's most respected multinational corporations. The largest of these cases in terms of fines and penalties was against Siemens in 2008.

Siemens, a German engineering corporation with worldwide operations, was fined $800 million by the SEC and the Department of Justice for paying $1.4 billion in bribes in several countries. According to the SEC, Siemens paid bribes in Venezuela to secure construction contracts on metro lines They also were involved in corruption in Iraq under the United Nations Oil for Food Program. They reportedly paid kickbacks to Iraqi ministries for purchasing power stations and equipment. They also used bribes to secure contracts to develop mobile telephone networks in Bangladesh and for the sale of medical devices in Vietnam, China, and Russia. Finally, Siemens was also found to be bribing Argentinean officials to secure national identity cards (SEC Press Release 2008).

These actions were not isolated to a few individuals within the organization. The SEC found that between 2001 and 2007 an elaborate scheme was developed company-wide to obfuscate the illicit payments, which involved employees at all levels, including senior management (SEC Press Release 2008). Siemens was a shocking, high-profile case not only because of the size of the settlement, but because of how pervasive the culture of corruption and unethical behavior was throughout the entire corporation. In addition to the $800 million in fines levied by the US, Siemens also paid another $800 million in fines to German courts, bringing the total fines and penalties to $1.6 billion (SEC Press Release 2008).

Daimler AG, another German firm, and the parent company to Mercedes-Benz, was also prosecuted for widespread corruption and bribery in at least 22 countries over a 10-year period. The SEC and Department of Justice found evidence of at least 200 transactions over this time period. These transactions were accounted for in dozens of fake ledger accounts known internally as the "interne Fremdkonten" (SEC Press Release 2008). They found that Daimler AG had used several different methods of paying bribes, including rebates on sales contracts that were sent to a government official instead of the purchasing firm, and through ghost sales intermediaries and cash desks (SEC Press Release 2008). The SEC ordered $91.4 million in disgorgement, and the Department of Justice assessed $93.6 million in fines on Daimler AG for these practices. This was the eleventh largest settlement value of any FCPA violation.

Ralph Lauren Corporation settled a case with the SEC and the Department of Justice in 2013 for bribes paid by a subsidiary in Argentina. This case was not one of the highest-netting cases in terms of fines and penalties, but was the first time a firm was able to achieve a non-prosecution settlement with both the SEC and the Department of Justice. This case was controversial because Ralph Lauren Corporation was quite disconnected from the corrupt acts of its subsidiary. Ralph Lauren Corporation had purchased a subsidiary in 2005 but did not restructure until 2009. In 2009, when Ralph Lauren Corporation went in to restructure its subsidiary, they found evidence that the subsidiary had been bribing local officials in violation of the FCPA. Within two weeks, the Ralph Lauren Corporation notified the SEC of the activity and offered prompt and complete cooperation. The general manager was found to have acted completely on his own volition, and there was absolutely no evidence that Ralph Lauren Corporation had tried to hide or promote the activity. Swift notification and compliance was noted as a reason for the non-prosecution deal that was offered by the SEC (SEC Press Release 2013). The SEC had found that the Ralph Lauren Corporation subsidiary had paid $593,000 to Argentine officials in the four-year period. The SEC ordered a criminal fine of $882,000 and a disgorgement of the $593,000 plus $141,845.79 in prejudgment interest for a grand total of $1,616,846 (SEC Press Release 2013). This case shows how costly an international investment can become under the FCPA even if the parent company does not have knowledge of the actions of the foreign subsidiary.

There are also reputation costs and business costs that come with criminal prosecutions under the OECD Anti-Bribery Convention and FCPA. For instance, under the FCPA, if a company is convicted criminally, they are no longer allowed to service government contracts. Ralph Lauren Corporation was lucky to successfully negotiate a non-prosecution settlement because it allowed them to avoid these types of additional costs that are associated with prosecution and conviction.

The FCPA prosecutions of the future

There has been an increase in the number of enforcements, and the level of fines and penalties. Figure 9.3 shows the number of enforcements by the Department of Justice, the SEC, and their combined enforcements since the FCPA was signed

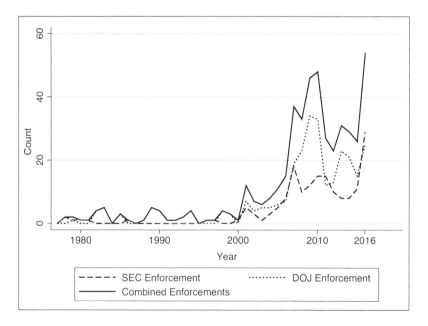

Figure 9.3 Number of FCPA enforcements by year

into law. Before the OECD Anti-Bribery Convention was agreed upon, there were fewer than 10 FCPA prosecutions per year, with some years having zero prosecutions. From the year 2000 onward, there is a significant uptick in enforcements, with a high of 54 in 2016. Beginning in 2007, the Department of Justice and the SEC have increased the number of prosecutions against firms involving mergers and acquisitions and successor liability. The increasing size of the penalties imposed for FCPA violations, and the willingness of the federal government to use its extra-territorial enforcement clause against corrupt acts that have no US nexus, have gained the attention of large multinational corporations.

Of the 10 largest penalties, 9 were against foreign firms. The culture of anti-corruption was championed by the US. Foreign firms have been slower to internalize the norm of anti-bribery for two primary reasons. First, bribery was quite common in the international marketplace until the late 1990s. The moral abhorrence of bribery and corruption was birthed out of particular events in US history. Other countries do not have a shared understanding of that historical experience, and is therefore not as prevalent in the social psyche. Second, until the late 1990s bribes were tax deductible in some states. Foreign firms were slower to learn that the FCPA applied to them as well. There was a 4-year adjustment period for foreign firms instead of a 20-year adjustment period that US firms had. This is increasing the costs of compliance for foreign firms, which is what the international anti-bribery regime was supposed to accomplish. US firms successfully lobbied the US government to make a deal that leveled the international playing field. This has been particularly problematic for firms doing business in China and India.

Forty-nine of the FCPA cases prosecuted since the signing of the OECD Anti-Bribery Convention involved corrupt activity in China, followed by Nigeria with 23 and Iraq with 21. Bribery in India was prosecuted under the FCPA in 16 separate cases, and 15 cases involved bribery in Russia. In 2008, $1.6 billion in bribes were disclosed in case settlements and $1.1 billion in 2016. The number of prosecutions, the value of the settlements, and the scope of the FCPA are expanding as an anti-bribery norm becomes internalized and a culture of anti-bribery spreads throughout the OECD countries. A bribery-free, international marketplace is a public good that improves marginal social welfare. Moving forward, multinational firms will need to pay closer attention to the policies and practices of firms they wish to acquire. The cost of compliance will increase and Greenfield investments may begin to look more attractive than mergers and acquisitions.

Notes

1 Stanley Sporkin has a long and noted career of service in the SEC, CIA, and as a US federal judge.
2 February 16, February 23 (Cover Story), August 9, August 18, September 13, Dec 12.
3 Each of these cases came to light during the course of the investigation, and were revealed to Japan and Belgium in 1976. In Japan, Lockheed secured the sale of 21 L-1011 aircraft to Nippon Airways and the sale of fighter jets to the Belgian government. The investigation found that Lockheed's bribery of foreign officials around the world totaled over $100 million.

186 *Jeffery Raymond Mistich*

4 The Church Committee was a Subcommittee on Multinational Corporations of the Senate Foreign Relations Committee, established in 1972.
5 122 CONG. REC. 30,336 (1976) (daily ed. Sept. 14, 1976) (citing Mr. Tanaka and Lockheed, WASH. POST, Aug. 21, 1976, at A10).
6 Daimler AG still had a net income of roughly 4.5 billion EU in 2010.
7 It was born under the Ford administration just following Nixon's resignation over Watergate, but not signed into law until Carter took office.
8 The three levels of analysis referred to here are the individual, domestic, and international levels.

References and further reading

Abbott, K.W. & Snidal, D. (2002) Values and interests: International legalization in the fight against corruption. *The Journal of Legal Studies*, *31*(S1), S141–S177.

Adler, T. (1982) Amending the Foreign Corrupt Practices Act of 1977: A step toward clarification and consolidation. *The Journal of Criminal Law and Criminology (1973)*, *73*(4), 1740–1773.

Anti-Bribery and Books & Records Provisions of the Foreign Corrupt Practices Act. United States Code. Title 15. Commerce and Trade. Chapter 2B. Securities Exchanges. July 22, 2004.

Cassin, R. L. (2011) 2010 FCPA Enforcement Index. *The FCPA Blog*. [Online] Available from: www.fcpablog.com/blog/2011/1/3/2010-fcpa-enforcement-index.html [Accessed 1st April 2015].

Crotty, J. (1997) Measures to address corruption problems in tax and customs administrations. *In Preparation for Presentation at the 8th International Anti Corruption Conference, Lima Peru, September*, *7*(11).

Department of Justice. Available from: www.justice.gov/criminal/fraud/fcpa/ [Accessed March 2014].

Department of Justice. (2010) Daimler AG and Three Subsidiaries Resolve Foreign Corrupt Practices Act Investigation and Agree to Pay 93.6 Million in Criminal Penalties. [Online] Available from: www.justice.gov/opa/pr/daimler-ag-and-three-subsidiaries-resolve-foreign-corrupt-practices-act-investigation-and [Accessed 1st December 2015].

Dobbin, F., Simmons, B. & Garrett, G. (2007) The global diffusion of public policies: Social construction, coercion, competition, or learning? *Annual Review of Sociology*, *33*, 449–472.

Elkins, Z. & Simmons, B. (2005) On waves, clusters, and diffusion: A conceptual framework. *The Annals of the American Academy of Political and Social Science*, *598*(1), 33–51.

Erbstoesser, E.R., Sturc, J.H. & Chesley, J.W. (2007) The FCPA and analogous foreign anti-bribery laws: Overview, recent developments, and acquisition due diligence. *Capital Markets Law Journal*, *2*(4), 381–403.

Farrell, H. & Newman, A. (2014) Domestic institutions beyond the nation-state: Charting the new interdependence approach. *World Politics, 66*(2), 331–363.

Gartzke, E., Li, Q. & Boehmer, C. (2001) Investing in the peace: Economic interdependence and international conflict. *International Organization*, *55*(2), 391–438.

Heiman, F. et al. (2014) Exporting Corruption Progress Report 2014: Assessing Enforcement of the OECD Convention on Combating Foreign Bribery. [Online] Avaiable from: http://issuu.com/transparencyinternational/docs/2014_exportingcorruption_oecdprogre?e= 2496456 /9826003 [Accessed March 2014].

The Foreign Corrupt Practices Act in the US   187

Kaczmarek, S.C. & Newman, A.L. (2011) The long arm of the law: Extraterritoriality and the national implementation of foreign bribery legislation. *International Organization*, 65(4), 745–770.

Keohane, R.O. (1982) The demand for international regimes. *International Organization*, 36(2), 325–355.

Koehler, M. (2012) The story of the Foreign Corrupt Practices Act. *Ohio State. Law Journal*, 73, 929–1013.

Koremenos, B., Lipson, C. & Snidal, D. (2001) The rational design of international institutions. *International Organization*, 55(4), 761–799.

Krasner, S.D. (1982) Structural causes and regime consequences: Regimes as intervening variables. *International Organization*, 36(2), 185–205.

Larson, W.L. (1980) Effective enforcement of the Foreign Corrupt Practices Act. *Stanford Law Review*, 561–580.

Martin, M.M. & Indek, B.A. (2014) The fourteenth annual AA Sommer, Jr. lecture on corporate, securities & financial law at the Fordham Corporate Law Center: The importance of independence. *Fordham Journal of Corporate & Financial Law*, 20, 1.

Martin, W.M. (2014) The fourteenth annual AA Sommer, Jr. lecture on corporate, securities, and financial law at the Fordham Corporate Law Center. *Fordham Journal of Corporate & Financial Law*, 20(1), 2.

Milliet-Einbinder, M. (2000) Writing off tax deductibility. *Organisation for Economic Cooperation and Development: The OECD Observer*, (220), 38.

Mistich, J. (2017) Honesty is the best policy: The origins of an international anti-bribery regime. *Unpublished PhD thesis Department of Political Science*. Florida State University.

Oatley, T. & Nabors, R. (1998) Redistributive cooperation: Market failure, wealth transfers, and the Basle Accord. *International Organization*, 52(1), 35–54.

OECD. (1986) Lynn Lambert Interview. Subject Reader, [Online] Available from: http://adst.org/wp-content/uploads/2012/09/OECD-Subject-Reader.pdf

OECD. (1994) Recommendation of the Council on Bribery in International Business Transactions. 829th Session, May 27th. [Online] Available from: https://www.oecd.org/daf/anti-bribery/anti-briberyconvention/1952622.pdf

OECD. (1996) Recommendation of the Council on the Tax Deductibility of Bribes to Foreign Officials. [Online] Available from: http://www.oecd.org/officialdocuments/publicd isplaydocumentpdf/?cote=C(96)27/FINAL&docLanguage=En

OECD. (1997) Revised Recommendation o fthe Council on Combating Bribery in International Business Transactions. [Online] Available from: http://www.oecd.org/officialdocuments/pub licdisplaydocumentpdf/?cote=C(97)123/FINAL&docLanguage=En

OECD. (2008) OECD and the United States: Sharing experiences for better economic policies. [Online] Available from: https://www.oecd.org/unitedstates/42125964.pdf

OECD. (2011) Convention on combating bribery of foreign officials in international business transactions and related documents. [Online] Available from: https://www.oecd.org/daf/anti-bribery/ConvCombatBribery_ENG.pdf

OECD. (2015) [Online] Available from: www.oecd.org/daf/anti-bribery/WGB-Enforcement-Data-2015.pdf

Olson, M. (2008) *The rise and decline of nations: Economic growth, stagflation, and social rigidities*. New Haven, CT: Yale University Press.

Oneal, J.R. & Russet, B.M. (1997) The classical liberals were right: Democracy, interdependence, and conflict, 1950–1985. *International Studies Quarterly*, 41(2), 267–294.

188 *Jeffery Raymond Mistich*

Richardson, M. (1993) U.S. to seek anti-bribery treaty: Finns' complaints may give 1970's idea a new life. *International Herald Tribune*. New York.

Russett, B., Oneal, J.R. & Davis, D.R. (1998) The third leg of the Kantian tripod for peace: International organizations and militarized disputes, 1950–1985. *International Organization*, *52*(3), 441–467.

Schneider, M., Scholz, J., Lubell, M., Mindruta, D. & Edwardsen, M. (2003) Building consensual institutions: Networks and the National Estuary Program. *American Journal of Political Science*, *47*(1), 143–158.

SEC. (2008) [Online] Available from: www.sec.gov/news/press/2008/2008-294.htm [Accessed 3rd November 2015].

SEC. (2013) [Online] Available from: www.sec.gov/news/press-release/2013-2013-65htm [Accessed 3rd November 2015].

SEC Historical Society. (2015) [Online] Available from: www.sechistorical.org/museum/galleries three-illicit.php [Accessed 1st December 2015].

Schreiber, J. S. (1967) *The American challenge*. Avon.

Shipan, C.R. & Volden, C. (2008) The mechanisms of policy diffusion. *American Journal of Political Science*, *52*(4), 840–857.

Sierck, A.W. & Watson, K.S. (1976) Post-Watergate business conduct: What role for the SEC? *The Business Lawyer*, 721–726.

Simmons, B.A. (2001) The international politics of harmonization: The case of capital market regulation. *International Organization*, *55*(3), 589–620.

Singer, D.A. (2007) *Regulating capital: Setting standards for the international financial system*. Ithaca, NY: Cornell University Press.

Stein, A.A. (1982) Coordination and collaboration: Regimes in an anarchic world. *International Organization*, *36*(2), 299–324.

Strange, S. (1987) The persistent myth of lost hegemony. *International Organization*, *41*(4), 551–574.

Time Magazine. (1976) Japan: Bribery Shokku at the top. Monday, August 9.

Time Magazine. (1976) The Lockheed mystery (contd.). *108*(11), September 13, 43.

Verdier, P. H. (2009) Transnational regulatory networks and their limits. *Yale Journal of International Law*, *34*, 113–231.

The Washington Post. (1976) Mr. Tanaka and Lockheed, Editorial. *A10* ["Tanaka"], August 21.

White, Mary Jo. (2013) The Importance of Independence. 14th Annual A.A. Sommer, Jr. Corporate Securities and Financial Law Lecture, Fordham Law School. Available from: https://www.sec.gov/news/speech/spch100113mjw).

10 The dynamics of corruption in Brazil

From trivial bribes to a corruption scandal

Ligia Maura Costa

Introduction

In the 21st century, combating and overcoming corruption is one of the most important challenges. Corruption is widespread and spreading all over the world. It represents a serious threat to the basic principles and values of any government. Corruption damages public confidence in democracy and threats to distort the rule of law. By diverting funds intended for the poor, corruption hurts them unreasonably. In addition to reducing economic growth, corruption may raise countries' macroeconomic and political instability. Fighting corruption is not easy though. This is particularly true in a globalizing world. Understanding the causes and designing the policies in the battle against corruption starts with a comprehensive analysis of the reasons and roots of corruption and its consequences. Accordingly, the study of corruption has been "multi-disciplinary", ranging from theoretical models to descriptions of corruption scandals. It has been studied as a political, economic, legal, cultural or moral issue. Many governments are either unable or unwilling to pursue anti-corruption campaigns and reforms. In fact, corruption is endemic in several countries. In these societies corruption becomes customary practice; its punishment may be arbitrary or the result of political payback. No one can deny that the gap is widening between those countries that can manage to control corruption and those that are not able to. It is a fact that corruption deteriorates investment and business conditions and reduces collective well-being. Corruption remains one of the main challenges of doing business in many countries.

Nowhere does corruption cause more damage than in developing and least developed countries. Corruption affects the efficiency and legitimacy of state activities and distorts the criteria by which public policies are decided (You and Khagram 2005). It arises at the boundaries of the public and private sectors (Rose-Ackerman 1978). Most definitions of corruption display the paramount role of the state. Among the most widely accepted definitions in the literature, corruption is generally defined as "the abuse of public office for private gain". It is a definition used by a diverse range of public institutions and nongovernmental organizations (NGOs), including the World Bank (WB) and Transparency International (TI). It is also consistent with the provisions of the United Nations Convention against Corruption (UNCAC), the only anti-corruption legally binding instrument that is

190   *Ligia Maura Costa*

global. Broadly speaking, corruption is conventionally understood as the misuse of public resources by public officials, for private gains. As per Nye's seminal work, corruption is a "behavior that deviates from the formal duties of a public role (elective or appointive) because of private-regarding (personal, close family, private clique) wealth or status gains" (1967, 416). It depends therefore upon the extent of the benefits and costs under the control of public officers. Bribes, kickbacks, "grease", and "speed" money are definitely the most used types of corrupt behaviors (Doh et al. 2003, 114).

Hardly a day passes without news regarding a corruption scandal somewhere in the world. Recently scandals in Brazil, Russia, India, China, Equatorial Guinea, Peru, South Africa, Egypt and elsewhere emphasize the extent of corruption globally, especially in emerging markets. Traditionally, emerging markets have been riddled with corruption, which has destroyed confidence in both public and private institutions. Mainstream scholars understand that corruption has a negative impact on sustainable economic growth in emerging markets (Rose-Ackerman 1978; Rose-Ackerman and Palifka 2016; Costa 2008; Thompson, 2013). Most of today's developing countries and least developed countries have corruption fully widespread and part of everyday life of their citizens. In fact, there is a link between corruption and underdevelopment, as corruption is responsible for the shortcomings and poor economic performance of several developing and least developed countries. Fortunately, one no longer believes that corruption "greases the wheels" of developing and least developed countries (Huntington 1968; Leff 1964; Nye 1967; Méon and Sekkat 2005; Power and Taylor 2011; Dreher and Gassebner 2013). Corruption is a social and global phenomenon that is not specific to emerging markets. Nevertheless, its negative effect appears stronger in developing and least developed countries as it is a major impediment to the progress and economic growth of these countries (Costa 2008; Costa 2012).

Over the last decades, most of the world's economic growth has occurred in four large developing countries – Brazil, India, Russia and China, coined by Jim O'Neil by the acronym "the BRICs" or the "BRIC countries" (2001). With a booming economy in the 2000s, it seemed that Brazil was on the fast track to become a developed country (Costa 2013). However, recent slow growth has not only reigned in this optimism, but it has also revealed just how widespread government corruption is throughout the country. Corruption is a hot topic in Brazil right now, but, actually, the issue of corruption is an old one. Concerns with corruption have been a cyclical problem in Brazil's history. Brazil became independent from Portugal in 1822. By the time Brazil became a republic in 1889, local oligarchy – called *coronéis* – established a patron–client relationship to produce blocs of votes in return for favors from the government (Green 2016, 47). In the 1980s, Brazil made its transition from military governance to a democratic government. Transition to democracy in 1985 nurtured high expectations on Brazilians of improved transparency and accountability (Power and Taylor 2011); unfortunately, it has not actually occurred as expected (Table 10.1). Many cases widely talked on corruption but not much action, making Brazilians

The dynamics of corruption in Brazil 191

Table 10.1 Brazilian cases of grand corruption or political corruption from 1987–2008

Name of the Case	Report
Railroad North-South	Irregularities in public bidding of a US$ 2.5 billion railroad were unveiled. The bid was cancelled.
Corruption Inquiry Committee	Inquiry committee was created to overlook irregularities in the disbursement of federal funds to municipalities. Despite accusations of abuse of power, charges have been dropped by the president of the lower house.
PC Farias	Paulo César Farias was accused of managing a kickback scheme in favor of President Collor. He has been convicted. This scandal served as basis for the impeachment of President Collor in 1992.
Regional Labor Court (TRT)	Judge Nicolau dos Santos Neto together with senator Luiz Estevão, owner of an engineering company, increased the constructions costs of the Regional Labor Court in São Paulo of over US$ 100 million.
SUDAM	Investigations showed a scheme of side payments to politicians at the federal agency Amazonian Development Superintendency (SUDAM).
Operation Anaconda	Operation "Anaconda" involved lawyers, detectives and judges who were selling judicial decisions and prison release orders.
Operation "*Sanguessuga*"	Members of the Congress received bribes to write individual budget amendments financing the purchase of ambulances with funds of the Ministry of Health. Seventy-two members of the Congress were involved in this scheme.
"*Mensalão*" (big montly payment)	During President Lula's first term in office, it was accused that his government paid members of Congress in exchange for legislative support. Several members of the government, politicians and businesspeople were found guilty and some are still in prison.

consider the entire system deceitful and illegitimate, with political lethargy as the consequence. During the 20th century, Brazil suffered with huge inflationary burden and high interest rates that resulted in bureaucratic governments, inefficient production and overwhelming restriction on imports and corruption. To generalize, clientelism in Brazil continued throughout the 20th century, and more than a few corruption scandals emerged. Several promises to clean up the system were made, without success (Roett 1978).

For instance, the first elected president after the military regime, Fernando Collor de Mello, was removed from office based on corruption accusations in 1992. He never faced one single day in jail. Later on, President Fernando Henrique Cardoso's two-term presidency was considered quite clean, but there were at least two major corruption scandals involving his administration. During the 2002 presidential race, Luiz Inacio Lula da Silva – known as Lula – has claimed to be clean and even included important measures against corruption in his campaign platform. In 2005, however, a scheme involving politicians and public officials to divert public funds in exchange of political support to Lula's government has emerged (Flynn, 2005), and it became at that time the biggest corruption scandal ever in the country called as "mensalão" (big monthly

192   *Ligia Maura Costa*

payment). The general prosecutor brought charges against 40 individuals (politicians and business people), and out of those 25 have been convicted and have faced jail time. Dilma Rousseff took over from Lula as leader of the Workers' Party and became president after the 2010 election. Since her first term in office, Rousseff's administration faced corruption allegations against several members of her cabinet, which were forced to resign. In 2014, federal police, prosecutors and judges have discovered the biggest corruption scandal in the country at the state-controlled oil and gas company Petrobras, the largest company in Latin America. The Petrobras scandal, dubbed "Operação Lava Jato" (or "Car Wash Investigation" in English), is, until today, the largest corruption probe in Brazil's history, and it seems far from its end.

With the recent economic growth based on rising commodity prices in the international market, a large number of untapped opportunities for business in Brazil have arisen. Yet, corruption has remained one of the serious issues to be tackled by the country. As per Girling's assertion, corruption does not disappear as countries move forward towards development, but rather that corruption only takes new forms (1997). Brazil is a good example of an endemic corrupt country that has experienced high economic growth rates and now risks sinking into a downward spiral of corruption. Recent economic slow growth has also revealed how widespread corruption still is throughout the country and the government. The Car Wash corruption scandal has splashed the reputation of the government, political parties, firms and the Brazilian society as investigations have revealed kickbacks paid to politicians, systematic bribes, distorted public decisions, money laundering and other related, illicit criminal activities.

That corruption exists in Brazil is a fact. Traditionally, corruption in the country was related to outdated legislation, a weak institutional framework, poor access to public information, lack of transparency, low public participation, the existence of conflicts of interest and the slow pace of justice of the judiciary system (Silva 1999; Lessig 2013). Based on legal, socio-economic and culture theories, this chapter focuses on the dynamics of corruption as perceived in Brazil as result of the recent spiral of scandals related but not limited to the state-controlled oil and gas company Petrobras. This chapter intends to respond to two traditional questions: What are the causes of corruption in Brazil? What are its consequences? In other words, the "causes" and "consequences" of corruption are closely interrelated and can hardly be separated. The purpose of this research is to answer to these and other questions using analytical narrative based on secondary data analysis, such as reports from the police, prosecutors, court hearings, judicial decision and the media. Large majority of the documents referred to in this chapter are publicly available at the websites of the Federal Police. The results of this study may explain the way that Brazil has been tackling corruption, through an analysis of selected aspects on recent corruption investigations and the influence of the new anti-corruption legislation on the results of the recent criminal cases. This study might help companies in formulating entry strategies in this emerging and challenging market where corruption is still far from being abolished.

Causes of corruption in Brazil

Corruption means different things for different people. The phenomenon of corruption is complex and has multiple causes. It is grounded in a country's history, its social, legal and cultural aspects, its bureaucratic traditions and its political and economic development. Corruption may take several forms, meanings and functions in different circumstances that range from single bribes to malfunction of an entire political and economic system. The main forms of corruption are bribery, embezzlement, fraud and extortion. These concepts may be partly overlapping and many times interchangeable. The causes of corruption have been seen either as a problem of politics or economics, or as a cultural, legal and moral problem. There is no disagreement among mainstream scholars that corruption pervades many societies and no remedy is available in the short term. In Brazil, corruption is an endless concern, with instances of corrupt conduct at all levels and across all branches of government. The Car Wash scandal illustrates that the country has an endemic corruption problem. In systemic or institutionalized corruption, corrupt practices are widespread, well known and implicitly tolerated. To a large extent, endemic corruption as faces Brazil is an indicator of a nonefficient state that must be comprehended within a larger theoretical bac/kground than that of simply poor governance (Cartier-Bresson 1997, 464).

Corruption is made possible, if not encouraged, by quite a few systemic problems. Sever/al causes helped to spread corruption in Brazil and make it normal practice in the country. To an extent, the causes of corruption vary from place to place. The causes of corruption in a dictatorship regime like Venezuela may not be the same as in a democracy like Brazil. Nondemocratic states are more vulnerable to corrupt practices as their leaders may form governments without using many checks and balances. In fact, democracies are less corrupt than other forms of government. But there are still some typical causes of corruption that are common to both democratic and nondemocratic regimes. The main general causes of corruption in countries are personal greed, poverty, poor education, drug trafficking, culture, weak institutions and lack of accountability, transparency and good governance. All of which helps to make corruption perceived as normal in a country. Corruption is eminent in a country where the need for people to accumulate wealth becomes widespread. The more they have, the more they want to have. In a democratic state the need for reelection may restrain the greed of politicians, but not necessarily. In Brazil, political power means winning elections and paying back other political parties to create coalitions. In contrast, corruption will be lower in rich and developed countries, where populations are richer more educated and literate. Drug users create demand for a drug market that fuels corruption. Many believe that corruption is a matter of culture. Some believe that corruption is a part of the framework of some societies and cannot be questioned.

Brazilian society has learned to live with corruption, even considering it as an integral part of their culture. Many consider corruption in Brazil as the result of a cultural aspect, whether it is the lack of separation between public and private or the mention of the "jeitinho brasileiro" or the "malandro". Culture cannot be

194   *Ligia Maura Costa*

ignored when discussing corruption in Brazil. But, besides that, corruption in Brazil has been also mainly related to outdated legislation, a weak institutional framework, poor access to public information, low public participation, lack of transparency and the existence of conflicts of interest and impunity perpetrated by the judiciary/legal system (Silva 1999). Corruption tends to flourish when there is a lack of accountability in the political and legal process, in the performance of civil servants and in the control of public resources. State intervention has increased during the Workers' Party ("Partido dos Trabalhadores – PT" in Portuguese) administration and may be add as another cause of corruption in Brazil. In fact, Ades and Di Tella state that corruption will be higher in countries with greater state intervention in the economy in the form of regulation, taxation or state commercial activity (1996). By and large, the root causes of corruption in Brazil appear to be the combination of all factors mentioned above together with wide differences in incomes.

Why have Brazilian officials, politicians and businesspeople misused in the recent past the public office for private gain more frequently and for larger payoffs than ever before in the history of the country? Part of the answer may be explained by the classic corruption equation: the expected cost of a corrupt act against the expected benefit. Impunity has properly been described as corruption's "evil twin" (Morris 2009, 9). The punishment of corruption offenses is obviously relevant. Until quite recently, the risk of getting caught and punished in Brazil was almost equal to zero. The legal and judiciary systems were neither effective nor efficient to battle corruption. Under Brazilian law, government ministers, governors of states and top politicians can be judged for crimes only in the privileged forum ("foro privilegiado" in Portuguese), represented by the Supreme Court or the superior court of justice, both are the highest judicial authorities in the country. Supreme court justices have an impressive caseload, and they are not only dedicated to criminal cases related to the privileged forum. It is true that a corruption trial in the highest courts is likely to progress much more slowly than in the federal court. And, unpunished politicians may degrade confidence in both political and legal systems. Besides, many argue that judicial institutions are not independent of political influences, in particular the Supreme Court and the superior court of justice. It is a fact that the majority of Supreme Court justices were appointed by Lula's and Rousseff's administrations. Brazilians have the perception that as the majority of supreme court justices have been nominated by leaders of the Workers' Party, they may be more sympathetic towards cases involving members of this party in judging Car Wash or similar corruption investigations than other judges deciding cases against individuals without privileged forum.

In 1995, Jeffrey Sachs and Andrew Warner observed a negative relationship between natural resources and economic growth, and asserted that natural resources are a curse. Furthermore, Ades and Di Tella (1999) suggested that in countries with large endowments of valuable natural resources – fuels, minerals and metals – corruption may offer greater potential gain to officials who allocate rights to exploit such resources. When Petrobras discovered one of the world's largest oil reserves – the pre-salt layer – in the Brazilian continental shelf, the country seemed to have hit the bonanza. But the good times did not last long for neither Brazil nor Petrobras. Brazil's Federal Police revealed that the state-controlled oil and gas giant was used as a cash cow for most parties in the government coalition. The majority of Petrobras' top executives were politically nominated by the government. Brazil did have a chance to achieve the Norwegian model of oil exploitation, and escape from the pitfalls of the Middle East or Venezuela and avoid the so-called Dutch disease. However, Lula's and Rousseff's governments seized the wrong path, and corruption and mismanagement have hit the company and the country hard. Clearly, democratic forms do not constantly triumph in controlling corruption.

Consequences of recent corruption scandals in Brazil

There is no disagreement among mainstream scholars that corruption can destabilize a country's economic performance, affect investment decisions, limit economic growth and cause distortion in competition (Husted 1999, 339). Corruption can undermine the legitimacy of governments and the confidence of nations. By its very nature, corruption is difficult to measure precisely. The most popular indices available are based on subjective perceptions, such as the Global Competitiveness Report (GCR) index by the World Economic Forum, the World Development Report (WDR) index by the World Bank and the widely known index compiled by the Transparency International (TI). The best available measure today probably is the TI Corruption Perceptions Index (CPI), published annually. The TI CPI considers the level to which public officials and politicians are perceived to accept bribes, take illicit payments in public procurement, embezzle public funds and perpetrate similar criminal offences. It captures the perception of business leaders, risk analysts and business journalists on the degree of corruption in almost 200 countries. Their score is the average on a scale of 0 to 100, where 0 would be entirely corrupt and 100 a clean country. In the 2014 TI CPI, Brazil scored 43 and ranked 69th. Most likely caused by the Car Wash investigation, Brazil scored 38 and ranked 76th in the 2015 TI CPI, reinforcing the link between perceived level of corruption and political turmoil in the country. In the 2016 TI CPI, Brazil moved up two points in its score (scored 40) and ranked 79th among 176 countries (Table 10.2), behind Turkey and Belarus, at the same level of China and India, and only slightly ahead of Albania, Bosnia-Herzegovina, Jamaica and Lesotho (Transparency International

Table 10.2 Brazil: Corruption Perceptions Index

BRAZIL		
	Score Index	*Rank*
2016	40	79
2015	38	76
2014	43	69

Source: Transparency International.

2014, 2015, 2016). Currently, the movement to fight corruption in Brazil seems to bring a more positive perception of the country.

In today's world, grand corruption or political corruption is one of the greatest unsolved legal challenges. Political corruption or grand corruption takes place at the highest levels of governmental authority. Politicians and state agents, instead of formulating and implementing laws and policies in the benefit of the society, are themselves corrupt (Moody-Stuart 1997; Doig and Theobald 2000). Widespread political corruption or grand corruption has the effect of rendering the whole system illegitimate. The tricky problem with political or grand corruption is the lack of political motivation to battle the problem. Politicians and top governmental authorities do not want to modify a system where they are the major embezzlers. Political corruption is destructive to the state's ability to implement developmental policies, to distribute resources, and consequently to transform the society and the economy accordingly. The effect of political corruption is that it renders the state helpless (Doig and Theobald 2000). In sum, corruption in government is a universal concern. Nowhere is that more true than in Brazil, where the Petrobras scandal has gradually converted into what is currently the world's largest-ever corruption scandal.

Following Rose-Ackermann's seminal work, privatizing state-owned companies may improve the performance of the companies and reduce corruption (1997, 35). The Brazilian oil and gas state-controlled giant used to be referred to as a "darling exception" to the overwhelming evidence of the weaknesses of state-owned enterprises towards corruption (Almeida and Zagaris 2015, 87). That's why Evans stated that Petrobras was "the most autonomous and corporately coherent organization within the state enterprise system" (1995, 172). Until three years ago, Petrobras was considered by many as one of the very few "cases of bureaucratic insulation against political exploitation" (Almeida and Zagaris 2015, 87). Not anymore after the corruption scandal that has shaken the company and the country.

It was in the 1950s, under President Getulio Vargas, that the Brazilian government created Petrobras with the slogan "*O Petróleo é Nosso*" (The Petroleum is Ours). Why has a corruption scandal involving one single company caused so much splash? Several reasons. First, it implicates the 15 largest oil companies in the world. Second, Petrobras is Brazil's largest company, accountable for almost 10% of the country's economy. Last but not least, the corruption scandal inside Petrobras implicates the highest political officials in the Brazil. Launched in March 2014, the operation code-named "Car Wash" was intended to investigate black market money dealers (called "doleiros" in Portuguese) who used to launder their criminal profits through small businesses, such as petrol stations and car washes. The investigation led to a top Petrobras executive named Paulo Roberto Costa, and to an intricate web of corruption that has shaken Brazil's foundations. To make a long story short, the Car Wash investigation unveiled the systemic political corruption in Brazil, took down one government and has left another one on the border of a constant breakdown.

This criminal investigation has revealed large-scale corruption of bribery, kickbacks, money laundering and illegal financing of political campaigns, initially involving Petrobras but later implicating several private companies, in particular engineering and construction firms, such as Odebrecht, the largest engineering company in Latin America, as well as the so-called national champions firms, such as the giant JBS, the globe's largest meat exporter. It has implicated top-level executives, bureaucrats, politicians, and businesspeople in general. Investigations discovered illegal payments of several billion US dollars to companies' top executives, politicians and political parties and public officials. Based on the investigation, prosecutors were able to place Brazilian multi-billionaires in jail, and to take a former president – Lula – into more than one court criminal proceeding related to corruption conduct in Petrobras. In reality, the Car Wash is the best illustration ever of efficient cooperation between the Federal Police, the Prosecution Office and the Judiciary at the federal level, with both unparalleled and scholastically unexplored changes in Brazilian society. It is also an example of effective international cooperation among Brazilian, US and Swiss authorities. For an idea of the size of the criminal operation, its first phase had the participation of roughly 400 federal police officers who carried out 81 search and seizure warrants, 18 arrest warrants, 10 temporary arrest warrants and 19 coercive measures orders in 17 cities and 7 states (Table 10.3), as per the website of the Federal Police (Policia Federal). The scale of the police operation was as massive as the state-controlled oil company itself, but this was just the commencement; the corruption was larger than anyone could have ever guessed.

Brazilian prosecutors have substantially profited from plea bargain agreements made with some of the suspects. The testimony of Paulo Roberto Costa (2014), former Petrobras Refining and Supply Director, displayed how large was the political parties' control over Petrobras' board of directors and how the scheme's proceeds were then divided. He stated that bribes were divided as follows:

> 2% was sent directly to the Workers' Party (to Mr. João Vacari Workers' Party treasurer) and the remaining 1% was transferred to the political group who has nominated him to the board, the Progressive Party (PP) [. . .] the remaining 1% was split as follows: 60% for the party, 20% to cover operational costs (such as companies to provide receipts, middlemen payments etc.) and 20%

Table 10.3 Locations of the "Car Wash" investigation, first phase

State	*City*
Distrito Federal	Brasília, Águas Claras and Taguatinga Norte
Mato Grosso	Cuiabá
Paraná	Curitiba, São José dos Pinhais, Londrina and Foz do Iguaçu
Rio de Janeiro	Rio de Janeiro
Rio Grande do Sul	Porto Alegre
Santa Catarina	Balneário Camboriú
São Paulo	São Paulo, Mairiporã, Votuporanga, Vinhedo, Assis and Indaiatuba

Source: Polícia Federal.

198 *Ligia Maura Costa*

to himself and, sometimes, to Mr. Alberto Youssef. The largest amounts of bribe were transferred directly to politicians.

Another plea bargain was particularly alarming. Julio Gerin de Almeida Camargo (2014), a consultant for the Toyo Setal construction and engineering company, revealed the massive size of the corruption scheme to be soon uncovered that included the cartel practices of Petrobras' supply and engineering companies, besides the payment of bribes and money laundering: "The rule of the game was: if you did not pay bribes [. . .], you would not succeed or you would not get contracts with Petrobras."

The "Car Wash" investigation confirmed that accused companies organized themselves to eliminate those companies that were not part of the "cartel club". Under the scope of this scheme, competition was transformed into artificial competition, where bids were adjusted in advance in secret meetings. Among the companies accused are the largest engineering and construction companies, such as Odebrecht, OAS, Camargo Correa, Queiroz Galvão, Mendes Junior, Andrade Gutierrez, Engevix, Iesa, UTC and Toyo Setel.

Corruption is a challenge for strengthening Latin American democracies and their economic development. The Car Wash investigation showed the involvement of presidents in Brazil and in other Latin American countries. The collaboration agreement of the engineering and construction company Odebrecht opened up a Pandora's box of serious corruption cases in the region and uncovered a well-established corruption network across Latin America's governments that includes Argentina, Ecuador, Mexico, Peru, Panama and Venezuela, among others. As a result, 10 Latin American countries signed with Brazilian authorities a joint international cooperation agreement to investigate the corruption schemes across the region. Recently some Latin American leaders have been arrested or formally charged.

The consequences of the corruption in Brazil are an element that cannot be exaggerated. For the last three years in a row, Brazil was the worst performing G20 country. In 2015, due in large part to corruption that led to political and economic uncertainty, Brazil has experienced its worst recession in history. Brazil's economy diminished almost 4% from 2014 to 2016. The majority of companies operating in Brazil from the oil and gas service companies and construction and engineering firms have been denounced by the Car Wash investigation. Since the Car Wash investigation, other corruption investigations have emerged, such as Operation Zelote, which tracks tax fraud, and operation Weak Flesh, targeting giant meat exporter JBS and poultry exporter BRF. Many companies linked to the Petrobras corruption scandal have filed for bankruptcy. Foreign direct investment in Brazil declined almost 12% during 2014 and 2015. Several top-level businessmen and politicians in Brazil are currently facing jail time (Table 10.4), and many in Latin America's governments have been arrested. One former Brazilian president has been sentenced to nine and a half years in jail, pending appeal; and two other living presidents are currently under investigation. One Brazilian president has been impeached as a side effect of the Petrobras corruption scandal. Last but not least, the Brazilian Supreme Court has banned corporate donations to electoral campaigns.

Table 10.4 Judicial work related to the Car Wash operation, January 5, 2017

Judicial Work	Total
Search and seizure warrant (in Brazil & abroad) *Mandados de busca e apreensão*	844
Bench warrant *Condução Coercitiva*	210
Preventive arrest warrant (Brasil e exterior) *Mandado de Prisão Preventiva*	97
Preventive arrest warrant *Mandados de prisão temporária*	104
Arrest warrant for a person caught in the act *Prisões em Flagrante*	6
Police officers involved in these operations	4,220
Police vehicles involved in these operations	1,320
Bank and fiscal secrecy breaches procedures	650
Data secrecy breach (telematic) procedures	350
Telephone secrecy breach procedures	330
Opened police investigations	326
Court proceedings initiated	1,397
Asssets blocked or seized	R$ 2,400,000,000.00* US$ 752,977,187.60
Repatriated assets	R$ 745,100,000.00 US$ 233,768,042.70
Amounts involved in the operations	R$ 12,500,000,000,000.00 US$ 3,921,183,537,580

Source: Polícia Federal, www.pf.gov.br/imprensa/lava-jato/numeros-da-operacao-lava-jato. Accessed September 1, 2017.

* 1 BRL = 0.3131 US$

In countries with systemic corruption, the legal framework is insufficient to assess and judge corruption cases. Systemic corruption calls for major reforms, in particular the legal and system. Significant progress has been made to improve the Brazilian legal framework in order to tackle corruption. The Brazilian Congress enacted the Clean Company Act in 2013 (Law No. 12,846 of 2013, regulated by the Decree No. 8,420 of 2014) in response to disclosure of widespread bribery. Based on the US Foreign Corrupt Practices Act (FCPA) and the UK Bribery Act, the Clean Company Act was designed to minimize the devastating effects of corruption. The Clean Company Act imposed civil and administrative liability on domestic and foreign companies for acts of corruption by their employees and agents. Besides the Clean Company Act, the Brazilian Criminal Code has been modified in order to provide for criminal liability for individuals who engage in bribery of domestic and foreign public officials. Other important legislation in Brazil includes Law No. 12,850/2013 (Law on Organized Crime), Law No. 9,613/1998 (Anti-money Laundering Law), Law No. 8,666/1993 (Public Tender

200   *Ligia Maura Costa*

Law) and Law No. 8,443/1992 (Federal Court of Accounts Law). Indeed, the Car Wash investigation may be a good example of how the anti-corruption system has improved and how institutions are stronger in Brazil. At the international level, since the beginning of the 21st century, Brazil became a party to the UNCAC, the only anti-corruption legally binding instrument that is actually global, and also was signatory to the OECD Anti-Bribery Convention.

Power and Taylor (2011) stated that scandals in Brazil involving politicians and top businesspeople become cold cases in courts and, subsequently, ended in impunity. This fact has helped to increase Brazilians' tolerance towards corruption. Impunity was the golden rule in the country, in particular for rich and powerful people. One of the reasons is the possibility of endless appeals after a conviction is judged. As per the Constitution of 1988, jail time is allowed only after all appeals have been fully exhausted, as a measure to defend civil rights. In corruption cases, it means delays and several postponements until prescription of the crime of corruption. Despite conviction, many have never faced jail time. Recently, the Federal Supreme Court ruled that defendant may start serving a sentence after an intermediate appellate court's confirmation of a criminal conviction from first district court. As per to the Supreme Course, it does not offend the constitutional principle of the defendant's presumption of innocence.

Conclusion

Is the Car Wash investigation the biggest corruption scandal in history? In today's modern history, the answer to this question is probably yes. This chapter examined corruption aspects in Brazil after the Car Wash investigation was launched in 2014. It analyses the main findings and outcomes of this criminal investigation. The recent corruption scandal in Brazil involving the state-run giant Petrobras has led to important disclosures regarding corruption practices, methods and mechanism not merely in the country but also in Latin America, as the scandal spilled out all over the region. Significant progress has been made in Brazil to improve the legal framework and institutional structures to tackle corruption. According to Gehlbach (2013), the detention of powerful elites' representatives under the Car Wash investigation is not, per se, a natural constraint to the well-known acts of corruption. If Brazil does not effectively address the corruption problem, chances are that the country would lose the opportunity that this investigation presents to fight corruption. Despite the new Clean Company Act, politicians have not yet been judged by the wrongdoings in Petrobras. Yet, politicians are protected by the privileged forum and have not faced the strength of the new law. There is no sign that the Car Wash investigation and related corruption investigation cases will change the mentality of current Brazilian politicians. But, it is true that the Car Wash investigation has increased Brazilians' frustration with political parties and politicians, and the institutions in general. Despite the fact that political parties are key players in a democracy, in the current context in Brazil, they are suffering a crisis of credibility as a result of the corruption in which they have been involved (Fleischer, 1996). Politicians, bureaucrats and businesspeople may challenge the

The dynamics of corruption in Brazil   201

new Clean Company Act and take the risk if they believe that paybacks are higher than the legal consequences. Corruption, dishonesty and unethical behavior represent serious threats to the basic principles and values, undermining public confidence in the institutions.

Public programs, government reorganization, law enforcement, political reform, transparency and strong institutions to battle corruption are some elements in a long-term process that has to be supported by the government from top to bottom (Pope 1997, 106). Corruption mismanages natural resources, harms the poor and weakens economies and societies. This assumption is true, and Brazil is a good example. Fraud, dishonesty and unethical behavior represent serious threats to the basic principles of government, undermining confidence in the country. The Petrobras scandal represents the face of a corrupt and destructive government. In contrast, it also represents a very positive aspect: the capacity of Brazilian law enforcement authorities to bring Petrobras suspects – bureaucrats and businesspeople – to be judged, convicted and jailed. Justice has been served. Politicians' names have continued to surface in corruption investigations; however, a blind eye is still protecting them. Justice has not yet been served.

References and further reading

Ades, A. and Di Tella, R. (1996) "The causes and consequences of corruption: A review of recent empirical contributions", *IDS Bulletin*, 27(2), 6–11 (https://opendocs.ids.ac.uk/opendocs/bitstream/handle/123456789/9246/IDSB_27_2_10.1111-j.1759-5436.1996.mp27002002.x.pdf;jsessionid=43E4FF0D384CFFAB66D7CAD90346D001?sequence=1 Accessed 1 September 2017).

Ades, A. and Di Tella, R. (1999) "Rents, competition and corruption", *American Economic Review*, 89(4), 982–993 (www.people.hbs.edu/rditella/papers/AERRentsCorruption.pdf Accessed 1 September 2017).

Almeida, M. A. de and Zagaris, B. (2015) "Political capture in the Petrobras corruption scandal: The sad tale of an oil giant", *The Fletcher Forum of World Affairs*, 39(2), 87–99 (https://static1.squarespace.com/static/579fc2ad725e253a86230610/t/57ec6f6fc534a5e78b120d0a/1475112816226/39-2_14AlmeidaZagaris.pdf Accessed 1 September 2017).

Camargo, J. G. de A. (2014) "Collaboration agreement October 31 2014" (http://politica.estadao.com.br/blogs/fausto-macedo/wp-content/uploads/sites/41/2015/02/dela%C3%A7%C3%A3ojulio.pdf Accessed 1 September 2017).

Cartier-Bresson, J. (1997) "Corruption network, transaction security and illegal social exchange", *Political Studies*, 45(3), 463–476.

Corruption Perception Index (2016) *Transparency International* (https://www.transparency.org/news/feature/corruption_perceptions_index_2016 Accessed 1 September 2017).

Corruption Perception Index (2015) *Transparency International* (https://www.transparency.org/cpi2015 Accessed 1 September 2017).

Corruption Perception Index (2014) *Transparency International* (https://www.transparency.org/cpi2014/results).

Costa, L. M. (2008) "Battling corruption through csr codes in emerging markets: Oil and gas industry", *RAE Eletrônica*, 7(1) (http://rae.fgv.br/rae-eletronica/vol7-num1-2008/battling-corruption-through-csr-codes-emerging-markets-oil-and-gas-ind Accessed 1 September 2017).

Costa, L. M. (2012) "Sustainable development in emerging markets & csr codes of conduct: Oil and gas industry in Brazil", *Journal of Operations and Supply Chain Management Special Issue*, 4, 44–66 (http://bibliotecadigital.fgv.br/ojs/index.php/joscm/article/viewFile/9563/8613 Accessed 1 September 2017).

Costa, L. M. (2013) *BRIC Countries from BRIC by BRIC to setting up a company: Cases, texts and legal materials*, volume one, Quartier Latin, Sao Paulo.

Costa, P. B. (2014) "Collaboration agreement No. 21 September 2 2014" (http://media.folha.uol.com.br/poder/2015/03/11/termo-de-colaboracao-021.pdf Accessed 1 September 2017).

Doh, J., Rodriguez, P., Uhlenbruck, K., Collins, J. and Eden. L. (2003) "Coping with corruption in foreign markets", *Academy of Management Executive*, 17(3), 114–127 (http://faculty.darden.virginia.edu/rodriguezp/document/10954775.pdf Accessed 1 September 2017).

Doig, A. and Theobald, R. (2000) *Corruption and democratisation*, Frank Cass, London.

Dreher, A. and Gassebner, M. (2013) "Greasing the wheels? The impact of regulations and corruption on firm entry", *Public Choice*, 155(3–4), 413–432 (https://link.springer.com/content/pdf/10.1007%2Fs11127-011-9871-2.pdf Accessed 1 September 2017).

Evans, P. (1995) *Embedded autonomy: States and industrial transformation*, Princeton University Press, Princeton.

Fleischer, D. (1996) "Political corruption in Brazil", *Crime Law and Social Change*, 25(4), 297–321.

Flynn, P. (2005) "Brazil and Lula 2005: Crisis, corruption and change in political perspective", *Third World Quarterly*, 26(8), 1221–1267.

Geddes, B. and Neto, A. (1992) "Institutional sources of corruption in Brazil", *Third World Quarterly*, 13(4), 641–661 (www.jstor.org/stable/3992381 Acessed 1 September 2017).

Gehlbach, S. (2013) *Formal models of domestic politics*, Cambridge University Press, New York.

Girling, J. (1997) *Corruption, capitalism and democracy*, Routledge, London and New York.

Green, D. (2016) "Corruption in Brazil", in Charles Funderburk, ed., *Political corruption in comparative perspective: Sources, status and prospects*, Routledge, London and New York, 41–70.

Huntington, S. P. (1968) *Political order in changing societies*, Yale University Press, New Haven and London.

Husted, B. W. (1999) "Wealth, culture, and corruption", *Journal of International Business Studies*, 30(2), 339–359.

Leff, N. H. (1964) "Economic development through bureaucratic corruption", *American Behavioral Scientist*, 8(3), 8–14.

Lessig, L. (2013) "Institutional corruptions", *Edmond J. Safra Research Lab Working Papers No. 1*, March 15 (http://papers.ssrn.com/sol3/papers.cfm?abstract_id=2233582 Acessed 1 September 2017).

Méon, P.-G. and Sekkat, K. (2005) "Does corruption grease or sand the wheels of growth?", *Public Choice*, 122, 69–97.

Moody-Stuart, G. (1997) *Grand corruption*, WorldView Publishing, Oxford.

Morris, S. D. (2009) *Political corruption in Mexico: The impact of democratization*, Lynne Rienner, Boulder, CO.

North, D. C. (1990) *Institutions, institutional change and economic performance*, Cambridge University Press, New York.

Nye, J. S. (1967) "Corruption and political development: A cost-benefit analysis", *American Political Science Review*, 61(2), 417–427.

The dynamics of corruption in Brazil 203

O'Neil, J. (2001) "Building better global economic BRICs", *Goldman Sachs Global Economic Paper No. 66* (www.goldmansachs.com/our-thinking/archive/archive-pdfs/build-better-brics.pdf Accessed 1 September 2017).

Polícia Federal (www.pf.gov.br/imprensa/lava-jato/numeros-da-operacao-lava-jato Accessed 1 September 2017).

Pope, J. (1997) "Enhancing accountability and ethics in the public sector", in Rick Stapenhurst and Sahr J. Kpundeh, eds., *Courbing corruption: Towards a model for building national integrity*, The World Bank, Washington, DC, 105–116.

Power, T. J. and Taylor, M. M. (2011) *Corruption and democracy in Brazil: The struggle for accountability*, University of Notre Dame Press, Notre Dame.

Roett, R. (1978) *Brazil: Politics in a patrimonial society*, Praeger, New York.

Rose-Ackerman, S. (1978) *Corruption: A study in political economy*, Academic Press, New York.

Rose-Ackerman, S. (1997) "The political economy of corruption", in K. A. Elliot, ed., *Corruption and the global economy*, Institute for International Economics, Washington, DC, 31–60 (https://piie.com/publications/chapters_preview/12/2iie2334.pdf Accessed 1 September 2017).

Rose-Ackerman, S. and Palifka, B. J. (2016) *Corruption and government: Causes consequences and reform*, 2nd ed., Cambridge University Press, New York.

Sachs, J. D. and Warner, A. M. (1995) "Natural resource abundance and economic growth", *National Bureau of Economic Research Working Paper No. 5398*, Cambridge, MA (www.nber.org/papers/w5398.pdf Accessed 1 September 2017).

Silva, M. F. da (1999). "The political economy of corruption in Brazil", *RAE*, 39(3), 26–41 (www.scielo.br/scielo.php?script=sci_arttext&pid=S0034-75901999000300004 Accessed 1 September 2017).

Thompson, D. (2013) "Two concepts of corruption", *Edmond J. Safra Research Lab Working Papers No. 16* (http://papers.ssrn.com/sol3/papers.cfm?abstract_id=2304419 Acessed 1 September 2017).

Transparency International (www.transparency.org/cpi2014/results, www.transparency.org/cpi2015, www.transparency.org/news/feature/corruption_perceptions_index_2016 Acessed 1 September 2017).

You, J.-S. and Khagram, S. (2005) "A comparative study of inequality and corruption", *American Sociological Review*, 70(1), 136–157.

11 "The theory of the world in-between"

Corporatism and mafia-ness in the new type of corruption in Italy

Davide Torsello and Maria Giulia Pezzi

> The theory of the in-between world, fellow . . . there are, how to say, the living above and the dead below, and we are in the middle . . . . This means there is a world, a world in between in which all people meet, and you say, is it possible that, that guy? Like, it is possible that, I don't know, tomorrow I can be at dinner with Berlusconi. It's impossible . . . . Do you get the idea? The world in between is where everything meets, where all persons, of a certain, of every, kind meet, all there. You are there, but not because of status, because you deserve it, not? Then, in the in-between world, even the guy from the upper world has some interest, that someone from the underworld does for him things that nobody can do . . . . That's the thing, and everything gets mixed . . . . Those who are below, in the underworld, are all the same.

Introduction

These words belong to a conversation from a police recording obtained in Rome in December 2012, which, along with several other similar testimonies, enabled the discovery of the criminal activities of a complex system that has been termed "Mafia Capitale" (Mafia Capital). This system is one of the most complex and sophisticated so far discovered: mechanisms of interaction between several and different actors, holding different roles, performing different criminal activities, such as violence, organized crime, extortion, usury, corruption and abuse of office. In the course of massive police operations in the Italian capital, the magistrates have issued 39 arrest warrants for suspects who are allegedly tied by a common organization, which the authorities describe as mafia-like but the suspects themselves do not, which has operated in Rome in the course of the past 10 years. It has been difficult to determine the overall financial scope of the activities, primarily because of the wide variety of practices. Due to the extraordinarily plastic and multilayered structure of this organization, Mafia Capitale is an example of how corruption, one of its main activities, has become diversified in its extent, scope, aims and targets, and has become a more "secure" practice thanks to the support of organized violence. Corruption of public officials is "structural" and has become the most profitable part of this system, as magistrates analyzing the case have argued, but it is increasingly problematic to study these forms of corruption by using the mainstream analytical categories that the social sciences have produced. One approach, developed in this chapter, is to look at the symbolic and factual construction and the organization of social interactions within this association, as well as, by extension, at the new forms of Italian public–private corruption.

The theory of the in-between world (*il mondo di mezzo*) is given expression among a lean, almost commonsensical delineation of the space in which the actors of the criminal group, those who benefit of the group's services and their potential competitors are located. The symbolic construction of this three-layered space is itself suggestive, but not to the point of indicating how corruption is changing in the Italian context (and arguably elsewhere). This chapter argues that the symbolism of the perceived social equality that criminal actors can achieve in the mondo di mezzo can be the key for understanding this new form of corruption. In other words, by paying attention to the ideas and ideologies of space (in socio-relational terms), one can have an idea of how corruption can become first a banalized practice (de Sardan 1999) and then a revolutionary mechanism of the reconfiguration of the power constellations dominant in Italian society. It is less important whether those who enter corruption deals are in a dyadic relationship, as the classical anthropological literature on clientelism had postulated some decades ago (Gellner and Waterbury 1977; Eisenstadt and Roniger 1984), or whether and to what extent the corruptor is able to influence the corrupted following his own agenda and rationality, as in the principal-agent theory (Klitgaard 1988; Groenendijk 1997). In the theory of the mondo di mezzo, every construction of the relationship between actors is brought down to the final proposition that, thanks to the in-between world, "in the underworld we are all the same". Corruption becomes then an (illicit) form of social empowerment, in which every deal is perceived as a mechanism of social exchange, and this is possible thanks to an accurate intertwining of activities, roles, tasks and duties.

This chapter is structured as follows. In the first section, we summarize some of the main anthropological approaches to the study of corruption, focusing in particular on those that emphasize the processual and transactional aspects of this phenomenon. In the second section, we deal with the cognitive and jurisprudence parameters through which the organization of Mafia Capitale is associated with other traditional mafia organizations. In the third section, we explore some of the mechanisms of social interaction that predominate in this organization and that render corruption a constantly changing social force. In the final section, we introduce the symbolism of corruption in the eyes of the magistrates and the criminals themselves.

Anthropological approaches to corruption

Ethnographic accounts of the role of the state in relation to corruption have taken different standpoints. These can be summarized as three perspectives: normative, hermeneutical and transactional. The normative approach analyzes the legislative and normative functions in which corruption becomes implanted in different societal contexts. In this perspective, corruption is seen as a violation of a social norm.

The state is portrayed either as a weak enforcing actor of anti-corruption norms and laws or, as a legislative agent of ad hoc norms to increase unaccountability.

In one of the most recent contributions to this approach, Nuijten and Anders (2007) have described "the secret of law", stressing the idea that the common Western-centric notion of corruption, grounded on the dichotomy between public and private interests, is of little help to anthropological investigations. They depart from the legal anthropological perspective that looks at law as plural and as profoundly influenced by social processes (Moore 2000). Corruption and law are not opposites but rather are constitutive of one another; just as legal prescriptions and their transgressions are not mutually exclusive. Because the possibility of transgression is always present in law, corruption is to these authors the very "secret of law", which defines fields of law's application and intervention, but meanwhile allows for its transgression in society. An approach that looks at law as the only cure against corruption is misleading because, among other things, law is plural, and it is only through empirical sensibility for its pluralism that corruption can be successfully detected through its nuances as an alternative form of legal order (Znoj 2007; MacNaughton and Wong 2007).

In this perspective, the state becomes an active participant in the process of setting the agenda for corruption and not a passive agent who fights against its effects. Law creates the sphere of legitimacy through which corruption is accepted or rejected, conceived of and exploited by those in power (Blundo 2006; Hsu and Smart 2007; Hoagh 2010). The hermeneutical perspective points at the sphere of governmentality rather than governance, individuating ground-level efforts to interpret political power (Foucault 2007). The focus of analysis should not be on whether the state has been able to set the boundaries between legality and illegality or morality and immorality, or whether the state makes use of corruption to obtain legitimacy, but instead on the discursive power of the notion of corruption.

This hermeneutic approach is present in Gupta's ethnography of the Indian case (1995, 2005). Gupta describes how local citizens in India use corruption as a form of discourse in order to access particular benefits that are scarcely allocated. For him, the political strategy consists of seeking information on ways to bribe properly, the amounts of money to be paid and under which interactional conditions bribes are needed to access services provided by state officers of local governments. This brings about the need to differentiate between two discursive uses of corruption in relation with governmentality. The first concerns the process of information-seeking about whom, how and when to bribe properly. The second corresponds to public talk – that is, the way through which professionals, media and prosecutors address corruption in their everyday and how their denouncements influence social ties of trust and solidarity (this concern will be discussed in the later part of the chapter).

Strategic reference to corruption in public discourses brings the state back into play, as Bailey (1969) and Boissevain (1974) indicated. The role of brokers and informed actors becomes crucial to understand how the management of information can be translated into power and influence (Scott 1972). Some ethnographic researchers have stressed this point (Wade 1982; Price 1999; Ruud 2000; Sewanta

2009). For example, in a study in Nepal that was based on a questionnaire, Sewanta has demonstrated how corruption is used by local citizens at the discursive level to differentiate among the performance and capacities of a number of institutions from the police to health services, the school and the post (2009). As Gupta had suggested, Sewanta likewise suggests that this discursive use does not necessarily lead local citizens to avoid engagement with state officials, but it actually works as a frame of reference to establish effective practices. On the other hand, the discursive construction of corruption eventually plays an important role in defining the judicial competencies and to legitimate its authority to combat this complex phenomenon.

The third perspective is transactional. Governance is not analyzed in relation to normative or hermeneutic aspects but as an interaction between different levels of political decision making and different social tasks in action. This approach has received comparatively less attention in mainstream political science literature, where the administrative, normative function of the state is at the heart of the debate. Even in the collective action theory (Olson 1971), where every actor is perceived as maximizing his or her own interests, and these interests can cumulate to foster or hamper corruption, transactional analyses of the tasks, roles and functions of the different levels of governance are a relatively new field. According to this perspective, corruption can be used to describe, by local actors, the functioning of the bureaucratic apparatus. One should not fall, however, into the teleological trap of considering corruption as an accepted practice by local people who cannot avoid it, because everyone is expected to be likewise corrupt (Banfield 1975). Rather, the main problem arises from the consideration that inefficient bureaucracies, pluralistic and comparatively weak legal mechanisms of enforcement of anti-corruption measures and low wages of public servants may all become breeders of corruption. However, stating that corruption becomes accepted as a practice in countries with weak institutional arrangements is a large simplification. Anthropological research has abundantly demonstrated that it is when corruption becomes "banalized", as de Sardan argues, that a distorted view of the functioning of the public sector comes into place (1999). This may have the effect of blurring the separation between private and public spheres, affecting the general idea of good governance, increasing local citizens' frustration about the perceived distance from the administrative centers and instilling in individuals a shared (false) awareness that face-to-face exchanges are the norm and even morally acceptable (de Sardan 1999). According to this perspective, corruption exemplifies a failure of the state to encompass local government spheres of activity, an incomplete bureaucratization process or a collusion of different sets of actors who make use of gaps in governance to compete or even cooperate for bribes (Torsello 2016).

The collusion of state and local government interests, and hence the transactional functions that corruption comes to acquire, are ways to express the tension between fear of delocalization of central power and dissatisfaction with strong state authority. This fear is often informed more by the visible, growing social inequality at the local level than by a shared knowledge of a corrupt state already present under the socialist regime (Uslaner 2008).

The mafia-ness of Mafia Capitale

The structure of the Mafia Capitale organization is impressive. It includes a leader, three key collaborators (one may say senior managers) – with respective tasks of organizing violent and intimidating actions, controlling corrupt exchanges as well as managing relations with the public administration and the political sphere – and a coordinator of the economic activities who manages relationships with companies. Down in the system hierarchy follow three entrepreneurs, three public officers, one organizer for logistics and several other participants, such as accountants, a fiscal expert, intermediaries of political authorities and of the business world and even a secretary. The only and surprising missing task is that of a banker, an old figure in the corruption activities of the last two decades, which has, because of more restrictive laws to control capital fluxes, been replaced by accountants and a wide range of consultants that typically grant access to offshore and shell companies around the globe. The interconnection and mutual dependence of these tasks and figures has been described by the magistrates as a long historical process that can be traced back to the activities of the criminal organization that has already operated in Rome since the 1980s, named Banda della Magliana. This organization has constituted a puzzling example of criminal enterprise in Italy because it has been extremely adaptable and plastic in its embrace though time of all kinds of activities (including corruption) with exponents from left-wing and right-wing parties (Abbate and Lillo 2015). In a sense, the findings regarding the Mafia Capitale have allowed the authorities to apply descriptions and images of mafia organizations to this system even though there is little evidence of collusions with more "traditional" mafia networks. The first step of the symbolic construction of the corruption activities in the mondo di mezzo system consists in how magistrates and police forces narrate the system.

One significant and early part of the inquest is dedicated to explaining the classical notion of mafia in the Italian jurisprudence tradition and to relate this with the description of the Mafia Capitale system. Mafia activities are defined by the coexistence of a number of "revealing indexes of mafia-ness": the secrecy of interpersonal ties, the spiritual kinship ties, the absolute respect for hierarchies, the shouldering of legal expenses by the clan and the widespread omertà as an indicator of subjugation to the system (Inquest 2014: 31–32). To this aspect, one can add another, less straightforward one, which is the control of a territory or a delimitated space. However, the use of these indexes is in itself a problematic approach in jurisprudence since it creates the basis for a number of sociological and cultural assumptions that do not need to be matched by facts, those that count at the end of the investigation. Hence, rather than assume that these indexes have a factual force, the magistrates take the view of indicating that the territorial rooting of mafia networks usually provides it the function of anti-state apparatuses, which may infiltrate into the public institutions and thus corrupt them. This organizational function is achieved by the mafia through the means of the above mentioned omertà, as well as the subjugation to violent practices. It is within this framework that the Roman organization can be considered as a form of mafia,

"The theory of the world in-between" 209

even if it is within "limited sectors and activities of social interaction" (Inquest 2014: 33).

Mafia Capitale presents a number of indexes of mafia-ness, such as the autonomously organized forms of crime and omertà, but in other terms, it differs from traditional mafia networks: it is spatially limited to the case of Rome; it includes different figures that covers fields as different as finance, politics, bureaucracy, business and organized crime; and it presents aspects of plasticity and rapidly changing structures that "meet at the mondo di mezzo" (Inquest 2014: 34–35). Unlike traditional forms of mafia, this system is, in its complexity, still fragile in the task of being recognized as part of the social fabrics that make up the in-between world. It is worthwhile to note how, in another wire taping, two of the members of the system were positively impressed by an article by *L'Espresso*, one of the most widely read Italian magazines, entitled "The four kings of Rome" (December 7, 2012):

> But this, this [article] on our work, it's a good thing . . . . They are more protected . . . . They are tranquil . . . . Even if, you know, talking to people, they run away. If you talk with a mole, yes, but [if it is one] who knows you already . . . when you have relationships with those who know you, if you are clever.
>
> (Inquest 2014: 35)

The wired text shows two elements that again work to build the symbolism of the in-between world. One is the preoccupation with a kind of marketing logic, in which the media coverage is, perversely, seen as positive for "publicizing" the range and type of activities in which the system is involved. Media empower the organization by attributing to it its capacities and fields of expertise. The second and even more significant element is that preoccupation is also expressed toward the potential misalignment of the system with forms of social interactions at a more general level: "they run away if you talk with them." Again, the transactional nature of corruption, in which the primary goal of the organization is to establish relations, to enter mechanisms of exchange that, in the eyes of the magistrates, may even render superfluous the acts of violence and intimidations on which the system has built its negative fame appear manifest.

The corporatism of corruption

In some of the classical social science literature on corruption, the illicit deal has often been viewed in terms of a dyadic relationship between two parts: the corruptor and the corrupted. Even in cases where the research focus has been on the implications at large in society, the relationship between citizens of the state or, in fewer cases, between actors and international organizations, there was barely the possibility that more actors would appear in a structured and corporative way (Kotkin and Sajó 2002). The Mafia Capitale case is rather unique in this sense: it provides a series of snapshots of a systemic corruption which is not, as some of the

210 *Davide Torsello and Maria Giulia Pezzi*

literature suggests, a practice of expression of malfunctioning bureaucracies or of weak states but of tight and extremely well-functioning interpersonal transactions.

Expressions such as "we are putting up a good team," "they can't touch us if we are a strong group," "we don't miss nobody in our group," or eventually "there is a group, and then there is a leader" are frequent in the wired conversations that the magistrates analyzed in their inquest. Reading these 1,156 pages, one gets the message that the true strength and novelty of the organization is that, like a mafia system, apart from well-recognized leadership, no one is singularly identifiable as the corruptor. There is a sense of corporatism that comes out of the efficient coordination among members of the organizations, who are able to summon the right person at the right moment, to menace when necessary, to put into contact public officers with entrepreneurs, to find semi-illicit or illicit ways to resolve delicate problems. In the case of the circulation of cash, for instance, limited by the new measures that Italian banks have introduced to decrease and control the use of cash for large transactions (in particular, concerning the 500 euro notes, the favorite in the corruption business), the organization is ready to find a way out. Personal connections of the member in charge of logistic arrangements have helped to change big denomination bills for small denomination bills through a circuit of connections with gasoline stands, who typically have an abundance of smaller bills. The gasoline business will later become an investment itself, when the organization has encountered the necessity to periodically launder part of its money. Again, thanks to a round of interpersonal connections, it is decided to invest in purchasing one or more gasoline stations, as well as truck washing plants.

In one case in 2013, the mayor of a small commune east of Rome had summoned a meeting with members of the organization through the member in charge of deals with the public administration. After a brief but explicative telephone call, the two – a lawyer and two others from the organization – decide to meet; the agenda is to prepare the details of a call for bids on a project of managing the refuse and recycling system in the commune. The mayor asked help to the organization to design the bid so that one of the companies controlled by them could be the winner, and not vice versa, as common wisdom would go. For this consultation, he allegedly received a bribe of 30,000 euro and his lawyer received a small honorarium of 1,500 euro which he kept on claiming all the times he was present in the meetings, and even if he even did not utter a word. The two parts designed the bids and the representative of the organization left. On the day that the bids were disclosed, however, it became clear that another company, with no connection to the organization, was ahead. A woman from the commune secretariat promptly informed somebody from the organization (it happened during the meeting for attributing the bid, which, by law, is a process to be held behind doors and in secret). The woman was very worried that the offer of the second company could actually be lower and hastily urged the organization to provide more documents in order to change the offer. All this was, of course, completely illegal. At this point, another organization member, an accountant, through an acquaintance, a businessman, was able in a turn of 20 minutes to contact the manager of the winning company. The manager was then put on the phone with the one from the organization responsible for dealing with the public administration that, without any menace or big explanation, obtained what he wanted. The second company stepped out and the bid was won. What remained was to threaten the zealous secretary and her collaborators, inviting them for lunch: as the wire tape says, "The girls are hungry; they deserve their meal."

The corporatism of the Mafia Capitale system is an expression of the ability to interlock a number of tasks that in the traditional forms of corruption were very costly and partly out of reach. There is evidence that initial capital for corrupting public administrators has been obtained through extortion and usury in the peripheral areas of Rome, targeting small businesses in particular. Drug dealing, on the other hand, and contrary to what the media assumed, was not in place. What allowed the members of the organization to feel "like a team" was less the violence that characterized the organization in a period precedent to its debut in public administration, however, and more the entrepreneurial activities which, like in the type of mafia organizations by Diego Gambetta (1993), have characterized the recent developments of the organization. Mafia Capitale has been promptly invested in paying out bureaucrats, rather than politicians as it was in the 1990s type of Italian corruption (Gomez et al. 2012). One innovative option chosen by Mafia Capitale has been the ability to individuate key bureaucrats, from Rome or neighboring communes, who have become beneficiaries of monthly installments – in other words, who receive denominated "salaries" from the organization for their services. These salaries may range from 500 euro to secretaries, to 1,500 to accountants, 3,000 to counselors and a range of 5,000 to 15,000 euros to managers. Some administrators, managers of public enterprises (such as in the business of refuse disposal), have gained over 100,000 euro per year for their collaboration with the organization. The perspective that "we are equal in the underworld and so we can aspire to the in-between world" is expressed in this strategy, which ensures "security" and fidelity as premiums to the administrators who open their doors to corrupt deals. In this perspective, the transactional approach to corruption becomes corroborated not only because of a form of perceived corporatism of the organization, which acts as a team, but eventually as mechanisms of social exchange, and chains of reciprocity (Appadurai 1986) are installed through official and illegal regular payments.

The migrant camp project

One particular case in which the organization shows its flexibility and outreach in several spheres of interaction with the public administration is the migrant camp project. In November 2012, members of the municipal council of the capital who are on the organization payslips inform the top layer that the project of building a camp for migrants, with a specialized structure for parentless children from North Africa, has been left out of the city budget for the coming two years. The budget is about to be approved, and due to the upcoming Christmas holidays there would be no more chances to approve the expense for 2013–2014. The news upsets the leadership, who is promptly informed but has less than 48 hours to react.

The sum at stake is high since the organization has invested 3 million euro in the project, without being assigned any work, and no bid being issued; the expected budget had been diverted to other interventions in the field of social security. At this point, the transactional strategy of the organization again becomes manifest. Using a number of interpersonal connections, the leadership arranges a meeting with the secretariat of the mayor pushing for a quick solution. This is also a favorable moment for the organization since in the coming spring the mayoral elections will be held. Support for the project can be traded for electoral support, the promise being to hold a number of electoral dinners in expensive restaurants, which takes place soon after the camp project gets the green light. Each of these dinners costs up to 1,000 euro per person, with the average overall expense ranging from 5,000 to 10,000 euros. On the top of this, and apart from the corruption of public officers who either are on the organization pay list or receive large kickbacks (10,000 to 30,000 euros), several thousands are transferred to three foundations that, among all, sponsor the electoral campaigns.

Not only is the organization successful at getting funding for the migrant camp in time; it also receives more than what was expected. The budget is revised (for the 112th time), and a portion of the reserve fund set up for emergencies is allocated to this and to another project. Altogether, the nomad camp (as it is officially termed) gets around 13 million euros for three years, more than what was expected, and it is a considerable gain if one considers that from another wiring it appears that effective construction of structures in the camp will cost just above 200,000 euros, whereas real food and managing costs are not esteemed in reality but are calculated to reach an average of 67 euro per person per day.

The opportunities that the migrant camp business offered the structure were at some point unexpectedly large. This case again is telling of how corruption is increasingly dependent on a number of conditions that determine patterns of social interaction and upon which depends the perceived strength and efficacy of the criminal organizations. Against the background of the typical 1990s corruption scandals that called for public outcry and that culminated in the Clean Hand Movement led by the charismatic figure of magistrate Antonio di Pietro, the new type of corruption has changed, evolving into less predictable and banal forms of transaction and interaction. Corruption in the 1990s pattern was a classic configuration of asymmetric power relationships, not so far away from the clientelistic pattern. The top of the configuration was occupied by the corrupted, typically a politician or high-class bureaucrat, who could influence decision-making processes via the party or inter-party executive assemblies (Della Porta and Vannucci 2007). In this structure, the corruptor (person or a group, such as a company) was more or less aware of the final destination of his bribe and was concerned mainly not to upset disappointed politicians who, in the larger scandals, represented their own parties. The number of figures and tasks involved in this exchange was much more limited, typically including the corruptor, an intermediary (usually a bureaucrat or local politician), a politician and in larger cases a party secretary, who often operated as "cashier" (*cassiere del partito*). This structure had strength and a weakness as compared to the one described in the case of Mafia Capitale. The strength was that it was difficult to get to the top of the structure since the hierarchy and strong separation of tasks and roles did not allow easy and direct interaction with key power holders. If this system "protected" the ultimate recipients of the bribe, it made it more difficult to include new members (such as other forms of intermediation) in the structure. The weakness of the old type of Italian corruption was that, once beheaded (as after condemnation of the former Prime Minister Bettino Craxi in 1994), the system was no longer viable since permission to acquire bribes had to follow a rigid party line. Moreover, at another point, the system was relatively more costly than the actual one. In particular, in the case of large transactions (such as construction business or pharmaceutical scandals), premiums had to be offered to other governing or even opposition parties in order to avoid leaking due to jealousies. The hierarchical structure of the 1990s corruption made the system insulated on the top but rather static and subject to the vagaries of party equilibriums, a well-known feature of the Italian political scene.

The symbolism of corruption

Anthropologists of some decades ago were led to distinguish between overt and covert culture and explicit from implicit culture. More general ideas (basic assumptions) are less accessible to verbal formulations because the social consensus in a community protects them from challenge and shifts the focus of discourse to more specifics that are at issue in normal social life. This creates the need for metaphors, which work as bridges (in cognitive and social forms of expression) between what is explicit and implicit of culture. Thus, one may expect that much of culture is not recoverable through ethnographic observation, but it needs to be built on the interpretation of how metaphors (and symbols) are used in the context of social life (LeVine 1984: 76–77).

Cultural meaning systems have at least four tasks: the representational, the constructive, the directive and the evocative. Respectively, they represent the world, they construct cultural entities, they direct one to do certain things and they evoke certain emotions (D'Andrade 1984: 96). These are always present to some degree in any system. Symbols represent either the physical thing that carries the meaning or the meaning carried by the physical thing. Even when applied to the mind, it is an internal image of some external form (D'andrade 1984: 103–104).

The transformation of corruption in recent years has had a perverse, but very direct, impact on its social functionality: it has gone from being an exclusive mechanism to being an inclusive one. The Tangentopoli era in the 1990s celebrated corruption at the level of the political parties that benefited from networks of large enterprises to assign contracts, privileges and monopolies. Corruption was an elitist and exclusive system for which the kickback (in Italian, *tangente*, and translated as "tangent") was the dominant metaphorical expression that not only defined a way of proceeding (by touching part of a curve area, difficult to grasp and predict), but mainly referred to the complex mechanism of interaction by which the tangent could come into contact with the curve – that is, the political world.

Today, corruption is less frequently metaphorized as tangent and is increasingly metaphorized as a "gelatinous system" in which different actors are immersed. The metaphor has changed substantially, from being the point at which two different lines meet to a system in which everyone is immersed in the same sticky liquid, which glues and unites, just like family ties. Corruption becomes, then, an expression of a system of social relations that does not seek to get closer to a distant goal (once the parties or their representatives) but rather is aware of its power of cohesiveness, of being able to keep different types of actors interrelated, under the form of a viscous and gelatinous liquid.

The theory of the mondo di mezzo has been acquired by magistrates with enthusiasm, similarly to the above-described mafia-ness of the organization. However, the mafia trope is not, to paraphrase D'Andrade, a case of representation of symbolism but of evocation. Magistrates in the inquest trace the possible links of the organization with elements of the traditional southern Italian mafias, but this is done more in the effort to link the denounced crimes to more serious crimes, such as those of association with mafia organizations (article 416bis). In this sense, the power of the symbolism of mafia in the exercise of a range of localized criminal activities – violence, extortion, blackmail, stalking and menacing – evoke the association between corruption and other forms of crime. One may argue that this process of signification is itself also directive since, in the complexity of the organization, it gives plenty of space to a firm division of labor, where tasks and roles are clearly set and directed from the leadership. Moreover, the strong inclusive character of the organization that can "count on right persons on the right time" confirms the directive feature.

On the representation side, however, the mafia metaphor becomes weaker. In one of the wire tapes quoted earlier, the leadership appears pleased by the "good publicity" that it has received from the media, in particular after publication of the special investigation by the magazine *L'Espresso* in 2012. However, the mistake that the journalist makes, attributing illicit earnings to drug dealing, along the line of all major mafia organizations, is quickly pinpointed by the wired interlocutors who are ready to comment, "he has not understood us. If we dealt with drugs, people would escape from us. Can you imagine? How do you work with people who stay away from you?" (Inquest, 35). There is, in the wired conversations, very little mention of doing business with other criminal organizations, and very little evocation of how a (potential) collaboration of this type should look.

Concerning omertà, one of the typical aspects of mafia-type organizations is the scarce propensity, in general, to call people by their names. Bosses and minor leaders have nicknames, some of them more and others less folkloristic. The evocative power of some of these nicknames has been a symbolic strength of mafia associative ties. Not only does it help to maintain hierarchy in its structure, but it also serves a second (surely not secondary) aim of reminding us of the true value of omertà at all social levels (Schneider and Schneider 2008). Nicknames are symbolic and evocative since they open up doors for meta-realities in which the real

"The theory of the world in-between" 215

heinous crimes are encapsulated by organizations led by leaders with terrifying and yet primarily familiar names.

The Mafia Capitale system is strikingly different in terms of its evocative power. First, its leadership is not evoked through semi-folkoristic or Hollywood-style names, but it uses personal names. Although surnames are usually avoided in conversations for obvious reasons, they are not always silenced. On the contrary, the evoking power of the organization can be symbolized by the overt use of names and surnames, which sometimes appear to emphasize the strength of the organization.

Moreover, from the wired material, it emerges that omertà is not actively sought or imposed from the top. It is more a choice of intermediaries and sometimes key political figures chosen in order not to be incriminated in the course of taped conversations. There is comparatively little fear in naming people than in letting investigative authorities trace the relationships with them. Conversations are rather abundant in the use of symbols, metaphors and euphemisms in a semi-conscious consideration that the probability that conversations may be wired is rather high. Nonetheless, conversations do take place because they are vital for these types of transactions, which are marked by adaptability to changing scenarios and the various tasks required by the coming into play of different and even new figures, but narrations are rarely evocative. Paying dues to a local bureaucrat is, for example, termed "let him gain his daily snack" (*fargli mangiare la pagnotta*), "let him suck all my blood" (*lasciarmi dissanguare per lui*), "he has his needs too" (*ha anche lui le sue esigenze*), or even in terms of a comparison with what active members usually gain. These externalizations are barely evocative in nature, as at times they look merely pragmatic. At times, they even describe a logic of "egalitarianism", which is part of the teamlike idea of corporatism, which of course leaves little space to systematic practices of omertà.

On the other hand, the mondo di mezzo system of metaphors is clearly telling of a more evocative symbolism. It is surely expressed in terms of representation of the world, with an evocative touch of transactional connectivism, a kind of inclusive Tolkien style (as the investigators argue) of association. In this style, not only does the mondo di mezzo connect spheres that are incompatible by definition (the world above and the one below), but it evokes a form of empowerment from below that anthropologists have detected in other socio-cultural connections where corruption is endemic, such as India (see Gupta 1995, 2005), Nepal, Africa and Indonesia. Not only is the mondo di mezzo a metaphor for inclusion, "perceived egalitarianism" and corporatism, it is also an evocation of an ideal type of society which, as the wired conversation in perhaps a lapse suggests, has been inspired by the kind of public morality which dominated Italy during the 20 years of Berlusconi's leadership. On July 20, 2017, the jury of the Court of Rome issued the final verdict on the Mafia Capitale case. The jury sentenced 41 among the accused, with the highest penalty set as 20 years of prison to the top members of the association. However, the verdict has confuted the existence of any type of mafia association. The motivations for this sentence have still not been issued.

Conclusions

Understanding the changing faces of Italian corruption is an endeavor that requires several analytical tools and theoretical approaches. For one thing, it is correct to state that the contribution of anthropology to this field, although shallow over the last three decades, has increasingly come to be strongly relevant, if not badly needed. Anthropological accounts of worldwide corruption have pointed out the need to revisit this timely topic through a so far neglected sensitivity for strategies of governance, on the grounds of mechanisms of social interaction and by looking at the hermeneutical aspects of a range of activities that are more often on the border between what is publicly perceived as licit and illicit. After the symbolic tradition of looking at culture as the sum of the cognitive, social and moral (including what it ought to be and what people believe it is) aspects of the social reality, corruption may easily become a lens for looking at several aspects. These are the following: (a) the functioning of political systems, (b) the limits and paradoxes of the "rule of law" argument and (c) the weakness both of the normative argument and of a sort of mainstream positivist idea that poor nations are corrupted and unequal because they are trapped in a status quo situation in which poverty and inequality generates corruption, which generates inequality and again poverty. To this aim, this chapter has taken into consideration the case of Italy, one of the 10 largest world economies, in which corruption not only is perceived as endemic in society but has recently been associated with a wider range of criminal activities that have unfortunately characterized the peninsula and produced abundant literature.

The case of Mafia Capitale, a multifaceted criminal organization that draws its main source of income from corruption, is particularly telling of how corruption can adapt to changing times. The relatively weaker salience of political parties, the styles of transnational governance, more accurate forms of control of criminal fluxes of capital and a pervasive intermingling of the private and public sectors are all pull-factors that have driven change. The increased and successful corporatism of the organization Mafia Capitale is one of the responses to these exogenous factors. The plasticity and strong inclusiveness of this organization have allowed it to adapt not only to changing historical conditions but more significantly to the needs of public administration, vexed in this country by continuous budget cuts and the declassification of its competences. One might argue that the omnipresent neoliberal paradigm has influenced not only ways in which the morality of the public administration in Italy is nowadays constructed but also its accent on transactional strategies, such as those evoked in the famous book from Boissevain (1974) on Malta. The transactional theory of corruption is not, however, about simply creating and maintaining connections. The theory shows, in the Mafia Capitale case, that an organization that has been attributed by the media and magistrate's narratives of mafia-ness (which can be more or less substantiated), has learned to, following D'Andrade (1984), combine evocative with directive aspects of its meaning systems.

The symbolism with which the beautiful metaphor of the mondo di mezzo has wrapped the Mafia Capitale system is the framework within which to situate the efforts of the two ontological constructs of the social meaning of the new version of corruption in Italy. The first, by the magistrates, is a form of mafia in which tradi-tional and archaic hierarchies and blood oaths are replaced by a gelatinous liquid that embroils different actors with different skills, competences and tasks. Corruption has turned, following a mafia-type of violent enforcement systems, into a mechanism, which brings together individuals creating an idea of sameness and equality, similar to the omertà mechanism, in which nobody would denounce anybody, because he has the same sticky liquid on his dress. This creates strong mechanisms of social exchange and chains of reciprocity that, being themselves present in the social facts as well as in the symbolism of the everyday, become more powerful, and hence, they grow well beyond the "banalizing" effect described by de Sardan in the African case (1999). On the other hand, the symbolic construction of the mondo di mezzo, oper-ated by the criminal actors themselves, does a similar job. It helps to create an image of a world that, again through mechanisms of exchange, bridges and binds sectors of society that are, in Italy as in many other Western countries, miles and miles away. The symbolism of an in-between social space thus becomes the most powerful metaphor in which every single piece of the game is necessary and has its power of connecting upward. In a system as socially complex and symbolically simple as this, it becomes very hard to argue that corruption may be controlled through more accurate and severe legislations or more attentive police investigations.

References

Abbate, L., & Lillo, M. (2015) *I re di Roma. Destra e sinistra agli ordini di mafia capitale.* Milano, Chiarelettere.

Appadurai, A. (1986) Introduction: Commodities and the politics of value. In Arjun Appa-durai (ed.), *The Social Life of Things* (pp. 3–63). New York, Cambridge University Press.

Bailey, F. (1969) *Stratagems and Spoils.* New York: Shocken Books.

Banfield, E.C. (1975) Corruption as a feature of governmental organization. *Journal of Law and Economics, 18*(3), 587–605.

Blundo, G. (2006) Dealing with the local state: The informal privatization of street-level bureaucracies in Senegal. *Development and Change, 37*(4), 799–819.

Boissevain, J. (1974) *Friends of Friends: Networks, Manipulators and Coalitions.* Oxford: Basil Blackwell.

Costantini, F. (2014) "Ordinanza Di Applicazione Di Misure Cautelari 30546/10 R.G. Mod. 21." Tribunale di Roma, Ufficio VI GIP.

D'Andrade, R. G. (1984) Cultural meaning systems. In R. M. Adams, N. J. Smelser, & D. J. Treiman (eds.), *Behavioral and Social Science Research: A National Resource: Part II* (pp. 197–236). Washington, DC, National Academy Press.

della Porta, D., & Vannucci, A. (2007) *Mani impunite: vechia e nuova corruzione in Italia.* Roma and Bari, Editori Laterza.

De Sardan, O. J. P. (1999) A moral economy of corruption in Africa? *The Journal of Mod-ern African Studies, 37*(1), 25–52.

Eisenstadt, S., & Roniger, L.M. (1984) *Patron, Clients and Friends. Interpersonal Rela-tions and the Structure of Trust in Society.* Cambridge, CUP.

Foucault, M. (2007) Security, territory, population: lectures at the Collège de France, 1977–78. Palgrave Macmillan UK.

Gambetta, D. (1993) *The Sicilian Mafia: The Business of Private Protection.* Cambridge, MA, Harvard University Press.

218 *Davide Torsello and Maria Giulia Pezzi*

Gellner, E., & Waterbury, J. (eds.). (1977) *Patron and Clients in Mediterranean Societies.* London, Duckworth.

Groenendijk, N. (1997) A principal-agent Model of corruption. *Crime, Law and Change,* *27*(4), 207–229.

Gomez, P., Travaglio, M., & Barbacetto, G. (2012) *Mani Pulite.* Milano, Chiarelettere.

Gupta, A. (1995) Blurred boundaries: The discourses of corruption, the culture of politics and the imagined state. *American Ethnologist, 22*(2), 375–402.

——— (2005) The discourse of corruption, the culture of politics and the imagined state. *American Ethnologist, 22*(2), 375–402.

Hoagh, C. (2010) The magic of the populace: An ethnography of illegibility in the South Africa immigration bureaucracy. *Political and Legal Anthropology Review, 33*(1), 6–25.

Hsu, C., & Smart, A. (2007) Corruption or social capital? Tact and performance of guanxi in market socialist China. In M. Nuijtel & G. Anders (eds.), *Corruption and the Secret of Law: A Legal Anthropological Perspective* (pp. 167–190). Aldershot, Ashgate.

Kotkin, S., & Sajo, A. (eds.). (2002) *Political Corruption in Transition: A Sceptic's Handbook.* Budapest, CEU Press.

Klitgaard, R. (1988) *Controlling Corruption.* Berkeley and Los Angeles, University of California Press.

LeVine, R.A. (1984) Properties of culture: An ethnographic view. In R. Shweder & R.A. LeVine (eds.), *Culture Theory: Essays on Mind, Emotion, and the Self.* New York, Cambridge University Press.

MacNaughton, E., & Wong, K. (2007) Corruption judgements in pre-war Japan: Locating the influence of tradition, morality and trust on criminal justice. In M. Nuijtel & G. Anders (eds.), *Corruption and the Secret of Law: A Legal Anthropological Perspective* (pp. 77–98). Aldershot, Ashgate.

Moore, S. (2000) *Law as Social Process.* Hamburg, LIT.

Nuijten, M., & Anders, G. (eds.). (2007) *Corruption and the Secret of Law: A Legal Anthropological Perspective.* Aldershot, Ashgate.

Olson, M. (1971) *The Logic of Collective Actions: Public Goods and the Theory of the Groups.* New York, Schocken Books.

Price, P. (1999) Cosmologies and corruption in (South) India. *Forum for Development Studies,* (2), 315–327.

Rothstein, B. (2007) *Anti-Corruption: A Big Bang Theory.* Quality of Government Institute Working Paper Series 2007:3. University of Gothenburg.

Ruud, A. (2000) Corruption as everyday practice: The public-private divide in local Indian society. *Forum for Development Studies, 2,* 271–294.

Schneider, J., & Schneider, P. (2008) The anthropology of crime and criminalization. *Annual Review of Anthropology, 37,* 351–373. [Online] Available from: http://doi.org/10.2307/20622630.

Scott, J. (1972) *Comparative Political Corruption.* Englewood Cliffs, NJ, Pr.

Sewanta, K. (2009). Local level perception of corruption: An anthropological inquiry. *Dhaulagiri Journal of Sociology and Anthropology, 3,* 163–174.

Torsello, D. (ed.). (2016) *Corruption in Public Administration: An Ethnongraphic Approach.* Cheltenham, Edward Elgar Publishing Ltd.

Uslaner, Eric M. (2008) *Corruption, Inequality, and the Rule of Law.* New York, Cambridge University Press.

Wade, R. (1982) The system of administrative and political corruption: Canal irrigation in South India. *The Journal of Development Studies, 18*(3), 287–327.

Znoj, H. (2007) Deep corruption in Indonesia: discourses, practices, histories. In M. Nuijtel, & G. Anders (eds.), *Corruption and the Secret of Law: a Legal Anthropological Perspective* (pp. 53–76). Aldershot, Ashgate.

12 Belarus

Do stones thrown into a marsh make rings?

Pavel Sascheko

Introduction

Every year between 1,100 and 1,200 bribery offences are reported to be committed in the Republic of Belarus (National Statistical Committee 2017), but only some corruption offences can be considered corruption scandals. Any corruption scandal involves several necessary elements: the act of corruption, a disclosure the corruption in the mass media and a public reaction to the disclosure of the situation (approval or disapproval). But it is obvious that revealing a corruption act in mass media is not necessarily the resolution. It is quite usual for official institutions to track public opinion. Thus, certain events revealed can lead to changes in respect of Belarusian legislation, governance, development of state programmes, etc. In this regard, it can be expected that a corruption scandal plays a role of a stone that makes "rings" in state governance, and it inevitably leads to some serious consequences, which can be compared to "rings on the surface of a lake". But sometimes a scandal can be compared to a "stone thrown into a marsh", and in this case "making rings" can be problematic.

This chapter aims at addressing of corruption cases which can be recognized as scandals and highlighting outcomes and policy changes arising from these events. Different sources of information can be used to collect data about corruption events, to trace their consequences and to establish causation between the event and its impact on governance. It should be noted that information about corruption scandals can be found in mass media, documents concerning legislative proposals and debates or in statements of public officials. Moreover, any political, managerial, economic and other governing decisions, as a rule, have a legal form. So, corruption scandals can lead to adoption, abolition or amendment of legal acts. These documents are usually publicly available, and direct reference to a corruption scandal, as for a reason for amending, adopting or abolishing legal acts is often made in them. It allows presuming a clear linkage between a corruption scandal and events regarding governance.

It is also necessary to take into account one more methodological point regarding the present study. Shestakov points out that publications in mass media reflect data which have criminological meaning (Shestakov 2006, 130). As Gorshenkov states, dissemination of information via mass media has some distinctive features if the information concerns criminality: a person who spreads such information has some legal knowledge, information disseminated has its legal implications and

220 Pavel Sascheko

mass media often receives it from juristic or other official state sources (Gorshenkov 2003). It should be also indicated that law enforcement bodies in post-Soviet countries consider dissemination of information about corruption in mass media as one of the important types of activity aimed at forming negative attitude of public opinion to corruption behaviour (Kongantiev 2008, 78; Kulmasheva 2011, 59). For instance, it is one of the duties of prosecutors in Belarus (Koniuk 2016, 58). In the majority of cases, the information on corruption is initially collected by law enforcement bodies and then disclosed to the public via mass media (during press conferences, via official websites, etc.). Information about corruption scandals is perceived by journalists and the public, taking into consideration the general tone and context of a publication, and their perception of what constitutes corruption.

It is necessary to take into account various articles of the Criminal Code of the Republic of Belarus (hereinafter referred to as the CC) to determine the legal meaning of corruption (National Assembly of the Republic of Belarus 1999). The Belarusian CC contains articles prohibiting bribe-giving (art. 431), bribe-taking (art. 430), mediation in bribery (art. 432), abuse of power (art. 424) and embezzlement of property by a public official (art. 210). There is no article in the Belarusian CC that defines and prohibits "corruption" as a separate criminal offence. So, it is complicated for a person without any legal background to identify such acts as abuse of power, such as embezzlement of property by a public official, as corruption offences.

Quite often the information provided by the mass media contains data on elements of the corruption criminal offence, type of misbehaviour of a public official, reference to an article of the CC of the Republic of Belarus or expert opinion of representatives of law enforcement bodies or advocates. Analysis of such information allows identification a pattern of corruption behaviour and its legal meaning in terms of anti-corruption legislation.

The legal definition of corruption is provided for by the Law of the Republic of Belarus of 15 July 2015 "On the fight against corruption" (National Assembly of the Republic of Belarus 2015). According to the law, corruption encompasses the following behaviour:

> the deliberate abuse by a public official, or a person equated to him/her, or by a foreign public official, of his/her official powers or the opportunities available to him or her due to his/her official position in order to unlawfully acquire property or other benefits in the form of service, protection or the promise of an advantage for himself/herself or anyone else;
> the bribery of a public official, or a person equated to him/her, or a foreign official, i.e. giving to him property or other benefits in the form of service, protection, or the promise of advantage for himself/herself or anyone else in order that a public official or a person equated to him/her or a foreign public official act or refrain from acting in the exercise of his or her official duties;
> commission of acts mentioned above in the name of or on behalf of a legal person or a foreign legal entity.

The law also contains provisions on conflicts of interest, declaration of assets, acceptance of gifts, limitations for public officials and so on. Violation of

Belarus 221

such rules constitutes corruption offences resulting in criminal or disciplinary sanctions.

In this chapter, an attempt is made to trace the link between patterns of corruption behaviour and legal aspects of their consequences regarding governance. Therefore, clear statements of high-ranking public officials in respect of consequences of corruption cases are taken into account, as well as economic, political and other contexts of the statements. An attempt was also made to trace which news causes the most emotional reaction of the public because it reflects an attitude of people towards the case, and high level of interest and active discussions are clear signs of a scandal.

The chapter is divided into two main sections. In the first section, corruption scandals in Belarus are defined and their patterns are described. In the second section, consequences of corruption cases and causation are explored with the primary focus on statements of high-ranking public officials and legal acts adopted, amended or abolished.

Corruption scandals in Belarus

At the first stage of the current study, the pieces of news published by the Belarusian Internet news resource "tut.by"[1] were examined in order to gather information on publications related to corruption in Belarus. The period of examination covered two years (June 2014–June 2016). This period was selected because the present chapter is focused on studying the legal consequences of corruption scandals. The legislative process takes a long time, and the investigation of corruption offences also needs to pass all the necessary stages (e.g. to detect guilty persons, causes of infringements, detain and prosecute the accused, etc.). After the scandal occurred, it was necessary to consider different ways of preventing similar acts, to draft a legal act and then to adopt it. In total, this process rarely takes less than one year, so corruption scandals that occurred after June 2016 were not the subject of the current study.

Since every article published on www.tut.by receives a "tag" reflecting its content, we used this tool to calculate the number of incidents involving corruption in the period of study (June 2014–June 2016). Initially, 696 news items on corruption were selected using this tag (news contains a broad variety of incidents including historical overviews, information on planned legislative changes, statistical data, etc.). After this, only those publications that specifically dealt with corruption acts or omissions (corruption cases) were selected from the total amount of publications with the tag "corruption". In total, there were 545 such publications.

Another important feature of tut.by, which is of great value for the present research, is the possibility of marking publications with likes and dislikes. To count interest of the community in a particular publication (as corruption scandals attract the attention of a large number of persons), the total number of likes and dislikes was summed up and was then used as a quantitative indicator of corruption scandals (see Figure 12.1).

From Figure 12.1 some distinctive "peaks" can be seen, which reflect the increase in public interest to a piece of information. The number of peaks reaching or exceeding the threshold of 200 "likes" and "dislikes" (summed up) was calculated, and it was discovered that only 25 publications on corruption cases reached the threshold. These publications are given in Figure 12.2.

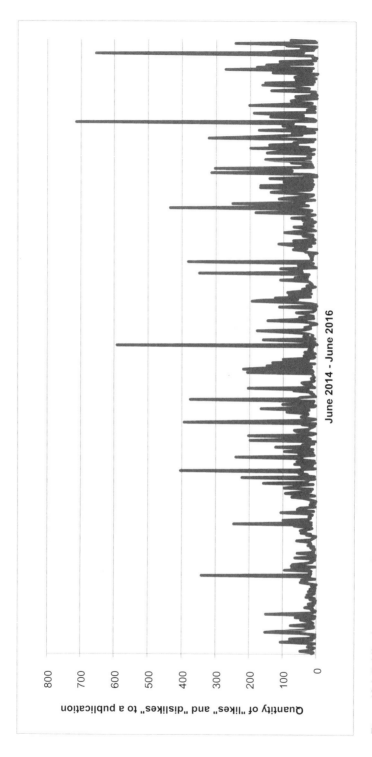

Figure 12.1 Publications on corruption cases (1–545)

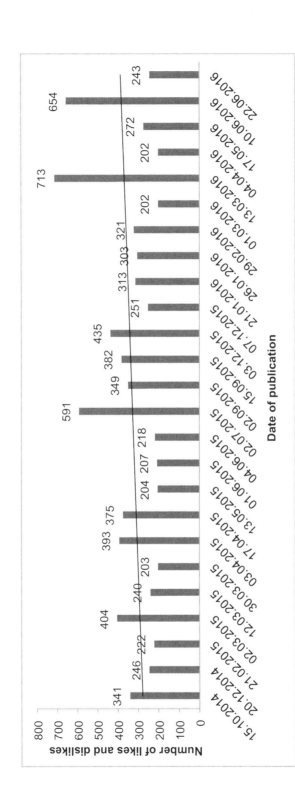

Figure 12.2 "Peak" publications

224 *Pavel Sascheko*

It should be noted however that though the "peaks" show the situations that were of special interest to the public, further analysis demonstrates that a corruption scandal usually receives special media attention, which results in a sequence of publications tracing the story. The majority of publications on corruption cases do not constitute a corruption scandal as they hardly attract any public interest. As Gorshenkov indicates, publications on corruption cases involving even high-ranking public officials (governors, vice-governors, ministers, members of parliaments, etc.) do not cause a sensation nowadays (Gorshenkov 2003).

The 25 publications on corruption, which were selected using the method mentioned above, were then analyzed as to their essence. It was discovered that some corruption cases were reflected in these publications several times, so the total number of scandals for analysis was reduced to 18. Brief information on each such case is given below to illustrate the specific situation that caused public interest:

1   The first case appeared on the news on 21 February 2015 (171 likes, 51 dislikes). Information was published on the possible compensation of moral harm for B., ex-chief executive of Russian potassium company Uralkali. He was arrested during his business visit to Minsk in August 2013 and charged with abuse of power. Afterwards, he was extradited to the Russian Federation. The web-site tut.by published more than 150 articles on the issue and even assigned it a special tag – "Potassium war".

2   The second case (peak publication: 2 March 2015, 348 likes, 56 dislikes) was titled "KGB discovered corruption scheme in Beltamozhservice". According to the information published, several bribe-givers and bribe-taker were arrested. The KGB informed that corruption acts had been committed for four years, and the deputy head of director general of Beltamozhservice received more than US$190,000 as a bribe. Later it was reported that the illegal activity involved the purchase of paper for copiers by Beltamozhservice. The case was covered by tut.by two times.

3   In the third case, an official of the anti-corruption department of the Ministry of Internal Affairs, S., was sentenced to 13 years of deprivation of liberty for bribe-taking (peak publication: 30 March 2015, 201 likes, 39 dislikes). It was disclosed that S. was arrested in December 2013. He received a bribe of US$30,000 for aiding companies in obtaining permissions for construction works. The case was reported by tut.by one time.

4   In the fourth case (peak publication: 30 March 2015, 174 likes, 29 dislikes), the Investigative Committee for the city of Minsk disclosed that it initiated the criminal case against P., head of Uzdenski district executive committee, and B., head of "Uzdenski agroservice". They were caught in flagrante delicto while receiving 8,000 euro from the representative of a well-known foreign producer of agricultural machinery for contract conclusion and for winning in a procurement procedure (a beetroot harvesting combine was bought). Bribe-givers were also detained (one of them was a German citizen). Case hearings began in January 2016. On 1 March 2016, P. and B. were sentenced to seven and six years of deprivation of liberty correspondently

Belarus 225

(in August 2016 B. died in a detention unit). In total, this case appeared on tut.by four times.

5   The publication about the fifth case appeared on 13 May 2015 (142 likes, 62 dislikes) under the title "Special services detained chief engineer of MWTP" (Minsk Wheel Tractor Plant). In the article, the press-service of the Investigative Committee of the Republic of Belarus stated that a criminal case was investigated against chief engineer G. and several other workers of Minsk Wheel Tractor Plant for abuse of power (paragraph 2 of article 424 of the CC of Belarus) and for receiving of a bribe (paragraph 1 of article 430 of the CC). In 2011–2015 they received bribes from organizations for assistance in supplying cutting tools. It reported about 80 instances of bribe-taking in total. In the news from 23 December 2016, the Investigative Committee stated that the investigation was over and that the case would be transferred to court soon. Finally, in February 2017 in a press release of Minsk Frunzensky district court, it was stated that the public prosecutor sought to punish G. with 10 years of deprivation of liberty. The case was reported five times.

6   The sixth case was in respect of detention of a person for misappropriation of money aimed at the construction of the cosmodrome "Vostochni" in Russia (1 June 2014, 167 likes, 40 dislikes). He escaped after the start of the criminal investigation in Russia, and several months later he was detained in Belarus. The interest in this case was provoked by the fact that the detained was driving a car completely covered with Swarovski crystals. The case was reported only once.

7   Borisovdrev case is the seventh case covered in mass media (peak publications: 15 October 2014, 311 likes, 30 dislikes; 20 December 2014, 211 likes, 35 dislikes; 17 April 2015, 345 likes, 30 dislikes; 4 June 2015, 201 likes, 17 dislikes; 2 July 2015, 551 likes, 40 dislikes). In 2007 modernization of the woodworking industry of the Republic of Belarus began. In 2012 and 2013 the President of the Republic of Belarus visited one of the plants involved, Borisovdrev, and at the time of the visit it was clear that the pace of modernization was far behind what had been the planned. So, sanctions were imposed on public officials of all levels, including high-ranking public officials. The criminal investigation was initiated, and in March 2014, M., the director of Borisovdrev, was detained. In accordance with the news, in October 2014 M. was accused of abuse of power committed in the course of fulfillment of a state programme for modernization of the factory. In December 2014, he was sentenced to three years deprivation of liberty. In April 2015, the Supreme Court of the Republic of Belarus shortened the term of imprisonment. The information on the release of M. under the amnesty law was published in July 2015. The case was covered in the news on tut.by 22 times.

8   The eighth case appeared in the news with the title saying that two heads of district executive committees were arrested (peak publication: 2 September 2015, 276 likes, 73 dislikes). They committed a criminal offence provided

226   *Pavel Sascheko*

for by paragraph 3 of article 424 of the CC of Belarus (abuse of power). In the subsequent information, it was clarified that their arrest was connected with their previous posts in the committees. Y., for instance, intending to minimize expenses, was forcing district organizations to sell him goods necessary to build his house with huge discounts. In September 2016, the criminal case was transferred to court. In May 2017, he was sentenced to three years of deprivation of liberty. The fate of the second head of district executive committee, B., remains unclear; there are no publications on the result of the investigation against him on tut.by. This case was mentioned on tut.by four times.

9   The ninth case concerns the corruption case on the customs station Kamienny Log (peak publications: 15 September 2015, 97 dislikes; 3 April 2015, 291 likes, 102 dislikes). On 15 September 2015, information was published that 40 customs officers working at Kamienny Log were detained because of their involvement in corruption. They invented a criminal scheme which induced cargo carriers to give bribes in order to expedite customs formalities. When they were arrested, more than US$2.2 billion was found at their places of residence. In April 2015, the president of Belarus specifically referred to the case in a meeting with authorities of customs offices. In January 2016, the head of the Oshmiany customs division (station Kamienny Log is a part of the Oshmiany customs division) was sentenced to seven years of deprivation of liberty. In March 2016, upon appeal, the Supreme Court of Belarus reduced the sentence to six years of deprivation of liberty. In November 2016, criminal proceedings against other participants of the case were started. In June 2017, mass media informed that the other customs officers involved were sentenced. This scandal appeared in tut.by's publications 15 times.

10   On 7 December 2015 tut.by placed information that several high-level officials had been detained, namely, first deputy head of the Belarusian railway company, M.; deputy head of Ministry of Agriculture and Food, P.; and the first deputy head of Ministry for Transport, R. (peak publication: 7 December 2015, 18:23, 185 likes, 66 dislikes). Earlier that day (at 13:11) the press-service of the Council of Ministers of the Republic of Belarus distributed information that M., P. and R. had been released from their posts. On 2 March 2017, it was published that the criminal case was transferred to court. As it was stated in the publication from 14 April 2017, the accused were involved in illegal activities in 2010–2015. They concluded several disadvantageous contracts that were detrimental to the interests of the state. M. was additionally accused of using his official position for organizing his wife's trips abroad by a car belonging to the company. He also illegally dug two ponds near his house, which caused damage to the environment. At the moment of writing, no further information is available on the case. This case appeared in publications on tut.by five times.

11   The so-called "Gomel meat" scandal is the eleventh case covered in mass media (peak publications: 21 January 2016, 279 likes, 34 dislikes; 3 December 2015, 354 likes, 81 dislikes). The case started in December 2015 when

tut.by published information from unconfirmed sources that around 10 officials in the Gomel region were allegedly detained for corruption offences such as abuse of power. Among those detained was the first deputy chairman of the local executive committee, M., and the head of Gomel meat plant, S. On 21 January 2016, the Investigative Committee confirmed that the case was being investigated against officials of Gomel meat plant, Gomel executive committee and Ministry of Agriculture and Food. The criminal proceedings were started by the KGB and transferred to the Investigative Committee for further investigation. More than 100 tons of meat had rotted because of improper storage conditions, and the convicted organized its distribution. The case appeared in publications on tut.by only two times.

12 In the twelfth case, mass media received information from regular users that a high-ranking police official had allegedly been detained for bribery. This information was subsequently confirmed by the Investigative Committee, which specified that the detained policeman occupied the post of the deputy head of Road Police for Vitebsk region and was detained for bribe-taking (paragraph 1 of article 430 of the CC) (peak publication: 26 January 2016, 261 likes, 42 dislikes). No information on the policeman's name was given. On 14 March 2017, mass media reported that the policeman was sentenced to six years of deprivation of liberty. The case appeared in publications on tut.by two times.

13 The thirteenth case in the list is connected with a piece of news about sentencing to long periods of imprisonment of several high-ranking officials of the Slutsk meat plant (peak publication: 29 February 2016, 190 likes, 131 dislikes). The case started at the beginning of April 2014 when the President of Belarus, during his visit to the Slutsk meat plant, was dissatisfied with complete mess and disorder, including rotten meat, which was found there. He ordered immediate actions to be taken to improve the situation and punish guilty persons (11 April 2014). Then it was reported that on 14 April 2014 management of the Slutsk meat plant had been detained for abuse of power, neglect of duty and exceeding of power. A new director was appointed on 16 June 2014. A total renovation of the premises of the factory was initiated. In September 2015, hearings against the accused started; they pleaded innocent. On 9 February 2016, the former director of the factory was sentenced to six years of deprivation of liberty and his deputy was sentenced to three years of deprivation of liberty. Another accused (the director of a transport company) was sentenced to four years of deprivation of liberty. In total, the scandal involving the Slutsk meat plant was mentioned on tut.by nine times.

14 The fourteenth case was connected with Naftan, a Belarussian petroleum refinery company (peak publications: 1 March 2016, 140 likes, 62 dislikes; 13 March 2016, 627 likes, 86 dislikes). The case started in February 2013, when top managers of Naftan were about to get more than 900,000 euro as a bribe, but they were detained by police officers. The information on the detention was revealed to the public only on 30 July 2014. It was confirmed

228 *Pavel Sascheko*

that a deputy director and several officials of Naftan, as well as officials of some other enterprises, were charged with abuse of power during conducting procurement procedures and execution of contracts. More than half a million US dollars, seven expensive cars and jewelry were seized. The sum of bribes exceeded 240,000 euro. The investigation was finished on 1 March 2016. On 13 March 2016, an open letter from the workers of Naftan to the President of the Republic of Belarus was published where they mentioned corruption cases and asked the government to take measures to improve the situation at the factory. In total, this case was covered by tut.by four times.

15 The fifteenth case reported is about the director of "Babushkina krinka". It was disclosed that on 4 April 2016 an official representative of the Investigative Committee was informed that a criminal case had been initiated against the director of the company. It was established that in 2015 she took a number of measures aimed at hiding the fact that a worker had been injured. Moreover, she signed an order stating that the injured worker had been on an unpaid leave on the date when he had been injured (peak publication: 4 April 2016, 140 likes, 62 dislikes). The case appeared on tut.by only once.

16 The sixteenth case in the collection of cases was reported in May 2016 (peak publication: 17 May 2016, 233 likes, 39 dislikes), when information appeared that judges of the Minsk Economic Court were involved in fraud and bribe-taking. They were arrested by the KGB and sentenced to long terms of deprivation of liberty. It was revealed in June 2016 that two judges of the Minsk Economic Court and four accomplices were involved in taking bribes and fraud in respect of insolvency procedures. They received bribes for designation of a crisis manager, choice of an expert, etc. It was reported that one of the judges received more than US$60,000 as bribes. The judges were sentenced to 11 and 13 years of deprivation of liberty (publication from 4 July 2016). In total, this case was covered by tut.by four times.

17 The seventeenth case is the Senator Sh. case (peak publication: 10 June 2016, 547 likes and 107 dislikes). It was indicated in the news that Sh., the director of Vitebsk broiler poultry factory (the state is one of the stakeholders of the company) and a senator (a member of parliament), was found guilty of abuse of power (paragraph 2 of article 424 of the CC). In accordance with the information published she bought combined feed in Lithuania on prices, which were much higher than prices for Belarusian combined feed and violated procurement regulations. She was deprived of the inviolability of a member of parliament and arrested on 14 August 2015 and then sentenced. After Sh. was released in the courtroom under amnesty law, she returned to the position of the head of the factory. In total, the Sh. case was covered by tut.by 28 times.

18 The eighteenth case involving Belarusbank officials appeared on the news in June 2016 (peak publication: 22 June 2016, 152 likes and 91 dislikes), when the head of KGB confirmed that the Deputy Head of Board of Management of Belarusbank had been arrested on 15 June 2016 for taking US$14,000 as a bribe. Criminal investigation on bribery (paragraph 3 of

article 430 of the CC of Belarus) was started. Soon information about the criminal investigation against other Belarusbank officials was published. In total, the issue of corruption in bank structure was covered by tut.by seven times.

The analysis of the 18 cases shows that the vast majority of cases that caused significant public interest involved abuse of power and receiving of bribes. The cases against high-ranking public officials in public and private sectors attracted more attention.

It can be concluded that to be recognized as a corruption scandal it is not enough to establish that there is one publication on the event. An additional criterion is needed to create the definition of a corruption scandal: the mass media must address the issue at least several times. In accordance with this approach, four cases were selected for further examination with regard to their consequences for governance in the Republic of Belarus. They are the Uralkali case (case 1, more than 150 publications on tut.by), the Borisovdrev case (case 7, 22 publications), the Kamienny Log case (case 9, 15 publications) and the senator Sh. case (case 17, 28 publications).

Consequences of corruption scandals in Belarus

Consequences of corruption scandals can be different: political, legal, economic, etc. They can be caused by a scandal or by a succession of corruption events. To detect the consequences, it is necessary to determine that consequences exist and to prove causation between scandals and consequences.

With the view of the detection of possible consequences of the corruption scandals mentioned above, statements of public officials in mass media, as well as legal acts, were examined. In order to establish that a consequence is caused by a corruption scandal, information about amendments to the legislation of the Republic of Belarus was used. Statements of public officials concerning plans to make amendments to legislation prove the link between a scandal and the amendments if these statements are made in connection with the corruption scandal or if participants of the corruption scandal are mentioned.

Is it important to note that many of the cases which were classified as corruption scandals and listed above reached their peak level of interest only in respect to special events covered by the media (e.g. peak news on cases 1, 2, 4, 5, 6, 8, 9, 10, 11, 12, 14, 16 and 18 were about detention of people accused of corruption, and cases 3, 13 and 17 were on sentencing the accused).

So it is evident that some of the events, which came into the focus of our research, had been initially on the news much earlier than when the "peak" publications appeared, and thus they had been under consideration of the public and officials.

For example, on 22 April 2014, the president addressed the Belarusian nation and the National Assembly of the Republic of Belarus with a message titled, "Strong economy and honest authority is a foundation for independence of the state and prosperity of the nation" (President of the Public of Belarus 2014). In

230   *Pavel Sascheko*

his speech, he stated that previous year he had been informed by law-enforcement bodies about corruption criminal cases, and he mentioned about 20 such cases. With a view of fighting corruption on a system level, some changes in the Belarusian legal system were announced.

Before April 2014, only five cases were considered as scandals in accordance with the methodology of the present study: 1 (arrest in August 2013), 3 (arrest in December 2013), 7 (arrest in March 2014), 13 (arrest in April 2014) and 14 (arrest in February 2013). The president directly addressed case 3 in the part of his speech where he discussed the negative situation where corruption appeared in the state bodies that were in charge of fighting it. He specified that the senior officer of the anti-organized crime and anti-corruption department of the Interior Ministry, S., assisted in obtaining construction permits in return for a US$30,000. The president turned attention to the following issue: S. received the bribe and provided assistance, but other people made the necessary decisions and gave permissions, so all guilty should be punished.

It is worth noting that three other cases (which do not appear in the list of corruption scandals above) mentioned by the president were about corruption cases in state bodies which are in charge of fighting against it. One is the criminal investigation against four officials of Department of KGB for Gomel Oblast who organized an investigation against a profit-making organization in the interest of business rivals. The second is a case of Deputy Prosecutor General A. who received a gold bar and a bottle of cognac as a bribe in return for termination of the criminal prosecution against the driver who was guilty in a deadly traffic accident (in connection with this case J., head of an investigative unit of the Minsk District department of the Investigative Committee, was also convicted of receiving a bribe). And in the third example, a criminal case on bribery was initiated against S., K., and M. who were officials of the Central district office of the Department of Investigative Committee for Minsk.

Case 7 (Borisovdrev) was also in the focus of the president's attention, though it was viewed in the context of broader problems with the whole woodworking sector of Belarusian economy, which was undergoing modernization. It should be mentioned that in 2006 the Edict of the President of the Republic of Belarus No. 538, "On measures for improving financial standing of unprofitable joint-stock companies", was adopted (President of the Republic of Belarus 2006). It contained a list of unprofitable entities (Borisovdrev, Homeldrev, Minskproektmebel and Fandok were included in the list) and measures for enhancing their financial status. Additional measures were indicated in the Edict of the President of the Republic of Belarus of 18 October 2007, No. 529, "On some measures for development of woodworking industry" (President of the Republic of Belarus 2007). Later the state continued its support of the entities.

During his visits to Borisovdrev and other plants that were undergoing modernization in 2014, the president took the view that their directors were not diligent and active enough in performing their duties. So, some immediate measures were taken (e.g. right after visiting Borisovdrev the Edict of the President of the Republic of Belarus of 8 November 2013, No. 502, "On liability for violation of

Belarus 231

executive discipline", was adopted) (President of the Republic of Belarus 2013). Under clause 4 of the edict disciplinary sanctions were imposed on some public officials who were in charge of implementation of assignments of the president regarding modernization of the woodworking entity Borisovdrev. An expert group was also created to control implementation of the program for modernization of woodworking industry.

However, as the problems were connected with the governance issues on the sector level, more severe measures were needed. They were additionally fostered by the fact that other sectors of industry where modernization of equipment was taking place were also posing problems. Right before the president's annual message on 11 April 2014, he visited the Slutsk meat plant (case 13), where he was astonished by the smell of rotten meat, dirt and litter on the territory and other signs of bad management.

It is no surprise then that in his message to the Belarusian nation and to the National Assembly of the Republic of Belarus on 22 April 2014 the president said that corruption is always accompanied by indifference in relation to managerial duties. Measures were to be taken to raise the responsibility of high-ranking officials and to stop their undue promotion after they disrupted the activities of entities and ruined companies. Though it was clear that the people involved in corruption should go to prison, the disruption of work was even more serious for the country in some cases taking into account losses. So, the president announced that a decree would be issued soon in order to solve the problem and provide personal responsibility of heads of organizations for all aspects of their job: from the safety of workers to the order in offices, premises and storage yards.

During his speech, the president referred to several instances of appointment of public officials involved in dishonest conduct on managerial positions. For example, the First Deputy Head of the Gomel Region Executive Committee, B., had been dismissed from the office for fraud concerning selling flats, but afterwards, he was appointed to the position of the First Deputy Director of the company "B elorusneft-Gomeloblnefteproduct". The former First Deputy Head of the Gomel City Executive Committee, R., who had been involved in the same criminal case on fraud concerning selling flats, was appointed the director of the subdivision of the erecting company "Trest Belsantekhmontage No 1". The former director of the "Executive Office of National Academy of Science of Belarus", S., concealed that he had been previously convicted, and he was appointed the deputy head of the executive committee for Zavodskoy district of Minsk. The president mentioned some other similar cases.

As a result, the Decree of the President of the Republic of Belarus No. 5, "On strengthening requirements to management and staff of organizations," was adopted on 15 December 2014 (President of the Republic of Belarus 2014). The decree provides some conditions for appointments, additional grounds for termination of contracts, disciplinary and financial sanctions that can be imposed for misbehaviour, etc. Under the decree, the maintenance of discipline and compliance with the requirements established regarding conditions of labour and equipment became one of the criteria for assessment of the activity of heads of public and private entities. But at the same time, heads of entities were entitled by the decree to establish additional payments from the profit of entities to staff without any limits with respect to the size of such payments. The decree also introduced that a contract can be terminated in case of violation of restrictions provided for anti-corruption legislation or violation of restrictions established by legislation for public servants.

In order to further implement the decree, several legal acts were amended or adopted. The Resolution of the Council of Ministers of the Republic of Belarus No. 68, "On approval of the Regulation on the procedure for endorsement of appointment of persons previously dismissed from the office because of discreditable behaviour on managerial positions", was adopted on 2 February 2015 (Resolution 2015). The law of the Republic of Belarus of 4 January 2010, No 108-Z, "On local government", was amended in 2016 (National Assembly of the Republic of Belarus 2010). According to the amendments to the law, heads of executive committees of districts are entitled to require imposing disciplinary sanctions on the staff of entities situated on the territory of the district and to approve the appointment on some managerial positions if the person appointing has been previously dismissed from the office because of discreditable conduct. Some other amendments to the legislation of the Republic of Belarus were made in connection with the adoption of the decree.

In the message to the Belarusian nation and the National Assembly of the Republic of Belarus on 22 April 2014, the President of the Republic of Belarus mentioned some domains where corruption cases were discovered: public procurement, licensing of advocates and realtors, judiciary, customs, construction industry, etc. He said that bribes, kickbacks and abuse of power had been detected in all fields of activity, and this required some steps to be taken, including: elimination of some functions of state bodies, development of a new system of state financial support and extensive use of tenders, enhancement of prestige of state service and an increase in the wages of public servants.

Particular attention was given to the process of reducing corruption in procurement procedures. The president said that though a complicated system of public procurement had been developed, the system did not present an obstacle for the Deputy Minister of Sport and Tourism who received bribes from profit-making companies for winning in tenders for delivery of sporting equipment.

The analysis of corruption cases, which occurred in June 2014–June 2016 and were included in the list of cases in the previous part of this chapter, demonstrates that violations of procurement procedures involving corruption were quite frequent (cases 2, 4, 5, 14, 17 and 18).

To improve the situation regarding public procurement procedures, the Resolution of the Council of Ministers of the Republic of Belarus of 22 August 2012, No. 778, "On some measures for the implementation of Law of the Republic of Belarus 'On public purchase of goods (works, services)'" was amended by the Resolution of the Council of Ministers of the Republic of Belarus of 27 January 2016, No. 68 (Council of Ministers of the Republic of Belarus 2012; Council of Ministers of the Republic of Belarus 2016). In 2016, it was reported that amendments to the Law of the Republic of Belarus of 13 July 2012, "On public purchase of goods (works, services)", were given their first reading by the House of Representatives of the National Assembly of the Republic of Belarus as well. Resolution No. 68 and the draft law contain provisions on electronic purchases, electronic procedures for complaints of participants and so on.

On 29 April 2015, in his message to the Belarusian nation and the National Assembly of the Republic of Belarus titled "Peace and Development", the president also announced that a draft law "On the fight against corruption" had been developed (Address of the President of the Public of Belarus 2015). It was elaborated taking into account the results of nationwide debates. The president noted that more than 300 proposals from people with regard to the text of the draft had been considered during the preparation of the law. This law was adopted on 15 July 2015.

New anti-corruption measures were prescribed in article 5 (system of measures on fighting against corruption) of the law, namely:

> use of procedures for hiring staff, selection, training and promotion of public officials in accordance with principles of the effectiveness of their activities and fairness;
> adoption of codes of ethics (standards of behaviour) of public servants and other state public officials;
> simplification of administrative procedures and reduction of their number;
> putting forward draft legal acts on combating corruption for nationwide debates;
> organization of anti-corruption education of public officials and people who study at educational institutions.

Article 22 of the Law of 2015 introduced some limitations concerning hiring of several categories of state and private public officials who were previously dismissed from public service because of discreditable conduct during five years after such dismissal (several exceptions were provided for by the law). This article of the law also prohibits the appointment of a person to a post of a state public official if he has previously committed an especially grave or grave criminal offence by using official power or an especially grave or grave criminal offence against interests of service.

Some limitations concerning obtaining pensions by public servants who have committed an especially grave or grave criminal offence against interests of service or committed an especially grave or grave criminal offence by using official power are provided for by Article 24 of the Law of 2015.

The Law of 2015 introduced the extended declaration of assets by public officials occupying positions of high authority (members of the National Assembly of the Republic of Belarus, judges of the Constitutional Court of the Republic of Belarus, judges, etc.). It put into effect new measures such as the confiscation of illicit enrichment that constitutes a significant increase in the assets of a public official occupying a position of high authority if he or she cannot reasonably explain the increase (article 36 of the Law).

234   *Pavel Sascheko*

The analysis of these and some other amendments introduced by the law demonstrates that not all of them are directly linked to corruption scandals. They were influenced not only by public debates and proposals to amend the draft law but also by the positions of different state bodies which took part in the legislative process. Though, of course, their staff, being members of the public, was influenced to some extent by the perception of the whole array of corruption scandals and corruption cases that had occurred in previous years.

Conclusion

Any corruption scandal has several key distinctive features, such as a corruption act or omission, publication about this act and public reaction to it. Taking into account that public reaction is the pivotal element of any scandal, which differentiates a scandal from other types of corruption events, it is important to measure the degree of the public's interest.

To this end, the number of likes and dislikes to a publication on a corruption case and the total number of publications were used to identify a corruption scandal. The present study shows that corruption scandals involve different types of public officials in public and private sectors. Information about corruption scandals published includes assessment of corruption behaviour from the Criminal Code point of view. However, no references to unethical behaviour, violation of codes of conduct, conflict of interests, transgressions in respect of the declaration of assets, etc. were found.

Most corruption cases, even those announced by the President of the Republic of Belarus, based on information from law enforcement bodies, do not receive any public interest. Taking into account the number of likes and dislikes, they cannot be considered as corruption scandals, because one of the key elements of a scandal – significant interest of public opinion – is absent.

The consequences of scandals comprise dismissal from office of the public officials involved and the conviction of criminals. Scandals lead to changes in Belarus with respect of governance, including amending legal acts in cases where scandals do involve high-ranking public officials or where they are connected with the implementation of economic programs, which are important for the state and are funded from the state budget. Some corruption scandals attract the attention of the President of the Republic of Belarus and are mentioned in his speeches as a direct basis for making measures and adoption of legal acts.

Amendments to the legislation are usually aimed at prevention of corruption by using different types of managerial, economic and other measures. Though all corruption cases studied were assessed in terms of criminal law through the prism of bribery offences and abuse of power, the consequences of the corruption scandals did not cause any changes in the Criminal Code of the Republic of Belarus regarding the criminalization of corruption. The state focuses on prevention of corruption because criminal law measures are well developed and are not able to prevent damage caused by criminal corruption offences.

Belarus 235

Thus, the corruption scandals that occurred in the Republic of Belarus made some "rings" in respect of governance. But, of course, the legal amendments and other consequences cannot be considered as results of corruption scandals only. State bodies took measures to prevent corruption based on a thorough analysis of the situation involving a wide range of corruption cases, taking into account best practices of fighting against corruption. It is directly provided for by the Law of the Republic of Belarus of 10 January 2000, No. 361-Z, "On normative legal acts" (National Assembly of the Republic of Belarus 2000). The law contains complicated procedures of amending legislation which includes requirements for the planning of adoption of a legal act, collection of information, elaboration of a draft, submitting the draft to state bodies for approval, conducting legal, criminological and other necessary examinations of the draft, etc. This procedure is designed to exclude the possible influence of random events on legislative procedures. So, an impact of corruption scandals on governance and legislative process in the Republic of Belarus should not be exaggerated.

Note

1 Tut.by is the most popular news resource in the Republic of Belarus, with a total audience of 2 million people monthly and around 966,700 unique users per day.

References and further reading

Council of Ministers of the Republic of Belarus. (2012) *Resolution on Some Measures for the Implementation of Law of the Republic of Belarus "On Public Purchase of Goods (Works, Services)"*. [Online] Available from: http://pravo.by/document/?guid=3871&p0=C21200778&p1=1 [Accessed 1st August 2017].

Council of Ministers of the Republic of Belarus. (2015) *Resolution on Approval of the Regulation on the Procedure for Endorsement of Appointment of Persons Previously Dismissed from the Office Because of Discreditable Behaviour on Managerial Positions.* [Online] Available from: http://pravo.by/upload/docs/op/C21500068_1423083600.pdf [Accessed 1st August 2017].

Council of Ministers of the Republic of Belarus. (2016) *Resolution on Introducing Amendments and Additions to the Regulation of the Council of Ministers of the Republic of Belarus of 22 August 2013 No 778*. [Online] Available from: www.government.by/upload/docs/file741a2a9258291aeb.PDF [Accessed 1st August 2017].

Gorshenkov, G.N. (2003) Foundation of Mass Communications Criminology. In: Shestakov, D.A. (ed.) *Criminality among Social Subsystems: New Conception and Branches of Criminology*. Yuridichesky Center-Press, St. Petersburg, 117–185.

Kongantiev, M.T. (2008) Ways for Improvement of the Effectiveness of Cooperation of Head of Internal Affairs Body and Mass Media: Basing on Kyrgyz Republic Materials. *Law and Legislation*, 10, 77–78.

Koniuk, A.V. (2016) Coordination of Activity of State Bodies Fighting against Corruption and State Bodies and Other Organizations Which Participate in Fighting against Corruption. In: Koniuk, A.V. (ed.) *Combating Corruption*. Academy of Public Administration under the Aegis of the President of the Republic of Belarus, Minsk, 52–62.

236   *Pavel Sascheko*

Kulmasheva, I.F. (2011) Cooperation of Prosecution Service Bodies and Mass Media in the Sphere of Law Instruction. *BULLETIN: Academy of the R.F. Prosecutor General's Office*, 5(25), 58–62.

National Assembly of the Republic of Belarus. (1999) *Criminal Code of the Republic of Belarus*. [Online] Available from: http://etalonline.by/?type=text&regnum=HK9900275 [Accessed 1st August 2017].

National Assembly of the Republic of Belarus. (2000) *Law on Normative Legal Acts*. [Online] Available from: http://pravo.by/document/?guid=3871&p0=H10000361 [Accessed 1st August 2017].

National Assembly of the Republic of Belarus. (2010) *Law on Local Government*. [Online] Available from: http://pravo.by/document/?guid=3871&p0=H11000108 [Accessed 1st August 2017].

National Assembly of the Republic of Belarus. (2015) *Law on the Fight against Corruption*. [Online] Available from: www.pravo.by/upload/docs/op/H11500305_1437598800. pdf [Accessed 1st August 2017].

National Statistical Committee of the Republic of Belarus. (2017) [Online] Available from: www.belstat.gov.by/ofitsialnaya-statistika/solialnaya-sfera/pravonarusheniya/godovye-dannye_7/prestupnost-v-respublike-belarus/ [Accessed 28th July 2017].

President of the Public of Belarus. (2014) *State of the Nation Address to the Belarusian People and the National Assembly*. [Online] Available from: http://president.gov.by/en/news_en/view/alexander-lukashenko-to-deliver-state-of-the-nation-address-on-22-april-8550/ [Accessed 1st August 2017].

President of the Public of Belarus. (2015) *Address of the President to the Belarusian People and the National Assembly*. [Online] Available from: http://president.gov.by/en/news_en/view/belarus-president-to-address-nation-parliament-on-29-april-11303/ [Accessed 1st August 2017].

President of the Republic of Belarus. (2006) *Edict on Measures for Improving Financial Standing of Unprofitable Joint-Stock Companies*. [Online] Available from: www.pravo.by/pdf/2006-143/2006-143(107-130).pdf#page=3 [Accessed 1st August 2017].

President of the Republic of Belarus. (2007) *Edict on Some Measures for Development of Woodworking Industry*. [Online] Available from: www.pravo.by/pdf/2007-252/2007-252(005-021).pdf#page=6 [Accessed 1st August 2017].

President of the Republic of Belarus. (2013) *Edict on Liability for Violation of Executive Discipline*. [Online] Available from: http://president.gov.by/ru/official_documents_ru/view/ukaz-502-ot-8-nojabrja-2013-g-7351/ [Accessed 1st August 2017].

President of the Republic of Belarus. (2014) *Decree on Strengthening Requirements to Management and Staff of Organizations*. [Online] Available from: http://president.gov.by/ru/official_documents_ru/view/dekret-5-ot-15-dekabrja-2014-g-10434/ [Accessed 1st August 2017].

Shestakov, D.A. (2006) *Criminology: New Approaches to Crime and Criminality: Criminogenic Laws and Criminological Legislation: Counteraction to Criminality in the Varied World*. Yuridichesky Center-Press, St. Petersburg.

13 Conclusion
Lessons learned

Omar E. Hawthorne

Global impacts of corruption scandals

Corruption, in everyday life, means that a public official abuses or misuses his or her office for private gain. Corruption scandals emerge when someone, whether internal or external, discovers and leaks or shares the information pertaining to an act of corruption. Societies always distinguish between acceptable and unacceptable behaviours or practices. Every society, therefore, tends to have a shared understanding of what constitutes corruption in each context (Anderson 2007). Corruption is a dynamic and adaptive phenomenon in any culture. The framing of corruption and corruption scandals has to be context specific. Internationally, there is, to date, no single, universally accepted definition of corruption. Nonetheless, the most commonly used definition refers to corruption as the abuse or misuse of public or entrusted power for private or personal gain.

Corruption scandals have become an important aspect of politics over the last two decades. Notwithstanding, countries have made great progress in taking on the fight against corruption whether at the global or domestic levels. There has also been an improvement in anti-corruption regulation and enforcement in a host of countries. Yet still, corruption scandals seemingly continue to rise at an even greater frequency. But, within the last two decades it has seemingly been more prevalent than usual, and corruption scandals are overturning governments and leading to stricter laws.

The impacts of corruption scandals have been global. In the global economy of interdependence and interconnected economies, a corruption scandal in one country is likely to have an impact in others; either because of the involvement of a trans-national corporation or the movement of money across countries. Based on the countries and issues covered in the text, it is clear that governance and corruption remain controversial and misunderstood topics. But, as Kaufman (2005: 81), in "Myths and Realities of Governance and Corruption," notes; they are now given higher priority in development circles and by the corporate sector that includes multinationals. The 'business as usual' or 'corruption greases the wheel' debate is no longer tolerated. Increasingly we are seeing some donors and international financial institutions (IFIs) working more and more with emerging economies to

238   *Omar E. Hawthorne*

help reduce corruption and increase citizens' voices, general equality and account-ability (Kaufman 2005: 81).

The work of the contributors herein reiterates the findings of the OECD in "Putting an End to Corruption" in that corruption undermines sustainabil-ity. It endangers private sector productivity by setting incentives to allocate resources to unproductive activities and by deterring innovation and the emergence of new companies. Furthermore, corruption hinders public sector productivity by biasing decisions in public expenditures, by impairing the skills and professionalism of the civil service and by reducing public resources available to support productivity in the economy. And corruption is a threat to inclusive growth by undermining the opportunities to participate equally in social, economic and political life and impacting the distribution of income and well-being. Corruption also erodes trust in government and public institutions, rendering reform more difficult. Often, when a corruption scandal is used to win a political election, politicians do so by arguing that they will be tougher on corruption than those they seek to replace, but frequently they end up in a corruption scandal themselves. While corruption is widely disapproved of, some corrupt politicians continue to win elections. The comparative literature does not provide clear systematic answers to this "paradox of corruption" (Kurer 2001). Corruption scandals seem to be more pervasive in some societies in comparison to others – but, once the scandal comes to light, it often leads to public outcry and some attempt at legislative or policy reform.

The chapters herein have shown that corruption occurs in many forms; petty or administrative corruption, grand corruption, corruption with institutions and unjust or locally unacceptable practices of the international community. Fur-thermore, as the UNDP (1997) *Corruption and Good Governance* discussion paper notes; corruption restricts investment and holds back economic growth and it undermines programmes designed specifically to aid the poor. The poor are harmed by systemic corruption, but the causes of poverty seem more funda-mental and deep-seated. It is difficult to document a simple relationship between the distribution of income and the level of corruption. Furthermore, in states with no social safety net and few economic opportunities for the very poor, the bribes collected by civil servants can perform a redistributive function, albeit one that is very inefficient and inequitable. Poor families that have a relative in the government benefit, while others are made worse off. By examining various corruption scandals throughout the chapters of this text it has been shown how corruption challenges development and policy agendas. But also how, to some degree, corruption has seemingly become standardized and institutionalized in many societies. The works of the contributors highlight the fact that corruption cannot be eradicated simply by legalizing payments and transferring public func-tions to the private sector. Corrupt tax and customs officials undermine the ability of the state to raise revenue. Procurement contracts that are obtained corruptly may be inflated in value to reflect the bribes paid. Corrupt privatisation robs the government treasury of needed funds.

Conclusion 239

A common tread in a number of the chapters and the corruption scandals examined herein is that the state intervenes in the economy to lay out a framework for the economic and social activity. The state can also be an instrument of repression. It can restrict the behaviour of individuals and groups beyond that needed to further public aims. It can benefit narrow but powerful groups with access to legislatures and chief executives. Top officials may organize the state to enrich themselves. Even when a state's aim is broadly democratic, public policies can be implemented in wasteful and incompetent ways (UNDP 1997: 1). Subsequently, with the volume of corruption scandals and seemingly lack of accountability and/or change in some instances, it should be noted that corruption cannot be expected to wither away just because a reform government has taken power or because economic growth is vigorous. As long as officials have discretionary authority, corrupt incentives will remain and can be especially harmful to fragile new states. Reformers will have to take concrete action, not just assume that entrenched habits will disappear with a change in top personnel. Those who benefited from the corrupt regime must not be permitted to hold back change.

One of the lessons to take away from this text is that corruption is not a problem that can be attacked in isolation; noting that a criminal law approach that simply searches for bad apples or big fish and punishes them is not sufficient. Without holistic reforms the bad apples or big fish will be replaced even sooner than the big fish or bad apple is imprisoned while at the same time assuming that the criminal justice system is efficient and the individual is convicted. Notwithstanding, the state may need to establish credibility by punishing highly visible corrupt officials. However, in many instances, it appears as if the goal of such prosecutions is to attract notice and public support but not to solve the underlying problem. Klitgaard (1988) recommends "frying a big fish" for just this reason. In developing countries such as Jamaica, Kenya, Nigeria and others, the frying a big fish approach is often needed, noting that in many instances public official act with impunity and there is rarely ever any consequence. Structural and procedural reform requires a set of credible anti-corruption laws that outlaw whatever types of payments are viewed as acceptable tips or gifts to public officials. Such payments should be legalized and made subject to reporting requirements. The UNDP (1997: 105) proposal that one test of the cultural justification for payments is the acceptability of proposals to make such payments public is noteworthy. The possibility that payoffs may motivate officials to work more efficiently suggests that in particular cases illegal bribes might be converted into legal incentive-pay schemes.

As shown in relations to corruption scandals in the text, such as those in Brazil, Nigeria, Kenya, Belarus, Jamaica, Trinidad and Tobago, amongst others, corrupt practices taking place within public institutions can also have many different manifestations, such as the selling and buying of positions, facilitation payments for intrastate procedures, theft and embezzlement of public resources, etc. Patronage-based appointments are some of the main forms of corruption

240 *Omar E. Hawthorne*

when you assess the recruitment of high officials. Furthermore, clientelism and favouritism in the contracting of human resources have been identified by contributors to this work as another factor contributing to the perception of corruption in a number of areas such as job creation, securing contracts, international aid, etc.

Anti-corruption measures

Former United Nations Secretary-General Kofi Annan, in a message to the First Conference of the States Parties to the UN Convention against Corruption (UNCAC), expressed that in many ways large and small corruption hurts us all. It impedes social and economic development. It erodes the public's trust, hurts investment and undermines democracy and the rule of law. It facilitates terrorism, conflict and organized crime. The effectiveness of any anti-corruption measures will also depend on the fundamental underlying assumptions we make about the nature of people. With the nature of the corruption scandals in the countries in this text, do we assume that human beings are inherently good and will see the merit in avoiding corruption because of the negative impact on society? Or is it a case where we assume that people are inherently evil and in a Hobbesian 'state of nature'? There is no doubt that corruption scandals continue to plague countries in every region of the world. Brown, (in Bracking 2007: xi), posits that there are some who would argue that corruption, like prostitution and poverty, will never be truly eradicated and that, while bureaucracy and its rules are essential safeguards, there are special occasions when in order to make an omelette, many bureaucratic eggshells must be broken. As for Sandholtz and Koetzle (2000: 31), corruption, like the poor, will probably always be with us. Thus, the manner in which we as a society recognize and deal with the issue of corruption, its effects on development, growth, sustainability and well-being of others, is intrinsic to the overall growth of society. The world today is less tolerant of large-scale corruption because democracy, free and fair elections and press freedom have become the norm in developed and developing countries. Corrupt officials have to find more ways of concealing their improprieties and the proceeds thereof, which makes it all the more difficult to gauge actual levels of corruption with any real degree of accuracy. Undoubtedly, reforms are needed.

Throughout the countries examined, the anti-corruption initiatives and their success are somewhat limited and or seemingly slow. Further the success of anti-corruption initiatives will depend on a number of factors, such as who owns the anti-corruption efforts being undertaken, the type of leadership being provided from the highest levels of government and, importantly, the capacity of the countries themselves to implement anti-corruption strategies and campaigns through effective detection, investigation and prosecution.

There are many challenges in the complex relationship between policy, conditionality, political development and corruption. The discourse undertaken by governments and the level of continuity when government changes in a country

Conclusion 241

in continuing anti-corruption reforms shows growth, but if and when corruption scandals are used to remove an opponent from office without legislative growth and/or continuity of legislative reforms then it continues the cycle of political point scoring. Moreover, if anti-corruption rhetoric lacks tangible results, it may reinforce popular cynicism about politics. A corruption scandal that leads to resignations and prosecutions serves as a ritual of catharsis and relegitimation. However, if their protagonists remain unpunished, corruption scandals become part of a de-legitimizing spiral in which the credibility of democratic norms is further undermined (Chubb and Vannicelli 1988: 138–9). Mainstream politicians have also unscrupulously manipulated popular fixations on corruption.

Obsession with corruption can also drain political life of its content. Political discussion has degenerated from substantive policy issues into accusations of corruption and promises of integrity throughout Central and Eastern Europe (Bogdanov 2005). By weakening state legitimacy, anti-corruption rhetoric has proven counterproductive. Mark Philp (2002: 79) finds that:

> Western agencies have often shown a lack of sensitivity in their willingness to supply a lexicon of corruption to political forces in transition states which, rather than assisting in the process of cleaning up government, has simultaneously armed political groups with a resource that they have no incentive to use responsibly and has further weakened the legitimacy of these states both domestically and in the international community.

Bissesar, in assessing the management or mismanagement of corruption using Trinidad and Tobago as a case study, has presented that while the parliament has established the necessary processes for oversight, the success so far in curbing corruption by governmental agencies within the country has been poor. The author probes and tries to arrive at explanations for the limited success of the parliament in fighting corruption in the twin-island state. It focuses specifically on one committee, the Public Accounts Enterprises Committee, which has oversight for ministries/state enterprises and service commissions. She illustrates and goes on to conclude that in the case of Trinidad and Tobago, one major flaw seems to be that government members far outweigh the opposition members, and that even the role of the chairman is extremely limited. The interactions between members as well as the governance arrangements between the parliament and the civil society are, out of necessity, the subject of discourse for another work. With the challenges in providing oversight of the administration of the government, Bissesar attributes this as a reason why Trinidad and Tobago's perception of corruption is 101st out of 175 of most corrupt countries globally.

The role of the media

Throughout this text it has been shown that there is not one specific issue that leads to a corruption scandal. The media's involvement of societal actors has been

242 *Omar E. Hawthorne*

shown to be highly relevant in a number of cases. Throughout the text, watchdog journalism triggered investigations that led to corruption scandals. Moreover, since most measures of corruption are based on perceptions, it may be that the relative prevalence of scandals in some countries determines whether a country is considered corrupt (Balán 2011: 475). There have been many instances of politicians involved in corruption scandals who have continued to have successful electoral careers. As Balán (2011: 460) so eloquently puts it, corruption scandals resist interpretations that label them as either negative consequences of growing levels of corruption or positive outcomes of more effective control mechanisms. Corruption scandals are a consequence of the way in which political systems channel conflict and dissent within government coalitions. In other words, scandals are a by-product of political competition.

In Belarus, Pavel Sascheko aptly interrogates the consequences of scandals and whether corrruption scandals lead to the dismissal of compromised public officials involved and the conviction of criminals. Scandals, Sascheko argues, led to changes in Belarus with respect of governance, including amending legal acts in cases where scandals involve high-ranking public officials or where they are connected with the implementation of economic programmes, which, he argues are important for the state and are funded from the state budget. Some corruption scandals attracted the attention of the President of the Republic of Belarus and are mentioned in his speeches as a direct basis for implementing measures and the adoption of legal acts. In Belarus, like other countries in the text, corruption scandals in deed seem to impact legislation. Amendments to the legislation are usually aimed at prevention of corruption by using different types of managerial, economic and other measures. Though all corruption cases studied were assessed in terms of criminal law through the prism of bribery offences, or abuse of power offences, the consequences of the corruption scandals did not cause any changes in the Criminal Code of the Republic of Belarus regarding the criminalization of corruption. Sascheko concludes that the corruption scandals that have occurred in the Republic of Belarus made some "rings" in respect of governance. But he also posits that the legal amendments and other consequences cannot be considered as results of corruption scandals only, in that state bodies took measures developed to prevent corruption based on a thorough analysis of the situation involving a wide range of corruption cases and by taking into account best practices of fighting against corruption.

In some of the countries, such as Jamaica, Kenya, Nigeria, amongst others, examined in this text, the leaking of information comes from both the opposition and government insiders. Thus, when analyzing the lack of incentives to blow the whistle and constraints upon potential informants, (Balán 2011: 459) contension that most corruption scandals are triggered by competition among government, is relevant. In that, often when insiders leak damaging information about other political actors it can be viewed as part of intra-government political competition for power and resources. Present analysis of the politics of corruption scandals reveals that scandals are more likely to occur under

Conclusion   243

specific configurations of inter-party and intra-party or coalition competition. As Balán (2011: 459) rightfully notes, denouncers are generally government insiders.

The relevance of corruption and scandals cannot be overstated; a view that is supported by public opinion data showing that corruption is listed among the most important issues dominating the political agenda. One tendency highlighted in some of the chapters is that legislators and policymakers often attempt to respond to corruption scandals by either campaigning for new anti-corruption measures and or making legislative changes. For example, Jamaica amended its law to facilitate investigation by the Dutch authorities. Holmes, in Chapter 4, when examining corruption scandals in post-Communist Russia, assessed the way in which these scandals have been dealt with in Russia and their wider implications for policy and noted that they differ in each case. For Holmes, Putin's very first act as [acting] president was to pass a decree granting immunity to any Russian president, past or present, and his family. Legislatively, if this act remains valid, it might one day be used to protect Putin himself. Holmes also referred to Bill Browder's claim that [Putin] is the world's wealthiest person (Morris 2017). Substantively, Holmes argues that there is little doubt that the primary original beneficiary of this was to be Yeltsin, in that, although this decree can be criticized, it could be argued that Putin's action was intended to bring closure, much as the post-Stalin Soviet leadership allegedly engaged in one last show trial (of Stalin's secret police chief and then deputy premier, Lavrentii Beria) to symbolize the end of the Stalin terror regime, or as the Chinese leadership did with the trial of the 'Gang of Four' to bring a symbolic conclusion to the Cultural Revolution.

The policy impact of the Magnitsky case has been much greater outside of Russia than within it, and as Holmes posits, no noteworthy policy changes have emanated from Moscow in light of the Magnitsky affair. On the other hand, the US imposed sanctions against Russia – the so-called Magnitsky Act of 2012 – following Magnitsky's death. This act led to the naming of prominent Russians who are said to have been involved in serious human rights abuses, including Magnitsky's death, and who have had assets in the US frozen and are banned from entering the US. Putin's retaliation in this case was a ban on what, by many accounts, was the selling of Russian infants to US citizens for adoption. Of the corruption scandals examined, a pointed conclusion for Holmes is that several of the corruption scandals in Russia have had international ramifications; especially in the US. Thus the Yeltsin scandal in its broader sense (i.e. including those in his immediate entourage) was linked to the major Bank of New York money-laundering scandal. The Magnitsky case not only resulted in the 2012 Magnitsky Act but continues to resonate in 2017 with Donald Trump Jr.'s claims that his June 2016 meeting with Russians was mostly about repealing that act.

Torsello and Pezzi, in examining corporatism and mafia-ness in the new type of corruption in Italy, posits some interesting analysis. Importantly, and a salient point, is that changing faces of Italian corruption is an endeavour that requires several

244   *Omar E. Hawthorne*

analytical tools and theoretical approaches. Furthermore, for Torsello and Pezzi, it is correct to state that the contribution of anthropology to this field, although shallow over the last three decades, has increasingly come to be strongly relevant, if not badly needed. Anthropological accounts of worldwide corruption have pointed out the need to revisit this timely topic through a so far neglected sensitivity for strategies of governance. This should be done on the grounds of mechanisms of social interaction and by looking at the hermeneutical aspects of a range of activities that are more often on the border between what is publicly perceived as licit and illicit. The interesting chapter on Italy forces readers to grasp the theory of the world-in between as Torsello and Pezzi positions it. Noting that, the case of Mafia Capitale, a multifaceted criminal organization that draws its main source of income from corruption, is exceptionally telling of how corruption can adapt to changing times. The relatively weaker salience of political parties, the styles of trans-national governance, more accurate forms of control of criminal fluxes of capital and a pervasive intermingling of the private and public sectors are all pull-factors that have driven change. Additionally, for the authors, the increased and successful corporatism of the organization Mafia Capitale is one of the responses to these exogenous factors. The plasticity and strong inclusiveness of this organization have allowed it to adapt not only to changing historical conditions, but more significantly to the needs of the public administration that is vexed by continuous budget cuts and the declassification of its competences. Perhaps one of the most interesting takeaways from Torsello and Pezzi's chapter is, as they put it, the symbolism of an in-between social space thus becomes the most powerful metaphor in which every single piece of the game is necessary and has its power of connecting upward. In a system as socially complex and symbolically simple as this, it becomes very hard to argue that corruption may be controlled through more accurate and severe legislations or more attentive police investigations.

In Kenya, Magu's chapter makes a strong case in highlighting that corruption is a part of the Kenyan landscape, and that graft permeates all levels, from the local chief, police, doctor, and all the way to Goldenberg, a global web of connected networks, countries, companies, banks and shady deals that have included smuggling gold. The fight against corruption in Kenya has travelled a long, torturous and unsuccessful road. The international donor community has been active by being at the forefront of pushing for better governance through a bevy of threats, coercion and incentives. Among others, the World Bank, IMF, bilateral and multilateral donors, institutions such as Transparency International, and to some extent, domestic sources against runaway corruption have been staunch advocates on the public's behalf. Kenya has ratified several regional, continental and international conventions against corruption, including UNCAC. However, it can be argued that Kenya's ratification of these instruments is simply to save face, rather than to implement a concerted program of reducing graft, despite the clear positive outcomes linking good governance and economic development with reduced corruption.

Conclusion   245

Subsequently, there has been a lack of will, administratively and politically, to address corruption. Some of those accused of corruption, e.g., Nicholas Biwott, linked to Goldenberg, or Ministers Murungaru and Mwiria, steadily and gradually find their way back into government. This has seemingly been a trend across several countries in this work; notably Jamaica, Nigeria, Trinidad and Tobago, Belarus and others. Additionally, when governments attempt to make legislative change, even with a majority of representative in their respective legislative houses, the will to make comprehensive legislative reform is seemingly lacking.

Williams-Elegbe, in examining high-profile grand corruption cases in Nigeria's oil sector between 2007 and 2017, demonstrated the billions of dollars lost due to corruption and the costly effect as a contributing factor as to why Nigeria remains an underdeveloped country, and, according to a 2015 UNDP report, the poverty rate of Nigeria is a staggering 62.2 percent. There is a mutually reinforcing relationship between poverty, corruption and politics in Nigeria, and for the grand corrupt, state resources are the only way in which they can retain the political power necessary to remain wealthy and powerful. Nigeria, a country rich with oil resources, is underdeveloped with high poverty rates. But, as Williams-Elegbe rightly states, oil resources are the single largest source of public wealth in Nigeria, and unless there are changes in the structure and nature of Nigeria's political organization and system, it is always going to be the case that Nigeria's oil wealth will be plundered by Nigeria's elite. The scandals examined by Williams-Elegbe show that despite Buhari's best efforts, Nigeria still has a long way to go before the oil sector is free of corruption scandals. The culture of corruption did not emerge overnight, and thus it will not be solved easily. Strong measures need to be put in place to stamp out corruption. If one assesses the billions of dollars siphoned off in Nigeria, as revealed by the numerous corruption scandals, one can only imagine the corruption level that has yet to be revealed via a scandal. Nigeria's 2016 whistleblowing policy has led to the recovery of some of the state resources that had been siphoned off, but much is left to be done.

Alleyne and Chandler's chapter on whistleblowing in the Caribbean is pointed, and a pivotal finding from their study is that, contrary to the beliefs of those who oppose whistleblowing, whistleblowers are not motivated by self-interest, but rather seek to make a positive and significant contribution to organizations and by extension the society. It has been argued that whistleblowers have helped to save billions of dollars and numerous lives through their disclosures of pertinent information with reference to fraud, corruption, mismanagement and wrongdoings committed by public and private organizations, government and their officials, thereby protecting citizens, employees and consumers. Additionally, for the true benefits of whistleblowing as an anti-corruption strategy to be realized, the relevant authorities need to address the two biggest issues in the Caribbean: its culture and the personal costs associated with whistleblowing. Addressing these issues will serve to give potential

246   *Omar E. Hawthorne*

whistleblowers and other employees within organizations the confidence to know that there are concerted efforts towards eliminating corruption at the organizational and national levels.

The works of the chapters show that successfully preventing corrupt behaviour requires a comprehensive approach that addresses all levels of government and also reaches out to the private sector. Safeguards and integrity frameworks have to be put in place. Risk areas of corruption such as public procurement have to be specially scrutinized, in particular large-scale infrastructure projects or major sports or cultural events. The financing of political parties and electoral campaigns has to be adequately regulated to avoid undue influence and policies captured by narrow private interests. Transparent, strong and accountable governance frameworks are critical to preventing corruption in countries at all levels of development.

By most industrial countries laws, foreign bribery is a crime, but the research has shown that companies still engage in foreign bribery and are often only found out when a corruption scandal has emerged. As economic interdependence increased dramatically from the late 1970s through the late 1990s, the lack of policy coordination on anti-bribery legislation led to policy discrepancies between states that were problematic for many practical reasons in addition to the normative concerns associated with bribery. Furthermore, as Mistich highlights, policy coordination between states and cooperative institutions have long been studied under a rational choice framework. Bribery is a complex issue, and combating it requires coordination across social, political and economic actors. To add to this complexity, each of these elements varies across space and time.

One of the interesting dynamics of Mistich's chapter is the level of cases analyzed from the Foreign Corrupt Practices Act and Extra-Territorial Enforcement of an International Anti-Bribery Regime. In that, what gave the regime teeth was a US amendment to the FCPA with an extra-territoriality clause. Knowing that this revision to the FCPA was moving through the US Congress is one of the things that encouraged the OECD member states to finalize the agreement. Congress passed this amendment in 1998. It extended the jurisdiction of the FCPA to include all firms registered with the Securities and Exchange Commission. This meant that foreign firms that do business with the US were now subject to penalties if they violated US law, even if the transaction had no US nexus. Mistich's assessment of a 2010 case, an example that involved the prosecution of Daimler AG for their bribery of foreign officials in at least 22 countries, but not in the US is key. Daimler AG is a German firm according to a DOJ 2010 News Release. Daimler AG's corrupt activities took place in countries other than the US, but they were nonetheless fined $93.6 million and agreed to a disgorgement of $91.4 million of profits related to these activities.

Further analysis of the global impact of corruption scandals can be examined from Mistich's chapter where he notes that 49 of the FCPA cases prosecuted since the signing of the OECD Anti-Bribery Convention involved corrupt activity in China, followed by Nigeria with 23 and Iraq with 21. Bribery in India was prosecuted under the FCPA in 16 separate cases, and 15 cases involved bribery in

Russia. In 2008, $1.6 billion in bribes were disclosed in case settlements and $1.1 billion in 2016. The number of prosecutions, the value of the settlements and the scope of the FCPA are expanding as an anti-bribery norm becomes internalized and a culture of anti-bribery spreads throughout the OECD countries. A bribery-free, international marketplace is a public good that improves marginal social welfare. Moving forward, multinational firms will need to pay closer attention to the policies and practices of firms they wish to acquire.

Reider-Gordon, in his assessment of the US pharmaceutical and medical device industry, posits that it has been extensively studied and documented in the social sciences as well as medical journals that physicians prescribe far greater volumes of drugs from a paying manufacturers of drugs, devices, biological, and medical supplies (MDBSs), eschewing generics and even rival brands from companies that have not provided direct benefits to that provider. Likewise, the undue influence and outright engagement in bribery by the industry in the US is well documented. Many scholars, researchers, investigative reporters, policy makers and citizen groups have detailed at length the forms pharmaceutical and medical device industry corruption has taken, the negative impact it has had on healthcare providers (HCPs) and the healthcare landscape, from medical schools to the costs of medications.

Additionally, Reider-Gordon's chapter shows that little has changed despite decades of mounting evidence, and thus it is time to act. To address this endemic corruption in US medicine, a federal law that stands alone and does not depend on the success of failure of any other act, should be enacted. Such a law would ban all forms of transfers of value (gifts, cash, hospitality, sponsorships, grants, reimbursements, trainings, CME, funding patient advocacy organizations, funding medical research, interpreting the results of clinical trials, shaping medical school training, all of it) from MDBSs to HCPs (including nurses, physician assistants, and ancillary providers). And, this, Reider-Gordon argues, would force the MDBS to reform how they compensate their sales and marketing teams. MDBS are not going to change their winning formulas willingly. To do so would conflict with their primary goal of maximizing profitability. The fines by regulators are but a proverbial drop in the bucket. However, if the legality of their behaviour is changed then the stakes become much higher. Potential loss of operating license, debarment from federal contracts or as suppliers under Medicare/Medicaid and more will then become real and meaningful risks. Banning all forms of payment by MDBSs to HCPs does not just relieve the HCPs of undue influence and conflict-of-interest (COI) dilemmas; it would substantially alter how the industry responds in the marketplace. Furthermore, for Reider-Gordon, telling shareholders it is illegal for the company to engage in any quid pro quo provides the answer to cease engaging in the practice and elevates the penalties for those who dare to flaunt the law. With the October 2017 Trump administration's declaration of the opioid crisis as a Public Health Emergency, thus it is a matter of wait and see; the specific laws and policies to be implemented to address the loopholes on how to fix this and other issues will be defining.

Another recommendation from the works of the contributors clearly shows that there is a greater need for promoting international cooperation between law enforcement institutions. As the global economy becomes more interconnected, it is more important that countries are able to cooperate to detect, investigate and sanction corruption. The Brazil case is a perfect example of this. The corruption scandals wreaking havoc through Brazil's political system has not only toppled the first female president of the country, it has also embroiled her replacement, with a former president charged and convicted for corruption. This Brazilian scandal spans the country and includes neighbouring countries. The role of the media in investigating and exposing corruption is pivotal. Additionally criminalization by itself is not sufficient; enforcement is the truest means of deterring and putting an end to bribery.

Whistleblowing is indeed one of the most vital tools in the fight against corruption. It must be encouraged and whistleblowers must be protected. Alleyne and Chandler posit a few recommendations that should be implemented throughout organizations to ensure that whistleblowing can become an effective anti-corruption strategy. First, organisations need to implement more protection and support mechanisms in order to encourage staff to come forward and whistleblow. If staff members feel protected they will be more willing to come forward and report any wrongdoing by their colleagues that they witness.

Additionally, organizations should look to create a culture and an environment that encourages whistleblowing. This, the authors propose, can be done through the provision of training programmes to help them deal with situations when wrongdoing may occur and also to enhance certain characteristics that influences whistleblowing; for example organizational commitment. Also important is the creation of financial incentives for valid whistleblowing (e.g. reward systems) and allow anonymous whistleblowing through the provision of trusted and confidential reporting mechanisms. Organizations can also seek to recruit ethically minded individuals who are most likely to report wrongdoing when it is observed. This can be done using personality and integrity tests to ascertain the characteristics that potential employees possess (Alleyne and Pierce 2017).

The corruption scandals have shown that corruption in many of these countries is largely used as an instrument to acquire and maintain economic and political power at all levels. Opportunities are often lost to integrate anti-corruption dimension with state-building perspective into the increasing number of policies, programmes and legislation. Corruption delegitimizes the state, and thus it must be identified and addressed or it will continue to be limited and will only address corruption on the surface and not the core problem. Traditional anti-corruption mechanisms are insufficient because many corrupt practices are not isolated individual acts but instruments for the benefit of groups and networks. Added, the discrepancies between legal and socio-political definitions of corruption need to be overcome.

Good governance is the key, but unless there are improvements in capacity, accountability and corruption reduction, other reforms will have limited impact. Overall, better governance is associated with greater country competitiveness.

Conclusion 249

Research has shown that transparency helps improve governance and reduce corruption. These are essential ingredients for better development and faster economic growth to which the international community and countries should pay closer attention. Corruption is a 'business', and a profitable one for many who engage in it. The scandals examined throughout the text show the 'marrying/pairing' of political and politically connected individuals engaged in various corruption scandals and that little to no punishment is meeted out once a scandal has unearthed their political misdoings. Undoubtedly, some countries are openly trying to stem corruption, but until most countries engage in strict public disclosure of assets and incomes of candidates running for public office, politicians, legislators, judges, public officials and their dependents, corruption will flourish. There is no doubt that what is also needed is full disclosure of political campaign contributions by individuals and firms, public disclosure of all parliamentary votes, legislation, addressing conflict of interest laws, separating business, politics, and legislation. There is a long way to go in terms of getting meaningful reforms but it must be done. The impact of corruption is global. If nothing else, the scandals show the global nature of corruption, and thus a bolder approach is needed to help stop corruption.

References and further reading

Alleyne, P. and Pierce, A. (2017) Whistleblowing as a Corporate Governance Mechanism in the Caribbean. In *Snapshots in Governance: The Caribbean Experience*, edited by A. M. Bissessar and S. Ryan, pp. 176–98. Trinidad and Tobago: University of the West Indies.

Anderson, M. (2007) Anti-Corruption Mechanisms Causing Conflict? Paper presented at The Nexus: Corruption, Conflict & Peacebuilding Colloquium, Fletcher School, Tufts University.

Balán, M. (2011) Competition by Denunciation: The Political Dynamics of Corruption Scandals in Argentina and Chile. *Comparative Politics*, 43 (4), 459–78.

Bogdanov, L. (2005) Politicheskiat Risk Raste s Otkaza ot Ideologia v Partiite. *Dnevnik*, 10 February.

Bracking, S. (ed.). (2007) *Corruption and Development: The Anti-Corruption Campaigns.* New York: Palgrave Macmillan.

Chubb, J. and Vannicelli, M. (1988) Italy: A Web of Scandals in a Flaw Democracy. In *The Politics of Scandal: Power and Process in Liberal Democracies*, edited by A. S. Markovits and M. Silverstein, pp. 122–50. New York: Holmes & Meier.

Huntington, S. (1968) *Political Order in Changing Societies*. New Haven: Yale University Press.

Kaufmann, D. (2005) Myths and Realities of Governance and Corruption. MPRA Papers No. 8089. Available from: https://mpra.ub.uni-muenchen.de/8089/1/MPRA_paper_8089. pdf [Accessed 25th September 2017].

Klitgaard, R. (1988) *Controlling Corruption*. Berkeley: University of California Press.

Kurer, O. (2001) Why Do Voters Support Corrupt Politicians? In *The Political Economy of Corruption*, edited by A. K. Jain, pp. 63–86. London and New York: Routledge.

Morris, D. (2017) Vladimir Putin Is Reportedly Richer Than Bill Gates and Jeff Bezos Combined. *Fortune*, 30 July. [Online]. Available from: http://fortune.com/2017/07/29/

250 *Omar E. Hawthorne*

vladimir-putin-russia-jeff-bezos-bill-gates-worlds-richest-man/ [Accessed 7th August 2017].

Nichter, S. (2014) Conceptualizing Vote Buying. *Electoral Studies*, 35, 315–27.

Philp, M. (2002) Political Corruption, Democratization, and Reform. In *Political Corruption in Transition: A Sceptic's Handbook*, edited by S. Kotkin and A. Sajó, pp. 57–80. Budapest: Central European University Press.

Sandholtz, W. and Koetzle, W. (2000) Accounting for Corruption: Economic Structure, Democracy, and Trade. *International Studies Quarterly*, 44 (1), 31–50.

UNDP (1997) *Corruption and Good Governance: Discussion Paper 3*. New York: UNDP.

Index

Note: **Boldface** page references indicate tables. *Italic* references indicate figures.

AA Oil 131
Abacha, M. S. 129
Abubakar, A. 131
accountability, lack of 7, 11, 17, 21, 99, 109, 115–116, 194, 239
Accountant General of the Federation 127
Ades, A. 194
Adoke Bello, M. 129–131
adoption policy, Russian 67
Affordable Care Act (ACA) 155–156, 159–160, 164
African Regional Ministerial Workshop on Organized Transnational Crime and Corruption 89
African Union Convention on Preventing and Combating Corruption 8
Africa Peer Review Mechanism (APRM) 90
Agnew, S. 172
Ajaokuta-Kaduna-Kano gas pipeline 134
Akinseye-George, Y. 35
Ali, J. 46
Alleyne, P. 10, 37–39, 47, 245, 248
Aluko, K. 131–133
Amafagha, K. *see* Etete, D.
Amendment to the Obligation to Leave and Prohibition on Entry Act 67
American Medical Association (AMA) 153, 160
AML/CFT Standards 20
Anders, G. 206
Anechiarico, F. 9
Anglo Leasing scandal 80–83, 89
Annan, K. 240
anti-bribery legislation, US and international: cases and outcomes, recent 182–184; clustered decision making and 178; evolution of

171–178; implementing 162–164; Lockheed scandals and, 12, 171–173, 185n3; OECD Anti-Bribery Convention and 171, 175, 177–178, 181–182, 184; overview 12–13; theory 178–182; transfers of value and 155–156, 160, 163, 165n9; Working Group on Bribery in International Business Transactions and 177; *see also* Foreign Corrupt Practices Act (FCPA); *specific law*
Anti-Corruption Cases Trial Monitoring Committee 137
Anti-Corruption Commission 85
Anti-Corruption and Economic Crimes Act 88
Anti-Corruption Investigations Bureau (ACIB) 20
anti-corruption legislation: in Belarus 232–235; in Brazil 199–200; challenges 240–241; in Jamaica 97–98, 116, 243; in Kenya 87–90; lessons learned 240–241; limits of 240; in Nigeria 135–137; in Russia 66–68; Trafigura Beheer scandal and 107–108; in Trinidad and Tobago 16–21; US 145–147, 162–164; US pharmaceutical and medical devices industry and 145–146, 162–164; *see also specific law*
Anti-Corruption Police Unit (ACPU) 87
anti-corruption rhetoric 241
Antigua corruption scandal 10, 41–43
anti-money laundering (AML) 20
Anwar, M. 36
Apter, D. 4
Arthashastra (Kaultilya) 2
Asian Development Bank 6

252 Index

AstraZenaca (pharmaceutical company) 157
Atkinson, P. 109
Atlantic Energy Brass Development Ltd 131–133
Atlantic Energy Drilling Concepts Nigeria Ltd 131–133
Axenergy Limited 128

Babushkina krinka (company) 228
Bacarese, A. 89
Bachan, R. 46
Bad Ad Program 149
Bagoo, A. 46–47
Bahama's corrupt activity 40, **40**
Bailey, F. 206
Balán, M. 3, 242–243
Banca del Gottardo 60
Banda della Magliana 208
banking industry and extra-territorial clause 176–177
Bank of New York money-laundering scandal 68, 243
Barbuda corruption scandal 10, 41–43
Baru, M. 134
Becker, G. 5
Beck, P. 5
Begovic, B. 17–18
Belarusbank scandal 228–229
Belarusian railway company scandal 226
Belarus's corruption scandals: anti-corruption legislation and 232–235; Babushkina krinka 228; Belarusbank 228–229; Belarusian railway company 226; Beltamozhservice 224; Borisovdrev 225, 229–230; case information 221, *222*, *223*, 224–229; consequences of 221, 229–234, 242; Criminal Code and 220, 234, 242; Decree of President of the Republic of Belarus No. 5 and 231–232; dissemination of corruption information and 220; Gomel meat 226–227; incidence of 219; Kamienny Log 226, 229; Law of the Republic of Belarus and 220, 232–233, 235; Law of the Republic of Belarus No. 361-Z and 235; Ministry of Internal Affairs 224; Minsk Economic Court 228; Minsk Wheel Tractor Plant 225; Naftan 227–228; overview 13–14, 219–221, 234–235; peak levels of 221, *222*, 224, 229; "Potassium war" 224; publications on corruption and 221, *223*, 224, 234; public procurement procedures and 232–233; Resolution of the Council of Ministers of the Republic

of Belarus No. 68 and 232; Road Police for Vitebsk 227; Senator Sh. 228–229; Slutsk meat plant 227, 231; Uralkali 224, 229; Uzdenski 224–225; Vitebsk broiler poultry factory 228
Beltamozhservice corruption scandal 224
Berezovsky, B. 70
Bernard, Prince of Belgium 171
Big Pharma *see* US pharmaceutical and medical devices industry
Biomet 157
Bissessar, A. M. 9, 241
Biwott, N. 91, 245
black market money dealers (*doleiros*) 196
Block 245 oil field 129
Boissevan, J. 206, 216
Boko Haram 122
Bonica, A. 100
Borisovdrev corruption scandal 225, 229–230
Borodin, P. 61
Brady, H. 111–112
Brazil's corruption scandals: anti-corruption legislation and 199–200; "Car Wash" 13, 192–193, 195–196, **197**, 198, **199**, 200; causes of 193–195; Clean Company Act and 199–201; clientelism and 190–191; consequences of 195–200; Corruption Perceptions Index and 195, **195**; Criminal Code and 199; as cultural aspect 193–194; democratic government and 190–192, 195; Dutch disease and 195; economic growth and 190; Federal Police and 195, 197; Federal Supreme Court and 194, 200; foreign direct investment and 198; grand corruption 190–191, **191**; international cooperation in combating 248; lessons learned from 4; *mensalão* and 191–192, **191**; oligarchy and 190; Operation Zelote 198; overview 13, 189–192, 200–201; patron-client relationship of government and 190; Petrobas 192, 194–198, 201; punishments and 194; recent 190–191, **191**
Bretton Woods institutions 79, 87, 244; *see also specific name*
bribe gifts 151; *see also specific scandal*
Bribe Payers Index 7
bribery 5, 12, 150–151, 178–179, 185, 246; *see also specific scandal*
Bribery Act 199
bribery game 179, *179*
BRIC countries 190
Bristol-Myers Squibb (pharmaceutical company) 157

Index   253

Browder, B. 66, 71n10, 243
Brown, D. 240
Buhari administration 12, 135–137
Buhari, M. 120, 135, 137, 138n12
Bulls Eye Security Coke 114
Burbridge, D. 87

Camargo, J. G. de A. 198
Cameron, D. 120
Campbell, C. 102, 104–106, 109, 114
Campbell, L. 109
Carballo, M. 44–45
Cardoso, F. H. 191
Caribbean corruption scandals in financial
   sector: Colonial Life Insurance
   Company 10, 43–45, 48; Commission of
   Enquiry and 44, 46; Commissioner for
   Co-operative Development and 45–46;
   Corruption Perceptions Index and 34,
   40–41, **40**; defining corruption and
   35–36; Director of Public Prosecutions
   and 46; Hindu Credit Union 10,
   44–48; impact of 36, 50; interpreting
   corruption and 35–36; overview 10,
   34–35; prevalence of 34; problem of, for
   governments 50; Stanford International
   Bank 10, 41–43, 48; types of corruption
   36; whistleblowing and 37–40, 47–49,
   245–246
Caribbean Financial Action Task Force
   (CFATF) 20
Carter, J. 173, 178
"Car Wash" scandal 13, 192–193,
   195–196, **197**, 198, **199**, 200
Catchick, P. 150–151
Cater, C. 9
Center for Global Financial Integrity 9
Center for Responsive Politics 160
Central Authority of Trinidad and Tobago
   18–19
Central Bank of Kenya 80
Central Bank of Nigeria (CBN) 128–129,
   135–136
Centre for Public Policy Alternatives
   124–125
Ceresney, A. 150, 156–157
Chaika, Y. 67
Chandler, M. 10, 245, 248
"chickengate" 90–91
China's corrupt activity 9, 185, 246
Choudhry, N. 151–152
Christie, S. 108–109
Church Committee 172, 186n4
Church, F. 172–173
Clean Company Act 199–201

Clean Hand Movement 212
CL Financial (CLF) 44
clientelism 190–191
Clinton, H. 67
clustered decision making 178
Coke, C. 11, 98, 109–111, 113–114
Coke extradition 11, 98, 109–114, *110*
Coke, L. 113
Cold War 2, 79, 86, 174
Colin Campbell Our Candidate (CCOC)
   bank account 102, 104–108
Collor de Mello, F. 191
Colonial Life Insurance Company (CLICO)
   corruption scandal 10, 43–45, 48
"coloured revolutions" 70
combating the financing of terrorism
   (CFT) 20
Commission of Enquiry 44, 46
Commissioner for Co-operative
   Development (CCD) 45–46
Commission for the Prevention of
   Corruption 98
Committees Office of the Parliament 30
Common Market for Eastern and Southern
   Africa (COMESA) 89
Commonwealth and Foreign Territories
   Act 19
composite indicators 7
conflicts of interest (COI) 150–152, 160,
   162, 247
Congo Free State 8–9
Consumer Protection Act 39
Convention on Combating Bribery of
   Foreign Public Officials 103
corporatism of corruption 209–211
corruption: accountability and, lack
   of 194; challenge of combating,
   current 189; comprehensive approach
   to preventing 246; corporatism of
   209–211; corruption scandal versus
   3; as cost of doing business 5–6, 85,
   179, 249; cost of 189, 245; defining
   6–7, 35–36, 189–190; delegitimization
   of government and 248; demand-and-
   supply analysis of 7; as derivative of
   evil 104–107; discussion of, facilitation
   of 2; etymology 2; experience-based
   indicators of 7; factors contributing to,
   fundamental 21; globalization of 8–9,
   88–89; hermeneutical perspective of
   206; historical perspective of 2; impact
   of 5–6, 189–190, 249; incidence of,
   global 190; international cooperation
   in combating 248; interpreting 35–36;
   manifestations of 1–3; measuring

254 *Index*

6–7, 68; multi-dimensional nature of 17–21; multi-disciplinary research on 189; overview 9–14; perception-based indicators of 7; pervasiveness of 5–6; petty 77; pluralism of law and 206; political campaigns and 5, 107, 249; reform 239, 248–249; regional activities and initiatives combating 8; risk areas of 246; strategic reference perspective of 206–207; symbolism of 205, 213–216, 244; synonyms 2; transactional perspective of 207; types of 1–2, 17–18, 36, 238; varieties of 193; *see also* corruption scandals; grand corruption; *specific scandal*
Corruption and Good Governance (UNDP) 238
Corruption and Government (Rose-Ackerman and Palifka) 9
Corruption Perceptions Index (CPI): Brazil 195, **195**; Caribbean 34, 40–41, **40**; establishment by Transparency International 6; Jamaica 98; Kenya 78; Russia 57; Trinidad and Tobago 21, 31n4; use of 6–7
corruption scandals: catharsis rituals and 241; corruption versus 3; defining 3–4; features of, key 83–84, 234; impact of 14, 237–240, 246–247, 249; media and 241–249; politics and 4, 97, 237–238; power struggles and 4, 248; recent 10; stages of 3–4; *see also* lessons learned; *specific scandal*
Costa, L. M. 13
Costa, P. R. 196–197
Country Performance Assessment ratings 6
Court of Appeal 109
Crane, A. 35
Craxi, B. 213
Criminal Finances Act 67
Criminal Law Convention on Corruption 8
cultural meaning systems 213
Curacao Shell plant sale 102

DaCosta Commission 98
Daimler AG 176, 183, 246
Dakar Declaration on the Prevention and Control of Organized Transnational Crime and Corruption 89
D'Andrade, R. G. 214
Daniel, T. 89
Darrow, J. 161
da Silva, L. I. L. 191–192, 194–195, 197
Dauphin, C. 105

David, J. 42
Daylian, C. 158
Decree of President of the Republic of Belarus No. 5 231–232
Deferred Prosecution Agreements (DPAs) 157
Défi Américain, Le (Servan-Schreiber) 172
Della Porta, D. 105
del Ponte, C. 60
demand-and-supply analysis of corruption 7
de Maria, W. 7
democratic governments 2, 5, 98, 190–192, 195, 198
Demske, G. E. 164
Department of Justice (DOJ) 111, 133, 145–146, 149, 157, 181–185
de Sardan, O. J. P. 207, 217
detailing 12, 147–150, 155, 158
Detsy, A. 151–152
di Pietro, A. 212
Director of Public Prosecutions (DPP) 46, 103–104, 115
Di Tella, R. 194
Dodd-Frank Wall Street Reform 39
Doig, A. 47
drug dealing 211; *see also* Coke extradition
Dudus *see* Coke, C.
Duke Oil Limited 134
Duma 64, 66–67
Duprey, C. L. 43–44
Dutch disease 195
Dutch Penal Code 103
Dyachenko, T. 61, 69

East African Association of Anti-Corruption Authorities (EAAACA) 89
East African Community (EAC) 89
economic collapse (2008), global 39
Economic and Financial Crimes Commission (EFCC) 122
Economic Forum (2008) 57
Egmont Group of Financial Intelligence 20
Eldoret International Airport 84
electronic citizen services (e-Citizen) 91
Elizabeth II 120
Elkins, Z. 178–179
Emenalo, B. 127
Employee Code of Conduct and Employment Agreement 109
ENI 129–131
Enill, C. 47
Enron, 35
Enweremadu, D. U. 123
Esipisu, M. 82

Estonia's anti-corruption legislation 67
Etete, D. 129–131, 138n3, 138n9
Ethical Criteria for Medicinal Drug
  Promotion 162–163
Ethics and Anti-Corruption Commission
  (EACC) 85, 88
Eurobond debt instrument 79–80
Eurobond scandal 89
Euromarine scandal 89
European Court of Human Rights 64–65
Everhart, S. S. 36
Exchange Bank 81
Executive Flexible Premium Annuities
  (EFPAs) 44
experience-based indicators of corruption 7
Extradition Act 19
Extra-Territorial Enforcement of an
  International Anti-Bribery Regime
  176–177, 182, 246

False Claims Act (FCA) 146–147, 149,
  165n12
FATF Recommendations 20
Federal Bureau of Investigation (FBI) 42, 61
Federal High Court 131
Federal Ministry of Finance (FMF) 136
Financial Industry Regulatory Authority
  (FINRA) 43
Financial Intelligence Unit (FIU) 20
Financial Times article on year of
  corruption 2
First Caribbean International Bank (FCIB)
  104, 108
First Mercantile Securities Corporation 82
Food and Drug Administration (FDA)
  148–149
Force Publique 8
Foreign Agents Registration Act (FARA) 111
foreign bribery 150, 246; *see also specific
  scandal*
Foreign Corrupt Practices Act (FCPA):
  amendment to 176; Clean Company
  Act and 199; in combating corruption
  8, 246–247; contesting of, by business
  interests 179–182; cost of compliance
  185; cost of conviction to company 184;
  Daimler AG and 183; enforcement of
  157, 180–181, 184–185, *184*; extra-
  territoriality clause of 5, 12, 176–177,
  182, 246; historical perspective of
  171–172; Lockheed scandals and
  12, 171–173, 185n3; multinational
  corporations and 178; Nigeria and 185;
  passing of 163, 174, 178; prisoner's

dilemma and 179, *179*; prosecutions
  of future 184–185; public trust in
  government and, decline in 173; Ralph
  Lauren Corporation and 183–184;
  regulatory policy and 180; restrictions
  on 174; Russia and 185; scope of
  145–146; Siemens and 183; Stryker and
  158; US pharmaceutical and medical
  devices industry and 156–158; US trade
  and 174
foreign direct investment (FDI) 181, 198
Foreign States Order 103
Freedom House 6
Freedom of Information Act 19
free press 2

Gambetta, D. 211
Ganeev affair 62, 67
Ganeev, V. 62, 64
gas subsidy scam 126–128
GATT 174
Gazprom (Russian corporation) 62
Gehlbach, S. 200
gift economy 161
Girling, J. 192
Githongo, J. 83
GlaxoSmithKline (pharmaceutical
  company) 157
Gleander, The, articles 100
Glencore (company) 102
Global Competitiveness Report
  (GCR) 6, 195
Global Corruption barometer 6, 120
Global Integrity Index 6
globalization of corruption 8–9, 88–89
Goldenberg scandal 11, 78, 80–82, 85,
  88–89, 244–245
Golding, B. 102–103, 107–108, 110–114
Gomel meat scandal 226–227
Goodman, B. 154–155
Gorokhov, N. 64–65
Gorshenkov, G. N. 219, 224
Gould, D. J. 35
government: client-patron relationship of
  190; corruption and delegitimization of
  248; democratic 2, 5, 98, 190–192, 195,
  198; good 248–249; grand corruption
  and 123; nondemocratic 193; poor
  99; public trust in, decline of 100,
  172–173; Westminster Whitehall model
  of 17, 112
Government Accountability Office
  (GAO) 162
Graham, J. W. 38–39

256　*Index*

Graham's principled organizational dissent model 38–39

grand corruption: in Brazil 190–191, **191**; Central Bank of Nigeria 128–129; challenge of, legal 196; enforcement of laws against 122–123; Etete, Adoke, and oil companies scandal 129–131; government and 123; impact of 121–123; judicial corruption and 122–123; in Kenya 81; kerosene subsidy scam 124–126; Madueke, Aluko, and Omokore scandal 131–133; Nigeria National Petroleum Corporation contracts 133–135; Nigeria's problems with 120–123; petrol subsidy scam 126–128; police corruption and 122; Transparency International and 120–122

Grassley, C. 155

Grouse, L. 152

Gryzlov, B. 62

GSK (pharmaceutical company) 152–153

Gulf Cartel 42

Gupta, A. 206–207

Guyana's corrupt activity 40–41, **40**

Harnarine, H. 44–46

Harrison, D. 115

Hatchard, T. 89

Hawthorne, O. 2, 11, 14

healthcare providers (HCPs): billing of time with company reps and 158; conflicts of interest of 150–152, 247; denial of gift-taking by 152–153; detailing and 12, 147–150, 155, 158; FDA oversight and 149; financial arrangements with MDBSs 148; foreign 157; gift-taking by 150, 159; impact of corruption in industry on 163, 247; industry guidelines and 153–155; opioid crisis and 247; Sunshine Act and 155–156, 160; transfers of value and 155–156, 160, 163, 165n9; *see also specific name*

Heidenheimer, A. 9

Hempstone, S. 86

Henry, D. 150

Heritage Foundation 6, 40

hermeneutical perspective of corruption 206

Hermitage Capital Management Company 62

Hinds, N. 104, 109

Hindu Credit Union (HCU) corruption scandal 10, 44–48

Holman, M. 81

Holmes, L. 10, 243

Holness, A. 114

household kerosene (HHK) 124

Human Rights Council 64

Huntington, S. 5

Hylton, M. 41

Ilyukin, V. 61

immunity from arrest and prosecution 59, 64, 66–67, 70, 123, 243

"in-between world" of corporatism and mafia-ness 13, 204–205

Independent Electoral Commission (INEC) 133

Independent Electrical Boundaries Commission (IEBC) 90

India's corrupt activity 185, 206, 246

Integrated Financial Management System (IFMIS) 86, 91

Integrity Commission 11, 98, 116

Integrity Commission Bill 41

Integrity in Public Life Act 19

Inter-American Convention Against Corruption 18

Interception of Communications Act 112

International Institute for Sustainable Development 124–125

International Legal Consulting v Malabu Oil and Gas Ltd 131

International Monetary Fund (IMF) 86–87

Iraq's corrupt activity 183, 185, 246

Istanbul Plan 8

Italy's corruption scandals: anthropological research and 205–207, 244; Banda della Magliana and 208; Clean Hand Movement and 212; corporatism of 209–211; Court of Rome and 215; Craxi and 213; culture and 213; current 214; drug dealing 211; "in-between world" of corporatism and mafia-ness and 13, 204–205; Mafia Capitale and 13, 204, 208–209, 211, 215–217, 244; mafia metaphor and 214; Mani Pulite 5; migrant camp project 211–213, 217; mondo di mezzo theory and 205, 209, 214–215; nicknames and 214–215; omertà and 214; overview 13, 205, 216–217; secret of law and 206; symbolism of corruption and 205, 213–216, 244; Tangentopoli scandal 5, 213

Iyer, N. 5

Index 257

Jacobellis v. Ohio 1
Jamaica Labor Party (JLP) 102–104, 107, 111, 114
Jamaica's corruption scandals: accountability and, lack of 99; anti-corruption legislation and efforts and 97–98, 116, 243; causes and contributions 100, 115–116; Coke extradition 11, 98, 109–114, *110*; Commission for the Prevention of Corruption and 98; Corruption Perceptions Index and 98; cost of 99; Director of Public Prosecutions and 103–104, 115; incidence of 98–100; Integrity Commission and 11, 98, 116; Integrity Commission Bill and 41; Jamaica Constabulary Police and 110; Jamaica Defence Force and 110; Jamaica Labor Party and 102–104, 107, 111, 114; listing of 99; Minister of Justice and 103; Mutual Assistance Order and 103; National Contracts Commission and 97–98, 103; Office of the Contractor General and 97–98, 102, 107, 114–115; overview 11, 97–98; politics and 97; poor governance and 99; Public Management Accountability Act and 97–98; relevance of 97–98; Westminster Whitehall model of government and 112; whistleblowing and 97; *see also* Trafigura Beheer scandal
JBS (meat exporter) 197, 198
Johnson, M. 9
Joint Select Committee in Trinidad and Tobago 22, **23–24**
Jonathan, G. 126, 128, 131–133
Jones, E. 100, 116
JP Morgan Chase (bank) 131
judiciary corruption 122–123

Kachikwu, I. 134–135
Kaczmarek, S. C. 182
Kamienny Log scandal 226, 229
Kaufman, D. 9, 237
Kautilya 2
Kenya Anti-Corruption Authority (KACA) 87
Kenya Anti-Corruption Commission (KACC) 88
Kenya's corruption scandals: African Regional Ministerial Workshop on Organized Transnational Crime and Corruption and 89; Anglo Leasing 80–83, 89; Anti-Corruption Commission and 85; Anti-Corruption and Economics Crimes Act and 88; anti-corruption international conventions and 88–90; anti-corruption legislation and 87–90; Anti-Corruption Police Unit and 87; "chickengate" 90–91; Cold War and 79, 86; Corruption Perceptions Index and 78; cost of 11, 78, 80–81, 83–84; domestic impact of 79, 84–86; electronic citizen services and 91; Ethics and Anti-Corruption Commission and 85, 88; Eurobond debt instrument and 79–80; features of, key 83–84; foreign aid and loans and 86–87; globalization and 88–89; Goldenberg 11, 78, 80–82, 88–89, 244–245; grand corruption and 81; historical perspective of 78–79; impact of 79, 84–87; incidence of 77; innovation of 79–80; Integrated Financial Management Information System and 86; international impact of 86–87; Kenya Anti-Corruption Authority and 87; Kenya Anti-Corruption Commission and 88; Ministry of Interior and Coordination of National Government and 85; National Youth Service 80; Official Secrets Act and 78; overview 10–11, 77–78; petty corruption and 77; preventing and eliminating 90–92; Prevention of Corruption Act and 87; public safety and 86; state-owned enterprises and 79; tenderpreneurship and 80; Turkwell Hydro-Electric Power project and 85; UN Convention against Corruption and 89; Urban Infrastructure Project and 85; whistleblowing and 78, 81, 242–243
Keohane, R. O. 181
kerosene subsidy scam 124–126
Kibaki, M. 81–83
King, L. 42–43
Klebnikov, P. 69–70
Klitgaard, R. 239
Knight, K. D. 109
Koetzle, W. 2, 240
Kofele-Kale, N. 89
Kompromat (compromising material) 61
Kreikebaum, H. 34, 36, 47
Kremlin renovation 59–60
KUITP 85
Kuppusamy, K. 47
Kushner, J. 67
Kwaka, J. 88

258 *Index*

LaFrance, A. 159
Lalchan, Y. 46
Lambert, L. 176
Lashmankin and Others v. Russia 64
Lawan, F. 127
Law of the Republic of Belarus 220,
 232–233, 235
Lay, K. 35
Lazarenko, P. 60
Leff, N. 5
Lenin, V. 67
Lessig, L. 161
lessons learned: anti-corruption legislation
 240–241; from Brazil's corruption
 scandals 4; global impacts of corruption
 scandals 237–240; media's role 241–249
Levada Center website 65–66
Lexchin, J. 161
Lien, D. 5
Lightbourne, D. 111–113
Light, D. 161
Litvinenko, A. 70
Local Content Act 132
Lockheed scandals 12, 171–173, 185n3
Lowenstein, G. 158
Lowi, T. 3
Lula 191 192, 194–195, 197

Mabetex (construction company) 59–61
Madueke, D. A. 131–133
Mafia Capitale (Mafia Capital) 13, 204,
 208–209, 211, 215–217, 244
mafia metaphor 214
Magnitsky Act 67–68, 71n18, 243
Magnitsky affair 62–65, 67–69, 243
Magnitsky, S. 62–65, 69
Magu, S. 10, 244
Maher, M. 5
Malabu Oil & Gas 129–131
Manafort, P. 67
Manatt, Phelps & Phillips 111–112
manifestations of corruption 1–3
Mani Pulite scandal 5
Manley, M. 102
Mansfield, P. 150
Manson, K. 83
manufacturers of drugs, devices,
 biological, and medical supplies
 (MDBSs): anti-corruption legislation
 and efforts and 145–146, 162–164;
 bribe gifts and 151; civil actions
 and settlements and 157–158, 165n12;
 conflicts of interest and 150–152, 160,
 162; Deferred Prosecution Agreements

and 157; denial of gift-taking by
healthcare providers and 152–153;
detailing and 12, 147–150, 155, 158;
documentation of 247; exportation of
marketing strategies and 157; FDA
oversight and 149; industry guidelines
and 153–155; influence of 148, 247;
kickbacks and 148–149; market 145;
Open Payments Program and 161–162;
regulation of 145–146, 154; reporting
requirements 156, 165n11; self-
regulation and 154; Sunshine Act and
155–156, 159, 161–162, 164; transfers
of value and 155–156, 160, 165n9;
transparency and, limits of 158–162;
whistleblowing and 155; *see also* US
pharmaceutical and medical devices
industry

Maore, M. 83
Marcos, F. 60
Martelli, C. 5
Matiang'i, F. 81
Matten, D. 35
Mauro, P. 85
Mead Johnson Nutrition 157
media: corruption scandals and 241–249;
 democratic governments and 98, 100;
 free press and 2; social 3–4; *see also*
 specific name
Medicaid 147, 155, 163, 247
Medicare 147, 155, 163, 247
Medvedev, D. 57, 63–69
mensalão 191–192, **191**
Miceli, M. P. 37
migrant camp project 211–213, 217
Mills, G. 97, 99
Ministry of Interior and Coordination of
 National Government (Kenya) 85
Ministry of Internal Affairs (Russia) 65, 67
Ministry of Internal Affairs corruption
 scandal (Belarus) 224
Minsk Economic Court corruption
 scandal 228
Minsk Wheel Tractor Plant 235
Mistich, J. 5, 12, 246–247
mondo di mezzo theory 205, 209, 214–215
Money Laundering Act 108
Moscow Criminal Investigation
 Department 62
Moscow Police 65
Moskovskii Komsomolets article 62
Muite, P. 81
multi-dimensional nature of corruption
 17–21

Index 259

multi-disciplinary research on corruption 189
Murray, D. 48
Murungaru, C. 91, 245
Mutonyi, J. 87
Mutual Assistance in Criminal Matters Act 18
Mutual Assistance Order 103
Mutunga, T. 88
Mwangi, O. G. 81
Mwiraria, D. 83, 91, 245

Naftan (petroleum refinery company) 227–228
Nash equilibrium 179, 181
National Action Plan in Nigeria 137
National Contracts Commission (NCC) 97–98, 103
National Crime Agency 132
National Youth Service (NYS) scandal 80
Nations in Transit 6
Navalnyi, A. 63, 65–66, 69–70, 71n16
Near, J. P. 37
Nepal corrupt activity 207
Netherlands, Kingdom of 103, 107–108
Netherlands National Police Agency (KLPD) 114
Netherlands-Nigeria Bilateral Investment Treaty (BIT) 130
Newman, A. L. 182
New Partnership for Africa's Development (NEPAD) 90
Nicholls, C. 89
Nicholls, C. Q. C. 121
Nigeria Agip Exploration 129, 130–131, 138n8
Nigeria National Petroleum Corporation (NNPC) 102, 125, 128, 133–135
Nigerian Constitution 123
Nigerian House of Representatives 131
Nigerian National Bureau of Statistics (NBS) 120
Nigerian Oil and Gas Industry Content Development Act 132
Nigerian Petroleum Development Company (NPDC) 132
Nigeria's corruption scandals: Anti-Corruption Cases Trial Monitoring Committee and 137; anti-corruption legislation and efforts and 135–137; Buhari administration and 12, 135–137; Central Bank of Nigeria 128–129, 135–136; challenges of preventing 245; cost of 126, 245; Economic and Financial Crimes Commission and 122; Etete, Adoke, and oil companies fraudulence 129–131; Foreign Corrupt Practices Act and 185; GDP growth and 9; grand corruption problems in 120–123; immunity from arrest and prosecution and 123; judiciary corruption and 122–123; kerosene subsidy scam 124–126; Madueke, Aluko, and Omokore scandal 131–133; National Action Plan and 137; Nigeria National Petroleum Corporation contracts 133–135; Nigerian Constitution and 123; OECD Anti-Bribery Convention and 246; Open Government Partnership and 137; overview 11–12, 121, 137; pervasiveness of 120; petrol subsidy scam 126–128; police corruption and 122; whistleblowing and 136
Nixon, R. 171
nondemocratic government 193
nongovernmental organizations (NGOs) 189
Nordio, C. 5
North African migrant camp scandal 211–213, 217
Novartis AG (pharmaceutical company) 157
Nuijten, M. 206
Nyong'o, A. 81

Obaje, A. 130
Obasanjo, O. 102
Oberthur, C. 83
Oblast, G. 230
obscenity legal case 1
Odebrecht (engineering company) 197–198
OECD (Organisation for Economic Co-operation and Development) 162, 175, 181–182, 246
OECD Anti-Bribery Convention 12, 100, 105, 171, 175, 177–178, 181–182, 184, 246–247
OECD Anti-Corruption Network for Eastern Europe and Central Asia (ACN) 8
OECD Convention on Combating Bribery of Foreign Public Officials in International Business Transactions 8, 151, 163
OECD Guidelines for Multinational Enterprises 103
OECD Working Group on Bribery in International Business Transactions 177
Office of the Contractor General (OCG) 97–98, 102, 107, 114–115
Office of Prescription Drug Promotion 149
Official Secrets Act 78

260   *Index*

O'Gilvie, J. 114
oil prospering license (OPL) 129
Okogbule, N. S. 152
Okoth, S. 88
oligarchy 190
Omnibus Foreign Trade and
  Competitiveness Act (OFTCA)
  174–175, 178
Omokore, J. 131–133
O'Neil, J. 190
Onnoghen, W. 137
Ontario Oil and Gas 128
Open Government Partnership (OGP) 137
Open Payments Program 161–162
"Operação Lava Jato" *see* "Car Wash"
  scandal
Operation Zelote 198
Organisation for Economic Co-operation
  and Development *see* OECD
organizational factors contributing to
  corruption 21
Orthofix International (company) 157
Osei, P. 98–100
Osinbajo, Y. 135
Otedola, F. 127

Pacolli, B. I. 60, 71n5
Palermo Convention 90
Palifka, B. 1, 9, 84
Panama Papers 4, 9
Paris Club 86
Parker, G. R. 100
Parliament of Trinidad and Tobago 16,
  21–22, **23–24**, 24–26, *27*, 28
Patient Protection and Affordable Care Act
  155–156, 159–160, 164
patronage-based appointments 239–240
patron-client relationship of government 190
Pattni, K. 80–81
Pattni, V. 80
Paulwell, P. 109
People's National Party (PNP) 11, 100,
  102–103, 105–109
perception-based indicators of corruption 7
Persad-Bissessar, K. 46
Petrobas (oil and gas company) 192,
  194–198, 201; *see also* "Car Wash"
  scandal
Petroleum Corporation of Jamaica (PCJ) 102
Petroleum Products Pricing Regulatory
  Agency (PPPRA) 126, 138n5
petrol subsidy scam 126–128
petty corruption 77
Pfizer 148

Pham-Kanter, G. 149, 160–161
Philips, P. 111
Philp, M. 241
PhRMA 153–154
Pickersgill, R. 109
Pierce, A. 38–39, 47
Pierre, A. 46–47
pluralism of law 206
Police Complaints Authority (PCA) Act 19
police corruption 61–62, 64, 122, 227;
  see also specific scandal
policy 66–68, 180; *see also specific law*
political campaigns and corruption 5, 107,
  249; *see also* Trafigura Beheer scandal
Political Corruption (Heidenheimer and
  Johnson) 9
Political and Economic Risk Consultancy 6
Political Risk Services 6
politics and corruption scandals 4, 97,
  237–238; *see also specific scandal*
Politkovskaya, A. 70
Polterovich, V. M. 21, 26
Ponzi scheme 43
"Potassium War" 224
Poverty Reduction and Growth Facility
  (PRGF) strategies 79
power struggles and corruption scandals 4,
  248; *see also specific scandal*
Power, T. J. 200
premium motor spirit (PMS) 124, 126
Prevention of Corruption Act 19, 87, 90
Pricewaterhouse Cooper (PwC) 125, 128
principled organizational dissent model
  (Graham) 38–39
prisoner's dilemma 179, *179*
Privy Council 109
Proceeds of Crime Act 19
Protected Disclosures Act 97
Public Accounts Committee (PAC) 22, 24
Public Accounts Enterprises Committee
  (PAEC) 9, 16, 22, 24, 26, 28, 241
Public Management Accountability Act
  97–98
Public Oversight Commission 63
public trust in government, decline of 100,
  172–173
Pursuit of Absolute Integrity (Anechiarico) 9
Putin, V. 10, 57–59, 61–64, 66–70, 243

Rachagan, S. 47
raiding (*reiderstvo*) 61, 69
Ralph Loren Corporation 183–184
Ramnath, G. 46
Reconciliation Committee 128

regulatory policy 180; *see also specific law*
Reider-Gordon, M. 12, 247
rent-seeking 5, 85–87, 92, 104
Resolution of the Council of Ministers of the Republic of Belarus No. 68 232
response stage of corruption scandal 3–4
Richardson, P. 9
Riley, S. 47
Road Police for Vitebsk corruption scandal 227
"roofing" (*kryshevanie*) corruption 61
Rose-Ackerman, S. 1, 5, 9, 84, 196
Rousseff, D. 192, 194–195
Russia's corruption scandals: adoption policy and 67; anti-corruption demonstrations and 70; anti-corruption legislation and 66–68; "coloured revolutions" and 70; Corruption Perceptions Index and 57; defining corruption scandal and 58–59; *Duma* and 64, 66–67; Foreign Corrupt Practices Act and 185; Ganeev affair 62, 67; immunity from arrest and prosecution and 59, 64, 66–67, 70, 243; impact of 63–68; international ramifications of 68; Klebnikov's murder and 69–70; Kremlin renovation and 59–60; Magnitsky affair 62–65, 67–69, 243; Medvedev and 57, 63–69; Ministry of Internal Affairs and 65, 67; Moscow Criminal Investigation Department and 62; Moscow Police and 65; Navalnyi's efforts against 63, 65–66, 69–70, 71n16; OECD Anti-Bribery Convention and 246–247; outcomes of 63–66; overview 10, 57; police corruption 61–62, 64; policy and 66–68; Public Oversight Commission 63; Putin and 10, 57–59, 61–64, 66–70, 243; raiding (*reiderstvo*) 61, 69; "roofing" (*kryshevanie*) 61; Russian people's view of 68; US presidential election (2016) and 67, 71n4; "werewolves in epaulettes" 61–62, 64; Yeltsin and 59–61, 64, 68, 243

Sachs, J. 194
Sah, S. 158
Samociuk, M. 5
Samuda, K. 111
Sandholtz, W. 2, 240
Sanusi II, L. 128
Sarbanes-Oxley Act 39, 146
Sartori, G. 29–30

Sascheko, P. 13–14, 242
scandal, defining 58
Schollhammer, H. 35
SciClone Pharmaceuticals 157
secret of law 206
Securities and Exchange Commission (SEC) 8, 42, 48, 171–173, 181, 183–185, 246
Seeterram, C. 46
Seko, Mobutu Sese 9
Senator Sh. corruption scandal 228–229
Serious Fraud Office (Great Britain) 90
Serious and Organized Crime Threat Assessment (SOCTA) 150
Servan-Schreiber, J. J. 172
Sewanta, K. 207
Shabbir, G. 36
Shakespeare, William 2
Shell Nigeria 130
Shell Nigeria Ultra Deep Limited v Federal Republic of Nigeria 130
Shell Oil 129
Shell Ultra Deep 129–130
Shestakov, D. A. 219
Shevtsova, L. 69
Shower Posse drug cartel 110, 113–114
Siemens (company) 183
Simmons, B. 178–179
Simpson-Miller, P. 105–106, 109, 114
Singer, D. A. 180
Skuratov, Y. 60–61, 71n7
Slutsk meat plant 227, 231
Smith & Ouzman (S & O), Limited 11, 90
Smith, N. 90
social media 3–4
societal factors contributing to corruption 21
Somner, A. 172
South Africa's corrupt activity 80
Southall, R. 82
Southern African Development Community (SADC) 89
Sperling, V. 87
Sporkin, S. 171–172
spread stage of corruption scandal 3–4
Staddon, A. 25–26, 28–29
Stanford, A. 10, 41–43, 48
Stanford Financial Group 10, 41–43, 48
Stanford International Bank corruption scandal 10, 41–43, 48
Stark Laws 147, 149
state-owned enterprises (SEOs) 79
Stelfox, H. 151–152
Stewart, Potter 1
Steyn, G. 81

262 *Index*

Stigler, G. 5
Stone, C. 100
strategic alliance agreements (SAAs) 132
strategic reference perspective of
corruption 206–207
Strauss, D. 104
Structural Adjustment strategies 79
Stryker (company) 158
Suharto, M. 60
Sunshine Act 155–156, 159–162, 164
symbolism of corruption 205, 213–216, 244
Symposium on Corruption and Good
Governance 177

Tanaka, K. 171
Tangentopoli scandal 5, 213
Taylor, M. M. 200
tenderpreneurship 2, 80
terrorists 86
Teva Pharmaceuticals 157
Thompson, T. 3
Torsello, D. 13, 243–244
Trafigura Beheer scandal: amendment
of Jamaican law and 102, 107–108;
anti-corruption legislation and
107–108; campaign finance and 5,
100, 102; Campbell (Colin) and 102,
104–106, 114; cartoon illustrations of
101; Colin Campbell Our Candidate
bank account and 102, 104–108;
company's account of 104–107;
constitutional rights of claimants and
103–104; Court of Appeal and 109;
Dauphin and 105; derivative evil of
corruption and 104–107; Director of
Public Prosecutions and 103–104,
115; Dutch assistance in investigation
of 103; Employee Code of Conduct
and Employment Agreement and 109;
First Caribbean International Bank
and 104, 108; Golding and 102–103,
107–108; historical perspective in
Jamaica 102–103; Jamaica Labor
Party and 102–104, 107; Money
Laundering Act and 108; Netherlands
and 103, 107–108; Office of the
Contractor General and 102, 107,
114; ongoing investigation of 98;
overview 11; People's National Party
and 11, 100, 102–103, 105–109;
pivotal nature of 100; Privy Council
and 109; Simpson-Miller and
105–106, 109, 114; whistleblowing
and 108–109
transactional perspective of corruption 207

transfers of value (ToVs) 155–156, 160,
163, 165n9
transparency 158–162, 249
Transparency International (TI) 2,
120–122, 151, 189; *see also* Corruption
Perceptions Index (CPI)
Travel Act 146, 164n1
Treasury Single Account (TSA) 135–136
trigger stage of corruption scandal 3
Trinidad Express Newspapers article 46, 48
Trinidad and Tobago Newsday article
48–49
Trinidad and Tobago's corruption scandals:
allegations 21, 31n6; anti-corruption
legislation and efforts and 16–21;
Colonial Life insurance Company
10, 43–45, 48; Committees Office of
the Parliament and 30; Corruption
Perceptions Index and 21, 31n4;
economic development and 41; factors
contributing to 21, 31n5; Hindu Credit
Union corruption scandal 10, 44–48;
historical perspective of 16–17; impact
of 41; international conventions in
combating 18; Joint Select Committee
and 22, **23–24**; in 1960s and 1970s
31n1; Opposition members of
parliament and 29–30; overview 9–10,
16, 28–29; Parliament and 16, 21–22,
23–24, 24–26, *27*, 28; Public Accounts
Committee and 22, 24; Public Accounts
Enterprises Committee and 9, 16, 22,
24, 26, 28; Regulation Committee and
22; Sessional Select Committees and 22;
special initiatives combating 20; treaties
in combating 18, 31n2; Watchdog
Committees and 22; Westminster
Whitehall model of government and 17
Trinidad and Tobago Transparency
Institute (TTTI) 48
Trump, D. 59, 71n8, 247
Trump Jr., D. 67–68
Tullock, G. 5
Tumber, H. 4
Turkwell Hydro-Electric Power (HEP)
project 85
tut.by 221, 235n1

UNDP 238–239
Union minière de Haut-Katanga 8–9
United Nations Convention against
Corruption (UNCAC) 8, 18, 89, 151,
162, 189–190, 200, 240
United Nations Convention against
Transnational Organized Crime 90

Index 263

United Nations Economic Commission for Africa 90
United Nations General Assembly 8
United Nations Office on Drugs and Crime (UNODC) 120, 151
United Nations Oil for Food Program 183
Universal Satspace Corporation 82
University of Pittsburgh Medical Center and Schools of the Health Sciences 163
Uralkali corruption scandal 224, 229
Urban Infrastructure Project 85
Uruguay Rounds 174
US anti-corruption legislation 67, 145–147, 162–164; *see also specific law*
US insurance industry 164
US pharmaceutical and medical devices industry: Affordable Healthcare Act and 155–156, 159–160, 164; anti-corruption legislation and efforts and 145–146, 162–164; conflicts of interest and 150–152, 160, 162; Deferred Prosecution Agreements and 157; documentation of 247; Ethical Criteria for Medicinal Drug Promotion and 162–163; Foreign Corrupt Practices Act and 156–158; gift economy and 161; guidelines 15–155; Open Payments Program and 161–162; overview 12, 145; PhRMA and 153–154; physicians in denial and 152–153; reform recommendations 247; regulation of 145–146, 154; self-regulation and 154; Sunshine Act and 155–156, 159–160, 164; transfers of value and 155–156, 160, 165n9; transparency and, limits of 158–162; Vermont and 156; whistleblowing and 155; *see also* manufacturers of drugs, devices, biological, and medical supplies (MDBSs)
US presidential election (2016) 67, 71n4
Uzdenski corruption scandal 224–225

Vannucci, A. 105
Vargas, G. 196
Varieties of Democracy 6
Veselnitskaya, N. 67
violent non-state actors (VNSAs) 86
Vitebsk broiler poultry factory scandal 228
Vitol SA Inc. 102
Vostochni cosmodrone 225

Wabukala, E. 91
Waisbord, S. 4
Wanjigi (businessman) 83
Warner, A. 194

Watergate 11, 171–172
Watkins, S. 35
Wazana, A. 148
Weber, M. 69
"werewolves in epaulettes" scandal 61–62, 64
Werner, S. 58
Westminster Whitehall model of government 17, 112
Whistleblower Bill 136
Whistleblowers Law 97
Whistleblower Unit 136
whistleblowing: benefits of 49, 245; in Caribbean 37–40, 47–49, 245–246; culture encouraging, developing 248; decision to blow whistle and 37–38; defining 34–35, 37; factors influencing 37–38; Graham's principled organizational dissent model and 38–39; impact on corruption and 47–49; importance of 4, 248; interpreting 37; in Jamaica 97; in Kenya 78, 81, 242–243; leaking information and 242–243; legislation 39, 136; manufacturers of drugs, devices, biological, and medical supplies and 155; in Nigeria 136; overview 10; personal costs of 38–39, 49–51, 245; predictors of 39; recommendations for 49–51; retaliation against 49; Trafigura Beheer scandal and 108–109; US pharmaceutical and medical devices industry and 155
Williams, E. 44–45
Williams-Elegbe, S. 11, 83, 245
Working Group on Bribery in International Business Transactions 177
World Bank (WB) 6, 8–9, 83, 85, 87, 189, 195
World Bank Institute 9
World Development Report (WDR) 195
World Economic Forum 6, 195
World Health Organization (WHO) 162–163
Worldwide Governance Indicator 6
Wrong, M. 81
Wydler, L. 43, 48

Yakubu, A. 133
Yanaty Nigeria Limited 128
Yaroslavl website 63
Yeltsin, B. 59–61, 64, 66, 68, 243
Young, G. 41

Zenon Oil 127
Zhang, W. 152